Alone on Guadalcanal

Woods

Australian Diary

for

1942

5th Year of Publication

No. 9

Two Days on a Page

5/-

JOHN ANDREW & CO.

Printers and Publishers

21 PHILLIP STREET, SYDNEY

Alone on Guadalcanal

A COASTWATCHER'S STORY

Martin Clemens

NAVAL INSTITUTE PRESS
Annapolis, Maryland

Library of Congress Cataloging-in-Publication Data
Clemens, Martin, 1915–
    Alone on Guadalcanal : a coastwatcher's story / Martin Clemens.
        p.   cm.
    Includes index.
    ISBN 1-55750-122-x (alk. paper)
        1. Clemens, Martin, 1915–   —Diaries. 2. World War, 1939–1945
—Campaigns—Solomon Islands—Guadalcanal. 3. World War, 1939–1945
—Personal narratives, British. 4. Military service, Voluntary
—United States. 5. Intelligence officers—Great Britain—Biography.
I. Title.
D767.98.c53   1998
940.54'26—dc21
[b]   98-34092

Printed in the United States of America on acid-free paper ∞
05 04 03 02 01 00 99 98   9 8 7 6 5 4 3 2
First printing

Frontispiece: Martin Clemens's bomb-battered diary.

FOR ANNE AND OUR CHILDREN,
CHARLOTTE, VICKY, ALEX, AND MARK

Vouchsafe to those who have not read the story,
That I may prompt them; and of such as have,
I humbly pray them to admit the excuse
Of time, of numbers, and due course of things,
Which cannot in their huge and proper life
Be here presented.

—Shakespeare, *King Henry V,* act 5, prologue

CONTENTS

FOREWORDS

In his account *Return to Paradise,* James Michener observes of the test to which British colonial administration was put during World War II:

> When war broke, these German-Australian–trained natives killed missionaries, betrayed coastwatchers and sold American pilots to Jap soldiers who beheaded them. On British islands not one white man was betrayed. Not one. The fidelity of the Solomon Islanders was unbelievable.

Unless and until the Cold War becomes the hot war, it becomes increasingly clear that its outcome depends in large measure upon our ability to earn and deserve and command such fidelity. We must command it not only from our immediate allies, but from peoples who may not share our English language and culture but who do share our belief in the right of the individual.

We American Marines were presented with that fidelity and support at Guadalcanal. Obviously, since it was there when we arrived, it had been earned by others. Britain's colonial servants, such men as Martin Clemens, had earned and deserved that loyalty from the natives over a period of years, and so had it to command when it was needed. Somehow, these colonial servants had cut through the barriers of race and language and culture to reach the heart and affection of the Solomon Islander. I believe they achieved this by force of character, by example and personification of the virtues of our western philosophy.

When a competitive society and philosophy, in the form of the Japanese military, overran the Solomons, there was little left of the western world's local prestige. Our only alliance with the Solomon Islanders depended upon faith. That faith was proclaimed by Martin Clemens, and others like him, who stayed behind the exodus of Europeans, in hiding from the Japanese, but in constant contact with his native charges.

He had no tangible resource at hand, save his personal example, with which to champion the faith he asked those natives to bear. In their eyes, the initial Japanese conquest of Guadalcanal might well have appeared decisive and final. Yet with his faith and example, and a long accumulated storehouse of trust and loyalty, he was able to sustain the native population in expectation and hope for the white man's eventual victory. Many trying months later, he was still sustaining a friendly and faithful population and so could offer help when my Marines landed on Guadalcanal. During the ensuing decisive weeks, when we were so often only one battalion and one day ahead of the Japanese countermoves, we relied heavily upon information brought to us by Martin and his charges. There were instances when that information and support was a substantial portion of the margin of victory.

As we look to the future we must ponder how to make and keep faithful allies for the world struggle. We can well look to the past to see how one man, representative of his service, by his personal example sustained one small but vital alliance. That it has gone thus far unheralded is reason enough for this book.

Gen. Alexander Archer Vandegrift, USMC, 1953

IT IS A GREAT PLEASURE to write an introduction to Martin Clemens's spirited account of great days on Guadalcanal. Although I only reached the Pacific a few weeks before General Vandegrift and his Marines landed in the Solomon Islands, I was privileged in the months that followed to see much of the campaign, and I can vouch for the accuracy of the vivid, truthful picture of it contained in this book, from the beginning of August 1942. Of events before that, I have no knowledge.

Before the Marines arrived on the scene, Colonel Marchant, the resident commissioner, and his stalwarts must indeed have felt alone and abandoned in the bush, and that at a time of dire and dreadful defeat in the Middle East, in Malaya and Singapore, at Pearl Harbor, in the Philippines, and, as it seemed in those black days, wherever the enemy was able to strike at the overstrained, outnumbered or unready forces of the alliance, which then looked anything but grand.

But, even if the Germans were at the gates of Alexandria and the

Japanese advancing almost unopposed across the Pacific, the district commissioner must still be in his district; the responsibility for law and order, for such public services as there were, for indeed pretty well everything that happened, must be discharged. If things looked dangerous or difficult beyond the ordinary, why, all the more reason to call on the DC to deal with them—he was there, he always had dealt with difficulty and emergency, and surely a mere enemy invasion was not going to defeat him now! And, of course, it did not, as you can read in these pages; and when the time came for the counterattack, for the chance to hit back, he became intelligence officer, guerrilla leader, pilot at sea and guide on land, and a great many other things; and all the time he continued to administer his district from inside the Marines' position as he had done from a hiding place in the bush, in spite of the enemy.

It was on the island of Guadalcanal that the Japanese advance to the south was first held and then turned back. It was a heroic, an epic struggle against odds that must have seemed, and often were, overwhelming, if only the U.S. Marines had known the meaning of the word, in a climate like a Turkish bath, in mud, rain, and misery, while malaria, malnutrition, and dysentery took almost as heavy a toll as the enemy's weapons of the weary but indomitable men. Americans will surely be very proud when they read this plain tale of how fine men finely led stood in the line of duty and prevailed against great odds. But for the British people, and especially for us of the Colonial Service, it has a special appeal of its own; for we know that many Americans have an instinctive dislike and suspicion of "colonialism," which they suppose to be a system of oppression and exploitation of backward people. When the counterattack in the Pacific started we could not avoid being conscious of this attitude of mind. But as the months passed there came a change.

The unconscious, instinctive, critical attitude changed to respect, admiration, and in the field of personal relations, to comradeship, mutual regard, and indeed, often affection. Early incredulity, derision, or distaste gave place to appreciation and understanding of our task among weak and primitive people, of the reasons why the loyalty and devotion to Britain of those simple, ignorant, often savage folk was so real, so staunch, in many cases so heroic—for what does heroism mean, if the story of Sergeant Vouza is not heroic? And that was one story only, of many.

The causes of that change were plain enough to see and simple; they lay in names such as Marchant, Fox-Strangways, Kennedy, Clemens, Sukuna, Trench, Thakombau, Horton, Waddell, Josselyn, Vouza, Andrew, Dovu —the catalogue alone would fill a stout volume.

Among the blaring, screaming hatreds, platitudes, and meannesses of our present state, when to turn on the radio is to hear little but wars and rumours of senseless wars, abuse of old allies or "cynic selfishness and heartless greed," when the world seems to have lost all sense of real values, it does the heart good to hark back to a story like this. A story of brave men and high adventure, of the trust and loyalty of simple folk, of hardship, danger, and privations shared, of duty seen simply and done without question, of allies content each to do his honest utmost as time and circumstances demanded, neither counting the cost nor discounting the other man. A fine story, simply told with humour and modesty, by one who played his part in it with courage, endurance, and a cheerful steadfastness which earned the admiration of General Vandegrift, his staff and Marines, expert judges of these qualities.

Sir Philip Mitchell, K.C.M.G., M.C., 1953

PREFACE

CHOOSING A TITLE for this book presented some difficulty. Had Richard Tregaskis not taken it, "Guadalcanal Diary" would have been the obvious choice. In prewar days, district officers in the Solomons were required to keep diaries, and I therefore kept one as the district officer, Guadalcanal. (See frontispiece.) These diaries were supposed to contain the dull details of usual routine government work. As times became abnormal, mine suffered a considerable metamorphosis and became a more personal story. This book is based primarily on that diary, or rather the personal part of it. However, Tregaskis got away with the title, long before I had even handed in my gun and tin hat, and I had to think of something else!

At first I was not in favor of *Alone on Guadalcanal* as it was not true in the literal sense. Eventually, however, I decided on it, because it does describe how I felt during the long months of waiting, when I never saw another European face. Mentally and spiritually we all felt very much alone.

When I say *we,* I mean that considerable number of whites—government officers, planters, missionaries—who were present on Guadalcanal, having chosen to remain behind for various purposes. As time went on, most of us made tracks from the shore into the timeless jungle. Our only hobby was writing letters to each other, suggesting, subtly or otherwise, that the other fellow was much better placed than oneself. This gave us a small measure of comfort, and kept our spirits up.

When I returned home to England after the war was over, the Pacific struggle did seem very far away. People knew far more about the war in Europe, and tended to leave the Pacific as being an American affair. Occasionally I found kindred spirits who had been in Burma and who had heard of our war, and now and again a former POW from Malaya who knew quite a lot. However, I felt genuinely ashamed of the abysmal ignorance generally displayed. Some didn't know of what our war had consisted; some didn't know that parts of British territory had been won back.

I hope only that this book will help to delineate what happened at the beginning of the war in the islands, before any help came, and to demonstrate why, in the Pacific, Guadalcanal had to be held before any advance could be made anywhere. This, perhaps, requires some explanation.

It took the Japanese only about two months to occupy Southeast Asia more or less completely. The Allied position in January 1942, with Malaya about to fall and the American fleet shattered, was desperate. Hastily recalled Australian divisions, veterans of desert warfare but with no experience in fighting in the jungle, were retreating over the Owen Stanley Range in New Guinea; in the absence of any air power, apart from a few gallant Catalina patrol planes, that meant that we had no offensive force from New Ireland to New Caledonia, a distance of nearly two thousand miles. Our few remaining ships were being sunk in the Makassar Strait.

Although the strategic focus at that time was on New Guinea, where the weight of Australian arms on the ground was being forced back by a single Japanese brigade, expert in jungle warfare, the hinge of the system lay in the outer islands. If Japan retained Guadalcanal, she could send planes to subdue the New Hebrides, while her navy occupied the islands. New Caledonia could then be neutralized and all shipping routes between Australia and America cut. Important centers, vital to the war effort, would come under aerial attack, and the position would be extremely grave. The only way of preventing this debacle, and the division of the Allies, was the occupation of Guadalcanal.

No mean venture, this. Owing to the tragic losses in Malaya, and Britain's entire preoccupation with the European theater of war, no troops were available for this dangerous task. (I have been given to understand that the grand plan eventually envisaged the commitment of a division of Royal Marines.) In the event, the Americans were asked to fill the breach; nobly they did so, in the person of the U.S. Marines, who came from the East Coast, the West Coast, and American Samoa.

Even when the 1st Marine Division had landed—three regiments, together for only a few weeks—we did not know whether we should be able to drive back the Japanese. The issue remained in doubt until, "by the Grace of God and a shoestring," we just managed to hold the enemy's all-out attack in November 1942. General MacArthur and the Australians were doing much the same thing on our left wing, at Buna-Gona in New Guinea.

If someone had told me, even in November 1941, that six months later I would be running about in the jungle, barefoot, and with a beard as camouflage, I would certainly not have believed him. When the time came, however, there we were! I soon found how few the necessities of life really are, and how precious they become, when you are deprived of them.

You can get used to such deprivations, especially such things as lack of sleep, living in the same clothes day in, day out in a sweaty climate, or even no food; but when you return to a more normal life you cannot but realize how glorious are the delights of deep, sound sleep, with the knowledge that no one is after you. Loss of weight, on the other hand, did not seem to affect me very much. I lost forty-two pounds in less than six months, but I soon regained it, once I reestablished contact with Sydney's glorious oysters and good Australian steaks.

It was a grave risk keeping a diary, albeit a personal one, especially once the Japanese had taken up residence; but having kept it for so long I found it hard to stop, and as I traveled light and carried no records other than my wireless telegraph log it had its uses. At first I tried to keep it a factual account of what I did personally, but military matters soon crept in, especially when there was nothing else to record. From time to time I also put down what I thought about things, as I had no other European with whom to converse. During the later stages of the campaign, when I should really have stopped keeping it, I naturally did not record details of our own forces or of their intentions; in order to give a clearer picture, however, I have now incorporated these into the story, either from memory or from reports and correspondence, where they are necessary to the understanding of what was happening and to preserve continuity.

Many years ago I was told by a very eminent friend of mine, a professor and a divine, that to publish a personal story such as this one, parts of which no one could verify, was a very great responsibility. (When you have read this book, you may agree that this was but one more risk!) I make no claim, however, for historical detail or accuracy. I have not attempted to tell the story of everything that happened on Guadalcanal during those fateful months, nor even included everything I did myself. During the occupation, writing the diary helped to fill in long periods of anxious waiting when there was little else to do; but I was often too busy, or too tired, to make up my diary every day, and the record therefore cannot be complete.

That those of us who faded into the jungle were able to emerge after our long wait was, in the main, due to the sorely tried but unswerving loyalty of the Solomon Islanders. As far as I was concerned, these were not only the scouts and the boat crews, who daily carried out miracles of deception, but also other government employees, who had less spectacular jobs, and the villagers, Christian and pagan alike, who hid us and fed us and at times got killed impartially by both sides, owing to the constantly varying fortunes of war. There is no doubt that the enemy did receive help from a small number of natives, but within my knowledge they were men who either had, at some time or other, got against the law or were kept in a state of intimidation by the Japanese.

Enemy occupation was a strange thing to the islander; goodness knows, it is strange enough to anyone. His ancestral wars had consisted of small raids, usually amphibious, followed by the feasting of the victors on the vanquished. Some of the older people, having seen the suppression of headhunting in the Solomons and then the eviction of the Germans from New Guinea and Bougainville Island in World War I, no doubt thought the British invincible. It would have saved all of us a great deal of trouble if we had been.

By contrast, the Solomon Islander had little respect for the Japanese. Their pearl fishermen used to steal, between the wars, the shells off his family reefs before they had properly matured, thereby not only filching his means of livelihood but destroying it for years to come. Here they were, in force, and the British were running before them. This was baffling and unsettling, and many were the natives who, now that anxious times were upon us, begged me to tell them what was to happen. All that I could say was that, someday, someone would rescue us from our sorry plight, and that, until that happy day, I intended to stay with them.

It was not much to offer, but it was accepted, and it all came true. Do not ask me why, because I do not know. As a token of that faith, I ran up the Union Jack wherever I happened to be; and though I must admit that as aerial visitors became prevalent it sometimes had to fly under a shady tree, yet it flew higher than the Japanese flag at Lunga ever would. It now hangs in my school library; I treasure it still.

That we were able to be of some use to the Allied war effort during our long wait was due, to a great extent, to the skillful planning of the Royal Australian Navy's Naval Intelligence Division, and especially to the foresight of Eric Feldt, who had such a great deal to do with thinking out the teleradio idea and enabling us to pass on the intelligence that we were able to collect. His people, and we of the Protectorate Government service, occasionally got on each other's nerves later on in the war, but that was due, I think, to an excess of zeal and an anxiety to get things done on both our parts. In spite of this professional rivalry, we never failed to share our grog—whenever we had any. (Eric Feldt's excellent book, *The Coast Watchers,* and Walter Lord's *Lonely Vigil* are probably the only authoritative works on the subject. Feldt's book, however, is a plain, unvarnished, and extremely modest account of the overall picture, and it gives some idea of the general organization. Lord's work gives a more personal view of individual coastwatchers in the Solomons. This book is quite different, being an entirely personal story.)

That our saviors were the U.S. Marines will always be remembered in the Solomons, and particularly on Guadalcanal, where Americans dug in for the first time, as far as I know, on British colonial territory. It was a privilege to work with them, and they became our lasting friends. Acknowledgments are due to the men of the United States Marine Corps photographic section, who not only allowed me to reproduce their official photographs but sent me a beautiful full-plate collection of them. Thanks in particular are due to Jim Whitehead, who very kindly made the selection for me. (I only wish that he had included a photograph of himself, as duty officer, D-2 section. Had he done so, I might have appropriately included his smooth features in the illustrations!) Special thanks are also due to Sgt. Robert Howard, who took many of the pictures, certainly all those taken outside the tiny area held by the Marines. It was his duty to take some of them, but nevertheless, thank you, Bob!

The first draft of this book dates from the early 1950s. At that time there were many military history books on the market, and I was unable to interest a publisher in it. Over the years, other efforts were made to get the manuscript into print; these too, for various reasons, did not meet with success.

In January 1994, while trout fishing in Tasmania, I met John Randolph, the editor of *Fly Fisherman* magazine and a veteran of the 2d Marine Division. He soon discovered who I was and got straight on to why I had not written a book on Guadalcanal. I told him of the efforts I had made, including most recently an inquiry to the Naval Institute Press. John kindly offered to contact them; this time the inquiry met with a positive response.

A most energetic supporter of this project over the years had been Stanley Jersey, an Army Air Forces veteran of the Solomons and the leading student of the postal history of U.S. forces in the Pacific. Stan thought I should have an agent in the United States. He suggested Joel Bromberg, an experienced editor who had handled military history and done philatelic research on the Solomon Islands. Joel's liaison efforts were rewarded when the Naval Institute Press accepted the book for publication.

There remained the problem of creating a coherent whole from three different drafts of the manuscript. Working with those, my diary, and considerable documentary material and correspondence, Joel did a marvelous job of editing and rewriting, and performed research and fact checking as well. His wife, Irene Bromberg, who had expertly keyboarded the drafts to enable editing on computer, proofread my final manuscript. Without the two of them, and Stan Jersey prodding in the background, there would have been no book.

Many Marines, who have become good friends over the years, keep asking me if I am going to write a book on Guadalcanal. Well, chaps, here it is.

The effect of modern war, as I have already mentioned, was bewildering to the primitive islander; but if, in the Solomons, where there are so many distinct Melanesian races and cultures and so many languages, it made him realize that in the face of adversity all must pull together, and that, instead of thinking of himself as a Guadalcanal man, or a Malaita man, he had to consider himself a Solomon Islander, he did derive some little benefit from that harrowing experience. Apart from acquiring a little ready cash, he gained little else.

Martin Clemens

Alone on Guadalcanal

Guadalcanal and Martin Clemens

by Allan R. Millett

ALTHOUGH THE MOUNTAINOUS volcanic islands of the former British Solomon Islands Protectorate (BSIP) are thirty-five hundred miles from the great naval base at Singapore, they took on a strategic importance in 1941–42 that confounded the some five hundred Europeans who inhabited them. The geopolitics of war mystified the ninety-five thousand Melanesian natives who had lived under British administration since the late nineteenth century. A great island city of commercial and naval significance that shaped the history of all of South Asia, Singapore anchored the western end of the Malay Barrier. The islands of the oil-rich Dutch East Indies extended the Malay Barrier eastward along the Equator. The island chain—part of the great circle of volcanic lands that rings the Pacific Ocean—continued to Australian-administered Papua and New Guinea and thence to New Britain Island to the north, which ended in the port of Rabaul. Still west of the international date line, the Barrier continued with the Solomons. Whoever controlled the Solomons could interrupt maritime and air traffic from the United States to Australia. And for the United States the route to the Philippines passed through the Malay Barrier, for the Naval Arms Limitation Treaty of 1922 had conceded to

Japanese control most of the islands between the international date line and Manila. The strategic linkage between the defense of Singapore and the Philippines doomed the Solomons to their improbable role as a major theater in World War II.

Within the global concepts for the defense of the British Empire after World War I, the defense of the Malay Barrier against Japan focused on Singapore, whose importance to Malaya was matched by its importance to the defense of Burma and India. The Imperial General Staff, a Commonwealth committee dominated by its British members, believed that an Australian commitment to Singapore was essential, even though the British assumed that they might get some help from France, the Netherlands, and the United States. None of these potential allies, however, seemed willing or able to contribute much to deter or defend against a Japanese offensive into what Tokyo called the "South Seas Resource Area" or, more grandly, the "Greater East Asian Co-Prosperity Sphere."

The coming of war in Europe in 1939, followed by the devastating defeat of France in 1940, threw all the plans for the defense of the Asia-Pacific British Empire into the trashbin designed for all strategic wishful thinking. When Winston Churchill became prime minister in 1940, he brought a sense of strategic realism to the office, but not a complete conversion to facing facts. In his calculus, defense of the Mediterranean, the gateway to the overvalued resources of India, took priority over defense of Singapore, and he drew the bulk of the volunteer Australian Imperial Force into the maelstrom of war in the Middle East. Australia sent two divisions to the Middle East, its first formed for war in 1940, then a third. A fourth (the 8th Division) went to Malaya in 1941. Australian naval and air units also moved to the Middle East or, in the case of aircrews, all the way to Great Britain to participate in the defense of Great Britain or the strategic bombing of Germany. Before Pearl Harbor, Australian and New Zealand soldiers (the "Anzacs") were fighting and dying in Greece, Crete, Libya, Somalia, and Egypt. Given the combination of apathy and sense of ravishment that characterized Australian defense policy in 1941, it is little wonder that the defense of New Guinea and the Solomons assumed almost no priority in Australian military planning.[1]

If the Australians had few forces with which to defend the Solomon Islands other than the white-officered native police and scratch formations of European militia, they could at least create an intelligence organization that could report enemy air and ship movements. After a 1922 review of Australian defense responsibilities conducted by an interservice committee, the Naval Intelligence Division of the Royal Australian Navy created a network of civilian observers throughout New Guinea and the Solomons, with similar positions along Australia's northern coast. Since it did not have a reliable portable radio, the Naval Intelligence Division could do little to support its volunteer observers until, in the late 1930s, it purchased a battery-powered combination telegraph-voice radio for distribution to the coastwatchers. The system had limitations that made portability and communications relative terms. The "teleradio" could be broken down into a receiver section, a transmitter section, a speaker section, and other smaller modules, but it also required large batteries, a battery charger, chemicals for the battery charger, and other support equipment. With luck and strong porters, the teleradio might be divided into loads for ten men. It also worked best from higher elevations (line of sight), but even then its range still fell into a four-hundred-mile (voice) to six-hundred-mile (tapped code) envelope, which meant the establishment of many stations within relay range of one another. Nevertheless, the distribution of teleradios finally gave the coastwatchers some way to report their sightings in time-urgent terms.

With the outbreak of war in 1939, the director of the Naval Intelligence Division, Cdr. Rupert B. M. Long, RAN, assigned a fellow World War I naval veteran and enthusiastic Australian civil administrator in New Guinea, Lt. Cdr. Eric A. Feldt, to bring the coastwatcher organization to war readiness. A close friend of Feldt's and a loose manager, Long gave the energetic, intense Feldt plenty of autonomy. Fortunately, he also gave him effective support. As a senior naval staff officer at Port Moresby, Feldt recruited more coastwatchers, conducted training sessions, distributed supplies, and infused a paper organization with a real sense of mission. Before the war with Japan, he visited almost every team in his network, which extended all the way to Rabaul, New Britain Island, and the straits south of New Ireland Island. As Long and Feldt predicted, any Japanese offensive would make Rabaul (defended by the only Australian Army battalion in the whole region) its principal objective. The southern Solomons were not a pressing priority. Under Feldt's direction, the coastwatchers, collectively known as "Ferdinand" to honor the bull in the children's story who watched and waited, numbered about one thousand in late 1941, manning one hundred stations linked by radio and resupplied by the Royal Australian Air Force. The cordon of observers stretched twenty-five hundred miles from the northern coast of New Guinea to the New Hebrides.[2]

The area covered by Ferdinand had six regional subdivisions, one of which was the southern Solomons, administered by Resident Commissioner William S. Marchant from his headquarters in Tulagi, the small port on an island of the same name. Marchant also headed the coast-watchers stationed on the larger islands of his domain: Ysabel, New Georgia, and Guadalcanal. Feldt concluded that Marchant had too many responsibilities, so he sent Sub-Lt. Donald S. Macfarlan, RANR, to Tulagi to take de facto control of Ferdinand. He later sent his most trusted assistant, Lt. Hugh Mackenzie, RAN, to Vila, Efate, New Hebrides, to establish a new central reporting site for the southern Solomons. Marchant's station moved with the Resident Commissioner to Malaita when the Japanese approached. There Marchant's professional radio operator received reports from Guadalcanal, recoded them, and sent them to Mackenzie. As Deputy Supervising Intelligence Officer, Solomons, Mackenzie reported directly to Feldt at his headquarters at Townsville, Queensland.

When the Japanese advanced into the southern Solomons and began to bomb Tulagi, Marchant displaced for Malaita and tried to take Macfarlan and his radio with him, but the determined young Scot refused to abandon his four subordinate posts. One of these coastwatchers was a middle-aged storekeeper on Savo, Leif Schroeder, who, betrayed by some Melanesians, eventually fled to the western tip of Guadalcanal. Macfarlan himself went to Aola, Guadalcanal, with Clemens and then organized his team (reinforced by a jungle-wise miner, A. M. Andresen) with Kenneth D. Hay. A veteran of World War I and known for his large appetite, Hay managed a plantation for Burns, Philp & Company (South Sea) Ltd., which, with Lever Brothers, dominated the island's cash crop economy of coconuts and copra. This team observed the coastal plain of the Lunga River on the northern shore of central Guadalcanal. The second team, formed in late March near the island's western tip, had another exotic, aging islander for its *kiap,* or boss, F. Ashton "Snowy" Rhoades, also a plantation manager. Schroeder joined Rhoades after his escape from Savo. The third Guadalcanal coastwatcher team manned a station at the island's administrative headquarters, the northeastern coastal town of Aola. This team had a leader of a much different sort, another Scot and a member of the British professional colonial civil service, District Officer Martin Clemens.

When I visited Australia in 1995 to teach a too-short session at the Australian Defence Force Academy (ADFA) in Canberra, I wanted to meet Martin Clemens. As a historian of the United States Marine Corps and the biographer of Gen. Gerald C. Thomas, USMC, who had served on Guadalcanal as the operations officer and chief of staff of the 1st Marine Division, I regarded Clemens as one of the heroes of the Guadalcanal campaign. My judgment showed no originality. Every Marine I ever knew—personally or through his writings—regarded Martin Clemens with respect and affection because he had contributed so much to the division's successful operations on Guadalcanal.

When I started to work on my biography of General Thomas, I learned very quickly a central lesson for all Guadalcanal historians: consult Martin Clemens. As I already knew from reading other people's books, Clemens had kept a diary and notebook throughout his service on Guadalcanal, a priceless source of information and opinion on the American side of the campaign. I opened a correspondence with Major Clemens, and he very generously sent me portions of his diaries and notes as well as his opinions about the major commanders and staff officers of the 1st Marine Division. The more research I did, the more I found his views accurate, prudent, understanding, and candid. During our correspondence, I noticed that his address was "Toorak." Somehow I assumed that Toorak must be an isolated ranch of sheep and cattle in Queensland or New South Wales. My hosts at ADFA, Professors Peter Dennis and Jeffrey Grey, with great humor (was it humour?) told me that Toorak was an affluent and very smart suburb of Melbourne.

On the other hand, I found it appalling that Peter and Jeffrey did not know that Martin Clemens was—at least among Marines—the most famous Australian warrior of them all, a figure of greater consequence than Field Marshal Sir Thomas Blamey, Breaker Morant, or Mel Gibson.

Of course, I soon realized that Martin Clemens was not a "real" Australian, since he had "come out" from Great Britain as just another colonial administrator for the Solomons and had served, albeit with honor, on the periphery of the Australian war effort. Being a saint to the veterans of the 1st Marine Division did not automatically bestow on him a special place in the pantheon of heroes remembered in Canberra's Australian War Memorial.

During a long weekend graciously granted by the ADFA history department, I finally met Martin Clemens at his home at Toorak in July 1995. As Peter and Jeffrey had predicted, my family and I found the Clemens home, Dunraven, anything but primitive. Anne and Martin Clemens could not have been more hospitable to my wife and me and our five-year-old daughter. The Clemenses wined and dined us, and we got some special tours of Melbourne, including the war memorial. Naturally, we talked a great deal about Guadalcanal and veteran Marines, many of whom Major Clemens had seen often at division reunions and trips to the United States since World War II. Though plagued with arthritic knees, Martin set the pace, full of enthusiasm for the World War II commemoration, golf, animal husbandry, the livestock business, children and grandchildren, and his comrades of the British Solomon Islands Protectorate Defence Force. I found it easy to imagine Martin as he was when he walked out of the jungle on 15 August 1942 and into the life of the 1st Marine Division. Marine officers who saw him remembered him as active, highly intelligent, articulate, handsome, and obviously courageous in an understated way. At eighty, Martin Clemens was still the same man.

Born in Aberdeen, Scotland, on 17 April 1915, Warren Frederick Martin Clemens grew up in a household of high standards and low means. His father played the organ and directed the choir at Queen's Cross Presbyterian Church, but he died in 1924 when Martin was nine years old. His mother, a Martin from the herring fishing center of Peterhead, managed to send him to boarding school in England with the help of scholarships and her family. After nine years at Bedford School, Martin became a scholarship student at Christ's College, Cambridge University. His university experience at Christ's College mirrored his record at Bedford School. Not distinguished in any one thing, except rowing, he was very good at many. As a student in the natural sciences, he made marks good enough to win honors and the prestige of a "leaving exhibition." He then did advanced work in animal husbandry and botany in an additional year beyond his graduation in 1937. Although he followed a scientific curriculum, he also enjoyed his course work in the arts and letters. The fact that his academic advisor was Sir Charles Percy Snow may have had something to do with his academic interest "in two cultures." Martin was never an academic drudge, however. He rowed with distinction on the Cambridge crew and participated in a wide range of social activities and sports.

In 1937 Clemens sought and won an appointment in the British Colonial Service, which allowed him to remain a year at Cambridge for the service's training course and some graduate study. He received a posting to the Solomon Islands in August 1938 for a three-year probationary appointment on the island of Malaita. He specialized in development projects such as road building and agricultural land use that directly helped the islanders. In due course he passed his qualifying examinations for full status in the Colonial Service and moved to San Cristobal as a district officer in November 1941.

Concerned that Great Britain was at war but he was not, Clemens volunteered for military service during a short leave to Sydney, which coincided with the attack on Pearl Harbor. Even a war with Japan did not alter his civil service status, but it did change his assignment. Clemens returned to the Solomons to evacuate the Europeans and Chinese from Tulagi, where he found the town in flames and chaos from a bombing by long-range Japanese four-engine amphibian patrol bombers. Meeting with Resident Commissioner Marchant and Lieutenant Macfarlan amid Tulagi's ruin, he agreed to cross the Florida Strait to Guadalcanal and the island's district headquarters at Aola and take over as district officer and coastwatcher on 28 February. Clemens's first job was a challenge, for he had to finish off the evacuation of the Melanesian plantation workers to their home islands. Their European managers had left them in a rush.

Anticipating that the Japanese would soon reach Tulagi, Clemens organized his coastwatcher detachment around his Melanesian native police and administrative personnel and set up his radio (ZGJ4) and messenger contact with Rhoades and Macfarlan when they got organized. In March 1942 Clemens learned that he had been appointed a captain in the British Solomon Islands Protectorate Defence Force (BSIPDF), a militia of police and volunteers that might conduct guerrilla warfare. The military rank, which Lieutenant Commander Feldt arranged for the coastwatchers, was supposed to protect the coastwatchers from charges of spying and to qualify them for pay and benefits under military regulations. Most of the coastwatchers became officers or enlisted men in the Royal Australian Naval Volunteer Reserve, but Clemens went into "the army." Given Japanese treatment of prisoners, in uniform or not, the military rank would have meant little if Clemens had been captured in his role of behind-the-lines intelligence operative. In any event, he had no badges of rank, no uniform, and no military identification papers.

On 1 May 1942 Clemens received a coded message from Marchant that Tulagi, again under bombardment, could no longer serve as regional capital or a way station for messages to Feldt's headquarters at Townsville. The Japanese landed on Tulagi two days later, part of the general advance to the south that was supposed to end with the capture of Port Moresby, New Guinea. The carrier task force of the Imperial Japanese Navy that entered the Coral Sea, however, ran into a similar U.S. Navy carrier task force (two fleet carriers) and fought a battle on 7 and 8 May. It was a tactical victory for the Japanese, since their naval aviators sank the *Lexington* and damaged the *Yorktown* at the loss of the light carrier *Shoho,* but with one of his fleet carriers damaged and half his carrier aircraft gone, Rear Adm. Hara Chuichi decided to fight another day. The First South Seas Offensive came to an end, but the Japanese did not withdraw from Tulagi, even though they themselves had been the target of an American air raid on 4 May, a raid that had caught the Japanese unloading enough equipment and food for a long and luxurious tropical occupation. Already prepared for working from the mountains above Guadalcanal's coastal plain, Clemens and his scouts stayed along the coast long enough to rescue the two-man crew of an American torpedo plane, then took to the hills. Martin Clemens could hardly have known he was about to walk into a central role in the war against Japan.[3]

Although the Battle of the Coral Sea kept the Allied position along the Malay Barrier from becoming untenable, the Battle of Midway a month later (3–6 June) provided a momentary change in the strategic sea state of the Pacific war. No greater opportunists ever wore the uniform of the United States than Adm. Ernest J. King and Gen. Douglas MacArthur, and no two senior commanders could be more persuasive and unrelenting

in the pursuit of their military (and personal) goals. King and MacArthur
—separated by the distance between Melbourne and Washington—could
not have been closer in their conviction that America's *real* war was the
crusade against Japan, not the halting efforts of a coalition of national
misfits against Nazi Germany. With the better part of the Japanese Combined Fleet's carrier force hors de combat after Midway, King and
MacArthur argued to the U.S. Joint Chiefs of Staff and through them to
the Allied Combined Chiefs of Staffs that the Allies had a unique opportunity for an offensive in the South Pacific.[4]

Although the Joint Chiefs remained skeptical about the idea of a
Pacific offensive, they could find no powerful reason to oppose the King-
MacArthur concept, especially if it could be mounted with forces already
in the theater. At the very least a limited offensive would preempt any
additional Japanese move south to disrupt the sea lanes and base structure
essential to the buildup in Australia. MacArthur had a more ambitious
goal, the recapture of Rabaul, but only he viewed this objective as realis-
tic, given the balance of forces in the South Pacific. When the Joint Chiefs
approved a Pacific offensive on 2 July 1942, they expected only limited
operations in eastern New Guinea and the southern Solomons.

The organization of the Allied war effort in the South Pacific encour-
aged caution. MacArthur commanded all Allied forces (Australian,
American, and the remnants of the Dutch defenders of the East Indies) in
the Southwest Pacific theater. President Roosevelt needed a hero to defeat
Japan, not a goat for the fall of the Philippines, so MacArthur, darling of
the "Asia First" Republicans, stayed and returned. Control of the sea
lanes to Australia, however, was Navy business, and King had no desire to
give MacArthur or any other general permanent control of any major
portion of the Pacific Fleet, commanded from Honolulu by Adm. Chester
W. Nimitz and a new hero after Midway. The South Pacific theater,
which included the southern Solomons, remained under Nimitz, who
also held the joint command of commander-in-chief, Pacific Ocean Areas.
Nimitz's regional commander was Vice Adm. Robert L. Ghormley, USN,
who regarded the King-MacArthur offensive plan as near-madness.
When it came to precise plans and the assignment of forces, MacArthur
and Ghormley were bidding for many of the same air and naval assets.
One of the most precious of these assets was intelligence, and when it

came to "information warfare," the Allied commanders had much to trade, provided they decided to keep the Japanese, not each other, the primary enemy. Part of the intelligence domain that now had to serve two masters was Ferdinand, whose members waited, watched, and tried to avoid the Japanese.

Admiral Ghormley's headquarters did not pay much attention to Lieutenant Mackenzie's observers' reports because it, like the rest of the U.S. Navy, had come to believe that the best intelligence came from Japanese radio messages, analyzed by the staff of the Navy's Communications Security Service, Office of Naval Communications (Op-20-G). For two decades the work of the radio intelligence experts in the Navy had grown in credibility while the Office of Naval Intelligence had fallen in usefulness and esteem, in part because it lost some of its best (and scarce) Japanese-language experts to the radio intelligence business. Although the radio intelligence community deserved part of the responsibility for the surprise at Pearl Harbor, the sum of the intelligence failures of December 1941 rested on the more conventional intelligence experts who ran air and submarine patrols, collected reports from military and civilian human intelligence agencies like the Office of Naval Intelligence and the FBI, and scrutinized photographs and newspapers. The victories at the Coral Sea and Midway, moreover, gave the radio intelligence experts a halo of success and indispensability. The combination of radio traffic analysis and cryptography became the coin of the intelligence realm in the Pacific war, and the U.S. Navy controlled most of this treasury, code-named ULTRA.[5]

MacArthur, however, was not without his own assets, including some ULTRA material, and they included several agencies tied to the Australian armed forces and then into the Allied Intelligence Bureau (AIB). MacArthur appointed an Australian Army colonel as AIB head with an American colonel as deputy. Ferdinand fell under the general supervision of the AIB, even that part of Ferdinand which operated in the South Pacific theater. As the AIB developed its own ULTRA organization in 1942, Col. Spencer B. Akin, the U.S. Army's Signals Intelligence Service representative in MacArthur's headquarters, sent a special intercept detachment to Townsville, where it established a post near Feldt's Ferdinand station. Although this arrangement gave Akin some advantages in his code-breaking and traffic-analysis operations, it also provided the ULTRA operation some useful "cover" since allies and enemies alike might assume that Ferdinand alone was generating all the communications business in Townsville. Under MacArthur's bureaucratic protection, Mackenzie's team in Vila could operate with considerable autonomy, and what information and analysis it shared with Ghormley's staff (information flowing both to and from Townsville) was a free good for ComSoPac. Although Ghormley had his shortcomings as a commander, he appreciated good intelligence work, had good relations with British naval intelligence from earlier assignments, and had served as a pioneer of naval aviation photography. Ghormley soon concluded that the Ferdinand observers knew their business since their reports proved accurate—that is, planes that took off from the airfields on New Britain, Buka, and Bougainville arrived over targets to the south as predicted. His staff could also see that coastwatchers' reports matched their own radio intelligence and sometimes filled its voids, especially when the Japanese Navy changed its call signs and codes in JN-25, the Operational code that American cryptographers could read—in time and in parts. By July 1942 ComSoPac accepted Ferdinand reports as gospel.[6]

As it started to form in the fertile mind of Rear Adm. Richmond Kelly Turner, USN, the chief operational planner of King's staff, the Navy concept for an operation in the southern Solomons assumed that Tulagi, now a Japanese anchorage for patrol craft and amphibian aircraft, should be recaptured. Turner's eyes rode the waves and scaled tall mountains with a single glance without settling on any other focus of effort. Assigned to command the amphibious task force in the South Pacific, Turner and his staff could not decide where to take their landing force, the 1st Marine Division, recently arrived in New Zealand for extended training. Using Mackenzie's reports from the three Guadalcanal teams, Ghormley convinced Turner that the key objective was the northern coastal plain at the Lunga River, where the Japanese had started to build an airfield. Through June 1942 small parties of Japanese had examined the region, and on 6 July the engineer forces and supporting troops arrived in strength. In accordance with IGHQ Navy Director 109 from Tokyo, Operation SN had begun. At a minimum the new base on Guadalcanal would anchor the defense of the southern Solomons, and it might serve as an essential part of a second South Seas offensive. Operation SN was about to meet Operation Watchtower.

From his varied observation posts from the mountains south of the Lunga plain, Martin Clemens watched the Japanese go to work on their airbase. The two other teams watched and reported, too. All three teams faced a common problem, a shortage of supplies and a growing sense that the Melanesian population, much of it impressed as laborers on the airfield, was shifting its loyalty to the Japanese. Outdoor living on the run wore the coastwatchers down, including Clemens, who bore the official responsibility for keeping the peace with his native constables. There were still Europeans on the island, priests and nuns of several Catholic missions, some gold miners, and people who had simply missed an opportunity to leave Guadalcanal. The Japanese became one of two enemies, as Clemens and his team found their caches looted and their movements observed by Melanesians of doubtful loyalty. Mackenzie's messages demanded more and more information about the Japanese situation and details about the terrain and weather. Macfarlan told Clemens "something big" was in the offing. The coastwatchers grasped this warning with fervent hope. The frequency of their transmissions, however, gave Japanese radio intelligence teams a greater opportunity to locate their transmission sites and to send patrols after them.[7]

Clemens's information-gathering system on Guadalcanal depended upon cooperative native islanders, who would make reports of Japanese activity to an island police officer or government agent, who then forwarded the information to Clemens for consolidation, evaluation, and communication by radio to Malaita and then on to Vila. The key position was the "sub-coastwatcher," and Clemens worried about the enthusiasm of some of his "police boys." In June 1942, Malaita District Officer C. N. F. Bengough sent him a formidable reinforcement, Jacob Charles Vouza (1900–1984), a police sergeant major, who had joined the BSIP Armed Constabulary in 1916 and retired in 1941. Clemens thought that Bengough had done him no favor, since he knew from personal experience that Vouza liked being his own boss and imposed his own justice on the islanders. Moreover, although Vouza came from the village of Volonavua, near Koli Point, he had served on Malaita for more than twenty years, and Clemens doubted that he had the personal contacts and intimate knowledge of the area his duties required. Trusting in loyalty and experience, Clemens sent Vouza off to cover the crucial Koli Point region. Vouza proved to be his most effective subordinate, although he still fought his war as he saw fit.

In his headquarters at the Hotel Cecil in Wellington, New Zealand, Maj. Gen. Alexander Archer Vandegrift, USMC, had just survived a local earth tremor when he received a no less thunderous message from Admiral Ghormley to fly to Auckland the next day, 26 June 1942. Known throughout the Marine Corps as "Sunny Jim" for his calm disposition in moments of stress, Vandegrift already suspected why Ghormley wanted to see him. His communications security officer, 1st Lt. Sanford B. Hunt, USMC, had been reading ComSoPac's most classified incoming message traffic, even "information" copies, and Hunt had seen Admiral King's message of 24 June to Admiral Nimitz that King believed the Joint Chiefs of Staff would approve his proposal for an offensive in the southern Solomons (Tulagi) and the nearby Santa Cruz Islands. King told Nimitz that MacArthur and Ghormley should work out the detailed plans and organize the task forces for the offensive, which might begin as soon as 1 August.

Vandegrift said nothing to the three staff members he took with him to Auckland: Lt. Col. Gerald C. Thomas, USMC, the division operations officer; Lt. Col. Frank B. Goettge, USMC, the division intelligence officer; and Lt. Col. Edward W. Snedeker, USMC, the division communications officer. The Marines found Ghormley and his staff appalled by the implications of King's message. Vandegrift's staff judged the implied mission—that the 1st Marine Division would land somewhere against the enemy in five weeks' time. The division's first convoy had barely reached New Zealand, and other units were still at sea. Moreover, all the ships had been loaded for an administrative landing, not an amphibious assault, and in any case were not numerous enough to carry all the division's personnel, weapons, and equipment. In addition, the division was really untrained above the battalion level, and it lacked one whole reinforced infantry regiment (the 7th Marines), which had been sent earlier to defend Samoa. The conferees urged Ghormley to see MacArthur and at least get the Joint Chiefs to lengthen the preparatory period. One immediate task that faced the Marines was to learn as much as possible about the Solomons. "There was little information immediately available either as to the character of the theater of operations or the enemy strength and activity therein."[8]

Vandegrift and Thomas returned to Wellington to start the awesome task of preparing their division for an amphibious assault, but they dispatched Goettge to Melbourne to learn as much about the Solomons as possible. The preliminary meeting in Auckland identified Guadalcanal as a potential objective, more important than Tulagi since it could provide an airfield. Ghormley's own intelligence staff had seen some AIB analysis that suggested that the Japanese had an airfield underway. In his first "appreciation" of the situation, Colonel Thomas identified Guadalcanal as the key objective. In the first week of July 1942, Guadalcanal (code-named Cactus) became the focus of Allied planning. During his intelligence odyssey to Australia, Goettge looked for Guadalcanal experts, and the AIB started rounding up plantation personnel, South Seas mariners, and assorted visitors to the island's northern coast. Goettge learned about Ferdinand and asked the AIB for more information from the coast-watchers, but he did not have the time for a trip to Townsville to see Feldt before returning to Wellington with his gaggle of self-proclaimed experts on 15 July. Vandegrift wanted more information, and Thomas thought the islanders provided more questions than answers. Having a proposal to send a ground reconnaissance team to Guadalcanal vetoed by Ghormley, they settled for a photographic and aerial reconnaissance by two trusted associates, Lt. Col. Merrill B. Twining and Maj. William B. McKean. A former brigade intelligence officer, Twining was Thomas's assistant D-3, and McKean served as the Marine planner on the staff of the commander, Transport Divisions, South Pacific Force, Capt. Lawrence F. Reifsnider, USN.

By taking an exciting ride over Guadalcanal on a B-17P stationed at Port Moresby, Twining and McKean closed the contact between the 1st Marine Division and Ferdinand, for they had to fly to Townsville to get their copies of the aerial photographs, supplemented by the most recent information provided by the Guadalcanal coastwatchers. They came away from their meeting with Feldt convinced that his organization could provide the answers to most of their questions, and Feldt gave them very good news when he said he thought AIB's and ComSoPac's estimate of the Japanese force ashore on the Lunga plain was much too large, closer to three thousand than five thousand. He gave Twining detailed sketch maps of Lunga, Tulagi, and Gavutu that showed gun positions, fortifications, and support installations. He told the Marines that he had already instructed Mackenzie at Vila to communicate directly with his American counterparts there, which included the headquarters of all ground-based Navy aviation. This headquarters in turn prepared target lists and photographic guides for the carrier air groups that would support the landing, now scheduled for 7 August. In their talks with Feldt, the Marines learned that one of their sources was Martin Clemens. Feldt identified Clemens by name and gave Twining the code and authenticating information that would allow the Marines to call Clemens directly when they went ashore. He also gave Twining the impression that Clemens was injured. (Actually the injured party was Macfarlan, who had broken his foot and might need rescue.) The Marines began to think of Clemens as *their* local intelligence officer.[9]

In his aerie in the mountains, Martin Clemens waited impatiently for more information, more signs of an Allied operation. Except for mounting Japanese work on the airfield, he could see nothing that indicated that the Japanese expected an invasion. Understandably, neither Mackenzie nor Feldt told him anything about the landing. Running short of patience and supplies, Clemens tried to cajole the Melanesians into cooperation; he trusted only his personal staff and police, and he feared that even some of them might be ready to switch allegiance. Clemens had no instructions except to survive, provide information on the Japanese by his weakening radio, and wait.

In the meantime, the 1st Marine Division staff put the finishing touches on its operations order, which it sold to Ghormley as ComSoPac OpO 1-42 on 15 July 1942. Admiral Turner arrived to find that his nominal superior and his landing force commander had produced a fait accompli at his expense, but he could not find enough time or flaws to change the order. It called for simultaneous landings on Tulagi and Guadalcanal on the morning of 7 August. The actual landings, which stressed speed and surprise, would be preceded by a brief but brisk air attack from the carriers of Vice Adm. Frank Jack Fletcher's Task Force 61 and a shore bombardment by the warships of Rear Adm. Victor A. C. Crutchley, RAN, whose six cruisers and fifteen destroyers would escort Turner's amphibious force.

For Vandegrift there was still the problem of the scheme of maneuver on Guadalcanal, for which he remained directly responsible. The Tulagi-Gavutu landings would be commanded by his assistant division commander, Brig. Gen. William H. Rupertus. Since the Tulagi landing looked (and was) the most immediately difficult, given the defenses of the 3d Kure Special Naval Landing Force, Vandegrift assigned Rupertus his toughest infantry, the 1st Raider Battalion (Lt. Col. Merritt A. Edson), the 1st Parachute Battalion (Maj. Robert H. Williams), the 1st Battalion, 2d Marines (Lt. Col. Robert E. Hill), and the 2d Battalion, 5th Marines (Lt. Col. Harold E. Rosecrans). Since Admiral Turner would not release the two remaining battalions of the 2d Marines (a regiment borrowed from the 2d Marine Division) to the 1st Marine Division, Vandegrift had only five infantry battalions to land on Red Beach, the landing site east of the Lunga River. He had no margin for error—and he still didn't feel as if he had a good grasp of the terrain.[10]

The Australian and British islanders of Ferdinand and other units of the AIB might have helped, but accident of timing and personality deprived Vandegrift of the best available Allied advisors. In Vila, Mackenzie assigned two young, bright RANVR officers to Rupertus's headquarters, Dick D. (C.) Horton and Henry Josselyn, in order to establish a new reporting team on Tulagi and to set the stage for the reestablishment of the colonial government. Horton had been Clemens's predecessor as the Aola district officer and knew Guadalcanal well since he had been a "walking" *kiap*. Of the Australians who accompanied Vandegrift—or were assigned out to his regimental commanders—the most assertive was Charles Widdy, the manager of the Lever Brothers plantation at Lunga, quickly commissioned a temporary pilot officer (second lieutenant) in the Royal Australian Air Force. Widdy may have known coconuts, but he knew little about the distances on Guadalcanal, the names of rivers, or the relative heights of two pieces of key terrain, the "grassy knoll" that thrust up from the jungle east of the Lunga, and Mount Austen, a considerable ridge miles from the objective area. Suspecting that Widdy had confused them all, Vandegrift and Thomas had Goettge arrange more aerial photographic coverage of the area, but the photographs went astray in the military mails between Australia and the amphibious task force. In sum, Vandegrift still needed more local help.[11]

Although the landings of 7 August went more or less as planned, Vandegrift and his staff found little cause for optimism about their future on

Cactus in the next week. First, Admiral Fletcher, arguing that he was short of fighters and fuel, cut his carrier task force's presence from four to two days while the Japanese air counterattacks took no holiday. Next, a Japanese naval force of cruisers and destroyers slipped into the area and devastated Admiral Crutchley's covering force, which lost five of six cruisers and two destroyers in a night action off Savo Island, 8–9 August 1942. Now completely naked to air attack, Turner ordered his captains to unload as much as they could and weigh anchor on 9 August. With Turner's task force went much of Marine direct access to ULTRA intelligence, for the U.S. Navy's advanced base communications unit did not disembark, which, given the peril of the situation, was understandable. Not until 15 September did Navy communicators feel that Guadalcanal was secure enough for a naval communications station that could process ULTRA transmissions. Then the Japanese, who had switched to a different variant of JN-25 on 14 August, proved to be reluctant victims. The only good news was that the airfield, named Henderson Field by the Marines, became marginally operational on 13 August, which meant that the 1st Marine Aircraft Wing (Brig. Gen. Roy S. Geiger) could begin operations, including some reconnaissance flights, a week later. It also meant more contact with the outside intelligence world, at least by messenger. Unfortunately, the 1st Marine Division crippled its own intelligence operations through Frank Goettge's enthusiasm and Vandegrift's lapse of judgment when presented with a plan "to do something." This episode—the ambush and massacre of the Goettge patrol on 12–14 August—created a special need for Martin Clemens, whose only thought at the time was to get into the Marines' lines and get some rest and decent food—as well as a real bath.[12]

Desperate for prisoners as soon as he landed on Guadalcanal, Frank Goettge found the first POWs produced by the Marines a disappointing source of information since they were either Korean laborers or low-ranking Japanese naval construction personnel. He learned that the defenders (still uncounted to his satisfaction) had fled to the west, beyond the Matanikau River, like the Lunga a major waterway from the mountains to the sea. A handful of prisoners from Tulagi offered no help. Meeting with his senior subordinates on Guadalcanal on 9 and 11 August, Vandegrift impressed them with his firmness and confidence in ultimate victory, but it was also clear that information about the Japanese force from any source was in short supply. Goettge's D-2 section, led by a charismatic intelligence chief, 1st Sgt. Stephen A. Custer, looked for more POWs. Spurred by the testimony of one Japanese naval engineer rating that some of his comrades along the Matanikau would surrender, Custer volunteered to take a Marine patrol to the place he thought he would find more defectors. Frank Goettge persuaded Vandegrift that the patrol was a risk worth taking. Even so, the composition of the patrol showed poor judgment since Goettge chose himself as the patrol leader, assisted by Sergeant Custer (an ominous name for an intelligence expert) and Capt. Wilfred Ringer, the 5th Marines intelligence officer. Other officers and enlisted men of the division and 5th Marines intelligence section joined the patrol, including a medical officer and 1st Lt. Ralph Corry, a Japanese language officer and former radio intelligence cryptographer. Ambushed as soon as it came ashore at the mouth of the Matanikau, the patrol fought until annihilated. Only three enlisted men managed to escape by swimming along the coast, an experience made so harrowing by the sea, sharks, and Japanese that one of them went mad. Two relief expeditions found no bodies, but lots of hostile Japanese.[13]

Now having lost the bulk of his division's intelligence section and that of one of his two infantry regiments, Vandegrift still did not have a sense about what sort of opposition his division and Roy Geiger's airmen faced. The 5th Marines pushed patrols out to the Matanikau and confirmed a Japanese force to the west, and the 1st Marines patrols to the east on 13 August discovered an American Catholic missionary, who said the natives had seen Japanese east of the Marines' perimeter. The division needed someone far more knowledgeable about the terrain and the situation than the British-Australian "advisors" who had accompanied the division ashore. To be fair to Charles Widdy and his colleagues, Goettge had recruited them for their knowledge of the beaches, tides, sandbars, currents, and access roads, not their tactical knowledge and great experience off the coast, of which they had little. Widdy's credibility fell when he got the creeks and rivers east of the Lunga confused in name and fordability. It seemed obvious that one of the two coastwatcher teams near the Marines' perimeter should come in, but just how this task should be accomplished left a great deal to doubt and chance.

The Marines had received more news about Clemens on 10 August, when Sergeant Major Vouza and ten islanders came into their positions with a Navy pilot whom they had rescued. Assured by their British-Australian advisors that the Melanesians were friendly and part of the Ferdinand scout system, Vandegrift issued orders to his Marines that the Melanesians were valued allies and should be hurried to the D-2 section whenever they came in, which would be in daylight hours only. Frank Goettge, still alive on 10 August, probably played the key role in alerting the division that there were "friendlies" outside their lines. Vouza also reported that Clemens was available, mobile, and eager to reach the perimeter for food and supplies. He volunteered to meet Clemens outside the perimeter and bring him in.[14]

Aware that Japanese stragglers fleeing the Lunga plain might run into his coastwatchers or that unfriendly Melanesians might betray the teams to the Japanese, Mackenzie radioed the three teams to consider working their way to the Lunga perimeter, but he gave them no further guidance. In truth, the Rhoades-Schroeder team (VQJ8) was too far away and now burdened with refugee Catholic missionaries; they would have to be evacuated by sea, a sea largely controlled by the Japanese. The Macfarlan-Hay-Andresen team (VQJ10) had two Europeans who could travel overland only with great difficulty, Macfarlan with his bad foot and Hay with his great stomach. Clemens, on the other hand, had two good but sore feet (he had no boots) and a stomach that got smaller every day. Although he had been battling a jungle fever, he thought he could get into the perimeter if someone would summon him and give him directions on when and where to meet the Marine outposts. He certainly needed some advice about how to avoid the wandering Japanese. In the meantime, Mackenzie had much more pressing business. The disaster at Savo Island and the prospect of growing Japanese naval and air attacks, even a counterlanding, created a critical need for prompt coastwatcher warnings from the northern and central Solomons. On 14 August Mackenzie and a team of three arrived by plane with a radio and supporting equipment and set up station KEN in a dugout near the northwest corner of Henderson Field, with phone lines to the division headquarters and to the Marine Air Group 23 operations center, which coordinated air defense.

Taking the designation DSIO Lunga, Mackenzie established contact not only with his agents to the north, but also with teams VQJ10 and VQJ8 in the mountains. He ordered these teams to stand fast and report any Japanese movement reported to them along the Lunga perimeter.

Presumably, he would have given similar orders to ZGJ4, but Clemens's radio had quit working for lack of power, and Clemens himself had already entered the 1st Marines' lines east of the Lunga River along the misnamed "Tenaru River," which was actually the Ilu. Clemens came in from the hills believing he had permission to do so. On 10 August Macfarlan had forwarded a message from Widdy that the Marines wanted more local expertise in their headquarters. The same message promised that further instructions and an "execute" would follow. Macfarlan told Clemens to be ready to move since he could and Macfarlan couldn't. He sent Clemens his dress shoes. Clemens needed little urging, but he heard nothing more until 13 August, when a Melanesian messenger brought a sodden note directly from Widdy. A 1st Marines patrol would meet Clemens along the eastern coastal track. First met by a party of fifty Melanesian policemen and bearers led by Jacob Vouza, a bearded Martin Clemens and his ten "boys," Clemens wearing Macfarlan's dress shoes and tattered bush clothes, joined the 1st Marine Division on 15 August 1942.[15]

Martin Clemens's contributions to the operations of the 1st Marine Division are described in his own diary and autobiography and the personal and official testimony of his Marine comrades. At his own suggestion, the 1st Marine Division asked Resident Commissioner Marchant to appoint him British liaison officer to the division headquarters while he retained his civil post as district officer, Guadalcanal, which probably pleased Charles Widdy, whose first priority was the survival of the Lever Brothers property and his Melanesian workforce. What is also clear is that Clemens was no longer a member of Ferdinand and played no role in Mackenzie's operations during the campaign for the southern Solomons. Mackenzie managed to bring Macfarlan and Andresen in from the hills in early October. Without the knowledge and approval of Vandegrift, he sent a commando party led by Dick Horton from Malaita (without Marchant's knowledge) to a rendezvous on the northwestern tip of Guadalcanal to rescue Rhoades, Schroeder, thirteen priests and nuns, and one U.S. Navy aviator. Clemens and his BSIPDF scout force had no part of the operation since they belonged to Vandegrift, who was furious when he learned of Mackenzie's action.[16]

As the island's senior civil servant, Clemens had a delicate dual mission that could be accomplished only in close collaboration with the Americans,

which was to eject the Japanese while at the same time saving Guadalcanal's civilians and property. The wise direction of the Melanesians
meant reducing their exploitation by the Japanese, who eventually flooded
into Guadalcanal at a total strength of 31,400 soldiers of the 17th Army. It
also meant keeping the Melanesians out of the considerable harm's way
created by American artillery and airpower. The best way for Clemens to
aid his people and the Marines was to integrate himself and his native
police force into the very heart of the operations of the 1st Marine Division, which is precisely what he did. His release from Ferdinand, as well
as his close working relationship with the division staff, probably
influenced his dealings with his fellow British islanders and the Australians on Guadalcanal, some of whom probably misunderstood his sudden appearance on 14 August.

Vandegrift himself took an immediate liking to the young Scot, a
Commonwealth companion to Capt. James C. Murray Jr., the intense,
cerebral Yale graduate who served as Vandegrift's adjutant. Vandegrift
remembered Clemens as "a remarkable chap of medium height, well
built and apparently suffering no ill effects from his self-imposed jungle
exile." On 17 August a correspondent with the Marines, Richard Tregaskis, found Clemens scrubbed, clean-shaven, and newly clothed in
someone else's shorts and stiff khaki shirt—and even wearing rank tabs.
He had joined the division headquarters and was telling charming stories
at his own expense about his life in the bush. He told the correspondent
nothing about his intelligence role, only that he was supposed to govern
the Melanesians. 1st Lt. Herbert C. Merillat, USMCR, the division press
officer and historian, thought Clemens might have set off a wave of envy
among the other Anglo-Australian officers because of his quick admission to Vandegrift's inner circle. A former Rhodes Scholar who shared
many of Clemens's interests in sport and the arts, Merillat became a close
friend. He shared the other officers' appreciation of Clemens's grace
under fire, but also understood that he was an essential member of the
division staff, not some court jester who traded his charm for access to
Vandegrift's outdoor shower, whiskey supply, and food. In fact, the division headquarters staff lived little better than a battalion headquarters,
and it had to endure the same bombing and shelling.[17]

In an assignment he largely defined for himself, Martin Clemens became an essential part of the 1st Marine Division "brain trust" that ran the ground war. The key members of this group were Thomas, Twining, and Snedeker from start to finish of the division's service on Guadalcanal, which ended in December 1942. Clemens worked most closely with the reconstituted division intelligence section, headed by Lt. Col. Edmund J. Buckley, USMCR, the intelligence officer of the 11th Marines, the division's artillery regiment. Buckley was an amateur, and it showed, but Thomas and Twining, both former intelligence officers, easily filled the void. The analysis of Japanese documents and the interrogation of prisoners (still in very short supply) remained with Capt. Sherwood F. "Pappy" Moran, USMCR, a former missionary and YMCA secretary in Japan. Clemens sent his scouts forth to find material for Moran to work on. The headquarters group obtained another member when Lt. Col. Merritt A. Edson brought his 1st Raider Battalion over from Tulagi. Later, as colonel of the 5th Marines, Edson remained a key advisor.[18]

In a major division reorganization in late September, Clemens gained another ally and lifelong friend, Col. William J. Whaling, who enjoyed a Corps-wide reputation as a hunter, woodsman, crack marksman, and fearless combat veteran from World War I. Promoted out of his billet as 5th Marines executive officer, Whaling remained on Guadalcanal when Vandegrift sent some other colonels home because Thomas, now the division chief of staff, wanted Whaling to command a special group of scout-snipers, reinforced by Clemens's police scouts and bearers. The "Whaling Group" would have few permanent cadre, but it would train and deploy Marine volunteers, who then returned to their parent battalions as thoroughly schooled patrol leaders. Whaling's principal training device was actual long-range patrols of several days' duration and night operations in which the Melanesians played a central role as scouts and bearers. They also proved the scourge of Japanese stragglers and unwary sentries. With Marchant's political support and arms and equipment furnished by the Marines, Clemens's force grew to number several hundred Melanesians, and Clemens quickly replaced Widdy and Father Emery de Klerk, S.M., as the islanders' key representative. Marchant even sent Clemens an assistant, 1st Lt. David Trench, a British officer seconded to the BSIPDF. Even the arrival of Maj. John V. Mather, AIF, the liaison officer with the 7th Marines, did not reduce Clemens's role at headquarters.

Clemens made an immediate impact on the 1st Division staff's ability to checkmate the Japanese encirclement of the Henderson Field perimeter. Under the concealment of darkness and facing no effective naval opposition, the Japanese 17th Army started to land reinforcements on 19 August. Clemens provided essential information on the terrain east and south of the perimeter, and his scouting network brought in daily sightings. The first Clemens contribution was in correcting and amplifying the crude sketch map the division staff used, supplemented eventually with aerial photographs. Clemens's scouts then reported that a reinforced Japanese infantry battalion had landed at Taivu Point, a report verified by a patrol from the 1st Marines. Captured on 20 August on a scouting mission, Jacob Vouza survived torture, questioning, and "execution" to return to the perimeter with more warning. Expecting an attack, the 1st Marines prepared a blazing welcome for the "Ichiki Detachment," which it slaughtered along the Tenaru River on the night of 20–21 August. Marine morale and confidence soared.

More islander reports to Clemens confirmed the massing of another assault force, the better part of the Imperial Japanese Army's crack 35th Brigade ashore at Tasimboko on 1–5 September. With Martin Clemens and his scouts, Merritt Edson and two Raider companies raided Tasimboko on the night of 7–8 September and fought a stiff battle with the rear elements of the "Kawaguchi Detachment" before withdrawing by sea. The documents and material captured at Tasimboko convinced Thomas, Twining, and Edson that the Japanese would attack the thin Marine lines on the southern edge of the perimeter, east of the Lunga. The redeployment of the 1st Raider Battalion with the rifle companies of the 1st Parachute Battalion countered the Japanese and produced the ferocious three-day battle remembered variously as the Battle of Edson's Ridge, Raiders' Ridge, or Bloody Ridge, on 12–14 September.[19]

Although scout reports assisted 1st Marine Division operations west of the Lunga perimeter, "the Matanikau Front," in September and October, Clemens made his greatest contribution by helping plan and execute joint Marine-Army operations against the Japanese positions between Koli Point and Aola. Although the Japanese no longer posed a great offensive threat from this sector, they maintained their own intelligence network of observers and radios along the coast and into the jungle, including observation posts along the long spine of Mount Austen itself. They also maintained an enclave of two thousand soldiers at Koilotumeria. In addition to the Japanese, General Vandegrift also had to cope with Admiral Turner, who thought that if one enclave was good (Henderson Field–Lunga), then two would be better (Aola). Building another airfield and defending it with stray Marine and Army reinforced infantry regiments became Turner's obsession. Vandegrift could not persuade him that the Aola enclave was unsuitable because of soil and drainage problems and a dispersion of scarce combat troops. Clemens joined the debate as a guest expert and helped reinforce the engineers' assessment that Aola would be a builder's nightmare. Turner, however, already had troops ashore, so Vandegrift's challenge was to get them out of Aola and up to the Lunga enclave. Again, Clemens helped sway the argument in Vandegrift's favor.

Working with Thomas, Twining, and Buckley, Clemens participated in a scheme to cleanse the Aola-Koli region of Japanese intelligence outposts and one regimental base camp and to recover some of the troops at Aola. The plan involved the 2d Raider Battalion (Lt. Col. Evans F. Carlson), whose August raid to Makin Island had produced ambiguous results and ambivalent feelings about Carlson, a controversial commander who enjoyed a personal friendship with President Franklin D. Roosevelt. (Carlson's executive officer was Maj. James Roosevelt, USMCR.) The 2d Raider Battalion had a tough mission: mop up any Japanese who escaped on offensive from the Lunga enclave. Reinforced with Clemens's scouts and bearers, commanded by John Mather, the 2d Raider Battalion left Aola on 4 November and reached Henderson Field on 4 December, having marched 150 miles through the jungle. The raiders left piles of dead Japanese behind them, killing about 450 with the loss of only 17 Marines. Aroused by Jacob Vouza, the Guadalcanal islanders in effect rose in rebellion and added uncounted more Japanese dead to the score. By the time the 2d Raider Battalion reached the Lunga perimeter, the Japanese presence in eastern Guadalcanal had ended and the Aola enclave was as dead an issue as the Japanese.[20]

As the American presence on Guadalcanal increased to include the better part of two Marine divisions and two Army divisions, Clemens's own role expanded and set the stage for the rest of his distinguished wartime service. He became British liaison officer to the U.S. 14th Corps, the Army command that completed the campaign for Guadalcanal in January 1943. Promoted to major in December 1942, Clemens also became the commanding officer of the Special Service (Commando) Battalion, BSIPDF, a composite battalion formed of Solomon Islanders, Fijians, and Tongans and officered by Europeans, some of them junior officers in the British Army. Clemens's battalion opened a jungle warfare school on Guadalcanal for all Allied reconnaissance and commando units. Attached to American and New Zealand units, the South Pacific Scouts, as the battalion became known, served with distinction in the landings in the central Solomons. Clemens himself led a desperate mission into the jungles of western New Georgia to find the isolated 1st Marine Raider Regiment and make a full appreciation of its situation. Making the fifteen-mile trek with one American bodyguard and one BSIPDF sergeant, Clemens found the Marines, then returned with Col. Harry B. Liversedge's recommendation that he not just be resupplied (he was), but reinforced (he wasn't) or be withdrawn (he was). For this action and his work on Guadalcanal, the commanding general, U.S. 14th Corps awarded Clemens the Legion of Merit for distinguished service. His own government had already awarded him a Military Cross for Heroism on Guadalcanal.[21]

Clemens remained in the Solomons as a civil administrator after the campaign withered away in early 1944 with the isolation of the Japanese bases on Bougainville and New Britain islands. (Until the end of the war Australian forces besieged these sick and starved garrisons, even though the crucial Pacific war operations had moved thousands of miles westward.) By the time the war with Japan ended in September 1945, Clemens had become fully engaged in the political, social, and economic reconstruction of the Solomon Islands until he finally received permission to take some leave in Great Britain. Even though he had to find a ride home in New Zealand, he first had to go to Australia to retrieve his passport. The trip had fateful consequences since he met Miss Anne Turnbull of Melbourne, the daughter of a prominent "squatter" or large landholder and cattle and sheep rancher. The Turnbull family had paid a high price in World War II since Anne's fiancé had perished in the air war against Germany, and both of her brothers were lost in the war against Japan. Anne and Martin Clemens were married in 1948 after Clemens's service as deputy district commissioner, Samaria and district commissioner, Gaza, Palestine Protectorate. Danger and political challenges continued to follow the Clemens family, which eventually included one son and three daughters.

Before his retirement from the British colonial service in 1960, Martin Clemens served for twelve years on Cyprus, where he became the commissioner of Nicosia and Kyrenia (1951–57) and defense secretary (1958–60), with a year off to attend the Imperial Defence College, London (1958). Placed on the Queen's Honors List in 1956 as an officer of the Order of the British Empire (OBE), he moved to the rank of commander (CBE) upon his retirement. Clemens's retirement at the age of forty-five while he still had a bright future in the British Colonial Service had its roots in the fading fortunes of the Turnbull family. Under Australian land-use regulations, a male heir or a reasonable substitute thereto (sons-in-law qualify) had to assume responsibility for the grazing lands held in leasehold from the government. In addition to providing a more secure social and educational life for their children, Anne and Martin Clemens had to return to Australia to keep an eye on their family business. Given his education and experience in the Solomons, Martin Clemens quickly established himself in the Australian stock-raising community, winning many awards for the excellence of his cattle and sheep. Dividing his time between his home in Toorak and his stations in Queensland, he continued his passion for boating, golf, trout fishing, horseback riding, and the arts. He became a Liberal Party organizer and a major participant in veterans' associations. He found special meaning in two of these groups, the Guadalcanal Solomon Islands War Memorial Trust and the 1st Marine Division Association. He never overlooked an opportunity to help the Melanesians who had served under his command in the BSIPDF, and he worked with success to obtain a knighthood in 1979 for Jacob Vouza, his stalwart sergeant major who had survived capture and torture by the Japanese on Guadalcanal. Upon Sir Jacob's death in 1984, Clemens organized the drive to place a memorial in his home village.[22]

Postwar recollections enhanced Martin Clemens's stature to Homeric proportions. The novelist T. Grady Gallant, serving as a young Marine artilleryman in 1942, remembered that his battery commander briefed his men before the 7 August landing that a special British officer and his Melansian scouts awaited them on Guadalcanal. This officer would supply critical information on the terrain and Japanese.[23] In the official Marine Corps commemorative history of the fiftieth anniversary of the Guadalcanal campaign, Clemens became "a fabled character . . . strolling out of the jungle into the Marine lines. He had watched the landing from the hills south of the airfield and now brought his bodyguard of native policemen with him."[24]

Once upon a time, Marines all over the world stood to attention whenever a veteran of the harrowing Samar, Philippines campaign (1901) appeared in a mess. "Stand, gentlemen, he served on Samar!" The tradition died with the veterans. Perhaps someday the veterans of Guadalcanal will receive the same honors, although Marine Corps tastes in social matters have turned distinctly egalitarian. Nevertheless, Guadalcanal veterans —and the people who write books or make movies—still recognize that we should all stand, rhetorically speaking, for Martin Clemens, one of the men who shaped the first great Allied counteroffensive in the Pacific war.

Notes

1. Jeffrey Grey, *A Military History of Australia* (Cambridge: Cambridge University Press, 1990), 125–61.

2. "Coastwatchers," in *The Oxford Companion to Australian Military History,* ed. Peter Dennis, Jeffrey Grey, Ewan Morris, and Robin Prior (Melbourne: Oxford University Press, 1995), 154–55; Eric Feldt, *The Coast Watchers* (Melbourne: Oxford University Press, 1946); Walter Lord, *Lonely Vigil: Coastwatchers of the Solomons* (New York: Viking Press, 1977). See also Peter Ryan, *Fear Drive My Feet* (Ringwood, Victoria, Australia: Penguin Books, 1992).

3. Interviews with W. F. Martin Clemens, Toorak, Melbourne, Victoria, Australia, 21–23 July 1995, supplemented with contemporaneous scrapbooks and correspondence and amplified by Clemens in an autobiographical summary, December 1996, in the author's possession.

4. Grace Person Hayes, *The History of the Joint Chiefs of Staff in World War II: The War Against Japan* (Annapolis, Md.: Naval Institute Press, 1982), 136–53; Ronald H. Spector, *Eagle Against the Sun: The American War with Japan* (New York: Free Press, 1985), 184–87; H. P. Willmott, *The Barrier and the Javelin: Japanese and Allied Pacific Strategies, February to June 1942* (Annapolis, Md.: Naval Institute Press, 1983), 3–170.

5. Ronald Lewin, *The American MAGIC: Codes, Ciphers and the Defeat of Japan* (New York: Farrar Straus Giroux, 1982); W. J. Holmes, *Double-Edged Secrets:*

U.S. Naval Intelligence Operations in the Pacific during World War II (Annapolis, Md.: Naval Institute Press, 1979); John Winton, *ULTRA in the Pacific* (Annapolis, Md.: Naval Institute Press, 1993); Jeffrey M. Dorwart, *Conflict of Duty: The U.S. Navy's Intelligence Dilemma, 1919–1945* (Annapolis, Md.: Naval Institute Press, 1983); John Prados, *Combined Fleet Decoded: The Secret History of American Intelligence and the Japanese Navy in World War II* (New York: Random House, 1995); and Capt. Wyman H. Packard, USN (Ret.), *A Century of U.S. Naval Intelligence* (Washington, D.C.: Naval Historical Center, 1996).

6. Edward J. Drea, *MacArthur's ULTRA: Codebreaking and the War Against Japan, 1942–1945* (Lawrence: University Press of Kansas, 1992); Col. Allison Ind, USA, *Allied Intelligence Bureau: Our Secret Weapon in the War Against Japan* (New York: David McKay, 1958), 3–64.

In addition to the secondary sources above, see Office of Naval Communications, "The Role of Communication Intelligence in the American-Japanese War," vol. 3, "The Solomon Islands Campaign," 21 June, 1943, NSA/CSS Cryptologic Documents, World War II, RG 457, NA, copy in the historical files, U.S. Army Military History Institute, Carlisle Barracks, Pennsylvania; and "Intelligence," Commanders in Chief United States Pacific Fleet and Pacific Ocean Areas, Command History, 1941–1945, Operational Archives, Naval Historical Division.

7. Feldt, *Coast Watchers,* 58–87, and Clemens diaries and autobiography.

8. Headquarters 1st Marine Division, "Division Commanders Final Report on the Guadalcanal Operation," pts. 1–5, June 1943, copy in the Marine Corps Historical Center Archives, Washington Navy Yard (hereafter cited as 1st MarDiv, "Final Report"). The quote is from pt. 1, 3.

For the Guadalcanal campaign as experienced by the 1st Marine Division, the official history is Lt. Col. Frank O. Hough, Maj. Verle E. Ludwig, and Henry I. Shaw Jr., *History of U.S. Marine Corps Operations in World War II, vol. 1, Pearl Harbor to Guadalcanal* (Washington, D.C.: Historical Branch, G-3, Headquarters, U.S. Marine Corps, 1958), 235–374.

Of all the secondary accounts, two stand out: Brig. Gen. Samuel B. Griffith II, USMC (Ret.), *The Battle for Guadalcanal* (Philadelphia: Lippincott, 1963) and Richard B. Frank, *Guadalcanal* (New York: Random House, 1990), both of which use Japanese sources and formerly classified intelligence documents. I have also used many of the personal letters and oral histories provided by the 1st Marine Division's staff officers when I wrote *In Many a Strife: General Gerald C. Thomas and the U.S. Marine Corps, 1917–1956* (Annapolis, Md.: Naval Institute Press, 1993), a biography of the division operations officer (D-3) and chief of staff in the Guadalcanal campaign, especially my correspondence with the late Gen. Merrill B. Twining, USMC, the assistant D-3 and D-3 for the same period (June–December 1942). These sources are described in detail in *In Many a Strife.*

Of the memoir literature, one is in a class by itself: Gen. Merrill B. Twining, USMC (Ret.), *No Bended Knee: The Battle for Guadalcanal* (Novato, Calif.: Presidio Press, 1996). General Twining died on 11 May 1996 at ninety-three, almost simultaneously with the appearance of his memoirs.

9. Oral memoir (1966), Gen. G. C. Thomas, USMC, 221–24, Oral History Collection, Marine Corps Historical Center; Twining, *No Bended Knee,* 33–41, 1st MarDiv, "Final Report," pt.1, 23 and Annex E, "Intelligence."

10. 1st MarDiv, "Final Report," pt. 2, 1–14 and Annex G, "Intelligence." Thomas, oral memoir, 261; Maj. Gen. A. A. Vandegrift, memoir, 1962, Marine Corps Historical Center; Gen. M. B. Twining, "Vandegrift" and "Critical Decisions of the Guadalcanal Campaign," memoranda prepared for the author and in his possession, 1987. For reprises of their manuscript memoirs, see Gen. A. A. Vandegrift, with Robert Asprey, *Once a Marine: The Memoirs of General A. A. Vandegrift* (New York: W. W. Norton, 1964), and Twining, *No Bended Knee,* 42–60.

11. Thomas, oral memoir, 266–71; Feldt, *Coast Watchers,* 74–87.

12. Herbert Christian Merillat, *Guadalcanal Remember* (New York: Dodd, Mead, 1982), 91–100, which is based on his diaries and notes kept while an officer on General Vandegrift's personal staff; Col. Sanford B. Hunt, USMC (Ret.) to the author, 17 July and 8 August 1988, 8 and 9 February 1997; Martin Clemens, "A Coastwatcher's Diary," manuscript memoir, n.d. [1954], copy in author's possession, 69–72.

13. 1st MarDiv, "Final Report," pt. 4, 19 and Annex A, "Intelligence."

14. Ibid.; Merillat, *Guadalcanal Remembered,* 91–100.

15. Clemens, "Coastwatcher's Diary," 133–42; Feldt, *Coast Watchers,* 88–96.

16. Feldt, *Coast Watchers,* 96–97; Ind, *Allied Intelligence Bureau,* 38–41.
For their service in the Solomons campaign, MacArthur awarded Macfarlan, Rhoades, and two coastwatchers in the northern Solomons (Jack Read and Paul E. Mason) the U.S. Distinguished Service Cross, the Army's second highest award for heroism in combat.

17. Vandegrift, *Once a Marine,* 135–37; Richard Tregaskis, *Guadalcanal Diary* (New York: Random House, 1943), 107–8; Merillat, *Guadalcanal Remembered,* 88–90, 140, 150.

18. Millett, *In Many a Strife,* 182–92; Twining, *No Bended Knee,* 73–87; Maj. Jon Hoffman, USMCR, *Once a Legend: "Red Mike" Edson of the Marine Raiders* (Novato, Calif.: Presidio Press, 1994), 165–209; Merillat, *Guadalcanal Remembered,* 101–12; Clemens, "Coastwatcher's Diary," 142–68.

19. Clemens, "Coastwatcher's Diary," 168–75; 1st MarDiv, "Final Report," pt. 4, 8–13; Merillat, *Guardalcanal Remembered,* 129–45; Thomas, oral memoir, 356–65; Twining, *No Bended Knee,* 88–102.
For an authoritative history of the Raider battalions, see Maj. Jon T. Hoffman, USMCR, *From Makin to Bougainville; Marine Raiders in the Pacific War* (Washington, D.C.: Marine Corps Historical Center, 1995).

20. Thomas, oral memoir, 449–60; Twining, *No Bended Knee,* 139–46; Merillat, *Guadalcanal Remembered,* 222–23.

21. Clemens interview, documents, and autobiographical summary provided to the author, July 1995, confirmed by the service records, Australian War Memorial.

22. Ibid.

23. T. Grady Gallant, *On Valor's Side* (New York: Doubleday, 1963), 206.

24. Henry I. Shaw Jr., *First Offensive: The Marine Campaign for Guadalcanal* (Washington, D.C.: Marine Corps Historical Center, 1993), 18.

1

"And there we were . . ."

IT WAS, I recall, at the beginning of March 1942 that I was sitting in the district office at Aola on Guadalcanal, wondering what on earth to do with a crowd of native headmen who had come in from all over the island. And there they were, clustered round my desk, hoping I could put a stop to their fears.

What could I say to them? I had taken over the district only three days earlier. The headmen had heard that my predecessor, Dick Horton, had gone; now the only other European on the station had orders to go. Terrified of what the Japanese might do to them and their families, they wanted to know that I would not desert them. And there we were, undefended, with the Japs flying over us to bomb the RAAF advance post on Tanambogo Island, nineteen miles away. What to do? I puffed on my pipe and scratched my chin.

How could I explain what had happened? The Japanese were a people for whom the Solomon Islander had had little respect: he had known them as the scruffy sailors and pearl divers who robbed his reefs and spread disease amongst native women. How could the British be defeated by such people? Would we leave the islanders to their mercy? You cannot do it, they said; I sympathized with them. It seemed awfully close, and I felt terribly alone.

Trying not to show how moved I was, I wiped my brow and spoke quietly to the circle of anxious faces: "No matter altogether Japan 'e come, me stop 'long youfella." There was an audible sigh of relief. "Business b'long youfella boil'm [follow me], all 'e way, bymbye altogether b'long mefella come save'm youme. Me no savvy who, me no savvy when, but bymbye everyt'ing 'e alright."

"If you stick with me, someone someday will come and save us, and everything will be all right." It was a flimsy promise, and it was with a sinking heart that I made it; but we all shook hands solemnly, and felt a little better, and they went home.

Feeble though it was, that pledge was the basis for the tremendous show put up by the people of Guadalcanal during the dark days that followed. Had I not given it—more important, had they not believed it—I would not be here to tell this story now.

The Strange Land

I reflected on all that had happened since 1938, when I accepted an appointment as a Colonial Service cadet to the Solomon Islands. Back then, I was not sure just where they were. From my school days I recalled that Great Britain had annexed the southern Solomons to curb the excesses of the infamous "blackbirding" trade, which supplied native labor to the Queensland sugar plantations. I also vaguely remembered that the northern islands of the group had been acquired from the Germans by treaty.

Once I knew I was going, I read the delightful translation, by an early Lord Amherst of Hackney, of the Spanish account of Mendaña's voyage of discovery. On 7 February 1568, three months after he set sail from Peru, Alvaro de Mendaña found the Solomon Islands, so named because they were thought to be fabled Ophir, the source of gold for Solomon's temple. In April a party reached Guadalcanal, named after their leader's birthplace in Valencia. On 12 May Mendaña's company celebrated communion on a small headland they called El Puerto de la Cruz—to us, almost four hundred years later, it was Point Cruz, just west of the Matanikau River, which we gained and lost so many times during the fighting.

During my voyage out, I gathered from some fellow passengers that you just turned left out of Sydney Harbor, and after 1,750 miles the Solomons were the first group on the right. "Aah," they said, "just a little bit of a trip!" I continued my reading. New Guinea, the Solomons, and the New Hebrides stretched three thousand miles from west to east, forming a natural semicircular barrier some one thousand miles northeast of Australia. They were Australia's front-line defense toward Asia and the Pacific.

The British Solomon Islands Protectorate, as it was known, comprised an archipelago of more than nine hundred islands, extending nearly a thousand miles from northwest to southeast. The government consisted of a resident commissioner, a secretariat, a legal officer, several technical heads, and a district officer in each of the eight districts. Official mail came from Suva, Fiji, headquarters of the high commissioner for the Western Pacific, every six weeks. More urgent matters were dealt with by wireless.

The most westerly district, with headquarters at Faisi in the Shortland Islands, consisted mainly of the small islands lying in or about the Straits of Bougainville; it included the much larger Choiseul, named for a French naval explorer. The Gizo District comprised the New Georgia group, islands with attractive native names such as Vella Lavella, Kolombangara, and Gizo, site of the government station. To the east lay a large district centered on Ysabel (or Santa Isabel), another island named by Mendaña. In the center of the group were the two largest districts, both by size and by population. Malaita was long and narrow; Guadalcanal was shorter, but wider, and considerably higher. Between these two sleeping lions, the smaller district of Nggela, or the Florida Islands, curled round Port Purvis, perhaps the greatest harbor of the South Pacific, and the tiny island capital of Tulagi. Southeast of Guadalcanal lies San Cristobal, which, with Ulawa, Santa Ana, and Santa Catalina, formed another district, with headquarters at Kira Kira on San Cristobal's northeastern shore. The Santa Cruz District embraced the easternmost islands of the Protectorate; the government station was at Peu, on Vanikoro.

I first set eyes on the Solomon Islands from the masthead of the motor vessel *Malaita,* which did the run from Sydney to the Solomons and New Guinea. My brother cadet and I had worn down everyone with questions and exhausted the conversation; by then it was three in the morning, but we were too excited to sleep, so we climbed the mainmast and dreamily speculated on our future. It was a heavenly night—the moon shown brightly on the smooth waters ahead, and the Milky Way shimmered across the sky. Slowly, as the ship slipped silently on, we became aware of a heady perfume, wafted toward us on a breeze; then, out of the sea, there rose the rugged outline of the islands. It was an entrancing moment. Little did we think that, four short years later, there would be many times when we wished we'd never felt their fatal attractions.

I spent a few weeks at our administrative headquarters, Tulagi. Apart from Chinatown, our bazaar and ship repair area, the island was mostly a government preserve. Rainfall was high, so the houses, of wooden frame construction, had wide verandahs all round and hinged shutters to allow air circulation or keep out the rain. As the simplest and cheapest way to ensure a supply of fresh water was to collect it off one's roof, this, generally of corrugated iron, was treated with a nonpoisonous red paint, as were the square holding tanks that were usually mounted in back of the building. In order to keep out white ants, the foundations, either hardwood piles or short concrete pyramids, rose above ground; they were capped with metal plates, whose flanged edges projected downward. Some of the older houses had wooden piles up to ten feet in height, as an added protection against prowlers. Kitchens were small separate buildings in the same style. The offices were of substantially the same construction, but as most of them were at sea level they were hot as blazes to work in.

Across the center of the island ran a wide range of gray volcanic rock, and on this most of the dwelling quarters had been erected. They all had marvelous views, and picked up any breeze that might be blowing. Houses and offices alike were dotted about in beautiful, parklike areas, where their white paint presented a striking appearance amidst colorful hibiscus, croton, and bougainvillea, and the occasional group of palm trees. These areas were immaculately kept by prison labor.

As the island was so small, one had to walk everywhere. The local headquarters of Lever Brothers, on Gavutu Island, and of Burns, Philp & Company, on Makambo Island, were both ten minutes across the bay.[1] In consequence there was always a great coming and going by launch, and the government wharf, where Treasury and Customs were located, was the great gossip center, the equivalent of the village pump. Visitors from other districts would anchor their vessels close by, and if not invited ashore would sleep on board; some, especially old seafarers, preferred to do so.

Tulagi was surrounded by colorful reefs, and it was fascinating to explore them in a bathing suit and homemade glasses. These—ordinary pieces of glass cut to shape, in wooden frames with an elastic band—fitted snugly over the eyes; this allowed one to float face down and observe what went on. We usually took along a spear and an old sack, in case a fat fish swam by or a crayfish showed himself from a hole in the reef.

It was a pleasant place, but life there seemed so artificial, and I was impatient to get my teeth into something real. Soon, however, I was posted to Malaita, where I worked under the conscientious eye of the district officer, Norman Bengough.

The DO was responsible for practically everything. I learned what it meant to sit as the local magistrate; train police; keep prisoners' warrants; act as coroner; inspect labor on plantations, do accounts, and collect taxes; supervise medical work; captain the district schooner; and even, on occasion, serve as collector of customs, boarding ships that had entered district waters without having touched at any other port in the group. The district officer was also, it seemed, the settler of disputes, not only between different groups within the native population but also between Solomon Islanders and Europeans.

My duties took me all over the island. I traveled by ship, if possible, but the district officer, or a trip to Tulagi for mail or rations, always had first call on the schooner, and I often had to go by foot. As there were no towns, there was little reason for roads—and, with the heavy rainfall, dense jungle, and frequent rivers, it would have been prohibitively expensive to construct them. Thus, bush walking was over muddy jungle tracks, broken by streams and rivers. In such a climate my expensive boots soon collapsed, and I took to wearing cheap gym shoes; I slipped more, but with the aid of a stout stick I was able to get to the end of the trail safely. No matter how far I had to walk, however, the appalling humidity quickly left me sweltering in my own perspiration, and a change was always needed at journey's end.

We used to pad along in a long, silent column. A policeman, who knew the route, led the way, and I followed. Behind me came another constable, strong and sure-footed, who assisted me if the way was too slippery. We were followed by the carriers with our bedding and rations; they were supervised by the remaining police, who also kept an eye on any felons who had been sentenced to a term of imprisonment at any court held during the tour. These had the privilege of carrying the heaviest loads. The biggest burden was a heavy ironbound, padlocked box, which contained court and Treasury forms, registers, and silver money collected in payment of tax. We also had to carry tinned rations, to which were added whatever fresh fruit and vegetables we could find en route. The farther away we were from the coast, the less likely this was.

The work done was varied, and very interesting, but the walking got monotonous—the shady jungle was always the same, mile after mile—and I used to plan magnificent meals as I went along. It was a relief to emerge once again and see the sea, with a cool-looking white schooner riding at anchor: the district vessels were no luxury yachts, but they were infinitely preferable to walking through the bush, and there was usually fresh fish for lunch. After a plunge into the clear blue water, one could put on clothes and enjoy at least some of the benefits of civilization.

Guadalcanal

From Cape Esperance at the northern end to Marau Island at the southern tip, Guadalcanal is about ninety miles as the crow flies. It is some twenty-seven hundred square miles in extent. A lofty central mountain range of broken and difficult country rises steeply to eight thousand feet. The island is covered almost entirely by dense tropical rain forest, except for man-made clearings and the plains along the northern coast. Owing to the steep fall from the central massif, and to an average rainfall of two hundred inches per annum, there are many fast-flowing rivers. In consequence, walking any distance along the coast was most difficult, and it was easier to go by boat.

Guadalcanal is frequently hot during the day and rarely cool at night, but if one could avoid malaria, as I did, by taking regular prophylactic doses of quinine, one could keep remarkably healthy. It should be remembered, however, that this was under civilized conditions of regular food and sleep; living in a muddy foxhole, on two meals a day, was quite another story.

The northern shore has long, sweeping beaches of jet-black sand. Most of the coconut plantations were scattered along this coast, and the managers either rode horses or got about by truck. (The "green" coconut required for copra was often brought in by bullock wagon.) Several plantations had young rubber trees, which were coming into production when the war started. There were goldfields in the hills to the south, and one could take a strong truck most of the way across the grass from Berande plantation; but gold mining had not got far beyond the panning stage.

In the early days, when malaria was particularly virulent, Guadalcanal was known as the "Solomon Coast." It was also noted for the cannibalism of its native inhabitants and the generous hospitality of its planters. This latter tradition was being nobly carried on by Kenneth Dalrymple Hay, the host at Berande.

Apart from the planters, prospectors, and traders, who were of all nationalities, the other European residents of the island were the district officer and the missionaries. The Melanesian Mission (Church of England) and the Seventh-Day Adventists were easily outnumbered by the Roman Catholic Marist fathers.

Besides the Europeans, who amounted to about fifty persons, there were fifteen thousand Melanesians, speaking at least six distinct languages, living on the island—some by the sea, others within reach of it, and others, real bushmen, in scattered settlements in the mountains. Some were Christians, some were pagans, but cannibalism had more or less disappeared. Their diet, when wages were not coming in, consisted mainly of root vegetables such as yams, taro and panna, and sweet potatoes. These were supplemented near the coast by coconuts, and by plantains up the valleys. Bananas and oranges grew in places, and the pawpaw, or papaya, grew in profusion everywhere. The coastal people further supplemented their diet with fish, and pigs were also kept. In the hills one found both wild and domestic pigs.

Many Europeans found yams and taro a pleasant change, but it was so easy to import foods that most had their requirements shipped in from Sydney, growing only their fruit and some of their vegetables. The steamer also brought their mail, batteries for the radio sets, and new books to read. In the hot, damp climate, the only foods that could be kept for even a few months were canned goods. All employed islanders got a ration consisting largely of rice and tinned meat, which also had to be imported. Consequently, when the Japanese invasion came, there was little means of replenishing our stocks of food, apart from planting vegetables and waiting for them to ripen in four months' time. The village dweller did not normally plant more than he wanted for his own use, as he had to clear the jungle to do so, so there was no natural surplus of food. As a result, when inter-island ships were held up by weather and the plantation rice had been finished, it was difficult to get native vegetables as a substitute.

The government station on Guadalcanal was situated centrally on the northern coast, at Aola Bay. Although the DO who selected the site was a former naval officer, I never did think much of it. A safe anchorage is of great importance in the islands; Aola's curving bay, with its fringe of palms at each end, was pretty enough, but very open. When the north wind blew in, one's vessel had to seek shelter off Bara Island to the east, and to get ashore in a dinghy became a cross between surf riding and being ejected from a nautical jack-in-the-box. The land was level enough, but our naval friend had laid out the station in a rather peculiar way. Having marked out a six-hundred-yard beach line, he placed at each end a stone, and then took parallel bearings from them, at right angles to the beach. Luckily there were no villages in the hinterland, and it was only recently that arguments had arisen between villagers and government gardeners. On looking up the plans, I had to conclude that, as there was no rear boundary, the government station ran out to the sea on the southern shore!

The station was spaciously laid out into grass lawns edged by a wide variety of colorful croton hedges. One came first to the district officer's house, a pleasant frame building with shady verandahs and a tennis court. On either side were houses for other senior officers. Bougainvillea, hibiscus, and frangipani, the fragrant pagoda tree, grew round each house. Farther back, grouped round the parade ground, was a line of large, stately buildings in the native style. These contained the district office, court, police office and barracks, prison, other auxiliary offices, and stores. Walking on, one came to the playing field, where cricket and football games were held. Farther on were the main hospital building and, across the playing field, a neat row of native huts. These were the wards of the hospital; here people from all over the island came to be healed.

There was little else on the level, except one or two shacks, of palm leaf and bamboo, that Dick Horton had erected for the teleradio. From here the land began to rise, and it had been cultivated into terraces by the families of islanders employed by the government. Here pineapples, sweet corn, and tomatoes grew amongst the root vegetables. The path climbed steeply to a small plateau; on this had been erected a house for a married cadet, who had arrived just in time to help close down the Protectorate.

This house was an experiment, a product of Dick Horton's brain. It was an attempt to build a comfortable bungalow, using the native style of construction but adding modern conveniences. Later the house became, because of its coolness and commanding position, a convenient head-quarters for reconnaissances behind the Japanese lines and, much later, headquarters for several training units. Behind it the jungle lowered in interminable darkness.

It was a pleasure to live in such pleasant surroundings. Aola was a nat-ural night stop for those going south from Tulagi; they used to anchor off, bring up the mail, and, in return for the latest Tulagi gossip, take dinner off the district officer.

The area around Lunga was the center of all the trouble during the Guadalcanal campaign. The Lunga River, one of the largest in the island, has three mouths, and the Tenaru River, two miles to the east, is probably another. Through the ages, the action of the Lunga and of the Ilu, a mile east of the Tenaru, had formed a large, diamond-shaped delta, some three to four miles square. This, with the area east of the Ilu down to Koli Point, was open country, which had been acquired by Lever Brothers. I am not sure of their total holdings, but at that time they had three adjoin-ing plantations: Kukum (also spelled Kookoom), on the west; Lunga, intersected by the three river mouths; and Tenaru, to the east. All had coconut palms in full bearing. (Some of the trees must have been rather old, for part of the area was used as a cattle-breeding station, which fur-nished cattle to Lever's other plantations. These not only provided excel-lent beef but helped to keep down the growth between the palm trees and supplied manure.)

Much of the plains behind these plantations had suffered some sort of chemical leaching, and trees would not grow there except along the nat-ural water courses. The plains were covered with kunai grass, four feet high; in war this added greatly to the difficulties of scouting, and both sides avoided them whenever possible. Their main advantage was to our pilots, several of whom made emergency landings there, and found their way back.

Those Who Served There: The Coastwatchers

When I first arrived in the Solomon Islands, each district had a wireless set for communication with headquarters in Tulagi. After the start of the European war, Eric Feldt, who had recently been appointed head of the Islands Coast Watching Service, came round to see us all; further sets were provided, and the system for observing and reporting strange things gradually took shape.

In early February 1942, with the Japanese everywhere in advance, "Tulagiradio," our headquarters communications setup, was about to move to Malaita with the resident commissioner. Bob Taylor, the senior wireless officer, had been ordered to Australia;[2] his assistant, Tom Sexton, set up his station at the RC's new headquarters at Auki, and settled down to receiving our messages and sending on our reports down south. Norman Bengough spoke with us on the regular teleradio schedules while he was still at his Auki district headquarters. Sexton performed miracles with his equipment, maintaining regular contact with Vila in the New Hebrides, more than six hundred miles away, and also with Fiji, even farther across the Pacific. Of course, he used Morse code, while we amateurs did all our work on voice. The Australian naval people at Vila soon were listening day and night, and frequently picked up our immediate traffic direct.

Our all-metal teleradio sets had been designed for the Flying Doctor Service in northern Australia. They were suited to the tropics, and easy to operate and maintain; but they were not made for hiking, and I had a lot of trouble moving the heavy six-volt batteries and the charging motor. One also had to carry tools, fuel, oil, and spares. The vital part was the vibrator, one each for transmitter and receiver; they were temperamental things, and to this day I am quite unable to describe them technically.

As I have noted, we were all relative amateurs at this wireless game. The district officers had had some practice, but men like Rhoades and Kuper had to start from scratch. The former, a veteran of the Australian Light Horse in World War I, was a quiet but determined chap with a wicked gleam in his eye. A bit of a cricket player, he had early acquired the nickname "Snowy," after a famous Yorkshire cricketer. As Rhoades was a bachelor, and had no orders to the contrary, he stayed on to manage the plantation at Lavoro, at the western end of the island.

Geoffrey Kuper was the medical practitioner on Rennell Island at the

Coastwatchers in the Solomon Islands with
Their Call Signs and Locations, 1942

Coastwatcher	Call Sign	Location
C. N. F. Bengough, OBE; Capt., BSIPDF	ZGJ	Malaita (Auki)
W. F. M. Clemens, CBE, AM, MC, LOM; Maj., BSIPDF [relieved D. C. Horton, DSC Silver Star, (Br.); Lt., RANVR, 28 February 1942]	ZGJ4	Eastern Guadalcanal (to August 1942)
M. J. Forster; Capt., BSIPDF	ZGJ3	San Cristobal
H. E. Josselyn, Silver Star, DSC (Br.); Lt., RANVR J. H. Keenan, DSC (Br.); Lt., RANVR	NRY	Vella Lavella (from October 1942)
D. G. Kennedy, DSO; Maj., BSIPDF H. Wickham; Sgt., BSIPDF	ZGJ5	New Georgia
D. G. Kennedy G. H. Kuper, BEM; Sgt., BSIPDF	ZGJ6	Ysabel
D. S. Macfarlan, DSC (U.S.); Lt. Comdr., RAN K. D. Hay; Sub-Lt., RANVR	VQJ8	Central Guadalcanal (to October 1942)
H. A. Mackenzie, LOM; Lt. Cdr., RAN/DSIO	KEN	Central Guadalcanal (from August 1942)
W. S. Marchant, CMG, OBE; Lt. Col., BSIPDF	VQJ	Malaita (resident commissioner's HQ)
T. O. Sexton, LOM, MID; Lt., RANVR H. W. Bullen; Lt., BSIPDF		
P. E. Mason, DSC (U.S.), DSC (Br.); Lt., RANVR	STO	Southern Bougainville (to July 1942)
A. W. McCasker; Lt., RANVR L. Schroeder	—	Ontong Java (from December 1942)
W. J. Read, DSC (U.S.); Lt., RANVR	JER	Buka Passage, northern Bougainville
L. Schroeder; P.O., RANVR	—	Savo (Nagotana Is.; to May 1942)
L. Schroeder (May–September 1942) F. A. Rhoades, DSC (U.S.), Silver Star; Lt., RANVR (to October 1942)	VQJ10	Northwestern Guadalcanal
A. N. A. Waddell, DSC (Br.); Lt., RANVR C. W. Seton, DCM; Lt., AIF	DEL	Choiseul (from October 1942)
C. E. J. Wilson, district officer Mrs. R. O. Boye, BEM; Hon. 3d officer, WRANS	VQO	Vanikoro

outbreak of the Pacific war. Brought back to Tulagi when the Japanese began their southward advance, he was at Aola when I took over as district officer on Guadalcanal. As I had a second NMP, I agreed to let Kennedy have him. Young, keen, and energetic, Kuper kept tabs on the enemy and did a great deal of medical work too. But he had to be ready to flee at a moment's notice: another NMP, Hugh Wheatley, who was dispatched to the Shortlands in March with a teleradio to gather intelligence, was promptly captured by the Japanese. He was never seen again.

Don Macfarlan—"Macfarlan of the Glens," as we christened him—had come up as naval liaison officer in Tulagi. He had not been long in the islands and had no experience of the jungle or the Solomon Islander, but his cheerful disposition was infectious, and with optimism and a sense of humor he overcame everything that both nature and the Japanese could throw at him.

Norman Bengough had to put up with me as assistant for two years. He was not worried at all by the Japanese on Malaita, but in April 1943, while acting as resident commissioner, he went on a reconnaissance in a RNZAF Hudson bomber, and it was shot down and lost with all hands. Bengough was a hard-working, conscientious officer, and his presence would be missed.

Dick Horton, my predecessor as district officer, left the Solomons to join the RAAF, but instead returned in a naval uniform with the U.S. Marines. He did valiant work, and was later put in on Rendova, where he earned the DSC. With him on the Rendova trip went Henry Josselyn, who had been his assistant on Guadalcanal.

Donald Kennedy had the longest spell of all of us in the Solomons. He had far less space in which to maneuver than we did, but in the later stages of the New Georgia campaign he not only had visitors but was flown back to Guadalcanal for consultation. One of Kennedy's narrowest escapes came when he was out getting supplies in his schooner and found himself face-to-face with a Japanese landing craft. In the best Royal Navy tradition, he opened fire and rammed straight into the barge, which sank, and he got home none the worse. There were no enemy survivors.

Mrs. Ruby Olive Boye was to my knowledge the only lady coastwatcher in the show. She was married to Samuel S. Boye, the manager of the Kauri Timber Company on Vanikoro. We never met, but her voice remains one of my memories: she always sounded so cheerful and imperturbable that it did one good to hear her.

Michael Forster, the district officer at Kira Kira, never had any resident Japanese on his island. He carried on his normal duties throughout the Guadalcanal campaign and stayed on till he was due for leave and a relief was found for him. Kuper did the same.

The rest of us, however, eventually needed maintenance and repair. The resident commissioner, W. S. Marchant, became badly run down and was evacuated, a very sick man. Rhoades and Sexton retired with malaria and ulcers, but soon returned to carry out many another dangerous task. Macfarlan went out with malaria and jaundice, and even Kennedy, tough as he was, was approaching nervous exhaustion when he finally left the Solomons.

Those Who Dwelt There: My Shadow Army

I remember seeing, when I first arrived in Tulagi, papers in which we beseeched the British government to let us have some more ammunition and a few automatic weapons. I believe that these were actually on the way, but were diverted to Malaya. Thus, when the statutory British Solomon Islands Protectorate Defence Force was called out in 1941, our only weapons were those of the police. These amounted to not more than one hundred eighty .303-caliber Lee-Enfields and a few Lewis guns, most of which were in Tulagi. As a result, when we expanded our various forces, we could not arm them until someone arrived with some weapons we could "borrow."

When I took over as district officer on Guadalcanal, the police detachment had a total strength of nine.[3] Corporal Andrew Langabaea was in charge, with Lance Corporal Koimate as second in command. I had two constables first class, Beato and Peli; three second class, Kao, Deke, and Chaparuka; and two third class, Londoviko and Chimi. They were the only ones who had had any form of military or disciplinary training. Together with my medical practitioner, a Fijian, and my senior clerk, from the western Solomons, Andrew and his men were the backbone of the system.

As a policeman Andrew had been regarded as rather slow, but his steadfastness and loyalty under miserable conditions earned him the British Empire Medal. Promoted sergeant major, he went in with me in the first wave at Rendova in 1943, and was wounded in the shoulder. For that action he was awarded the Purple Heart, a decoration normally reserved for U.S. military personnel.

The first two recruits I signed on, in February 1942, were Dovu and Garimani. The former was a stocky bushman with an infectious twinkle in his eye. He was a square peg in a round hole when it came to parade ground work, but he feared nothing, had a sure aim, and could pick up a trail like the proverbial Indian. On patrols he was always there when the shooting started, and I shall never forget that wicked look as, pushing rounds into his magazine, he would mutter, "B'long Japan 'ere." There were four other notable recruits in the early days: Bunga, a former company sergeant major at police headquarters; Vura; Gumu; and Chaku. All four later ran patrols or small actions on their own.

We had twelve police rifles, my .22 Winchester, and a couple of pistols to start with. Seven rifles, left behind by the RAAF, were rescued in the nick of time, together with several boxes of very useful ammunition. Gradually, through such additions to our armory, we were able to arm the other government servants, such as gardeners, clerks, hospital dressers, and store workers. They carried on their jobs where possible, and became our "Home Guard." Our recruits had to get rifles from the Japanese—if they could!

Eroni Leauli, the medical practitioner, dispersed his drugs around the island, and until they ran out he operated several dispensaries. In between times, he reported whatever information came to hand and kept up morale amongst the Solomon Islanders.

My senior clerk, to whom I have referred above, was Daniel Pule (pronounced Pooláy). He was awarded the British Empire Medal for his excellent work in debriefing those bringing in information and compiling it into clear, well-arranged reports, which were sent by runner up to me in the hills. Daniel was also responsible for feeding the multitude and for keeping a record of what he did.

Bingiti, who had recently completed his training as a Native Agricultural Instructor, organized and ran the Tulagi and Nggela party. This entailed considerable risk, not only in getting onto Tulagi itself but in returning with the information across miles of open sea in a tiny one-man canoe. Although I have seen him as green as I felt on occasion, Bingiti normally wore a pleasant smile. He was awarded the Legion of Merit for a smart piece of work on a patrol with the U.S. 25th Division behind Munda in 1943.

Laena, the bosun of the cutter *Lofung,* was one of my trustier irregulars. He came from Faisi, in the Shortlands, and was much darker than the Guadalcanal men. Laena had been detailed to guard our little ships, secreted in the mangrove swamps at Marau Sound. A party of Japs spent several weeks there, and when they moved up he came too, and brought an accurate list of all their weapons.

Kimbo and Subaliligi were two of the hospital dressers. Both did good work, especially Kimbo, who coaxed some Jap soldiers into an ambush by selling them a fowl, then returned with their rifles and the fowl. Buru, another hospital dresser, opened a coast watch in the Russell Islands with Dick Horton in October 1942.

Li-oa, my gardener, had come with me from San Cristobal; owing to his quiet and retiring nature, he had been nicknamed Leo, the lion, by one of the planters. When he could no longer attend to formal gardens, he grew food in many impossible places. Later he became adept at slipping through Japanese lines with messages. True to the courage of his nickname, Li-oa volunteered for the landing at Rendova, and there he gave his life for his country.

Apart from those I have mentioned, there were only two others who had had any training. These were Anea and Tabasui. Anea, a mouse of a man, was the warder of the prison at Aola. He became the leader of the convict supply train to my bush headquarters, wherever that happened to be. Many times he was nearly swept away by flooded rivers, and once he became so paralyzed with fright that he could not walk, and had to be carried from the scene.

Tabasui was a totally different sort of chap. He came from our headquarters prison in Tulagi with a string of long-service convicts, all murderers. Tabasui exerted an iron discipline upon his charges by giving long lectures on the virtues of discipline. Later we found that his gift of the gab was not entirely suited to reporting, but stick him in a tight spot and he'd turn up trumps.

With the trained men as a skeleton force, each village on or near the coast was expected to report any strange sights or happenings. The scouts on coastal duty spent most of their time seeing that this was done, and teaching the villagers to be accurate. Corporal Koimate's role was to collect information from the village coast watch in front of him and report it to either Macfarlan or me, depending on the urgency.

Recruits were brought in to my bush headquarters, releasing others for scouting details elsewhere. They were well trained, first for local security, then in the accurate observation and estimation of enemy ships, planes, and actions, and, later, of parties, numbers, and equipment. This process became continuous.

When Rhoades set up business, I could spare him only two of my regulars, Peli and Chaparuka. To these he added two of his own recruits, Tuaveku and Kabini, both reliable men; for the rest he relied on the local headmen and the village coast watch, which was established right round the island.

By the time the Marines arrived, the organization had got into shape, and in November it numbered about seventy-five scouts in four sections. These represented the responsible people in each area of occupied Guadalcanal during the vital stages of the campaign. The village coast watch was their supplementary eyes and ears, and their grapevine telephone service. Each section could call upon sixty or more reliable men, who were prepared to turn out for anything in the way of guiding or scouting, carrying supplies or ammunition, or getting out the wounded. It was impossible to keep records of these splendid fellows, but they played their part in passing the Marines about the jungle, arranging contact with the enemy, and collecting pilots, both Allied and Japanese. By the time the high commissioner came up, in December 1942, we had about four hundred scouts on the payroll.

Those Who Stayed There: Others Who Remained Behind

To the tourist, Guadalcanal would be quite a large island. For those of us who had to hide there, however, it soon appeared to be woefully small. Although there were quite a few of us tucked away, with no roads, and with boat travel restricted, each group was virtually isolated. In fact, there were two strong reasons for maintaining this isolation. One was that the supply of European foodstuffs was fast running out. The other was that those of us who were reporting had to keep apart, both to see more and to keep the show going in case we were surprised by the enemy.

In Rhoades's area, at the western end of the island, were three mission stations: Visale, near Cape Esperance, to his right; Maravovo, to his left; and Tangarare, farther down the west coast, near Cape Beaufort. Visale was the headquarters of the Marist Mission, which was under a bishop of the Roman Catholic Church. The Right Reverend Jean Marie Aubin came from France, for which he had fought in World War I. He was a man of character, whose courage I admired. Bishop Aubin took the view, to which he was entitled, that he was a neutral, and there was therefore no question of his evacuating his headquarters. We had many friendly but determined discussions on the subject, for I felt that I could not be responsible for his safety if he remained at the coast. In the event, he stayed, together with Fathers Scanlon, McMahon, and Wall; several lay brothers; and a considerable number of sisters.

The Reverend Leslie Stibbard was in charge of the Melanesian Mission station at Maravovo. He and his assistant, Frederick Rowley, ran a boys' school and looked after the mission printing press, which caused us all great concern at one stage. At Tangarare, Father Emery de Klerk was ordered by the bishop to leave, but somehow contrived to miss the boat. From then on, in close cooperation with my scouts and the local islanders, he carried out many useful offensive operations.

It would be appropriate here to mention Leif Schroeder. An Australian, Lafe was an old "shellback" who had arrived in the islands in a square-rigged ship. He had run small vessels and prospected for various minerals, and when I arrived on Guadalcanal was keeping a trading store on Savo Island. Although I did not know about it till later, he was given a WT set by the RAAF chaps, to warn them of the arrival of enemy planes. Lafe was not an unqualified success on the teleradio, though, as he was very deaf.

In addition to managing Berande plantation, Ken Hay had assumed command of the corporate effects of Burns Philp, which had considerable properties on Guadalcanal and much merchandise in Tulagi. He also had the last case of whiskey on the island, and we had to be very polite to him! Before communications dried up, Ken was running a hot paper war, with the resident commissioner and his firm, over the latter's affairs. When I got notes from him he used to report progress on this, with evident satisfaction or disgust.

When the evacuation came, most of the professional miners and prospectors made their way south. There remained behind three old hands, who decided that they would go on working their leases. These were F. M. Campbell, a burly Australian, who had retired from the police force to run his plantation on San Cristobal; A. M. "Andy" Andresen, a Swedish former master mariner, who had a plantation on Ulawa Island; and H. Freshwater, usually known to his friends as "Bilge," who was an Englishman.

When sailing eastward along the north coast from Berande, one passed the village of Tasimboko on the shore, and then rounded Taivu Point. After this one was sailing southeast, and the next habitation worthy of notice was Ruavatu, another Catholic center. This was presided over by Father H. Engberink, who came from Holland. His assistant was Father Arthur C. Duhamel, from Massachusetts; there were also three sisters, Sylvia, Odilia, and Edmée. Led by Father Engberink, who was determined not to leave Ruavatu, they stubbornly refused all our efforts to evacuate them.

Continuing east past the Aola government station, one came to Rere plantation, where Frank Keeble stayed during the early days. Some miles beyond Rere is the Kau Kau River, the banks of which had been turned into a coconut plantation by Clarence E. Hart. Hart did not think that the enemy would bother him, so he carried on producing copra until he could no longer get laborers to work for him, and then retired up the Kau Kau. He was affectionately known as "Concrete Clarry," after a very funny story about him. Apparently he fancied himself an engineer, for he constructed a concrete culvert on his plantation. It looked very nice until the rains came, and then it was soon washed away, as he had forgotten to make a hole for the water to pass through!

At the eastern end of Guadalcanal is another island, Marau. On the mainland opposite was another Catholic station, which had been ordered by the bishop to remain. Father Jean Coicaud was in charge, assisted by Father P. van Mechelin. There were also three Australian lay brothers, Brother Ervan (P. J. McDonough), Brother James (Richard L. Thrift), and Brother Ephrem (Ephrem Stevens).

Brother James used to get messages to me from time to time, and it was through him that I passed any messages for the local islanders. When, early in 1943, the missionaries' evacuation was arranged, he sent me detailed instructions how to find their last bottle of brandy, which he had buried in the garden in case anyone passed that way again. It was a sweet and thoughtful gesture, which I found deeply touching.

Father Jean Boudard, a dear old man who knew, from his French upbringing, how to live on the land and take with a thankful heart what God gave him, was unharmed throughout the occupation and continued to minister to the south coast people at the Avu Avu mission station. Once I sent him a note saying we were getting rather hungry up in the mountains; though his reply took four days to reach me, attached to it, in a piece of newspaper, were a piece of his excellent French bread and a piece of his home-cured bacon! The bread would have been excellent, but for the fungus that had grown on it en route. There was nothing wrong with the bacon.

What concerned me most about Bishop Aubin's decision to remain neutral was that his stations had the birth registers, with the names of all the people in the area. The Japanese were trying to compile a register of everyone on the island; if they had demanded the birth records the missionaries would not have been able to refuse them. As it turned out they did not, but had they ever put together such a list, and then issued a no-movement order, I would have had to close down or greatly modify our scouting system.

The Little Ships

> Round thy mysterious islet, and behold
> Surf and great mountains and loud river bars,
> And from the shore hear island voices call.
> —*Robert Louis Stevenson*

Owing to the great distances between islands, communication and transport in the Solomons had always been by way of sturdy cutters and schooners, capable of riding out the worst storms and of sailing should an engine break down. The islanders, who are famous for their wonderful oceangoing canoes holding up to sixty people, preferred our little ships when it came to carrying cargo.

They varied greatly in size, shape, and condition. Most skippers took immense pride in a smart ship, but we had our "traveling dustbins," especially amongst the Chinese traders. The government had a considerable fleet of vessels, all of different sizes. Let there be no misunderstanding, however: our ships were very small, the largest being not more than twenty tons burden.

The government vessels—there was one in each district, plus several at Tulagi—were wooden craft varying in length from thirty to sixty feet.[4] They had Gardner diesel engines, easy for an islander to run, which gave them a speed of six to seven knots. They also had full sets of sails, which we used at every opportunity, except when negotiating tricky passages in coral reefs.

Largest of these was the *Tulagi,* the resident commissioner's ship. A topsail schooner about sixty feet long, she had a hold for cargo, a galley forward, and a commodious cabin aft, with showers and modern conveniences. *Tulagi* had beautiful lines above the water, and elegant topmasts, but she rolled like an old sea cow, and her worm-eaten stern was reinforced with concrete. During the occupation, her beautiful white-enameled sides were painted black to render her less conspicuous, and she was stationed at Malaita.

The *Ramada* was the pride of the district officer, Guadalcanal. She was about forty-eight feet in length and had a useful schooner rig. With the foremast set, she used to get along very well. *Ramada* took it green over the bows in a rough sea, but was really quite unsinkable. She had the same sort of accommodation as *Tulagi.*

Wai-ai, the Ysabel district officer's vessel, was similar in rig to the *Ramada.* Unfortunately, she was discovered laid up in a mangrove swamp and burnt out by the enemy. The *Gizo,* which had been stationed in the district of that name, had gone to Malaita when the place was evacuated. She was more of a launch, and best suited for lagoon work.

The *G. F. Jones,* named for a leading Seventh-Day Adventist, had been the flagship of the SDA mission. About forty-eight feet in length and of considerable beam, she was notable in that she had been built entirely of local timber by Solomon Islanders at the mission headquarters at Bilua in the Marovo Lagoon, southern New Georgia. After we began to use her for Marine reconnaissance parties, she was soon rechristened *Franklin D. Roosevelt Jones.*

Hing-Li and *Kokerana* were Chinese trading schooners of more or less traditional design. They were about forty-five feet long, and carried about fifteen tons of cargo. The former was sailed to the New Hebrides after she had done very useful work for me.

The *Ruana,* one of the largest schooners in the Protectorate, belonged to the Fairymead Sugar Company, which owned plantations on Malaita. She was hardly longer than the *Tulagi,* but she had a greater draft and was well fitted out, with a powerful diesel engine. *Ruana* was notable for the remarkable voyage that Butcher Johnstone[5] made in her to the New Hebrides. She was there, doing outpost communication work, when some bright spark ran her on a reef late in 1943. Too bad—she would have been very useful back in the Solomons.

Kombito was a large and fast vessel, the property of Lever Brothers. They used her for recruiting, and for repatriating laborers to their home islands. She had a crude oil diesel engine, which emitted dense smoke from an exhaust trained up one of the masts. In 1939–40, when there were German raiders in the Pacific, the *Kombito,* with her smoke plume trailing over the horizon, gave more than a few planters a nasty scare.

The *Guinair,* also known as the *Gynia,* was a queer, launchlike craft that had been a flying-boat tender for New Guinea Airways. She was grossly overloaded and sailed down from Bougainville by a group of refugees, flying before the storm. Taken over by the AIF, she was left at Marau Sound when they evacuated the Solomons.

Lo-ai, a small cutter with half a deck and cabin top, was sailed down from the Shortlands, where she had belonged to one of the firms operating there. She was in harm's way on innumerable occasions, but seemed to have a charmed life.

The *Rob Roy* belonged to C. H. V. (Viv) Hodgess, who owned Paruru plantation on Guadalcanal. She was laid up in the mangrove swamps at Marau Sound. Unfortunately, when we got her out again, in November 1942, her stern gland leaked, and she kept sinking.

Some of these ships were very pleasant on which to travel; some were frightful. It depended upon the vessel's age, and where the engine was placed. The weather, too, could be most trying: when it was good, it was very, very good, but when it was bad, it was horrid—in fact, so horrid sometimes that I would sit on the poop in a chair lashed to the rail, just waiting for it all to finish!

By November, when we had found that they could do all manner of vital things, most of the schooners had machine guns mounted fore and aft, and large white stars painted on their awnings or cabins to identify them for our own aircraft. These little ships were extremely useful—and often extremely lucky not to be blown out of the water by the enemy. At all times they were manned by native bosuns and crews. The Solomon Islanders, born and bred to the sea and used to canoes, were excellent and intrepid sailors, who would confidently take their vessels through the narrowest passage in the dark, if it was necessary; and there is no doubt that we could not have done without them.

2

In Harm's Way

AFTER THE OUTBREAK of war in Europe, the younger members of the administration longed to escape the fretting inactivity of the Solomons and do something more active, preferably in a military capacity. Hence, like the other junior district officers, I was frustrated that I couldn't join up. On the whole I had enjoyed my term of duty and had had some interesting experiences, but we could not see why we should continue to go round, holding court and collecting tax, when there was a war on at home. Had we not been in the Officers Training Corps at school? Had we not obtained certificates in tactics, and mastered company drill?

Consequently, when war was declared, Norman Bengough and I immediately wrote to offer our services to His Majesty. In reply we received only an acknowledgment. It soon became clear that the colonial establishment would not let us go, as our numbers were just the minimum required to run the Protectorate; all we were told, however, was that we were in a reserved occupation.

The final blow to our self-esteem was a circular that came round, informing us that if we did take French leave and get away we would incur a grave risk of not being reinstated after the war. This pronouncement got us all rather disgusted and very bitter.[1] Little did we know how soon the war would be at our doorstep.

Later on we again offered our services and asked for release for joining up overseas. (At that point we had not begun to think much about the Japanese.) The reply from officialdom was the same: we were in a reserved occupation.

November 1941, and I had spent over a year in charge of San Cristobal, having passed the cadet's apprenticeship and learned the administrative game. There I felt even more out of things: it was a much smaller, more isolated district, where one might not see another European for months on end. Normally, on completion of three years' resident service, one was eligible for six months' home leave; as my tour of duty was due to end, I put in for it.

The growing threat of war in the Pacific wrote paid to that hoped-for vacation. After much pushing and shoving, however, and a trip to Tulagi to plead my case, I wangled three months' "local" leave in Australia, "on medical grounds." Happy to escape the backwater of San Cristobal, I booked passage to Australia on the *Malaita*. At Tulagi, our "Home Guard," still without weapons, was training like mad: people at last had begun to realize that Japan might enter the war. But everyone seemed to agree that if she did the war in the Solomons would be over in a matter of hours, and that there was not much use in staying on if one could get away.

As I stood near the rail, watching Tulagi and the other lush green islands fade from view, I recalled with mixed feelings the lighthearted days of my last three years. The old hands said that the best view of the islands was from the stern of the steamer, and yet they always came back again. To me, it seemed futile to go to Australia, but it seemed just as futile to stay behind.

Such was the state of affairs when the ship arrived in Sydney on 7 December. From the papers we learned that Pearl Harbor was a flaming wreck. Jack Keenan, a patrol officer from New Guinea, joined me at the stern rail—there seemed to be no point in going ashore. What on earth would happen now? After solemnly debating the situation, we tore up a one-pound note apiece and cast them out into the harbor. I did not foresee needing them much longer.

We found Sydney in a complete panic. No one appeared to know any-thing, with one exception: all the armed forces recruiting agencies had been informed that cadets and officers of the Western Pacific administrations were not to be taken on. There seemed to be nothing to do until I got a return voyage to Tulagi or knew definitely that I could not go back to the islands.

Anxious to play some small role in the defense effort, I became a volunteer ARP subwarden; but after a week, with not even a practice alarm, and no equipment except a yellow armband, I gave it up. Then I tried to join up again; this time, as the news got worse and worse, the RAN seemed a bit keener to have me. Capt. H. M. Newcomb, RN, who was taking in chaps for training as Asdic officers, was persuaded to allow me to fill in a form. He was a little more enthusiastic when we found we had been at the same school.

My orders, though, were still to return to the Solomons, on the first available transport. I found some satisfaction in the fact that all civilian shipping had been requisitioned, and that the *Malaita* was now a trooper.

Everything changed on 22 January 1942, when the Japanese bombed Tulagi. It hadn't taken them long, I thought, to get to us, but as we had seen their reconnaissance planes in the Solomons back in November I did not feel that it meant very much. Mine was apparently the minority view, however, for after that matters rapidly came to a head. The dear old Burns Philp steamer *Morinda* was pulled off the Lord Howe and Norfolk run and gotten ready for an emergency trip to the Solomons. A coal burner, almost thirty years old, she always left a long smoke trail in her wake, so it was with some reluctance that I prepared to return to the islands.

On Friday, 30 January, some friends gave me a farewell party at Sydney's leading night spot, Prince's. An air of gloom hung over everything, and the sad farewells made me feel that, though I was the one going, the others felt far worse about it than I did. Or, perhaps, they just thought I was potty.

The next day, having got no instructions from the hierarchy, I boarded *Morinda* with two other Tulagi-bound passengers, Jack Blaikie and Victor Shearwin—Police and Treasury, respectively. It seemed rather past the time for police work or collecting taxes. The crew, who were jumpy, refused to sail until we got a third cook; we waited five hours while they shanghaied one ashore.

At last we were at sea. I for one was glad of it, since the question of my status had at least been settled, if not exactly to my satisfaction. Unfortunately, we did not get the wireless news on board, so we could not be sure what was happening. As things were moving so quickly, we might even find Tulagi occupied by the enemy. The young purser, Harry Lukin, fondly imagined that he could defend the *Morinda* with our only armament—a Vickers gun, mounted atop the bridge; the way the vessel flapped and creaked in the choppy sea, I thought one bomb would shake her apart.

A restlessness now pervaded the ship. Her master, Captain Rothery, and crew were very keyed up—*Morinda* was carrying fuel and bombs for the RAAF at Tanambogo—and we were so defenseless that I felt almost naked. The black uncertainty was appalling: no one liked being alone, and men betrayed their nervousness by talking too much. I became certain of something I should already have realized, that the captain had orders to evacuate women and children, and possibly men too. Why, then, were we going back?

Sunday morning, 8 February, was nice and sunny as we steamed up between Guadalcanal and Nggela toward Tulagi. Again there was that feeling of helplessness, and my stomach was tied in knots; it was only when we saw the *Kombito* standing off that the tension was relieved. I had to laugh at Macfarlan, in his white naval uniform and tin hat, with full web equipment dangling all round him. With his gray, drawn face, he was ready for a dirty night—and it looked as if he'd had one. There were also some RAAF men, armed to the teeth, and Father Wall, who appeared just plain scared.

This military demonstration, we discovered, was prompted by a Japanese bombing raid, which was due at 1100. It was now 1045, and suddenly the sunny grin was off our faces. Lukin went aloft to ready his little gun; I didn't think it would be of much use.

Slowly the *Morinda* steamed up Mboli Passage, and maneuvered as close to the mangroves as possible. Captain Rothery stopped the engines, and the awful, eerie quiet on board, as we faced, defenseless, our first bombing, was almost unbearable. All were hoping it was a mistake, but at 1100 to the second a shout rang out: "There she is—to the northward." We were told to lie down. A fat lot of good what you did.

The next few minutes were hell. It was a four-engined Kawanisi flying boat, said the experts, and it circled twice while we waited. We felt he couldn't miss; but, thank God, he did. The captain, peering through his binoculars, gave "Bombs away!" I didn't bother to look. The plane went over, and then the bombs—four in line, about fifty yards on the port bow. Then the awful waiting while he circled—four more, but farther off, and astern. Lukin opened up with his Vickers—it sounded like an automatic peashooter. The Kawanisi, of course, was just high enough to be out of range. He circled again, then went off at last.

Mac, his sense of humor undamaged, broke the silence: "Well, by George, I was the first down!" Rothery didn't want to stay, but at length we exited the passage and tied up at Gavutu.

The presence of many island vessels confirmed that we had arrived in the midst of a general evacuation. To this day, the memory of the scene on the wharf has remained with me—drawn faces, no islanders in sight, and piles of luggage and unpacked belongings. My first order of business was to report to the resident commissioner, so I got a launch and went over to Tulagi.

I found the place in a state of hysteria. The police force had been discharged, and Lever's had taken out its people on the *Kurimarau*.[2] Now everyone was looking out for himself, and looting appeared imminent. Worse, the resident commissioner was ignorant of the enemy threat: I suggested I return to San Cristobal, but Marchant said I must either go to Gizo or leave on the ship. The former course of action was out of the question, for the Japanese were already in the Shortlands. I saw Waddell and Miller,[3] who had demolished their stations and evacuated the western Solomons. Both said it was sheer idiocy to return to Gizo now.

Reluctantly, I returned and told the resident commissioner that I would be leaving, as I had already signed up with the RAN. I tried to get my gear, but all the offices were deserted. The general opinion was that the Japs would take only a few days to come down from Bougainville. The Solomon Islanders, on the other hand, seemed bewildered. Why couldn't we do something? Why send the rifles south? Well, I supposed, if senior men thought defense was useless, it might well be.

A typewritten letter from Ken Hay describes the chaos that ensued as people fled before the expected arrival of the Japanese:

4th. February 1942.
The Manager
Messrs Burns Philp and Co. Ltd.
SYDNEY.

Dear Sir,
   After the departure of your Makambo staff for Australia I visited Tulagi to obtain stores and upon my arrival at Makambo I found that all

administrative and police control had ceased after a few bombs had been dropped on Tulagi and that the locks of the Makambo stores had been broken and the stores looted. . . .

As there was no Burns Philp representative at Makambo I decided to remove all remaining stores to Berande for safety. So far I have removed a large portion of the stores and am continuing to carry on with this work whilst the opportunity still offers and will forward you in due course a list of the goods removed.

All your important ledgers, cash books etc have been sealed and cased and will be forwarded to you under the personal care of Mr. J. A. Johnstone by first opportunity.

Pending further instructions from you I am carrying on your store business from here and invoicing goods to known clients. . . .

I have secured your current invoice book and am forwarding with Mr. Johnstone copies of invoices as from the 24th of December 1941 to date.

If it is your wish that I continue with the work that I am carrying on I shall be glad if you will radio me all necessary authority and also notify the Government as at present I have no proper authority. I will go to Makambo to attend to shipping of produce etc if any ship arrives provided I can obtain labour to do the loading. I will be taking in approximately 3000 lbs of rubber to ship and will continue to produce rubber here and copra also if labour is available.

I have no cash to pay wages with but perhaps you could make arrangements to forward some if opportunity offers.

Your Faisi and Gizo staffs have arrived at Makambo and I understand that both stores have been destroyed. The following ships are at Makambo: Lowoi, Loefung, Maravo and Salicana. It is my intention to take over these ships and endeavour to remove all your benzine, kerosene and oil stocks out here and put them inland and build leaf houses over them. After this has been completed I will find hideouts for the ships and leave crews and rations with them.

I would like to place on record the invaluable help which has been given to me by Mr. J. A. Johnstone and Mr. C. V. Widdy in evacuating your stores and I have asked the former to call and give you first hand information on the matter. . . .

Yours faithfully
/s/ K. D. Hay

I went back to Gavutu. The evacuees were all at Makambo, but Captain Rothery had refused to come in that far. With things so disorganized, there was an awful shambles getting them over to Gavutu. Then Rothery refused to take people without tickets, absurd in such a crisis. Johnson and Blake[4] tried to get on board to tell him that *Morinda* was a government charter, but they were turned away. Finally the captain agreed to take a certain number.

Blake made an arbitrary list of those going and remaining. I was to remain, along with several other men; Blake, though younger than they, was careful to include himself amongst the evacuees. A near riot ensued, as the panic-stricken crowd rushed to elbow its way on board; one fellow, a doctor, had his shoulder dislocated in the melee. Ken Hay, who also was staying, had words with a plantation man who was to be left behind, and who moaned on and on about how his wife would be all alone in Sydney without him. Fed up with his complaining, Hay, whose own wife had been evacuated to Australia in December, snapped, "Sneak back up on the gangway"—which the man, leaving his luggage behind, promptly did. Glad to leave the ship after witnessing such a disgusting display, I returned by launch to an empty Tulagi; by that time our last touch with civilization, however ignoble and uncivil, had sailed away.

The resident commissioner, who had decided to relocate to Malaita, again asked me to go to Gizo: he was convinced that the Japs would come no farther than the Shortlands. Marchant had his orderly and one servant left; the Bishop of Melanesia, Walter H. Baddeley, also had decided to stay with him. I gave the bishop a pair of shoes—I felt I might not need them much longer.

At 1000 on 10 February, as the AIF began blowing up civilian marine stores, I left for Auki in the *Gizo*. Chinatown was the scene of much looting that day, as its residents frantically left Tulagi in overloaded cutters and schooners. I found Bengough very smug, however—he seemed to think he could carry on indefinitely, without even preparing a withdrawal. His refusal to face reality was maddening. I could not stand it, so I returned to Tulagi.

Finding the resident commissioner alone, I told him that Gizo definitely was not on. Finally, Marchant, no doubt having realized that he needed every hand he could get, offered me either Malaita or Guadalcanal; I chose the latter, as Horton and Josselyn held views similar to mine, though I knew that the former wanted to go off and join the RAAF. I was given no instructions, policy, or plan, other than "act as Intelligence Officer"; so I presumed that, with God's help and a toothbrush, we would do what we could.

The next day, after loading the *Ramada* with fuel oil, Henry Josselyn and I shared a tinned lunch on board with Ken Hay and Butcher Johnstone before weighing anchor at 1500 for Guadalcanal. Tulagi looked ghastly—every place was littered with smashed crockery and furniture. We tried to stop some Solomon Islanders who were loading canoes full of loot, but it was useless; Hay and Johnstone, who were going back to Berande plantation, were both very bitter about the way the evacuation had been handled.

En route, I said cheerio to the RAAF boys at Tanambogo. Their four Catalinas, and the AIF detachment that guarded their installations, were now our one slim line of defense in the face of the enemy.[5]

3

Clearing the Decks

That evening, we got to Berande. Along with Macfarlan, who had come with us from Tanambogo, we held a conference of war.

Everything was in an uproar. The peaceful place I had known but three months before had simply disappeared. In an appalling display of cowardice and irresponsibility, many of the plantation managers had abandoned their properties and fled, without even taking their books or securing their stores. Hundreds of laborers were left to fend for themselves, unpaid, with only a few weeks' rations. Most were Malaita men; they were confused and angry and had no means of returning home. The situation had deteriorated into widespread looting and a general breakdown of civil order; no dump of stores was safe any longer. But we could not provide guards for all of them: the police had other things to do.

The next morning several of the miners left for San Cristobal with Macfarlan, who was having a scout around. Johnstone and I went to Aola to report to Dick Horton, the district officer. We found him busy with the repatriation of the laborers. Several schooners were in, and Horton and Henry Josselyn had been busy fixing them up for that purpose.[1] That afternoon, Josselyn took a small convoy off to Malaita. We decided to send

Johnstone with him, to get the *Ruana* and put all the remaining civilians on board. They should be able to get to Australia somehow.

I spent the next two days checking our air warning system. Our lookout post was situated near the top of a giant banyan tree, from which the sharp-eyed watch could spot planes over Tulagi, nineteen miles away. (On calm days one could hear them farther away than that, though most of the men could not yet distinguish the sounds of the different planes.) When an air attack was expected, the lookout would give the warning signal on a conch shell, which could be heard all over the station. The alarm was confirmed with a red flag; a white flag signaled all clear.

Before dawn on 17 February, Henry and I left in the *Ramada* for Tulagi, chancing a dash in to pick up what was left of the Central Hospital's precious gear. We arrived, after a very wearing trip, in time to pay a call on Pilot Officer Hamer and the RAAF at Tanambogo. The news was ominous indeed—the Catalinas had reported eleven Japanese cruisers at Rabaul, New Britain, less than six hundred miles away—and his men were nervous and grim.

We sat out the morning raid in the mangroves. The Japs, who seemed to think that Tulagi was still occupied, expended tons of bombs on the old radio station there. It was, of course, not working, but the tall steel mast, which still stood, apparently gave them the idea that it was the center of communications. Tanambogo, with its almost invisible aerials, did the real work.

I was pleased that Lieutenant Russell, in charge of the AIF "Independos," had taken my advice and had his men move the oil drums around on the wharf at Tulagi to give an impression of activity there. They had even put up mock clotheslines, with washing hung out as if to dry. If we could keep up the deception it would spare the RAAF and the Catalinas and buy us vital time.

Just how precarious our position had become was made clear to me when we were tied up off the hospital. I was standing in the dinghy, which was full of medical stores and being pushed back to the ship, when two fighters suddenly zoomed over Tulagi. I felt quite naked: there was nothing I could do. Luckily they appeared not to have seen us. We spent the night at Gavutu, then got away quick and fast after breakfast, before the chance of a raid.

Back at Aola, Henry took our meager force on anti-landing-party practice. It wasn't very good training: we could spare little ammunition, so they fired only a minimal number of rounds. I hoped we would not have to defend this place if the enemy came.

On 24 February, Horton returned from Auki in the *Ramada*. Dick waited until the next day to break the news: after speaking with the resident commissioner, he had decided to go to Sydney and try to join the RAAF. I was the new district officer.

There followed three days of intense activity, as I prepared to take over the government station at Aola Bay. This allowed me to take stock of our slim resources. There was much ground to clear for gardens, so I tried plowing with bullocks, but with little success—there were just too many roots. In the midst of everything we got a message telling us to return eleven drums of diesel oil that we had brought out from Tulagi; this was incomprehensible—they were likely to get bombed there, and we needed all we had. Finally, on the last day of February, I completed my inspection of Aola and its defenses.

Josselyn had been supervising the return of laborers to Malaita. Determined to play a more active part in things, he had thought up a naval patrol scheme, which Macfarlan and Hamer supported and I had been prepared to join. The idea was to get the best of the government schooners, wait till the Japs arrived, report by radio as much as we could, and then make a dash for it. While I was taking over, Henry went off to Auki and put up the scheme officially; Marchant, however, felt unable to make an immediate decision, saying he would let us know in a day or two.

In a rather mutinous letter to an Australian naval friend, Lt. W. R. Milne, which was taken to Sydney by a refugee, I described our situation at that time, and my frustration with it:

> The Office of the District Officer,
> Aola,
> Guadalcanal, B.S.I.P.
>
> Dear Bill,
>   You will, by now, have heard all sorts of stories about the shambles up here and come to the conclusion that all is scuppered and finished. However a few of us, what were left when the rats went, are cleaning up the shambles, and living quite normally.

I got back to find that the Mor [i.e., the *Morinda*] was due to evacuate the whole place and that all who were staying were to be volunteers for intelligence work. This was entirely the R.C.'s idea as Fiji had told him to get out with the rest. He told me I could not go back to my old District as the bloke relieving me had offered to stay and he offered me a district where I had never been before and where the D.O. had burnt everything and ratted. It was bombed the next day. It didn't seem quite the place to take on at this stage of the game which I told him very plainly. . . . I also find that my recall could easily have been cancelled but wasn't because the Govt Sec retired into his shell and did nothing.

It appeared also that the N.L.O. MacFarlan and Clive Hamer, in charge R.A.A.F. A.O.B. [Advanced Operational Base] had quite divergent ideas as [to] what was to be done. . . . All through the R.C. has stuck his head in the sand and said that the Japs would never come here. In fact he still believes it. We are getting a weekly raid over Tulagi, which has been thoroughly looted. . . .

The R.C. has gone out to another station and thinks he is carrying on normal administration. For the last week or so I have been Acting D.O. here, but have spent most of my time with a convoy of five boats salvaging Govt property and oil fuel from Tulagi. We creep in at early dawn pack up and hide up before 10.30 which seems to be blitz time, usually called the Tannimboko [Tanambogo] Trot, after the R.A.A.F. depot here. They dropped a nice stick on the Mor as we arrived. . . .

I have salvaged quite a lot of my gear from Tulagi, but doubt whether I will ever get any of it away from here. . . . Still why worry about things like property as long as one is alive.

After the Mor went, we sent off an old 80 foot schooner [i.e., the *Ruana*] with 5 Whites and six Chinese. . . . I heard that they had reached Vila. It was their ambition to sail in through the Heads . . . but I expect they will leave her at Vila and get something more substantial. Williamson, one of the gold crowd and Cramer-Roberts, Theodore's offsider[2] weren't too keen on the ocean trip. The latter's luggage was a shirt & bottle of 5 oz of gold.

Of the three of us here, Horton we are sending off by plane to join the R.A.A.F. and Josselyn . . . and myself are trying to get signed on as temp s/Lieuts to run a naval patrol for snooping purposes. . . . The R.C. and the D.O. on his station seem to want to go on till they get caught which seems to us rather stupid. Hence the reactionary camp on Guadalcanal. MacF, N.L.O. is to w/t Eric Feldt at Townsville and see what can be done. The R.C., of course, wants us to go on active service without joining an armed force, which is the height of folly. After several show downs he has sent to Fiji to get us our release for the duration. . . .

The worst show here was put up by the managers of the Commercial firms, who shot off in a boat after the first two bombs, without even taking their books, paying off their labour, shutting their stores or anything. In the last week or two I have had to sort out, record wages owed, and repatriate about 1500 labour off the various plantations. It was no joke with small vessels. . . .

All the best
/s/ Yours ever
Martin Clemens

Latest All is at 6's & 7's. The R.C. got a boomer from H.C. Fiji, no release. . . . We have been asked to stay for intelligence & now we are asked to carry on the administration. If you can possibly speak in some-one's ear that the R.C. must be got out for the good of the war, for God's sake do it. At present he is trying to pull the scapegoat touch on us. *M.*

Even more unfortunate, at least for me, we had drawn the RC's attention to the fact that the government records were still at Gavutu.[3] Marchant ordered Josselyn to take them down to Vila in the New Hebrides, six hundred miles away, but refused to release a government vessel to do the job. So Henry commandeered Lever's auxiliary ketch *Kombito,* which despite engine problems was well suited for the task, as she had a big hold and was very seaworthy.

On 1 March, Donald Kennedy sneaked over from Ysabel in his cutter, *Wai-ai,* to discuss things. Kennedy was older and more experienced than most of us. He loved adventure, and as he walked up to the house I noticed that he was really enjoying the present situation. A New Zealander, of strong and independent character, Kennedy intended to stick it out, either on Ysabel or farther west, and report the situation as fully as possible. Worried, like the rest of us, about our lack of military standing, he had begun to address that problem: from the RAAF he had obtained a bush hat, which he had decorated with a red band and the gilded coat of arms off the helmet of his white civil uniform. To this original headgear he had added a formidable leather belt, from which hung a small automatic, and an elegant carved ebony walking stick. It gave him a rakish appearance.

We compared notes about what had happened and what we intended to do. As I had just done on Guadalcanal, Kennedy had given firm orders to all the people on Ysabel that if the Japanese came they were to have no dealings with them, in order to avoid being in the position of having to give information to the enemy.

Kennedy was as worried as I was about the reliability of our staff, especially his NMP, George Bogese. Highly educated, Bogese was a smooth talker and a born politician, but for some years he had been the problem child of the Medical Department, and we did not feel that he was very safe to have about. Kennedy therefore proposed that I give him one of my two medical practitioners; he suggested young Geoffrey Kuper, the son of an early settler. I was not very keen on the idea, but we discussed the matter fairly and decided that, as Kennedy had fewer police, he should have a reliable NMP. Reluctantly, I agreed to transfer Kuper: Eroni seemed a skilled medical man, and I felt he would prove as good.

We still had to figure out what to do with Bogese. I am sorry to say that this time we did not refer the matter to Auki. We decided to send Bogese on a mission to Savo Island, which had never had an NMP of its own. There was plenty of medical work to do there, and we felt that if he were fully occupied he would not get up to mischief. It was a decision we would come to regret.

The last thing was to arrange a rendezvous in case the worse came to the worst, since there was really no object in going out in different vessels if we had to flit. We chose a signal to indicate that fact over the air; it was some irrelevant code word, and I am afraid that I have quite forgotten it. Horton, having composed a letter of resignation, went off with Kennedy to Tulagi.

At 2130 on 3 March, Josselyn returned to Aola in the *Kombito*. Though very tired, he went back to Auki that night, to try to get a satisfactory answer to his proposal; but Marchant said his hands were tied. Henry sneaked over to Gavutu, picked up the records, and was away for Aola before the daily Jap flying boat came by. So much for our attempted foray into naval intelligence.

We spent the following day outfitting the vessel for her long trip. Reluctantly, I provided two weeks' rations: I could ill afford to spare our scarce stores of European food, when in Vila such things were more plentiful. A competent yachtsman, Henry had thoroughly prepared for the voyage, equipping himself with various pilot books, charts, and navigational instruments. On 5 March he weighed anchor and headed south in the *Kombito*.

If it hadn't been for Macfarlan, who had turned up, in the *Tulagi,* two days before, I should have felt rather like the last of the ten little Indian boys. Though the ship returned to Malaita before I could commandeer her, I was glad to see him, and happier still that he had got rid of his crew of miners, whom he had left on San Cristobal. Mac was a godsend: he could take over the teleradio schedule and keep me from being overwhelmed by the innumerable other things that never seemed to be done.

After all the tension of the previous weeks, Mac's presence on the station was very refreshing: he could tell a good story, and he had a great sense of humor, poking fun at everything. This included what he called "your bloody commandos": "If I raise my voice," Mac said, "they'll all vanish into the bush!" I replied that they'd get there a jolly sight quicker than he would.

The military situation was not very clear. We knew from Read that the Japanese had occupied or were using Buka, just across the passage from Bougainville, and that several Europeans had been captured. Mac had been with the RAAF at Tanambogo for a couple of days, but he could not stand the bombing, which by now had become a regular occurrence. As he had not seen much of anything on his reconnaissance, he decided he would stay with me until we got news of the Japanese approaching, then head for Berande and the hills. I offered him the hospitality of the place, which was, sad to say, gradually being depleted. He was still dressed in faultless whites, but soap was getting scarce, and I warned him that he would not be able to keep it up much longer.

Also with me was Dick Horton's cook, Michael, whom I had gladly inherited together with his pots and pans. Michael was a very pleasant and cheerful character, who appeared quite happy at improvising meals out of whatever came to hand.

Another constant companion was my little dog, Suinao. I had bought him as a pup on Malaita for the tremendous price of fifteen sticks of tobacco (about five shillings). His father, well aware of his position as the district officer's dog, was more like an Aberdeen than anything else; Suinao, who was named after a famous headhunter, had his father's coat and appearance but was longer in the leg, and therefore much handier in the bush, and at getting into and out of dinghies and up and down companion ladders. He was a companionable beast, accompanied me everywhere, and was a great watchdog, which was just as well! Like his father, he would strut into a village, and, if challenged, was usually successful in establishing his social position as top dog on the island!

Although the Japs had not, so far as we knew, progressed any farther in the last few days, their bombing had increased considerably. The Catalinas now spent the night anchored off, refueling and taking on bombs, then got away fast in the morning. We kept up our communications schedule on the teleradio—with the other coastwatchers, the RC on Malaita, and the RAAF on Tanambogo. The RAAF chaps, whose call sign was VNTG, kept a listening watch every morning; if my banyan tree lookout signaled that planes were approaching, I would dash for the radio shack and warn Hamer and his men. Soon the lookout messenger would come, at the double, with detailed information—"Twofella Kawanisi 'e come 'long west," for example, or "Sixfella got'm four engine 'e stop 'long west"— and it would be immediately sent out over the air in code.

It was just as well that I was so fully occupied, because if ever I did have a moment to think then black fear returned, and with it the unanswerable questions: What was going to happen, and what were we going to do? There we were, and it looked as though we would have to fend for ourselves, as best we could.

4

Visitors, Welcome and Otherwise

D URING MY first days on the job I was extremely busy on the station. Aola was far from ready for the Japanese: islanders had to be trained as lookouts, scouts, or messengers; alarm routines worked out; food grown and stored; and everything made ready for the inevitable siege, and possibly famine, to come. The grim routine was interrupted by visits from some of the few Europeans left on the island, who were making plans for a long stay.

One morning the warder came in to report that his prisoners had been giving him cheek. They had nerves, too, poor chaps, but they would not be free to run away if trouble came. I went down and explained the situation, and they appeared much relieved. Keeping order was a slow job, since the police were trying to become soldiers too. The anti-looting patrols were enjoying some success, but only if the culprits were tried straightaway. That meant more mouths to feed, as imprisonment was the only effective penalty I had. One patrol brought in six men who had been caught in the act. They were extremely truculent, but I charged them under the Native Administration Regulations with housebreaking and riotous behavior and gave them the maximum sentence.

Then Luvena, the headman of Tasimboko, whom I had thought fairly dependable, was hauled before me for breach of the peace by an indignant mob of people from his area. At first it looked as if he had been starting a private war of his own, but after examining about thirty rather belligerent witnesses I found that it was all a case of rumor and misunderstanding. This sort of thing was becoming more frequent; it was really rather disturbing.

A few other headmen did rather better, reporting that all was well in their area. One, from the far coast, sent a messenger to inquire whether I would be collecting tax there that year! He also wanted to bring in a few criminals, but I felt that for the time being they would probably do just as well where they were.

People came in from everywhere, seeking advice. Amongst these was a stream of Chinese refugees. A large party of them had taken up residence at Balo village, only a mile from my station; their motley collection of cutters and schooners made a lovely target. Mostly traders, these people had fled from Tulagi; they were even more scared than the islanders. Fear had made them arrogant: they kept demanding food and protection, which I could not provide, but they had no intention of remaining to meet the Japs if they could possibly avoid it. To me, they represented just a further drain on our diminishing stores. All I could say to them was that I hoped to find means to send them farther south.

Another problem was Frank Keeble, an alcoholic planter's assistant. I was rather annoyed that he had found his way over to Guadalcanal. He had fortified his nerves with copious drafts of liquor, and gabbled on about how he had been told to look after this or that property or plantation, which I was not inclined to believe. Clarry Hart had the keys to a trade store near Rere; Keeble claimed he could look after it. If he could manage to keep himself alive and out of harm's way down there, it would be best for everyone concerned. He would be no good in a tight place.

More looters were brought in; they were ripping corrugated iron sheets off the plantation houses and hacking away at the timber for the sheer joy of it. One of those whom we had not yet caught was an escapee named Talu, a convicted murderer. His crime was particularly shocking. Talu had been in jail with several other prisoners; one night, he had wakened up, seized his hardwood bed board, and stove in the skull of the man at his side.

The people of Guadalcanal were reputed to be not so fierce as those of Malaita. I recalled with a chill the eeriness of the Malaita bush villages, where strangers were treated with suspicion and everyone openly carried his tomahawk or spear. It was all very well to talk of democracy when you could telephone your lawyer to see if your rights had been infringed; but in the silent jungle, where a single policeman might pass but once every three months or so, might was right, and the strong ruled by fear. I hoped the Guadalcanal people would indeed prove more amenable, but it was very hard to judge at first, with everyone in a panic.

When not occupied with court or patrols, my "commandos" were fever-ishly improving our primitive defenses and keeping a sharp lookout for enemy planes or other manifestations of hostility. They were a mixed lot. Andrew Langabaea, the corporal in charge, was a short, solemn individ-ual with a powerful chest and a good chin. He was working jolly hard, and he had a thorough knowledge of the headmen and their idiosyncrasies. Married late in life, Andrew had an infant son, Wilson, named after an officer under whom he had served. He also had a big yellow retriever, Devil.

Andrew's deep milk chocolate skin looked pale against Daniel Pule, the office clerk. Daniel came from Roviana, in New Georgia. He had short, curly, jet-black hair, and was a real purply black in color. He was the only one, apart from the NMP and one other man, who could even attempt to write a proper letter or report.

I had one other detachment, also recently formed, at a little camp called Koilo, which guarded the approach to the goldfields. It had been opened to maintain law and order, but Lance Corporal Koimate, who was in charge, now had the almost impossible job of protecting the miners' stores while doing reconnaissance in the sector from Kukum to Berande. The miners were always complaining, but Koimate was loyal, and could be counted on to stick it out.

Of the rest, Beato and Londoviko ("Londo"), as might be expected, were Catholics; Deke and Chaparuka were also products of the missions; and the others—Peli, Kao, and Chimi—were, quite simply, pagans. All were excellent bushmen, and, on the whole, as cheerful a crowd as you could meet. This was the Aola garrison—the police force, my communi-cations staff, and everything else rolled into one.

The local prison was our main source of labor. It had been reinforced, when Tulagi was evacuated, by a number of lifers, every one a murderer, under the firm hand of Tabasui.

At that time I badly needed a ship, as I wanted to make a quick trip up to the plantations at the northwest end of the island, to prevent further looting and get the people to settle down. One of the repatriation fleet had dumped some laborers from Yandina, in the Russell Islands, at Visale, instead of bringing them to Aola. The men, who were given neither food, pay credit cards, nor instructions, naturally were very disgruntled, and they had vented their anger by thoroughly looting Aruligo plantation. The only thing to do, I felt, was go up there and get them home.

After thinking over the question for several days, I put in a request for a ship to the resident commissioner. This was turned down on the ground that all the spare vessels were still occupied with repatriation of laborers. (I did not believe that nothing else was available—it was just that they did not want me to get away, as Horton and Josselyn had.) Well, if repatriation was the real reason for not sending me a ship, they could not refuse me permission to requisition one of several good Chinese vessels that were under my thumb. There was one I rather fancied, a fifty-foot schooner named the *Hing-Li*. She was about the size of the *Ramada,* and had a good engine. The owner, whom the Solomon Islanders had nicknamed "Missionarie,"[1] was quite agreeable to my chartering her; this I did forthwith, without waiting for instructions.

I had *Hing-Li* painted gray by some of the former looters. We stocked her with rations and fuel, and I had an aerial made to fit, so that we could carry the teleradio. During the daytime we kept her out of the way, in the lee of Bara Island.

On 10 March, two lay brothers and two of the Marist fathers from the Roman Catholic mission at Marau came in. They were repatriating some laborers from Paruru, having taken over the plantation launch, *Rob Roy,* when Viv Hodgess was evacuated. I gave them tea, told them the news, and cautioned them to stay very close to the coast and keep the vessel hidden during the morning.

Two days later, having cleared up all outstanding cases in court and restored law and order in Tasimboko, I decided to make a quick trip to Rere to drop off Frank Keeble. It would be a relief to get rid of him—he was rather trying, and I had to keep my liquor under lock and key. At Rere I found, as I had suspected, that the store was locked up; Hart, however, did not appear.

I noticed that the Catholics from Marau had picked up some useful odds and ends. Rice, diesel oil, barbed wire, even boats were beginning to vanish; clearly the missionaries were taking advantage of the deserted estates and helping themselves to what they could. I doubted that they had authority to appropriate anything, but I couldn't be in more than one place at a time.

Just then a Chinese schooner, *Varuna,* arrived. I had dispatched her from Aola, with an anti-looting patrol, three days before, to see about the cutter from Berande plantation. Ken Hay had heard that the homestead at Rere had been looted, so he had sent his vessel down to investigate; she had not returned, and I imagined that he was getting quite concerned about it. I sent the *Varuna* off to Berande, to let Hay know that his cutter would be coming up under sail—her engine had broken down—and tell him what I had decided to do with my passenger. Leaving Keeble as caretaker, with some ill-spared rations, I returned to Aola, in time to see to the afternoon teleradio schedule. Tulagi and Tanambogo had been getting the usual air attack, but there was still no further news of what was happening farther north.

I was up at 0600 to deal with some cases of native custom dispute. This early start enabled Macfarlan and me to set out in the *Hing-Li* to get some matters fixed up at Berande and make an overnight dash into Tanambogo, where Mac wanted to discuss developments with the RAAF. Most of the miners had, at last, decided to pay off their laborers in order to save rations, and I had obtained authority to advance them cash for the purpose. At Berande, we found a couple of schooners at anchor; Mac, who did not know the local boats as well as I or my crew did, was a little concerned, until it was established that they were friendly.

The scene at Hay's house was rather amusing. For the first time since I had been in the Solomons, I saw the Melanesian Church bishop, Wallér Baddeley, who had come over from Malaita, and the Catholic bishop on the same verandah, actually talking together! Ken was running around in a flat spin, arranging meals, trying to moderate his language, and hoping that two prelates would not come to blows.

They had brought news from the top end of Guadalcanal and from Malaita. Both were worried about repatriation and looting, and both wanted supplies. They seemed to regard the times as inconvenient rather than dangerous. Bishop Baddeley had news from the resident commissioner that a small steamer called the *Mako* was coming up with supplies for the RAAF and to evacuate the remaining European civilians. I felt much relieved, because it would improve the food situation by reducing the numbers; it was then that I knew for the first time that, whatever happened, I would be staying behind. The bishops departed on their separate ways, and Ken, Mac, and I settled down to the usual Berande evening.

The next day brought more trouble. Early on, Ken's "Home Guard" reported two strange vessels coming from the west. There was no flag, but closer inspection through Mac's binoculars revealed their European identity. They had been sailed down from Kieta by seven evacuees—a mutinous, truculent bunch, ready to take the law into their own hands. One of the Parers, of the flying family, was with them. The men claimed that half a dozen enemy cruisers had anchored at the top end of Bougainville, and a shore party had surprised a couple of planters and forced the assistant district officer to flee his headquarters. One or two said that the arrival of a Kawanisi had forced them to move on earlier. The Japs were moving in, and these fellows were scared; but all the same we felt that their tales were a bit exaggerated.

I didn't like the situation. The men all were armed, and when Ken wouldn't sell them any large quantity of supplies they shot a couple of his goats and cooked them on the beach. They were out for themselves, and I doubted they would cooperate: they didn't seem to realize, or care, that we were still trying to maintain law and order in the Solomons. One of the older ones, a miner and an expert with explosives, had deposited his gold in the government safe, but when he came to get it he found that the district officer had gone. He had placed gelignite round the edges of the safe door, covered it with clay, and set it off, blowing it neatly open and recovering his hard-earned gold.

That afternoon, leaving Ken to protect his supplies, we sailed for Tanambogo. The RAAF chaps were very keyed up, but they seemed quite pleased to see us. I had brought a lot of pawpaws and pineapples, which they fell upon with happy cries. I had also brought some broken radio spare parts; the leading technical bloke fixed them up, at the cost of two especially large pineapples!

The Air Force boys did not think very much of the chances of *Mako*'s coming up, because the number of Jap planes, which now bombed them every morning, was increasing. After some discussion, Mac decided to have *Mako* routed to one of the bays in southern Malaita, so we sent off a message to the resident commissioner. The concentration of small boats taking evacuees would have to be done very carefully, and loading would have to be very rapid.

Mac decided to stay with the RAAF, where he could be in radio touch in case the *Mako* did arrive. Dashing over to Tulagi well before daybreak, I found that one lot of my belongings, left there when I had gone on leave, was in the government bond store. The door was very stout and the windows were barred, so I left the stuff there, as it would not be of much value in the changed situation. The most important things that we collected were a rice husker and winnower, by arrangement with Father Wall. They would be handy if we ran out of food and had to grow our own rice.

The old radio station was still standing, though rather pathetically. Most of the bomb craters were in open ground, but the blast from one bomb had knocked in the end of the wireless officer's house, and his fine collection of classical gramophone records lay scattered in the seedy grass, smashed to smithereens. It was rather sad watching the tattered labels blowing away on the breeze. There was still some washing hanging on lines behind one or two of the houses, so we moved it elsewhere, hoping to give the impression that the inhabitants were still there.

On 16 March we got away to Guadalcanal, well before morning raid time. When I arrived at Berande, Ken Hay was running up and down the verandah, almost, but not quite, speechless with rage. He had had authority in writing, so he thought, to keep a watching brief over the trade store and plantation at Rere. Unfortunately, Ken had mentioned this, and the fact that his cutter had broken down, to some of the Bougainville evacuees; they had wasted no time in going down there, and he had been powerless to follow.

There was a regular pandemonium between Berande and Aola—to rephrase Kipling's immortal line, boats, boats, boats, sailing up and down again! There was the Berande cutter, sailing back with her broken engine; there was my boat, the *Hing-Li,* and the two cutters from Bougainville; and there was the other Chinese schooner, *Varuna,* which, before the evacuees had arrived, had taken Hay's instructions to Clarry Hart not to give my careless caretaker the keys to the store at Rere. One of the Bougainville launches returned to Berande; though the men came ashore and demanded food they would tell us nothing of what they had done, and they left a guard on board. The other launch was still at Rere, and Hay was extremely anxious to know what they were doing.

Ken persisted so in his tale of woe that I agreed to take him down to Rere to see what had happened. He realized the risk he was taking, but he left in charge one of the more sensible evacuees, Rolf Cambridge, whom he had known for years and who was one of his firm's managers in New Guinea. This chap had refused to join the Rere expedition, having guessed the intentions.

The next day we steamed down the coast with a fair wind, stopping at Aola just long enough to pass the word to the Chinese that they would be evacuated on the *Mako*. The lookout reported that fifteen bombers had been over Tanambogo late that morning and given it a good pasting. (The planes' noise had spurred us on—we were lucky to have missed the show.) When we got to Rere, the Bougainville cutter was heaving her anchor. We shouted the news of the *Mako* and, as we could not stop them, dashed ashore to review the damage. Keeble was gone—he had taken the *Varuna* and was heading for Berande. Ken's language got very rich indeed.

There wasn't very much left in the store. The watchman, an islander, told us that our caretaker, after getting the keys from Hart, had sold most of the stuff to the evacuees. All the doors at the plantation had been broken; the watchman alleged that the Bougainville crowd had done it, but we couldn't prove it one way or the other. Also, they had killed several of the plantation's Java sheep, which did not grow a proper fleece and were therefore well suited to the tropics. We had hoped that they would continue to thrive on the plantation and serve as our last reserve of meat.

By the time we returned to Berande later that day, Keeble, keeping well out of my way, had already sailed back to Rere on the *Varuna*. It seemed his visit to Berande had been for liquor—and Ken nearly burst a blood vessel when Cambridge told him that, after our caretaker had whined for over an hour, he had given Keeble one of Hay's last two bottles of gin. I couldn't help feeling depressed at the awful waste. What a fine war effort!

There was never a dull moment. I had hardly arrived at Berande when one of the policemen from the goldfields appeared with several persons accused of looting, together with witnesses. I had to hold a hasty court bright and early the next morning, to let the witnesses and the police return to the hills. Then I dashed back to Aola, rushed ashore, saw to my radio schedule, and embarked again for Rere to catch my missing caretaker.

As I had expected, Keeble had consumed all the gin, and was now blotto. I tried, unsuccessfully, to get a sensible story out of him. We had checked up on a dump of fuel oil near Rere; as I had suspected, he had been using it for his cunning trips, which Ken and I were unable to control. We were pretty certain that Keeble had flogged a couple of fifty-gallon drums of diesel fuel—he had no money of his own, and it was unlikely *Varuna's* skipper would be running him up and down for nothing. I was furious: here we were, with the enemy at our doorstep, and he was stealing our precious fuel and using it for pleasure trips. I dragged Keeble on board and went straight back to Berande.

The lookout there reported that twelve planes had been over the Tulagi area again during the morning, and that the Catholic fathers, who were hot foot back to Marau in the *Rob Roy,* had seen planes over Lunga. So it looked as if the Japs were beginning to look around. Now that we had got the Bougainville party together again, we sold them the *Mako* story; thankfully they believed us, and left the next morning in one of the cutters for south Malaita to await *Mako's* arrival. It was unlikely that they would do very much damage there, and if they did the RC would keep a firm eye on them. They had certainly done enough damage on Guadalcanal.

Then we settled down to grilling our unfortunate caretaker, who was now more sober. Ken knew that Keeble had collected a suitcase, containing sixty-five pounds, from the wharf at Gavutu on evacuation day; the owner, MacStewart, had been the last man to get on board the *Morinda.* Of course, some of the money had been spent, and Ken's store was also owed for the gin and certain other things that Cambridge had let Keeble have on credit. Then there was the question of the store at Rere, and the fuel. Eventually we got Keeble to part with what was left, and sent a message south instructing Hay's bankers to pay over the amount to MacStewart. He was jolly lucky to be getting it at all—we had really wasted an awful lot of time over such a trivial matter, when there were so many more important things to do. We told the cause of all the trouble that we would send him back to Aola plantation, where I could keep an eye on him. I sent the other cutter off to tell Macfarlan what we had done, and what was happening on Guadalcanal. After the exhausting investigation and all the dashing about of the last two or three days, I was just about worn out, so I collapsed into a deck chair and almost immediately fell asleep.

About sunset I was awakened by a lot of noise. The cutter had returned with Macfarlan, hot foot from the "front line" at Tanambogo. They had

had it solid that morning, while the Catalinas were still at anchor. Luckily no vital damage was done, but they had counted fifty-six bombs on the island and around the planes. It was unfortunate that with all the running around I had not been at Aola to give them a warning, because Lafe Schroeder, who had been providing a ball-to-ball description of Jap plane arrivals from his hideout on Nagotana Island, near Savo, could not warn them either, as his set had been temporarily out of action.

Mac gave us a graphic tale of the raid. As it had been much earlier than usual, no one had got away in the launch, though the boat itself had managed to find cover. All the RAAF chaps except the bosun had had to sit it out. The slit trenches there were very shallow, and they had been lucky not to have anyone wounded. Mac's bon mot was that he'd pressed himself so close to the ground he had ricked his back. I was glad he could still laugh about it.

It was high time that I went back to my office to deal with matters there. Mac wasn't ready to come, so, taking the careless caretaker, the next morning I rushed back to Aola. Late that afternoon, Fathers McMahon and Palmer[2] returned in Bishop Aubin's ship, *Santa Ana,* and offloaded Macfarlan, having earlier left a private message for dispatch by teleradio. I hoped it would arrive all right: it had to go to Malaita, thence to Vila, and eventually to the Naval Intelligence Division in Melbourne, before reaching the ordinary civilian post office channels in Australia.

There were masses of other work to do too. Complaints of all kinds, holding court, and getting the teleradio batteries charged up were enough with which to start. At 1700 on 21 March, after a warning from Tanambogo, the *Ruana* arrived, having run the gauntlet on a relief mission to Buin, southern Bougainville. I thought the trip had been canceled as being too dangerous. She was manned by the RAAF and by Jack Webster, who knew the lay of the land. Until recently, he had been working at the goldfields.

Webster described his remarkable voyage in *Ruana* to the New Hebrides. They had departed Aola on 15 February. He claimed that he had been the only qualified sailor on board, but that, as he had been a gold miner for some considerable time, he was out of practice. (By all other accounts I had heard, he was in an alcoholic mist throughout the trip!) With Johnno the butcher in command, however, and other gold miners as crew, they got through somehow, and did not see any Jap planes or ships. They had a bad time when they ran into rough water at the north end of the New Hebrides. By then they had done over four hundred miles, but there was no sign of the expected land. Forced to circle for three days, they were extremely fortunate not to run aground on the reefs; just when they were about to turn back, unsuccessful, someone sighted land at long last. I could imagine their relief.

As passengers, or rather, on this occasion, as internees, were Dr. Kroening and his wife. Kroening had been a district officer in the old German administration; on the departure of the assistant district officer from Kieta he had taken control, and other Europeans had feared that he might cooperate with the Japanese. Smart work by Jack Read, the coastwatcher, had resulted in his being picked up and whisked out of harm's way. The AIF detachment on Bougainville apparently had thought better of evacuating, and the *Ruana* had brought stores up to them. Read was getting well dug in for a long stay.

Mrs. Kroening was allowed ashore to have a bath at my house. The rest of us sat on the lawn out front and listened to gold-mining stories: I had quickly changed the subject after dropping an awful brick and telling Webster, in complete ignorance, that I had heard the only real sailor on board had been pie-eyed throughout the voyage, and that I thought that was why they hadn't been able to find the New Hebrides. He had excitedly contradicted me, explaining that it could not possibly have been true, as he was the man! This was the first time I had met him.

The next day, just before the sun went down, the sound of an airplane close at hand suddenly shattered the unearthly stillness. We leapt to the nearest slit trench, but it was only one of our Catalinas zooming low over the station in friendly salute. There was no time to warn the nearby Balo villagers, and in spite of our shouts of "B'long youme" they all dashed off into the bush. Having recovered from the first alarm of the evacuation, the islanders were gradually getting jittery again waiting for something to happen. The uncertainty was intolerable to these simple folk, but I sympathized with them. It had become a long wait, and how long it would be no one could possibly know.

5

A Watcher in the West

A<small>FTER THE</small> *Ruana* departed for Auki, to pick up fuel oil for the trip south, I got down to mending a spare WT set that had been left behind by a DO from one of the evacuated western districts. Snowy Rhoades had repeatedly written me that he ought to have a teleradio: he intended to stay, and he would have a marvelous view of Japs approaching Tulagi. Horton and I had been keeping a set for spare parts, but after no success making representations to Malaita for another set I thought it better to go without spares and let Rhoades give the RAAF warnings while he could.

Though I was not keen on getting stuck at Lavoro, I had to show Snowy how to work the set. Macfarlan was keeping radio watch for the RAAF. I decided to go down at once, while the opportunity still offered: the sooner Rhoades got started, the better. After loading up *Hing-Li* and installing my radio, we left about lunchtime on 23 March, intending to pass Cape Esperance at night.

At Berande, Hay was full of exasperation. This time it was the government: the RC had asked him to declare his stocks of fuel oil and other supplies! I persuaded Ken to give me a small petrol engine and dynamo, for Rhoades to charge his batteries.

Just before midnight, we set out for Lavoro. It was a fine, still night. The calm made me shiver—it was almost palpable. The air seemed full of portents, a feeling that anything might come out of the west. As the sea was so flat, we kept very close to the land, and arrived at Lavoro in time for breakfast. Snowy met us down at the wharf, a large pipe in his teeth and his rifle over his shoulder. He was dressed in khaki shorts and a wide-brimmed hat cocked at a jaunty angle. Beneath his bushy eyebrows, his deep-set eyes twinkled with anticipation.

While the men were unloading, we had a "dekko" round the plantation. Most of it was on flat ground; behind this the land rose to a steep cliff, with the house on top of it. The view was magnificent—I could clearly see the Russell Islands, thirty-five miles away. Rhoades would be able to give the RAAF at least fifteen minutes' warning of approaching planes.[1] Snowy was full of belligerent ideas; I thought he would probably get a chance to experiment later on, but the main thing at the moment was to get the teleradio up and working, so I could get back to Aola.

We put extension wires onto both ends of the aerial and hoisted it between two coconut palms, which we hoped made it almost invisible from the air; certainly it was so on the ground from fifty yards away. There were slipknots so he could pull the aerial down in a hurry. After we had spent a morning assembling the set under my inexpert guidance, I could not help but feel amused at myself, rattling off technical terms like an instructor. Snowy soon got the idea, and we contacted Macfarlan by lunch-time; it was typical of him that he started, "Hi, Mac, have you heard this one?" Well, the set worked, and that was all that mattered.

We both worried about the difficulty of giving Snowy some sort of military status. Since the beginning of March, we district officers had been gazetted, by radiotelephone, as second lieutenants in the British Solomon Islands Protectorate Defence Force. The RC, as commanding officer, had taken the exalted rank of captain, the highest provided for under existing legislation. I understood that Marchant was trying to have this revised to suit the altered conditions, but in the meanwhile neither of us had the power to make Rhoades anything other than a member of the Defence Force. Then, too, there were no uniform regulations, nor was there any sort of uniform or distinguishing badge. Promising to take up the matter, I told Snowy that, now he had a teleradio, he could also agitate about it himself. I left him a formal note of appointment as "a member" of the Defence Force; we knew it would mean very little should he fall into the hands of the Japanese.

Rhoades readily agreed also to keep an eye on native affairs in the area. I told him that if he arrested any troublemakers—there appeared to be far more roaming about than I had expected—I would send police to collect them or risk another trip myself.

After a hasty goodbye, I dashed off to Visale for tea with Bishop Aubin. He still insisted on remaining neutral. I told him that, though I respected his ideas, even if I had a ship when the Japanese arrived she would probably be far too busy to answer any messages for help or evacuation. He appeared to accept this, and asked no more than to be left to carry on his work. In that case, I said, the less his priests prowled around the plantations "salvaging," the better, for they always seemed to leave in their wake a trail of false rumors. I also told His Reverence that neither Hay nor anyone else could spare him any more tinned food.

We were off after sunset. A pouring rain had obliterated all landmarks, and I overshot Berande, but just before dawn we spotted the light, and dashed ashore to pass the news. Ken had steaks for breakfast. I was glad of a square meal, for I had to spend the morning holding court: he had passed the word that I was coming, and the headmen had brought in a large crowd of malefactors.

When I got back to Aola at nightfall, I was dead beat. Mac was in good heart, and with his help manning the teleradio I was able to spend the next few days intensively "cleaning up." All the district headmen had been ordered to report the situation in their area every two weeks, and to bring in cases for court, so that all should see that we were still keeping law and order.

Corporal Andrew was busy training police recruits, and the cultivation of vegetable gardens and digging of slit trenches were going on apace with all available labor, even convalescents from the hospital. The headman from Marau reported that the Catalina not on patrol now spent the blitz hours there every morning; luckily the Japs hadn't started to wander about or look for fresh targets. Much to my annoyance, Bengough had sent over another fourteen Chinese to join our happy band. They said that he had refused to feed them. I knew he knew that our food supplies were scanty, so I sent him an indignant signal, but got no reply.

Mac and I talked every night. As we had to keep lights out, there was nothing to do but sit on the verandah and listen to the rustle of the coconut palms by the beach. I reminded him of an incident that I had related in Tulagi. It had happened at Aola, where I was spending an evening with Dick Horton on my way in from San Cristobal. At sunset, we were watching the police doing "flag down" when a small white airplane, at great height, streaked past our astonished eyes. We had no means of identifying it as it faded into the gloaming, but we knew single-engined planes were scarce as hen's teeth in Australia, and we had no airfields in the islands. There was little doubt that it had been a Japanese cruiser plane—the shape of things to come. All of us, I think, had felt a chill down the spine, but we had hardly realized the implications. We had yarned away about the shortcomings of our defenses and the inefficiency of our reconnaissance services, but none of us had known just how limited our resources were.

Mac and I laughed over Tulagi in those days. It was there that I had met him. He was only a reserve officer, and had never served outside Australia, but although he and the administration had differences of opinion he had got on very well with everyone. Mac had seemed to have a far greater appreciation of the fact that it was time something was done to prepare the islands for the inevitable war with Japan. To a certain extent, he had visualized what would happen once the Solomons were evacuated, and was more prepared than most of us to accept it. But he was concerned principally with coastwatching, whereas people like Horton and me had felt that there was no future in it, and had not welcomed the prospect of being taken prisoner before we could get in a lick at the enemy. I hadn't really known where my duty lay. I suppose I was still finding out.

After all the rushing about, Aola seemed a haven of rest; yet its very quietness, and the lack of callers, became ominous—was something about to break? A medical dresser, who had set out for Visale, returned unexpectedly. I felt strangely uncomfortable.

A few hours later, I had little time left to wonder why. On 30 March, at 1830, a message came in from VNTG—three Japanese cruisers and a transport had been spotted by the Catalinas off Faisi, in the Shortland Islands.

The effect on Mac was electric. Although this meant that a landing force was definitely headed our way, I did not expect it that night. "Never mind when, boy," he said, "they're coming, and that's good enough for me. I'm off!" And with that Mac packed up his gear, took his teleradio, and was off in *Hing-Li* up the coast to Berande, to go and set up camp somewhere in the goldfields. It took him thirty minutes. His departure was so precipitate that there was little time to protest; so, as he clambered on board from the dinghy, still in faultless whites, all I could do was wish him the best of luck, muttering, "Keep your skates on, mate."

I walked back up to the house, feeling rather lonely. It looked as if each of us would have to work alone. Mac would have excellent observation from Gold Ridge, however, and to keep the teleradios dispersed was the best policy. Apart from pushing out as much information on the Japanese as possible, my job would be to try to keep the administration functioning, and the population friendly throughout the island. It would not be an easy task.

I had also received orders to "deny all resources to the enemy," which in plain language meant a scorched-earth policy. Although there was little of any real value to an invading force, apart, perhaps, from ourselves and our teleradio sets, the Japs might try to work the plantations. To put a copra dryer out of action was rather difficult; if I had had the orders before, I could have visited most of the plantations on the Lavoro trip.

While I was pondering the problem, Rhoades, quite suddenly, went off the air. One of his last messages had been that the northwestern villages were running wild; now I had three reasons to see him, and in an instant the decision whether to take another trip to Lavoro had been made for me. It would not be so safe this time. The Japanese had waited a long time before coming to Faisi; would they keep moving, or would they consolidate again? It would be rather awkward to sail round Cape Esperance in my little schooner and find myself in full view of a cruiser or two en route to Tulagi at six times our best speed. I spent all night trying to puzzle out what to do; when on 1 April I found that Rhoades was still off the air I decided to chance my arm and go straightaway. It was All Fools' Day—who cared? Perhaps I'd have fool's luck.

Away we went. At Berande, Mac was still organizing his move inland, with Hay flapping about the Catholics' staying behind. In spite of what I had told the bishop, he had been asking for tinned meat. I told Ken I'd have another word with him. It was 2000 and pitch dark when I anchored at Visale in the pouring rain. From the lack of lights ashore I could see all the missionaries had gone to bed. Sending a message by dinghy to let them know who it was, I turned in on top of the cabin for a few hours' rest.

We heaved anchor at false dawn and left immediately; I could not spare the time to talk to the bishop. We had been running through the mist for half an hour when suddenly the ship leapt into the air and just as suddenly plunged down again, and came to a grinding halt. Most of us were thrown to the deck; one or two scouts sitting on the gunwales were thrown into the sea. The worst had happened: we had overshot the passage and taken a knife-edged reef at full speed. I had visions of losing the ship, the teleradio, and possibly some of the men as well.

In two ticks the bosun and Chaparuka were over the side, and after some diving they found that we had merely stripped some of the copper off the false keel. Only the last twelve inches was still aground; so, after everyone on the ship had been sent onto the bowsprit, Chaparuka and the bosun, standing on the reef, gave a mighty heave behind and we were clear, with no real damage done. It was fool's luck, after all. As he emerged over the gunwale, dripping wet, Chaparuka said, "Me thank God 'e stop 'long youme." "Him now!" I replied, in that classic pidgin English equivalent of "You're goddamned right!" We all heaved a sigh of relief.

It continued to rain softly, and we got to Lavoro without further incident. Rhoades had been having trouble with one of the vibrators; luckily I had learned, by trial and error, to fix them, and he was soon on the air again. We chatted all morning about native affairs, and how to keep the northwestern end quiet. I was very short of trained policemen, but promised to try to send him a couple. It was bound to be my last trip to the area for some time to come, so we had to fix everything. When all was done, we had a feed, and Snowy walked me down to the dock. We shook hands firmly and wished each other good luck; I wondered if I'd see him again.

On the way back I called at both nearby missions, "earth scorching." Reverend Stibbard, the Church of England missionary at Maravovo, was not very keen on destroying things: he accepted that it would be much better to evacuate, but was very reluctant to do anything without his bishop's orders. His food stores were well hidden, mostly in water tanks, and also the type for the mission printing press. I chatted that evening with Bishop Aubin at Visale, then snatched a bit of sleep as we lay at anchor there.

Next morning I called at all the plantations down the coast, from

Aruligo to Tenaru. From the beach, the homesteads looked the same as they had in peacetime, but it was quite a different story when one got closer. The laborers had looted everything of value, smashed the rest, and eaten most of the stores and livestock. I cannot remember the number of places at which I called—there must have been almost a dozen—but though I had not visited any of them before, and did not know the former residents, it was very sad to see all the properties in such derelict condition. We removed the flue pipes from the copra dryers and the distributor heads from the trucks, and dismantled any other machinery we could find.

About sunset we got to the Tenaru River, and anchored close to the black sand beach. All of us were very tired, and after arranging the watch I fell instantly to sleep. In the morning I waited long enough to check in on the teleradio, which I rigged on a coconut stump, just out of reach of the surf. No fresh move had been reported from the Japs at Faisi; so far, so good.

At Berande, Ken Hay was on his own, and comparatively amiable: he did not seem to have any immediate cause for exasperation, except the Japanese. It was there, I remember, that we drank the last known bottle of beer on Guadalcanal, draining our glasses after a solemn two minutes' silence.

Macfarlan had not yet gone bush; he had in fact gone across to Tanambogo, to have a final chinwag with the RAAF. There was such a lot to do, but I could not go straight on to Aola: I had to stay at Berande to hold court, and to tick off a couple of native priests who had been "undermining" Hay's morale by spreading false alarm and despondency amongst his staff.

Pressing on to Ruavatu, I had great difficulty explaining the scorched-earth policy to the fathers, who objected strongly as they had large quantities of copra that would have to be destroyed in due course. There was a Lever's plantation adjacent to the mission station, and I had to go there and do over the machinery.

At 1800 on 5 April I got back to Aola, quite relieved at having done all I wanted and suffered no interference. Corporal Andrew was waiting for me. His report was laconic: "Everyt'ing 'e alright." It was, too. Andrew had done a great deal while I was away. He had responded superbly—he was twice the man he had been when I first arrived at Aola—and I realized I was beginning to rely on him. The confusion was at last becoming organized.

6

A European Murdered

THE NEXT MORNING, Rhoades came in well on the air, thank good-ness, and I had a long talk with Bengough. My set was working well in spite of frequent moves. While I was away, my household, such as it was, had been transferred, lock, stock, and barrel, to the cadet's house at the back of the station, whence I could duck into the jungle, by a variety of routes, at short notice.

The final evacuation was at last beginning. Daniel Pule got the Chinese party mustered; many of the original 150 had already moved on to San Cristobal or south Malaita, and his tabulated lists now showed a strength of only 47. We had great difficulty persuading them that they could not take more than a small amount of money with them when they were evac-uated. I relieved them of as much of it as I could, giving them receipts to take to Sydney; I needed all the cash I could get to keep paying staff and police, even though there were few places where they could buy anything.

As Andrew had the station running smoothly, I refueled and provi-sioned *Hing-Li* for the eastern leg of the earth-scorching program. Sailing after lunch, I headed southeast, toward my first stop, Rere. We anchored at 1530. It did not take long to disable the equipment: I burned down the old copra dryer and gave instructions for the demolition of islander-built structures. Next morning I was very pleased to be able to do the radio "sched" with a quarter-sized aerial rigged between the schooner's masts; I kept my fingers crossed until Snowy's drawl assured me that VQJ10 was on the air. Wasting no time, we plugged on to Kau Kau.

I was not entirely prepared for the contrast. Clarry Hart was carrying on as if Japan had never come into the war. He still had eleven men working for him! Hart claimed to be producing ten to twelve tons of copra a month; he was also working Maronia, a small plantation nearby. It was baffling: I had been carrying out orders to deny all resources to the enemy, and here was Clarry Hart producing them, or at least one of them. He believed that he could get it shipped, too, if the Japs did not come too close. Who was right? The chief thing, for now, was that he seemed quite happy. I told him to get a jungle hideout organized forthwith. The northwest wind was blowing up a choppy sea, so, waving farewell, at 1300 we splashed out in the dinghy and, with the wind behind us and all sails set, scudded down the coast in fine style.

At Marau Sound, I anchored at the Catholic mission station, which I learned was called Makina. We went and inspected Hodgess's plantation at Paruru, on the other side of the strait, but there was very little left except the buildings: a certain amount had been looted, and the Catholics had taken away the rest. Luckily there was no copra. I had a word with the crew of one of the RAAF "Cats," which was sheltering there for the day. They did not, repeat, *not,* like the bombing, and they had a deuce of a lot of work to do keeping tabs on the Japanese. Their one day off each week was spent either going to or coming from the slit trenches on Tanambogo, unless they could get permission to come down to Marau.

The next morning I took the opportunity to wander around Makina with Brother James Thrift. Like the other two lay brothers he was a schoolmaster, for the main object of the mission was to run a school for the boys of the area. As in most mission schools, the boys worked in the fields in the afternoons, to provide their food. They had some excellent gardens, on good flat, alluvial ground, once riverbed, though there were too many stones for good plowing. I told them to plant up as much as they could, against hard times. The fathers had made no preparations for moving: they did not intend to go bush unless and until Bishop Aubin gave them the word. I remarked that, as it was extremely unlikely that the bishop would ever have the time or the necessary facility to give them the word, they should get used to the idea of having to make the decision for themselves. That, they said, they couldn't do. They were all very brave men, but . . .

We were back at Makina when another Cat appeared, the wild waving of its wings before it landed indicating that the crew had a message for me. It turned out that a supply vessel had arrived at Tulagi the day before, and was busy unloading stores.[1] That was good news. But a black cloud already hung over everything, for the teleradio had earlier brought some very bad news indeed.

The grim message, forwarded via Macfarlan and Bengough, gave me the cold shivers. It was from F. M. Campbell, who had stayed at the goldfields. Campbell wanted me to come there immediately: he suspected that a European had been murdered. It would be disturbing news if it was true, for if the murder of whites had started our chances of survival were slim, even if we did manage to keep out of the hands of the Japanese.

The dead man was a penurious old-timer called Billy Wilmot. An ex-sailor, he had settled in the Solomons, but hadn't done too well and eventually had drifted into odd jobs and beachcombing. When the price of copra fell, he had got a job on the goldfields, but had not held it very long. Advanced in years, he had lived alone in a small shack on the river, between Gold Ridge and Campbell's place, doing nothing. Most of the miners and the locals had had a soft spot for Billy, and would leave him food from time to time. It would be hard work finding the truth.

After bringing in the Marau district headmen for a pep talk, I decided that all the coastal villages would have to be evacuated at the first sign of enemy landings, and the people moved to secluded bush villages inland. Kennedy was trying the same thing on Ysabel. This would reduce to a minimum the possibility of the Solomon Islanders' contacting the Japanese. There was, I felt, a reasonable chance that most of the population would be loyal, but I had no doubt that the best of them, if closely questioned, might give away our whereabouts, under pressure of fear. The headmen agreed with the policy, and promised early action. Word went out to all other headmen of what they were doing.

We heaved anchor and ran up the coast to Aola. After a brief inspection in the dark, and a few hours' rest, I was off before dawn for Berande, to investigate Wilmot's death. On the way we saw the ship going down the channel, and although she was several miles out I climbed the rigging and waved like mad as she sailed away. "Give my love to Sydney!" I shouted, and swallowed hard.

At Berande I found my early start had been wasted, as Hay, who had promised to drive me across the plains, was in bed with malaria. Then my NMP, Eroni, whom I had brought for the postmortem, developed a violent toothache, so I packed him off to Auki in *Hing-Li*. I felt thwarted by these delays, because a quick inquiry into Wilmot's death was vital, to let us know where we stood.

Macfarlan, who had just returned from Tanambogo, told me of the marvelous luck they had had with the ship. She had remained hidden during the raids the first day, but the day after five planes had bombed her while she was close to the wharf at Tulagi. Luckily there were no hits. It was agonizing listening to Mac as he tried to contact the RAAF. Jap aircraft seemed to be over Tulagi in ones and twos practically all day, and VNTG was off the air for five hours. We thought that they had all hopped into the launch and gone to Nggela to the mangroves, and that the radio watchkeeper was pinned down in a slit trench. When we got through to them later on, however, they had a sad story to tell. They had no report on damage at Tulagi, but Tanambogo and Gavutu had had a real plastering. Obviously, the radio sets had survived, but the Japs now seemed to have a good idea of what was there. I felt very uneasy, and spent a sleepless night in gloomy speculation.

The next day we climbed onto Ken Hay's old Ford and bumped across the grass plains. It was pretty warm, but there was a dry breeze blowing, and all the scene wanted was a few giraffes to make it look like Africa. After the road ended, we had to walk three miles to Bamboo Creek, the first identifiable point of the mining area. We got to the police post at Koilo by 1100, and after a swim in the river and an early lunch we trudged on up the river to Campbell's. The river valley where he had his workings was quite wide and pleasant, but the riverbed made a rough path.

The miners had built simple shacks of native leaf, but unless it was raining they lived in the open, with plenty of blankets against the cold night air. We found Campbell, with his two sons, sitting comfortably in his deck chair smoking a large black pipe, as he had always done on San Cristobal. Freshwater and Andresen, the other two remaining Europeans, had come down to join the convention, and we settled in to a real old-fashioned tea party.

After we had exhausted discussion, Campbell and I got down to the Wilmot case. Wilmot's shack was a few miles up, so Campbell, who was no longer young, had sent his sons in his stead. Their photographs indicated a violent death. Billy's revolver had been on the table in front of him, and therefore everyone initially had assumed that he had blown his brains out.

Now, however, there were doubts. In the first place, the incident had occurred on Good Friday, when the people from the surrounding villages, most of whom were Christians, were at home. Second, Campbell, a former police officer, was suspicious of the blood marks all over the hut: in his experience, bullet wounds to the head did not bleed until after the impact, and then rather quietly. It was strange that here the blood had been splashed far and wide. In addition, Campbell had known Wilmot for many years, and in his opinion Billy was not the sort of person who would have taken his own life. Although he had not been much of a success, he had got on extremely well with the islanders, and had been respected by everyone in spite of his poverty.

The report of Wilmot's death had come from one of the very few men known to have passed his isolated shack that day. This fellow had worked for the old man for years, visiting him daily and occasionally cooking for him. A Christian, he had long been well known to many Europeans, and was as mild and peaceful as they come. On Good Friday, exactly a week before, the man had arrived at Campbell's about nightfall; he was in an awful state, and obviously had had a nasty shock. He had gone to Wilmot's to clean up and fix him an evening meal. From the door he had seen Billy collapsed over his table in a pool of blood, with blood splashed all over the hut. Scared out of his wits, he had not known what to do, and had come hot foot down to Campbell for advice.

After closely questioning everyone concerned, I decided that we would have to go up and dig the poor old boy out. I can hardly describe my feelings that night—I did not know what to make of the case, and I could not sleep. It would be hard work finding the truth, and even if we did discover what had really happened it would be even more difficult to find out who had done it.

Next morning, taking along Campbell's boys and collecting Kelemedi,[2] a Fijian with some medical training who was caretaker on one of the leases, I walked up to Wilmot's place. The trip there, via a short but almost vertical cut known as Keeble's Steps, took over three hours. It was not on any direct route, and local people only occasionally passed that way. Since the goldfields had been evacuated, passersby had been even fewer.

I found a one-room shack with two doors, set in a small clearing covered with dense long grass that showed no footprints. It was hardly furnished at all: a rough bunk bed against the wall, and next to that a fixed table, at which Wilmot had been sitting. A Penguin novel and his glasses were on the table, and they were covered with blood. His pistol, which also lay on the table, was quite clean. I wondered why. The holster hung on the wall behind. Although blood had run down onto the bed, there was far more spattered on the walls, not so much behind as to one side of the old man. There were even spots of blood on the opposite wall, twenty feet away. The only other thing was a clothesline on the other side of the room, on which hung an old undershirt with some peculiar blood marks on it. It was all very strange.

The pistol attracted my attention. Not only was there no blood on it, it also was well greased, and the grease was old. There were four rounds in the chamber, and the safety catch was on. The old servant, who seemed genuinely sorry about Wilmot's death, had told me that Billy had always kept the pistol close by him but that he had never seen him open it up. I inspected the grease around the mouth of the barrel; then, on a sudden inspiration, I went outside and fired a round into the air.

I found what I had suspected: grease had been pushed out of the barrel grooves by the round I had just fired. That confirmed that the pistol had not been used for some time. It was at least extremely unlikely that Wilmot had shot himself, greased the barrel, and put the safety catch on again; nor did it look as if anyone else had used the weapon recently. A chill ran down my back, and I went outside to where they had disinterred him.

It was raining hard, but even so the atmosphere was pretty nauseating, and all of us used eucalyptus-oil masks. As Campbell and I had suspected, decomposition during the last six days had removed most of the clotted blood from Wilmot's head. There before us was clear evidence that he had not been killed with a bullet: there were no holes, and no powder marks, but only a clean cut, starting over the left temple and extending over the left ear. There was a slight angle in the middle, and from the length of the cut we all agreed that it could have been made by two powerful strokes of a very sharp axe. That would explain the blood on the walls: the first blow would have splashed blood onto the wall nearby, and the second would have spattered more blood all over the place. Whatever it was had gone clean through the bone and severed a portion of the brain. The rain had washed the wounds clean, and made all strikingly clear.

Wilmot must have been reading at his table when someone came in. He probably took off his glasses, and while he was putting them down the intruder must have quickly swung his long-handled axe, which he had probably concealed behind his back, and brought it down hard on the old man's skull. This all tallied with the distances between bed and table. It was grave news indeed.

We took some more photographs, and then, in the pouring rain, hastily reinterred poor Billy; as no flowers were available, we planted epicure beans on top of the grave. After erecting a wooden cross at his head, we went back to the hut.

I had another look at the undershirt on the clothesline. There was another clue. The strange blood marks were not splash marks: they clearly showed the outline of an axe head of about the same size as the cuts on Wilmot's head. The other marks looked as if someone had wiped blood off his hands, perhaps to disguise the marks of the axe; but he had then hung the shirt the wrong way round. The evening mists were beginning to creep in, so we departed, shivering slightly inwardly, and trudged up to Gold Ridge to camp the night. It would be ideal for Macfarlan: there was a magnificent view of Tulagi Harbor and Tanambogo.

I felt very uneasy going to sleep that night, with visions of the corpse before my eyes. Was the murderer in the area, and were we also on his list? Was he a local man, or was he a wandering pagan who had settled an old blood feud by taking a European head?

In 1890, Charles Woodford, the first resident commissioner, had given the contemporary view of Solomon Islanders: "The main object of their lives is to take each other's heads. They are not, however, what can be called a courageous people. . . . They are like wild beasts, always prowling about for prey, but rarely attacking unless they feel that they have their victim in their power without risk to themselves."[3]

Woodford added: "In cases of attacks upon white men at any rate there is . . . an absence of the fear of future consequences. . . . But the prime motive for attacks upon white men and natives alike lies in the fact . . . that these people are primarily and emphatically savages, with some good points certainly, but in their nature reigns unchecked the instinct of destruction."[4]

Although many of the Solomon Islanders of 1942 obviously had come a long way from that sinister background, its presence could still be felt in the bush, and eternal vigilance was a necessity of life. Most of the plantation laborers came from Malaita, where the inhabitants were still mostly pagan and native custom, still very austere, died hard. A cause was attributed to most deaths, especially of persons who had not completed their normal span of life. This cause was laid at the feet of some "devil" or spirit, who had been asked to kill the man by someone antagonistic to him. The dead person's mother, father, or nearest relation consulted a *fa`atabu* (holy man) and mentioned the name of the one who he believed caused the death, or he could say merely that it was a stranger. In due course this person would be killed by the relation, or by a professional headhunter who had been given the contract or had heard that a reward was out for a head. If this did not appear possible, another life was necessary to balance matters, and a white person was considered especially good.

This was the old custom, and it was possible that one of the laborers, having gone bush when the others were repatriated, might have remembered some old death that needed squaring up and had taken it out on old Billy Wilmot, thinking that government control was over. Many murders of white men in the Solomons had happened in that way, with no apparent motive. Later the perpetrator had owned up, satisfied he had been correct in observing clan custom; but of course the dead man could not be brought back to life.

Next morning, all the headmen and people concerned turned up for the inquest. I spent all day trying to find out what had happened. Wilmot had been murdered, and now we knew how, but it was hard to establish the time of death. Since all the Christians had stayed in their villages on Good Friday, we were able to account for nearly everyone who lived within a day's walking distance. Only two or three men, including Wilmot's servant, had passed down the valley that day, and their alibis were very nearly perfect. One man had just the axe for the job, but it was perfectly clean, and it could not be proven that he had carried it on Good Friday. Finger-printing was out of the question.

It was a deadlock. After my experience on Malaita and San Cristobal, however, I knew that the perpetrators of this sort of crime found it diffi-cult to keep it to themselves. The only alibi about which there was any shadow of doubt belonged to the man with the axe; I held him in custody for further questioning, feeling that he might spill the beans later on. There was little else I could do except remove the man from the area and keep him under close watch. (As Campbell said to me later, if he knocked me off, at least we should know who had murdered Billy Wilmot!) Next morning it was a gloomy party that went down the river, with the suspect in front marching between two policemen.

Discussing the postmortem at Campbell's wasn't very cheerful, but we brightened up a little bit when mail arrived from Ken Hay. We sent the man back to ask him to bring the truck up the next day, and then I had a last try at getting the miners to evacuate. Both Campbell and Andresen had plantations on San Cristobal, and they would probably have been much safer there. But not a bit of it—they all reckoned that they would be happier where they were. Saying goodbye in the morning, I hoped I would see them again.

I spent some time at Koilo briefing my police, then walked to Bamboo Creek, where the truck was waiting. The drive across the grass was burn-ing hot, and it was a relief to get into the shade under the coconut palms of Berande. Ken had been keeping a pretty good watch over Tulagi, and as far as he could see nothing untoward had happened. All was quiet on the coast, and there was no sign or news of any enemy landings in the area. I made up my reports and coded them for next morning's radio schedule.

Since the evacuation, Hay had continued to produce rubber at Berande. He liked to think that he was helping the war effort, even if it could not be immediately shipped anywhere useful. As there was nothing else to do, Ken showed me how it all worked. The trees had only recently come into bearing, and they were yielding very well: Hay was producing about three hundred pounds of processed rubber a day. At dinner, we worked out how much Ken would have got if he'd shipped it out. It was quite worthwhile.

On the way back, I called at Ruavatu and tried once more to persuade the fathers to retire to the bush. They still refused to move. After the alarms and excursions of the past two weeks, I was dead tired, and I returned to

Aola, on 15 April, prepared to go to sleep for a week. Andrew, now promoted sergeant, greeted me. "All quiet, I hope, Andrew," I said. He smiled. "Yes, Sah, 'e all quiet, but tumas work 'e stop. Altogether 'long bush 'e no stop quiet. Plenty headman 'e come bring'm tumas man for court. Altogether steal, make'm fight, do'm no good. Altogether Catholic missionary no boil'm order b'long you for go 'long bush. Altogether say order b'long Bishop, mefella neutral, stop 'long saltwater. Headman b'long youme say altogether no hear'm talk b'long 'im, 'e hard work tumas for altogether stop quiet. 'Long station nomore everyt'ing stop goodfella, me shift'm house b'long you ontop, altogether plant'm tumas kaikai, everyone 'long lookout 'e no sleep."[5] "Number one, Andrew, number one," I said.

With this comprehensive report I was well satisfied. The district headmen were playing the game, and trying to maintain law and order. I was also glad to hear that news of the inquest on Wilmot had traveled before us, and that my prompt arrival on the scene had had a reassuring effect all over the island. But there was much lawlessness afoot, and though the headmen who had brought in the lawbreakers were fairly cheerful they were finding it very hard to assert their influence, and none of them made any bones about the difficulty of maintaining control. I lay awake wondering whether they would stick it out when the Japs arrived.

The cadet's house, to which Andrew had transferred my quarters, was very cool, and comfortable enough; but it was a little eerie at night, with the jungle close behind and our suspected murderer down on the station. I did not feel at all happy, and was no longer in the mood for sleep.

7

In Which We Prepare for the Worst,

and the Enemy Arrives

W HEN I GOT to the office the next morning, there was little need to stop and think what to do. The queues of people and their multifarious business, as well as the station accounts, would keep me busy for days to come. The reorganizing of stores and growing of food continued. Most important of all was the air watch. It had become a full-time job, and extremely efficient: the Guadalcanal men had responded very well to training. They had excellent sight and hearing, and by now most of them could distinguish the different planes by the sound of their engines.

Visiting headmen reported anarchy on the southern coast. While they brought a lot of malefactors to court, most complained that there were many other scalawags whom they could not catch.

At lunchtime a new character entered the scene. He was a small, quite bald man who blinked his eyes in an odd way. Charlie Bird was a master mariner, and one of the old hands. It was not quite clear from where he had come—I had heard that he had been standing by to evacuate the RAAF. Charlie was going down to San Cristobal in a Chinese schooner, *Sam Dak,* with some harebrained scheme for starting copra production there. He also made the sensible proposal, to which I agreed with alacrity, that he take our careless caretaker, Frank Keeble, with him.

Andrew and my "commandos" were feverishly busy, coaxing, persuading, or bullying the coastal villages to move inland, and to organize a Home Guard to report any enemy or strange activity along their section of the coast. (As observation was our main role, there was no question of forming offensive sections. We were far too short of arms to inflict damage on an enemy force, however small, and it would be far more useful to fade into the jungle and continue observing.) Most of them were keen to help, but they lacked resolution. The most difficult thing to tell them was what to expect, and what would be important.

The police had so much to do that I could not spare anyone to carry on the investigation of Wilmot's death, so I signed on four more police recruits for Aola and sent the four chaps relieved, in "plain clothes," off to Koilo. Andrew would have to train the new men in the military virtues in his spare time. I lost no sleep over the fact that I had no authority to engage them. One of the lads signed on was a stocky, reddish-haired bushman named Dovu, straight from the hills. Although he was completely untrained, I felt that he would be a useful member of the force in the future.

One quiet afternoon I found a bag of cement on the station. The cadet's house had no steps, and it seemed a pity to waste it. Remembering my Colonial Service course training, I set up the necessary wooden shuttering and made some very fancy steps. No sooner had I laid down my trowel than Leong, the doyen of the remaining Chinese colony, appeared. The burden of his lay was simple: "We have no food, we have no bedding, we're scared of the Japs, and we want a ship to come and take us away." I patted him on the back and tried to explain the situation, but all I could really say was, "Bad luck, old man, it may be worse tomorrow." What annoyed me about the remaining Chinese was that they were not prepared to do anything, not even to try to sail their schooners south; and so they went on, waiting and waiting—and for what?

I heard by teleradio that Rhoades had been commissioned a sub-lieutenant in the RANVR. Not that he had anything to show it: like me, he had neither a badge of rank nor a uniform. I myself was now a captain in the Protectorate Defence Force, yet I did not have even a plain khaki shirt, and my headgear was but an ordinary brown civilian hat. Macfarlan was the only one on the island in uniform. I sent Snowy a message of congratulation, inquiring whether he would call his shore station "HMAS *Brush-Turkey*."

On Friday, 24 April, we had a welcome visit from some of the RAAF, come to stay the weekend. The crash boat brought ten of them, together with Hay, Macfarlan, and Stackpool.[1] They all looked pretty pale and drawn, and seemed rather edgy. Like me and Mr. Micawber, they were waiting for something to turn up. Apart from the bombing, which was having its effect on them, there had been a complete lull in enemy activity. It was all quite strange: the Japs had been in the Shortlands for a rather long time, and it was reasonable to expect them to come farther south. There wasn't much good in sitting around getting morbid, so I got on with the entertaining and arranged a cricket match between the visitors and a combined station team. I was jolly glad to see them.

At sundown on Saturday, Andrew turned out our entire "force" and put on a parade. Although we had no music, they put on a combination of beating the retreat and hauling down the flag, and the guests were duly impressed! On Sunday our visitors departed in a much happier state, and I was left to deal with a new guest, Father Engberink, who stayed till nightfall. We went over all the old arguments: he would not move without word from the bishop, so he still had made no preparations for leaving Ruavatu, his main object being to protect the mission plantations and property, even if the enemy came. I told him quite plainly that I did not think the nuns would be safe, but I had no power to order them to go.

I spent Monday morning trying to deal with arrears in court, but was interrupted continually by the lookout, reporting attacks on Tanambogo. The RAAF had had another bad bashing. Poor devils, they had only a few Bren guns, belonging to the AIF, with which to defend themselves. If only they had had something more lethal, I am sure that they would have returned as good as they got.

The bombing had increased perceptibly in volume, and it was clear that plans would have to be readied for the evacuation of Gavutu and Tanambogo. On 29 April Charlie Bird called on his way back from San Cristobal. He was going to stand by to evacuate the RAAF in an aged coaster, MV *Balus*,[2] which had been hidden away in the mangroves at Dende, on the south coast of Nggela Island. Don Russell, the lieutenant commanding the AIF detachment, had asked for charts. They, too, were not unmindful of the fact that our time was limited, and he was getting the *Ramada* ready to flit.

For my part, I had finally admitted to myself that, sooner or later, I would have to evacuate Aola, and the sooner I made plans, the better. Consequently, I had made several reconnaissance trips into the interior, to find a spot where I could keep the teleradio going, no matter what happened. I chose a village called Paripao, eight miles into the dense jungle and about one thousand feet up, as our first point of retreat. It had enough tall trees to solve aerial difficulties and provide lookouts, and yet be unsuspected from the air. We used a palm tree for one end of the WT aerial; for the other we cut a long, straight sapling, erected it on a tabernacle, and carefully camouflaged it with long creepers. As the teleradio operation was paramount, I did not worry much about accommodation: the best camouflage was living in native villages, which could be quickly adapted and as quickly evacuated, leaving no trace of our occupation. We had a bolt hole for escape.

So much for my own worries. The lack of activity on our part must have made it clear to the Japanese that we had little in the way of naval forces in the area. Now they had at last decided to advance, and their forces were massing in the western Solomons.[3] There was not much we coastwatchers could do about it except sit and wait. I could not help recalling the words of Henry V, in the third act of Shakespeare's play: "We are in God's hand, brother."

The next few days were utter pandemonium. At 0700 on 1 May the RAAF crash boat arrived, towing one of the irreplaceable Catalinas. She had been damaged the day before: a Kawanisi, flying in very low over water and much earlier than usual, had evaded Schroeder's notice and unloaded its bombs round two planes, which were moored off Tanambogo awaiting radio instructions from Port Moresby. Macfarlan, Rhoades, and I had shouted ourselves hoarse on the teleradio trying to pass a warning, but we couldn't get through because the RAAF was busy taking orders from Moresby and the Cats were waiting to receive on a different frequency. The second plane had managed to take off across the bay, but not before a large hole had been blown in her wing; she never got into the air, and was eventually picked up by the Japanese Navy. Her pilot, Geoff Hemsworth, and his crew were never seen again.

Flight Lt. Terry Ekins, the Catalina's commander, introduced himself to me and the shivering crowd on the beach. He wanted to have his plane towed to shore, and talked about flying in a rigger to mend her; but a quick look convinced me that "our Cat" was quite unserviceable, and would probably be with us for keeps.

The first thing to do was to hide the Catalina. Anyone who has ever walked round one will know what a difficult task that was. We assembled the men of three villages and all hands from the station, but she was far too heavy to haul off the beach, so the police went to half a dozen other villages for reinforcements. Meanwhile, we dug a slipway across the beach and lined it with coconut fronds. By noon we had four hundred eager helpers; having organized different teams, either pushing the plane or pulling on ropes, we slid the Cat across the sands until her wings were close up to the trunks of the overhanging coconut palms. The noise was indescribable, each team grunting and yelling as they heaved. Then the tail was covered with coconut fronds and the temporary slipway obliterated. The operation raised morale to a certain extent, but the calm sea and an almost imperceptible drizzle gave an eerie impression of stillness, and the noise of the bombing at Tulagi sounded like a grim warning of the storm to come.

While this was going on, I had put my whole force on standby. It was just as well, for at 2000 I got a message from Kennedy that two large enemy vessels had been sighted three hundred miles from, and sailing toward, Tulagi. The Japanese were coming at last.

We were so busy that I did not hesitate to put the Catalina crew on the teleradio watch and the lookout and to give them other odd defense jobs. If Kennedy's message was correct, the two Jap vessels, whose estimated speed was fifteen knots, should get to Tulagi within twenty-four hours. It was obvious that we should have moved off the beach a long time ago; but there we were—sitting ducks! We worked on into the night, with guards listening for any strange sounds; there were, thank goodness, no visitors.

Early next morning, from the lookout, there were continuous reports of planes over Tanambogo and Tulagi.[4] We had no contact with the RAAF, who had gone to their hideout on Nggela. I saw six separate raids on Tanambogo; during one of them the crash boat, returning for the wireless operators, received a direct hit, and sank in a few minutes. The coxswain barely escaped with his life.

As the day wore on, it became clear that the Jap planes were out to destroy everything on Tanambogo. The little island was finished as an operating center: either it was so badly damaged that the boys could not put out the flames, or they were purposely burning everything and preparing to leave. I was doing quite a lot of burning myself, getting rid of redundant papers and other documents, ready to push off. A message came in that Macfarlan had at last gone bush—with the skids on—up to Gold Ridge, and Hay was following with the last known case of whiskey in the area.

On the station, I was, as usual, trying to do everything at once and encourage the others too. Andrew was doing his best with our defenses: he would appear every half hour to ask, "Which way me do 'long this one?" or to complain, about some medical dresser or crewman recently impressed as a soldier, "Thisfella sleep 'long night, 'e no savvy war 'e stop" (i.e., that war had come). "All right, Andrew," I would wearily reply, "you savvy show 'im!"; and off he would go with the malingerer, ready to work overtime. Poor Daniel, a bureaucrat at heart, wanted to take all his beautiful blue forms and vouchers when we went bush; I told him that for now the days of three copies were over and that he should concentrate instead on the state of our ration stocks, as the Cat crew made big holes in our diminishing supply of tinned goods. Eroni, a rifle slung over his shoulder, was busy packing up hospital stocks for dispersal to different parts of the island. Another of the few chaps doing something constructive was a cheerful Ysabel man called Bingiti. He had been trained as an agricultural instructor, and with those prisoners who could be spared he was busy planting up as much of the station land as possible with native vegetables, which we would soon be requiring for food.

Ekins and his operator worked like slaves at the teleradio, which was humming all day long. At different times, three cutters with Chinese aboard arrived from the west, via Berande, fleeing before the storm. The mob was all breathless with jitters—they had seen the enemy warships, and that was enough for them. I listened to what they had to say and sent them on down the coast.

We had a prearranged signal with VNTG by which they were to indicate that they had cleared out safely and were on their way. Ekins didn't know it, and I couldn't for the life of me remember what it was. I got quite worried: was it "bacon and egg," or "ham and eggs," or was it "liver and bacon," or "egg and sausage"? At 2330, with Tanambogo a red glow on the horizon, I was going down to the radio shack to call them, when Ekins's gunner rushed out: "They want you urgently." There was no need to ask who. I ran in and grabbed the mike. "VQJ4 to VNTG, VQJ4 to VNTG, over, over." Amidst the appalling background noise, I could just hear a faint voice wearily calling, "Stike and eggs, dammit, stike and eggs, dammit, VNTG calling VQJ4, stike and eggs." "Stike and eggs"—"steak and eggs," that was it! And that *was* it—Tanambogo was a base no more. I found it hard to accept. Had they seen the enemy ships, had the Japs arrived, had they got away safely? There were many questions asked at Aola that night, and not a soul shut an eye for wondering what would come of it all.

The only good news we had during that grim night was that the *Morinda* was to come to the south end of Malaita to pick up all the Chinese. "Thank goodness," I said to Ekins, "we can be rid of ours at last." And then, half jokingly, I added, "I'll have to send someone to see they don't come back; I don't suppose you'd like to volunteer for the job?" "Well," he said, "might as well do something to earn my living." "Bless you," I replied, "you can start organizing now." And so, in the middle of the night, the Chinese were chivied out and told the good news. They were divided into parties and put into three schooners, *Varuna, Jones,* and *Kokerana,* which were soon loaded down almost to the waterline.

At 0530 on 3 May, just as Ekins was about to sail, a squat black craft was reported from the direction of Tulagi. It was the *Balus* with the RAAF, lock, stock, and barrel. They had escaped the notice of the Jap aircraft because of low cloud and slight rain. There were about forty of them, as gray and haggard a mob as I'd ever seen; some were at the very end of their nerve. The men had hardly eaten the day before, and looked pretty well all in, but they did justice to the breakfast we provided. It had not been pleasant for them during the last few days: as they had sneaked out of Tulagi Harbor, three enemy cruisers and a destroyer had sailed in, together with the transports that Kennedy had seen the night before. The Japanese were here, all right—in block capitals. They now had at least fifteen ships in the harbor.

Most of the men rolled over and slept on the lawn in front of the house, while Flying Officer Peagham, who was in charge, and Charlie Bird and I made plans. I was bitterly disappointed when Peagham told me that he wanted to get all of them away as soon as possible. I argued as much as I could in favor of their staying on as guerrillas or coastwatchers, but in view of the rough time they had had it was not surprising that they wanted to leave.

Shortly after the *Balus* arrived, I sent Terry Ekins and his little convoy off to Su'u, Malaita, to meet the *Morinda*. Although I rather doubted that she would now risk the trip, I was anxious to get the Chinese off my hands.

I was very busy all day long with Charlie Bird and the RAAF. The Cat crew helped me get the *Balus* ready for her long trip, while I dashed up and down to the radio shack, sending out the movements of Jap ships and planes and picking up messages from Kennedy, who was checking the Japanese Navy somewhere at the south end of New Georgia, and Mac-farlan, who was now installed at Gold Ridge with a magnificent bird's-eye view right into the harbor. Snowy Rhoades, having retired to "HMAS *Brush-Turkey,*" was sending out a splendid signal. I struggled to get the "dope" coded up and sent out as soon as possible: a twenty-four-hour radio watch was being kept in the New Hebrides, and I hoped they were pick-ing up our "ball to ball" description of the Japanese arrival.

The evacuation of the resident policemen's families from the station was progressing smoothly, and many were the anguished farewells as loved ones left with their possessions on their backs to walk to their vil-lages. We kept it up all day, in case the Japanese Air Force came to call. There were planes rumbling in the area, but they did not come very close, and we could not identify them.

The AIF had spent most of the previous day helping smash and burn everything at Tanambogo and Gavutu, then stayed to cover the RAAF's retreat. Finally, we had a faint signal that they were sailing *Ramada* direct to Marau Sound, to rendezvous with the RAAF and transfer to *Balus* for the trip south. This was depressing, as another AIF detachment was still holding out in Bougainville, but I had no chance even to try to persuade them to stay.

There was an awful lot to do, and little time to think. Things were happening very fast, and the position was very grim. I was pinned to the beach by the teleradio, yet I would have to get everything hidden away in the bush quick and lively, as a fast launch would take only two hours to come from Tulagi. When the time came for the *Balus* to depart, about 2000, I wondered whether Ekins's Catalina crew would leave; but they were a good mob, and I was relieved when, to a man, they decided to stay and give me a hand until their captain returned from Malaita.

I stood with them on the beach. Everything seemed pretty final. The feeling of being left alone is never pleasant, and with the departure of the RAAF even Andrew was visibly shaken. The general opinion of the Solomon Islanders on the station was that, if this was war, they didn't like it: the Japs had arrived, they could cruise over to Aola in a matter of hours, and there had not been a sign that we had anything with which to stop them. About 2100 Bengough sent the message that the *Morinda* wasn't coming. I hoped the Chinese could be left on Malaita or could go on to San Cristobal. I knew I had been right in sending them.

That night, the third of May, was one of the most miserable in my life. None of us dared to go to sleep, in case some hostile visitor appeared out of the dark to catch us unawares. We had a constant series of alarms, which kept everyone on the alert, and I was up and down to the beach reassuring people all night long.

8

The Battle of the Coral Sea

Fᴵʀꜱᴛ ᴅᴀᴡɴ broke cold and still. As the fingers of light picked out our sentries—huddled, nodding figures, keeping a weary watch—the vast white cumulus clouds over Guadalcanal suddenly came alive with the roar of planes, and the familiar heavy rumble of bombs began to be heard from Tulagi. Andrew, himself hardly awake, shook me: "Sah, altogether Japan 'e catch'm trouble." We rubbed our sleep-starved eyes and perked up. Then there was a rush to the banyan tree. We didn't have very good binoculars, but it was obvious that Jap shipping in Tulagi was in serious trouble. I could hardly believe it—was it really true? As it slowly dawned upon us that it really was, a tattoo of sheer joy went out on the station drum. "Come and see," it said, "come and see!"

About 0800 the noise of airplanes from the north increased, and we rushed out to witness the magnificent spectacle of twelve dive bombers plunging down out of the clouds over Tulagi. There was a steely glint at the bottom of their dive; we guessed it was from the torpedoes that they were launching.[1] Another squadron of twelve bombers followed shortly afterward, and we spotted four fighters after 1230.[2] What a sight for sore eyes—it was the largest number of Allied planes that most of us had ever seen.

The attack went on most of the morning. Wave after wave of planes dove on the Jap ships, collected together in Tulagi Harbor; I was glad that it had not been mined. It was a great tonic for everyone, even if I could not tell them who the attackers were. After noon, happy in the knowledge that the Cat boys had the radio watch and the Japs were too busy to bother us for the time being, I sank down in my chair and gratefully dropped off to sleep.

At teatime I awoke with a start, to be told that the battle was nearly over. During the afternoon, fourteen vessels had been counted limping out of the harbor. Some were in poor shape, and apparently unable to fire back at our planes. Several reportedly had sunk between Tulagi and Savo, and others were badly listing. A pall of smoke hung over Tulagi, which appeared to be engulfed in flames; we raised a cheer as two Catalinas lumbered up the strait and added to the conflagration. I figured we should be fairly safe that night unless we were disturbed by survivors, and Andrew thought that the tutelary sharks of Savo Island would prevent many of them from interfering with us! We kept watch nevertheless, in the same way as the night before; but this time there was a ray of hope and encouragement. There was much excited talk on the station that the Japs were finished, and that an Allied landing force would shortly arrive; I thought all the speculation rather premature, but could not help wondering, if that were true, whether we should have any warning of it. I began to worry about Ekins, whose convoy hadn't returned; had he had trouble with the Chinese or the Japanese? Or had he been bombed by mistake?

At 0100 the night watch called out. It was one of Ekins's schooners, the *G. F. Jones,* with a sad story to tell. Not only had they waited in vain at Su'u for the *Morinda,* but Davis,[3] whom the RC had sent to supervise the loading, had pinched the *Kokerana* and shanghaied from Ekins the two police I had sent to help him. My one consolation was that they had managed to offload all the Chinese, who would henceforth be Michael Forster's problem on San Cristobal. Wouldn't *he* be pleased! I sent an indignant signal to Bengough about the "daylight robbery" of my "resources."

From first light, there were three or four Kawanisi flying boats cruising up and down; the alarms continued all day. They were big, lumbering aircraft, and I always got a slight chill when I saw the big red "meatball" painted on their wings. A large transport, probably a ten-thousand-tonner, was seen going into Tulagi. She probably had more troops on board: in spite of the bashing they had had the day before, the Japs were consolidating their position. Everyone was very jumpy, but I did my best to carry on as usual. Snowy Rhoades, who now was sending out a much better signal, passed on the news that he had retired into the bush. I sadly reflected that I was the last one on the beach, with a Catalina on my doorstep to give the Japs the line!

At last, at teatime, Terry Ekins arrived. He was very sorry for himself. On the way back the two remaining schooners had lost contact in the rain; Ekins, relying on the local bosun, had been woken by a terrific jolt, to find *Varuna* hard aground on Rua Sura, a reef some miles off the coast. The crew had labored all morning trying to get her off; the sea was pretty calm, but one of the Kawanisis had flown up and down all the time, and Ekins had had to direct operations from the cabin, to keep out of sight of the plane. Alas, the *Varuna* was so firmly on the rocks that by afternoon they had decided to abandon her. Ekins had stripped the vessel of as much gear as possible and brought it back in the dinghy. "I'm terribly sorry, Martin," he said, "but I'm better in the air." I gave the bosun a smartening up, as he knew the waters and had gone to sleep on the job. And so ended another busy day.

The next two or three days were even busier. In spite of our attacks, the Japs seemed to have established a flying-boat base at Tulagi; the sooner we could get away from Aola, therefore, the better. It was obvious that the Catalina was done for, as no one could come to repair her; so Ekins and his men would have to be evacuated. I had mentioned this in my rude message to Norman Bengough. For once, my signal got immediate results: at dawn on 6 May a small cutter, *Lo-ai,* arrived, to take Ekins south—with profuse apologies from Bengough, and his promise to return my two police as soon as they reached Auki and could be sent over.

Shortly afterward, the Cat crew, Ekins, and I were standing on the beach, watching our dive bombers dropping their loads on Tulagi, when suddenly three Kawanisis, obviously fleeing the scene, zoomed low right over the station. We ducked pretty fast, and hoped they had not seen anyone. Anyway, they did not return. They must also have missed the camouflaged Catalina on the beach.

A long signal came in from Macfarlan, who had seen the whole show on Sunday and Monday but now found it too cloudy for good observation. He said that there had been three cruisers, one destroyer, and twelve other vessels in the harbor. As far as he could gather, there were only two left after Monday's raid, but there were three "43s" operating out of Tulagi, along with a few high-speed floatplanes. These would stop our boat trips.

After a lot of argument, Ekins and his crew finally agreed that there was now no hope of their ever flying out the Catalina. The next morning, they stripped out the radios and other important parts, and stowed them on the *Lo-ai* for the trip to Kira Kira; one of their .303 machine guns poked out under the stern awning.

I spent most of my time on the teleradio, dashing out from time to time to see how things were progressing. The evacuation of Aola was now in full swing. All the police not on lookout watch, together with the prisoners, were packing everything up. Crates, boxes, bundles, even heaps of gear were piled under the jacaranda trees at the back of the station, where a solemn Daniel Pule, pencil and pad in hand, recorded each load as it departed for the bush on its way to Paripao. Our call for volunteers from the surrounding villages had been answered, and there were about four hundred men in the working party. Daniel's job was to sort the stuff into loads, allot them to carriers, and make a list of who had taken what. A policeman went with every thirty or forty carriers, and another checked the loads at Paripao village, where they would be stored temporarily until they could be safely stowed away. Government records, stationery, stores, tools, pots and pans, furniture, even bedding—the list seemed endless.

That day, and most of the next, were spent clearing the station. By lunchtime on 7 May, the nearby coastal villagers had begun to realize that they ought to evacuate too, and our supply of carriers began to dry up; but the heaviest work had been done.

Ekins was ready to go. We had our last meal together. He and his men had been a great help, and I wished they could stay; but they were airmen, and it was only natural that they would want to return to the fight. I solemnly wrote him out a receipt for Catalina number A24-23, from which they had taken all movable equipment, and told him that I would endeavor to dispose of her! On the BBC news just after lunch, there was some mention of a "naval battle in the Coral Sea, in which a lot of Jap ships had been sunk." We all wondered whether this was our show. If indeed it was, we felt that it was successful only insofar as it had rapped the knuckles of the Japanese: it certainly had not stopped them from turning Tulagi into an operations base, and driving our chaps away. At 1500, Ekins and his crew sailed for San Cristobal. I hoped that the *Lo-ai* would arrive in friendly territory, and they would be able to fly again.

Now the feeling of loneliness returned, for we really were on our own. As the swell, in timeless rhythm, thudded against the shore, Andrew, Daniel, and I stood, rather disconsolately, on the black sand beach, three desolate figures by the empty bay. Andrew glanced toward Tulagi. "Airplane 'e finish, Guvman 'long Aola 'e finish, altogether Japan 'e stop. More better youme go 'long . . ." He inclined his head over his shoulder to the dark green, steamy jungle, to which we would have to look for salvation. "Yes, Andrew," I said wearily, "but tumas work 'e stop."

For me, the issues now were clear. Here we were at Aola, and there were the Japs at Tulagi, less than twenty miles away. We would lead them as long a dance as we could. There was work to do on the beach, and masses of it. Unfortunately, the weather had cleared up, and I greatly feared that the Japs would see the flames as we disposed of the Catalina. Most of the Kawanisis kept morning hours, however, so we decided to get the job over and done with in the afternoon while we had the chance.

We surrounded the Cat with firewood and, when she was well alight, blew several charges, which broke her up. She burned for an hour and a half without exciting any attention; by then most of the fuselage was gone, and we were left with the very solid main plane, the two engines, and the tail plane. We got in amongst the remains of the main plane and fuselage with axes and hammers, until we had them pretty flat on the ground; several coconut trees had been cut down along the leading edge, so that the main plane would be overhung by the remaining coconut trees and difficult to see from above. Then we covered the skeleton with coconut fronds and creepers, which we hoped would soon grow over it. The next day we tried again to fire the tail plane, which still protruded from the trees; but this was not successful, and in the end the police dragged away the pieces and dumped them into the sea.

It was very sad having to destroy our own aircraft while the enemy sailed serenely above. The Kawanisis settled down to regular patrolling, and for the next few days they cruised up and down the coast, one after the other. Fortunately, they were not attracted by the wreck of the Catalina. So far, so good.

9

Some Unexpected Guests

O N 8 MAY, the patrol I had sent out to get information about Wilmot's murder came back with empty hands. This was not good news: either the local villages knew about it and were hushing it up, or it had been done by a stranger who had managed to sneak away unobserved. I decided to send two constables to Gold Ridge and have them bring down the man who had not proved his alibi.

Eroni, our medical practitioner, turned up at last from a trip along the south coast. He had lots of news: he had found two single-engined American fighter planes,[1] which had crash-landed on the shelving beach near Cape Henslow. The pilots had been rescued by a cruiser, which local villagers had seen close to shore; Eroni brought their parachutes, rubber dinghies, clocks, and compasses, all useful gear. According to their navigation boards—which should not have been left behind—the pilots' names were Plott and McCuskey.[2] It was not difficult to work out their approximate takeoff point, but I presumed their parent carrier was well on the move, and far away by now from the position indicated.

The *Fico,* one of the Bougainville launches, arrived from Auki with Sgt. Maj. Jacob Vouza, who brought a short note from Norman Bengough.

In February Vouza had retired, having finished his twenty-five years' service in the police; Bengough asked whether I would like to keep him on, as he did not want him at Auki. Vouza was the islander who had struck me most on Malaita, where he had been sergeant major of police. A strongly built man with piercing eyes, he had maintained a firm control over the force and compiled an excellent record. Vouza was extremely loyal, was well respected by Malaita men, and knew police work inside out; yet, at times, he was a startling individualist, who overcame difficulties in original ways. Like Bengough, I had always had implicit faith in him, so his sudden arrival was most strange and embarrassing. Although a native of Guadalcanal, Vouza had worked on Malaita for many years, and knew it better than any man; yet Bengough did not want him. Whether he had betrayed his trust was not indicated in the note, and I could get little from Vouza himself. To absorb him into my organization would have been very difficult, for though he was far more senior than any of my chaps he knew none of them, and was out of touch with current affairs on Guadalcanal. How to fit him into the picture would take a lot of thinking out.

A report came in from Marau. The AIF crowd, having evacuated Gavutu, had left the *Ramada* at Marau Sound, along with the *Gynia,* the other small launch from Bougainville; but they had left no message saying what they wanted done with them. All I could do was anchor them inside the mangroves at Marau. Some gear remained on board, and the *G. F. Jones* was sent to pick it up; everything helped. She brought back something else, too: *Ramada*'s boat crew reported that the RAAF had left behind a large quantity of ammunition and a teleradio, at Halavo, on Nggela Island. Hell's bells!

Fortunately, Bingiti was on Nggela. As became an old sea scout, he had an observant eye and plenty of common sense, so I had sent him there, on the last trip of the RAAF crash boat, to spy out what he could. He soon had his little organization going, and now a canoe brought the report that three cruisers, four destroyers, a seaplane tender, and a small cargo vessel were sent to the bottom on 4 May.[3] I sent him back a message to secure everything at Halavo and send it over when opportunity offered. Twenty-five miles by night in a single-seat canoe was a risky trip, but it was the only way I could get information from Nggela.

By this time everything possible had been removed from Aola station, except actual food and cooking requirements for a few days. Government

OFFICE OF THE RESIDENT COMMISSIONER,

BRITISH SOLOMON ISLANDS PROTECTORATE.

May 13th. 1942

COMMUNICATIONS

With the closing down of VNTG alternative arrangements
for maintaining communications have been made as follows:-

1. All Coast Watching reports will be collected by ZGJ from
    which station they will, if necessary, be transmitted beyond
    the Protectorate through the Headquarters Station.

2. Vila (YJX 2) maintains a twenty-four hour watch on 'X'
    frequency and urgent messages should be passed to that station
    on 'X'. They will acknowledge on 43.5 metres. All such
    messages should be repeated to ZGJ at the next normal
    schedule with an indication as th whether YJX 2 has
    acknowledged.

3. In the event of ZGJ and the Headquarters Station ceasing to
    operate ZGJ 4, which can be heard well by Vila, should act
    as collecting centre and transmit to Vila on R/T. All other
    stations should in such circumstances repeat messages which
    they have sent to YJX 2 on 'X' fequency to ZGJ 4 at the next
    session, indicating to him whether YJX 2 acknowledged their signal.
    In this event, VQO will stand by at all normal sessions and
    copy traffic sent in by ZGJ 4 to YJX 2, so that VQO can
    repeat to YJX 2 if necessary.

4. The arrangements in para. 3 will come into force only in
    the event of ZGJ and the Headquarters Station being no longer
    able to carry on communications.

Resident Commissioner.

Making sure the information gets through.

employees were paid as usual, but they were all now "Defence Force."
After much persuasion, every coastal village had formed a Home Guard
section, which was responsible for reporting any enemy or strange activity
along its part of the coast. These were now well organized. Another important duty all villages accepted—I could hardly force them to take it on—

was feeding any of my chaps passing their way, and furnishing runners to pass on written messages. This service helped immeasurably to ensure that information reached me as quickly as possible.

The next morning, the whole station was on its toes for a test evacuation. At 0700 I rang the alarm bell and everyone went to action stations, each party loading and departing as soon as ready. Twelve prisoners took the teleradio sets, batteries, and charging engine, and my brass-bound DO's box. We were on the march at 0720, and clear of the boundary twenty minutes later. The lookout blew one blast on the conch shell, which signaled the rear guard under Sergeant Andrew to retire, covering our retreat.

And so, across the river and up the bush trail, through Gombia and Gegende, to Seveni. Here we had a "smoke-oh" and the prisoners were sent back to get other loads. Local carriers took over, and we pressed on to Paripao. Before we got to Tanebuti, we had to cross a bottomless swamp. This was a queer fold in the hill structure, caused by volcanic action; it was, in fact, a drainage basin with no exit. Although a light scrub grew over it, you could not walk on the roots, which were very thin and sank under the slightest pressure. The locals had made a sort of bridge-cum-ladder over which to scramble; it was easy to take away. When this was done the place was quite impassable. The detour around it was very long, and hard to find.

I got to Paripao just after noon. Daniel Pule had got our bush headquarters well organized. One of the biggest houses, on the side farthest from the coast, had been taken over, and a place was waiting for the teleradio. He even had a supply of stationery laid out, and all current files in proper order—as if they mattered! Another house had been taken over as defense post and barracks; it was one hundred yards away, on the coast side. Michael was quite indignant that no provision had been made for his kitchen, but I told him that it would have to wait.

I got the teleradio set up and working well. The Kawanisis had been down south all day; in the late afternoon we saw them return to Tulagi. They must have been very busy searching for our navy, for though they doubtless heard us on the air every morning they hadn't investigated or attacked any coastwatcher since the RAAF had cleared out. That night, however, we saw a searchlight scanning the waters near Visale: I had been lucky to get Aola evacuated before the Japs interfered. As my bush headquarters was ready, and I could get off the station in twenty minutes, I could return to Aola until all local business had been cleared up.

There was no real need to keep watch that night, so I slept like a log and took it easy in the morning. I was pleased to see the Kawanisis going west: the fact that the "Guvman" had had to leave Aola was enough bad news for the locals for one day without any pestering of their villages by the Japanese Air Force. I spent the morning getting security posts laid out and checking the stowage of our heavy gear and stores, then returned to Aola after lunch with the teleradio. Sergeant Andrew had stayed behind with the rear guard, which was supposed to protect us from surprise attack and act as a collecting center for information. He was more than somewhat distressed that all the local villagers ran away at the slightest provocation. I reassured him by saying that if they could be sure to run away when the Japs arrived, it would be the best thing they could do for all concerned!

I had delayed making a decision on what to do about Vouza. As he had two months' leave owed to him, I had sent him off to his home at Volonavua, near Koli Point, to settle his family. His countrymen there, together with the Tasimboko crowd, came under the same district headman; they were a troublesome and, on the whole, unreliable lot, and I had asked Vouza to try to keep them quiet and see that they did their Home Guard duties properly. The *Fico,* which had taken him up the coast, had returned; we refueled her and sent her back to Malaita that night by a southerly route.

Early the next morning, while I was reading in the cadet's house, the lookout reported that the *Ramada,* which I had ordered laid up, had arrived from Marau. I expected the bosun would come and tell me, in due course, why he had returned without orders.

Survivors

Suddenly I heard the sound of boots crunching the gravel on the path outside. My heart missed a beat as, clad only in my bath towel, I grabbed my gun. Fortunately, there was no cause for alarm: it was Brother James Thrift, from Makina. He had brought an American pilot and his radio operator, whose torpedo bomber had been forced to land at sea for lack of fuel. Like their comrades, they had flown from the *Yorktown* on 4 May, but they had not been as lucky, and it took three days in a rubber boat before they reached the south coast, near Avu Avu. The last day a huge shark had paid them an inordinate amount of attention, snapping at the ends of their oars. Once ashore, they had walked to the mission station, where Father Boudard had fed them and told them they would have to go to the district officer. He had lent them a horse, which they had ridden down to Marau. There they had fallen in with Brother James; after they had spent the night at Makina, he had taken a chance and brought them up in the *Ramada*.

The pilot, Lt. Leonard H. Ewoldt, wore a khaki shirt and trousers, and two silver collar bars denoting his rank. His radioman, who appeared to be an enlisted rating, wore a blue shirt and dark blue dungarees; his name was Ray Machalinski.

The lieutenant had only one thing on his mind: "Could you please get us back to Pearl Harbor?" I said I'd see what could be done; in the meantime, I had some breakfast ready. Over a generous portion of Michael's steak and eggs, he told us about the attack on Tulagi on 4 May. I was naturally most interested to find out what had constituted the attacking force; as I had suspected, it was units of the U.S. Navy, about which I knew very little, but neither man would give us the names of any of the ships concerned. (At first I was a little offended, since we were working for them in a way; but then I remembered that I had no uniform, and that they probably had no idea who I was.) They had observed at least five direct hits on ships in Tulagi Harbor. Ewoldt said he had attacked a small cargo vessel near Savo Island and had seen her, and two other ships, go down.[4]

On the schedule that morning I also got a report from Lafe Schroeder, who had had a grandstand view of the whole thing. He reckoned that three light cruisers had been sunk: one near the entrance to Mboli Passage, and the other two on reefs inside the harbor. Ewoldt was very interested in our combined account of the battle, which he confirmed was exceptionally accurate; he was amazed to hear of our coastwatching setup, about which he had been told nothing. It was agreed that he and Machalinski would stay with me until I could get them away, so Brother James, after wishing them Godspeed, departed for Marau in the *Ramada*.

The two men were impatient to be off, but it was bound to be a few days before they could get away. I could not, however, very well give them work to do, as I had done with Ekins and his crew. Michael accepted, without a murmur, the fact that we had two houseguests at such an inopportune time.

Next day we got more information from Bingiti. There were graphic details of the last hours of the three Jap warships near Tulagi and how the sharks had had a field day amongst the hundreds of bodies floating on the blood red water. The smaller islands in the harbor, Tanambogo, Gavutu, and Makambo; the Melanesian Mission station, near the mouth of the Mboli Passage at Taroaniara; and Bungana, where the mission sisters used to live, had all been visited or occupied by the Japanese. It appeared that they had landed in considerable strength, and I sent the messenger off to Bingiti with a request to find out their numbers, if possible.

The worst news that Bingiti sent was a very strong rumor about George Bogese, the NMP whom Kennedy and I had sent to Savo Island. He had been observed going to Tulagi with Japanese survivors, but whether of his own free will or under duress remained to be seen. There was no doubt that more would be heard from him: he was no friend of the government's, and we could not but assume that he could give us all away. What I feared most was that he would bring an enemy party over to Guadalcanal to find us.

The following morning, while I was having great difficulty with the charging engine, a launch arrived from Nggela with some Guadalcanal men who had worked for the AIF detachment. Doing their best to dramatize the situation, they told us how the AIF had had to work against time to complete demolition, and how they had still been in the harbor when the Japanese fleet sailed in. They had stayed until the ships had started to anchor, then slunk out of the harbor under cover of approaching darkness; they had left very little behind for the enemy. I gathered that hundreds of Japanese soldiers, who had been landed from ships, had been killed by the bombing, and that the remaining troops had taken three days to heap their bodies together and burn them.

By dint of questioning each of the men separately and sifting their stories, I came to the conclusion that there were seven or eight hundred Japs still in the Tulagi area. They had a fair number of small vessels, probably landing craft; from various wild guesses I deduced that their speed was twelve to fifteen knots.

I was furious when I had learned that the cache of ammunition and the teleradio had been left behind, and I sent several of the party back that night to collect them if they could. The Japs had started wandering about on the mainland of Nggela, but they had not yet been to Halavo, and there was still a chance that we could pick up these things. I badly wanted to stop them from getting the radio, to prevent the enemy from discovering, at least for a time, our alternative, and perhaps still secret, frequency.

As soon as I had packed off the Nggela party, I gave the lookouts a piece of my mind for letting the launch arrive without warning. Although I knew that they had recognized it, I had no intention of letting slackness develop so early in the game.

10

"The district officer has gone."

I WAS STILL in a quandary about moving out of Aola. There I could live off fresh milk, meat, and fish, and conserve our meager supply of tinned rations. At the same time, I was not very happy about the possibility of George Bogese's visiting Guadalcanal with the Japanese. He had, I had heard, already taken a party of their officers on a tour of Nggela.

Alone Again

The solution to my problem was provided by a deputation, consisting of Eroni, Andrew, and Daniel. It would be much better, they said, for all concerned if I retired to Paripao. They could easily keep the reporting system going, and I was the only one who could operate the teleradio. These three men were exceptionally loyal, and they had been working very hard under the most trying conditions, so I could not ignore their feelings. Thanking them for their solicitude, I told them that I would probably go bush once everything was packed up and we had got the Americans away.

The Kawanisis had worked out regular patrol routes. We soon found out that they fueled and loaded bombs about 0500 each day, under the glow of powerful searchlights, and took off about 0730. Then came the news that an enemy vessel had been seen at Marau at 0300 one morning. It was clear that our own ship traffic, even along the coast, would have to be reduced to an absolute minimum: the area was no longer predictably safe. Vessels going across to Malaita would have to go at night, and by a roundabout route.

On 16 May, the two American airmen departed in the *G. F. Jones* for the New Hebrides, via San Cristobal. They would pass a message to *Gynia*'s crew at Marau to report to me. I gave them the compass off the Catalina, a few charts, and something to eat. (Ewoldt seemed quite confident; like Ekins, it was another plane he wanted, and he did not mind what he had to put up with to get it.) With them went the owner of the *Hing-Li*, Yip Tim, and his family. Ewoldt was pleased to be on his way back to Pearl Harbor, which I believe they reached only a fortnight after the USS *Yorktown*. Yip Tim, on the other hand, was thrilled to be increasing the distance between himself and the Japanese.

About midnight the AIF launch returned from Nggela.[1] Seven rifles, four bayonets, and twenty-five thousand rounds of ammunition, plus the teleradio, had been rescued, literally from under the nose of the Japanese: an enemy patrol had carried out a house-to-house search only five minutes after the launch had departed. What really pleased me was that teleradio: though I very much doubted whether the set was in working order, it was a matter of prestige not to let any of them fall into enemy hands.

The next day, I was very glad to see the morning Kawanisi heading for Malaita: I was busy charging my batteries, and the charging motor completely drowned out airplane noises. The drone had another unwanted effect: I fell asleep in the radio shack. In fact, I was quite exhausted—I hadn't had a good sleep for weeks. The problem was the business of keeping the watch at night. Sergeant Andrew and his men were doing extremely well, but they hadn't really been tested in this sort of emergency, and I did not think it was fair to leave the responsibility entirely to them. I could have slept for a whole day, but I dared not chance it: the morale of the local population was pretty low, and I could see plainly that my presence on the coast was regarded as a liability rather than a morale builder. If the Japs landed, all the islanders could flit silently into the night, leaving me none the wiser. I hoped it would never happen, but neverthe-less I just had to make the effort to walk round the station every hour or so.

It is amazing what you can get used to. I discovered that I could doze off in between hourly visits to my posts and sentries, yet wake at the slightest strange noise. After a bit I found that I was getting a little rest, and later that I was comparatively fresh when I got up in the morning.

George Bogese's collaboration had been confirmed. Every day there was more news from Nggela of his treacherous actions. The latest rumor was that he was going to escort the Japs to Kau Kau.

I finally concluded that I would do much better if I did retire to Paripao. The reporting system worked well, and my scouts and lookouts were doing a great job; I thought I could leave them to do it on their own. To go bush was not so good from the point of view of food, but we would be able to reduce considerably the number of people on static watch, and use them to patrol the island and pick up information from a much wider area.

On 19 May, therefore, I left Aola for good. I had assembled 190 carri-ers, to take every last useful thing off the station at one lift. All we needed there was the seaward lookout and two prowlers; six policemen could keep this going quite adequately, assisted by the few remaining Balo villagers. Much of the station was now green with the young vines of the yam, or the flapping elephant-ear leaves of the young taro plants, which were our only food reserve. The main office safe was too heavy to take; after emp-tying it, I left an old sock inside—just to give the Japs something for their labors, if they ever managed to open it! Having paid as many people as possible, I crammed the remaining silver into a "traveling" safe. It still needed four to carry it.

At 1330 a blast on the lookout's conch shell signaled that we were clear of the station, now deserted except for the rear guard. Eroni had gone the day before to a jungle hideout close by, so there was only Andrew to whom to say goodbye. "You stop goodfella 'long Paripao an no fright," he said. "Me lookout 'long here goodfella." We shook hands firmly. "Goodbye, then," I replied, "and best of luck." It was sad to be leaving. Civilization seemed to be slipping away.

We reached Paripao at 1730, all in good nick. The village was on a spur or saddle of land from which the ground fell away steeply on both sides; the earth there was red clay. The central path, which was really quite narrow, followed the ridge; on either side there was just room for a single row of houses, except on the seaward side, where the ridge widened out considerably.

The prison gang had been building stores for our bulk gear, of the same size and dimensions as the houses in the village. Thus we fondly hoped to escape detection. I also made alterations to the mast for the teleradio aerial, and draped more creeper round it. A good lookout post would be provided by a large canarium almond tree, which was about eighty feet high but was clear of branches for about forty feet. Round the lowest branch we put a lashing, and onto this we secured a pulley; it made a very good place from which to hang the Union Jack and not have it be seen from the air. The last flash of brilliance in our camouflage was added by Deke, who rushed into the village waving the top of a betel nut palm, which he tied triumphantly to the top of the radio mast! It wouldn't really fool an expert, but I imagined it would not look out of the ordinary from the air.

Apart from the vegetables that had been recently planted, there was a considerable stock of native vegetables in the station garden, and we tried to consume as much as possible in order to save nonrenewable rations such as rice and meat. All the chickens and ducks in the chicken run at Aola were also reinstalled at Paripao. I doubted that there would be much surplus food in the bush villages, and as far as I could see then I was quite right.

The canarium almond tree, which carried the flag, soon had a platform at the top, from which an air and sea lookout was kept twenty-four hours a day. I kept the watch down to two hours, lest someone get tired and miss something; if the lookouts wanted food and drink, they let down a basket on a long string. Accurate reports on Jap shipping were going to be very valuable, so I spent the next few days getting the men accustomed to the new routine. With an intermediary halfway between the tree and my house, the description of a ship leaving the harbor or a plane taking off could be coded up as it happened and radioed in a few minutes.

During a lull in enemy activity I paid a visit to Belaga, a village about six miles west of and much higher than Paripao, which was the home of Vakalea, the district headman of that area. From his house there was a marvelous view of Tulagi—you almost felt as if you were suspended over it. What annoyed me was that even from there I could see no sign of any activity. No Kawanisis had been about for the last four days, and I wondered what had happened to them. While at Belaga I got a message from Rhoades about some evil types whom he had tried to arrest but who had escaped his custody. He'd heard that they had threatened, quite openly, to go to Tulagi and let the Japanese know where he was.

On the Inside, Looking Out

My main occupation at Paripao was sorting and encoding signals for dispatch. What I actually saw did not take long, but the patrol reports coming in from east, west, and south—and, when a canoe could chance it, from Bingiti on Nggela—all had useful information, some of it in great detail, and that took much longer. To improve the quality of the reports, I gradually trained my regulars in the collection of evidence; they grew adept at sifting and combining the reports of the village Home Guard, and their results were then brought to me. This not only saved time but also increased security, by reducing the number of people who came to Paripao. Part of the vegetables dug up from the Aola gardens was stored in caches to the east and west, so that men bringing in reports could be given a feed before returning home.

Nggela had got too hot for Lafe Schroeder, and he had managed to evacuate Nagotana and join Snowy Rhoades. His eyewitness accounts of events in Tulagi would be missed, but the gap was practically filled by Bingiti, whose detailed intelligence was first class. While I was trying to precis about fifteen pages of Bingiti's reports, the resident commissioner, through ZGJ, asked for news of Nggela. In return I told him which places were occupied, where, what the Japanese defense points and bivouac positions were, and how many men were stationed at each. Following is a precis of a typical signal from Rhoades:

> Japs told Savo natives that they would eventually find all whites hiding in the bush by observing their lights by night and smoke by day from planes. Two German officers with Japs at Savo and one Jap sergeant worked at Gavutu who talks pidgin extremely well and who had been recognised with having been familiar with Solomons in peace time. This chap has a scar on his cheek. Japs at Nggela were pulling down churches and giving the vestments to the locals. They had also declared that there is no church law any longer.

The Japanese position at Tulagi during the latter part of May was covered by this signal from Bingiti:

From ZGJ4 to VQJ. Following is reliable report, not rumour. Tulagi residency not occupied. Flag flies from resident commissioner's office which is main Jap control centre. Superior official lives there together with several clerks. The sentries on government wharf are the only guard on island. Alarm sounded by whistle. Estimated that 500 Japs camped on island. Estimate prepared by actual counting. One 'usual' [Kawanisi] anchored near government wharf, other five anchored at Gavutu where Jap garrison of similar number remain under flag erected on top of island. All European establishments round the harbour and within easy reach have been ransacked but are now no longer occupied. Japs have not treated Nggelese well and they will not now work for them. Every time they visit a village Japs haul out the villagers' trunks and boxes and pinch their clothing. Supplies of food are being obtained by menace of arms. Launch went to Aruligo plantation for meat last Monday, but doubt whether they got any as all cattle were driven into the bush long ago. Nggelese are cooperating to the extent that they have been telling the Japanese that all white men have gone. As regards Savo, Japs told natives that they were short of food and clothing and that they were coming to collect pigs, fowls and produce from their gardens. They also let it be known that they were short of fuel oil and petrol. No further news of Bogese, but Savo natives told that Japs looking for more native medical practitioners to attend their wounded, of which there are large numbers. Japs told Nggelese to clear out and run away to another island as they would require all food that was being produced. Appears from all reports that Japs were greatly impressed by our aerial attacks on 4th May and are in constant fear of raids from our planes.

I continued to speculate about the Japs' next move. If they were short of food, as from all accounts they appeared to be, and if there were more than a thousand of them, they would soon run through any local stocks on Nggela. It was, therefore, likely that they would visit the plantations on Guadalcanal and kill cattle for meat: there were no cattle on Nggela, and the Japs had already helped themselves to the "episcopal" pigs at Taroaniara, the Melanesian bishop's headquarters.

On Saturday, 23 May, we heard bombing over Tulagi. It was confirmed a couple of days later by Deke, who returned from Gold Ridge. He reported that he had seen three planes attacking Tulagi on Saturday. Our teleradios were giving a certain amount of trouble, especially Rhoades's set, probably because it was much more humid inland. There were no official spares, nor any likelihood of any coming, so I sent him the spare valves from the RAAF set; the police messenger who took them called at Macfarlan's, where he picked up another gadget that Snowy required.

I was having trouble with my charging engine. It had been running almost continuously, and it really required decarbonizing, an exercise with which I was not too familiar. I was lucky in a way, in that I had recently acquired another charging engine; but it was rather an old one, and I had used it only while the other was being repaired.

The Japanese Air Force, it appeared, finally had got fed up looking for our nonexistent Navy and decided to take a closer look at the immediate area, for they now spent a lot of time flying up and down across the grass plains. Sometimes they flew very low, and on 26 May a signal from Macfarlan claimed that a plane had landed near Tetere. I rather doubted that, but the next day we had a good scare, as a report came in that the Japanese had actually landed at Tenaru. I sent Koimate and another one of the goldfields patrol to investigate the doings at Tenaru and Tetere.

After much patient searching, I signed on five Christian men in Tasimboko who appeared intelligent and reliable enough to go over to Nggela and reinforce Bingiti. It looked as if I would need more trustworthy fellows in their own area, too, but Nggela had the higher priority, for Bingiti had written that the Nggelese were very bad at producing accurate reports and that he did not find their intelligence very reliable.

A police messenger arrived from the station. There was still no sign of Japs at Aola. All were OK there, and their morale was much better—they all had plenty to do.

11

"Japan 'e come 'long Guadalcanal"

O N 28 May Lance Corporal Koimate reported that the Japanese had called at Tenaru and Lunga and at Mamara plantation, farther to the north. They had some sort of landing craft and had stayed only a few hours at each place, but they had fired many rounds from rifles and automatic weapons and killed a considerable number of cattle. The enemy could, and probably would, cause alarm and despondency along the coast. I wondered how my force would react, for now it was no longer a matter of just sitting and waiting. Our "splendid isolation" had been broken at last.

I shall never forget Koimate's message, which a light touch by Michael Forster at Kira Kira has fixed in my mind. Forster claimed he had sighted a "light blue" plane over San Cristobal. But then, he had been at Oxford, and no doubt regarded the light blue of my alma mater as being an appropriate enemy color!

Late the next afternoon we heard tremendous bombing from Tulagi. After all the reports had been collated, it appeared that twenty-four planes had taken part in the raid, which was repeated later that evening. Gavutu was in flames, and over the top there was a huge pall of black smoke, which indicated burning fuel. The Jap searchlights were in action during the later raid, but there was very little reply from their ack-ack; this may have been owing to a shortage of ammunition, as no vessels had been to Tulagi for the last two or three days. There was no damage to our planes.

The people of Paripao had been in a nervous state ever since we had arrived, and a dispute soon developed over the cutting of a branch of the almond tree that was being used as a lookout post. Nut trees, which produced a salable crop, were jealously guarded in the Solomons: compensation was demanded, and hot words had been exchanged before I got to the scene. I went down and managed to reach a settlement with them, after much plain language had been spoken and several villagers had expressed a desire to go over to Nggela to see the Japanese. They were all scared stiff that my presence there would inevitably cause the enemy to wreak vengeance on them; they were quite convinced that the Japs would call at Aola in a day or two and march straight up to Paripao.

Perhaps their fear was well founded, perhaps not; in any case, to steady them I said I would pay another visit to Aola, just to make sure everything was all right. I was also impatient to hear further news of the heavy raid on Tulagi. The next day, therefore, I went down to Aola. All was well, but Sergeant Andrew and his faithful rear guard also needed cheering up.

I got the news from the latest Nggela patrol. Macfarlan's estimate of twenty-four planes was disputed by Bingiti, who said that a lot of the noise during the first raid was caused by ack-ack, and that his lads had seen only five Catalinas. Most of the Japanese fuel oil and gasoline stores on Gavutu and Tanambogo had been badly damaged, however, and the causeway joining the islands had been severed. One of the Japanese antiaircraft gun pits had been burnt out. It was confirmed that there were three guns on Gavutu; the same number on Tanambogo; one on Makambo, where the gun crew were the only inhabitants; and four on Tulagi. The best description I could get of these guns, after cross-examining the scouts very carefully, was that the barrels, as measured by one scout during the night, were six feet long, and the shells were the size of small beer bottles. My guess was that they were three inches in diameter. None of us had ever seen an ack-ack gun.

The only ship to visit Tulagi Harbor for two weeks had been a small sloop armed with small guns, which had called on 26 May and left that night. No Kawanisis had been staying the night for some time, except one

                              Office of the Resident Commissioner,
                              British Solomon Islands Protectorate.
                                    2nd. June 1942.

          District Officer,
               Auki.
             ⌐ Aola.
               Tatamba
               Kirakira.

                    Administrative Playfair - Keywords

          The undermentioned Keywords will be used for
          Administrative messages transmitted in Playfair Code
          for the months as set out below:-

               July   1942   EXPEDITIONARY
               August 1942   OVERWHELMINGLY
               September 1942   RECAPITULATORY
               October 1942   UNDECYPHERABLE
               November 1942   HYPOCHONDRIAC
               December 1942   RAZORBLADES
               January 1943   PERTINACIOUSLY
               February 1943   INEXHAUSTIVELY
               March   1943   INCONTROVERTIBILITY

          You should acknowledge receipt by telegraphing the word
          Rabbits

                              Resident Commissioner.

The vital words.

that had holed its bottom on a reef near Gavutu. I was amused to hear that
the main Jap radio set was in the ruins of the Tanambogo mess, where the
RAAF had had theirs. It was also reported that the Japs had unfortunately
found a few more rifles that the RAAF had left on Nggela, and that they
had again been on Savo with a machine gun asking the locals about the
white men on Guadalcanal. The soldiers said that they would be coming
to look for them in two weeks' time. I did not like the sound of that.

The first of June was somewhat less than glorious. I sent out 240 code groups of good stuff, but it rained steadily in the afternoon and we missed a good raid on Tanambogo. A small cutter, *Christine,* arrived from Nggela with more AIF employees; her bosun told me the Japs were very concerned over their losses of diesel oil and gasoline in the last few days. In spite of this, three Kawanisis had begun regular operations again. Bingiti's Nggela watch, and Andrew's reporting center at Aola, were working well. The latter sent me up summaries of what was collected; if it was important enough to require more detail, the reporter was brought up, or I went down to Aola. I was very careful about this, as there had been a tendency afoot to use information as an excuse to be sent to Paripao, where they could check that I was still on the island; that wasted my time, and besides, such men were dangerous.

The following day I held an inquiry into the shortage of rations at the goldfields police post at Koilo. Lance Corporal Tagathagoe, who was in charge, had been extremely careless, and I had no alternative but to teach him a lesson and make him pay the value of the shortage. Another lad had nearly been captured by the Japanese at Tenaru, then had compounded the problem by running away, when he should have stayed close at hand to report what the Japs were doing. If I discharged him, which was what he deserved, he would be quite likely to desert to the enemy. I therefore gave him six months' imprisonment and employed him on lookout duties. Discipline was a very worrying problem under such conditions.

I had decided to take a chance and give all the headmen, and my own staff, their next three months' pay: silver was extremely heavy to carry, and payment of advance wages was very good for morale. I spent two or three days typing the pay sheets; our mobility would be increased if that work were over and done with.

It rained solidly most of the time. There was little wind, and there were no gaps in the fall of rain between our lookout and Tulagi, so our observation suffered. I was very busy anyhow, trying to pack up as many of the office papers as possible: we might have to be on the move, and I wanted to reduce what we had to carry to an absolute minimum. We heard several raids on Tulagi and on 4 June saw a big fire, which we hoped meant that the fuel oil was burning. The results of the bombing must have been good, for even through the rain a pall of smoke could be seen over Tulagi and Tanambogo for several days. Following this, however, there was a lull in our bombing, which lasted almost a week.

At Paripao, spare hands had been busy building a henhouse and planting more vegetable gardens. The food supply for the hefty policemen, who normally got at least a pound of rice and an eight-ounce tin of meat every day, was bad, and it would get worse. I had a small quantity of rice, and quite a lot of tinned stuff, but I was already eating a lot of sweet potatoes and taro. The hens would give us eggs, and occasionally provide our teeth with exercise, but to the policemen a chicken was a meal for only one!

I had long since consumed my usual smoking tobacco, and F. M. Campbell had sold me three blocks of Derby plug. It would have been difficult to drive a nail through them! Besides, the stuff was strong enough to make a donkey hiccough. The locally grown tobacco was of excellent quality, but it was usually badly cured, and the islanders twisted it into a huge plait as long and as thick as a man's arm. I used some to dilute the Derby plug. It wasn't exactly "my smoke," but it was better than an empty pipe.

The charging engine was beginning to pack up, and I had to decarbonize it at last. It was filthy inside, but fortunately it did not take very long to scrape off the tarry deposit of carbon. I had to send down to Ruavatu to get some valve paste for the two valves to make a proper job of it, and when the engine was all put together again it had the decency to work more smoothly.

I was getting anxious about the nonarrival of new code words promised by Bengough, so when on 7 June a messenger arrived from Aola to say that the *Gizo* had been sighted I was so impatient that I tramped down through the mud and collected the vital words and a lot of official mail. After the rude exchanges of messages that had occurred from time to time, it was a pleasant surprise to get a note from the resident commissioner telling me that our "Tulagi gossip column," as Macfarlan called it, was highly appreciated in the proper quarters. A less encouraging note instructed us not to send more than twenty or thirty code groups at one time, as it had been confirmed that the Japanese could find out our positions provided there was a certain length of signal. (I expected that their direction-finding equipment had located me by now anyhow, but I felt happier the less I was on the air.) Before going back to Bengough, the *Gizo* had to take the new code words to Forster on San Cristobal, then return to Aola. This route would give her the maximum cover from the coastline. We worked out departure and arrival times and warned them to keep very close to the schedule.

Sergeant Andrew told me that they had been so busy the last ten days they had not even had time to catch any fish, and had been living entirely on sweet potatoes. So, early next morning, we walked along to the back of Ruavatu plantation, where I shot a bullock and cut it up into quarters. Half went to Aola and the rest to Paripao, with a joint for the missionaries at Ruavatu.

I got back to Paripao at 1000; the lookout reported that all was quiet. Bingiti had reported that, owing to the size of the Tulagi garrison, the Japs had rations for only two or three weeks. I spent some time speculating on what their next move would be. Whether they had landed on Guadalcanal because they were seeking food, or whether for a more sinister purpose, remained to be seen.

That morning I had a signal from Rhoades, which at the time struck me as rather humorous, though now I cannot see why. It ran something like this: "Japs again at Savo complete with one machine gun and tin hats, enquiring for whereabouts of white men on Guadalcanal. Said they would go there in two weeks' time—stop—Japs also at Tenaru and Kookoom joy riding on horses Friday last—nearly caught police boy." What made me laugh was the image of the Japs, riding after my unfortunate constable. Lever's would have been disappointed with the performance of their horses!

Shortly after breakfast on 10 June, there was another jolly good raid, which must have caught the Japs unawares. Just then I happened to be interviewing two of Bingiti's scouts, who had brought the pleasing news that the earlier raids had caught many Japanese out of their slit trenches; two hundred had been killed, and their wounded completely filled the aid station. I hoped the postmortem information on these raids would be of use.

I still had great trouble with the indispensable charging engine, which seemed to be developing an asthmatic cough. Daniel thought there might be water in the benzine, so we tried filtering it through my bush hat. (The hat had been "acquired" from the RAAF; it didn't look awfully military, but it was far better than the brown homburg in which I had returned from Australia.) The filtering brought about a great improvement, and the hat survived.

As regards a uniform, I had one pair of drab shorts, but my khaki shirt, after repeated washing, had faded to a very pale canary yellow. I tried dyeing it with coffee and tea, but they didn't give it much color. Then I tried soaking it in a muddy solution of red earth; this was more successful, but it made the shirt very scratchy to wear, and the color did not last very long. I was all right for long hose, and my last pair of shoes and one pair of gym shoes were still holding out. When on the move I had a leather belt and a short-nosed .38 pistol, which someone had left behind at Aola. I also had a Webley .45 that I had picked up somewhere, but such a cannon was not made for bush walking.

When I was about to go to Aola I had sent one of the scouts down to the Bokokimbo River, far below the Paripao ridge, to see if there were any river fish worth eating. As there were so many good fish in the sea, the coastal people rarely fished in rivers. My researcher returned with a very handsome beast, which weighed about six pounds: it had large, horny scales, similar to the tarpon's, and it was slightly flattened, like a bream. When cooked it had fairly firm flesh and a good taste. This was the first river fish that I or most of the scouts had ever had; we all felt that we wouldn't mind eating it again, and hoped it could be caught farther inland. Life was pretty tedious, but it could have been worse.

12

"When creeping murmur . . . !"

Now entertain conjecture of a time
When creeping murmur and the poring dark
Fills the wide vessel of the universe.

—*Shakespeare, King Henry V, act 4, prologue*

An Unnecessary Alarm

FOR SOME DAYS I had been expecting Eroni from the southern end of Guadalcanal. Following my policy of maximum dispersal, he had built himself a hideout about a mile to the west of Aola in the middle of dense jungle, and from here he visited his three dispensaries. On 11 June, I got a note from him at last.

The message was a great shock. Eroni reported that the Japanese had arrived at Rere and taken one of the SSEM missionaries, whom I had thought to be safely in the bush on Malaita. If this was true, my watch had failed not only in not reporting the arrival of the Japs but in letting the missionary wander about without my knowledge. It boded very evil, and from a mood of quiet optimism and almost smug satisfaction I was plunged again into despondency.

It was 0700 when I got the bad news. I hurriedly pounded out a warning on the teleradio. Though Aola and the immediate area were twice reported clear, I became extremely anxious, and had the locals at Paripao and at Belaga, the next village, standing by in case we had to flit. I sent a warning to Father Engberink at Ruavatu and had my ammunition hastily removed farther from the village to a previously prepared spot.

At 1600 Aola was again reported all clear, and I began to wonder whether I should clear out before nightfall or remain in Paripao until I got more news. Then came another note from Eroni: the whole thing was completely false. Mounting indignation gave rise to black rage. I got the teleradio working and canceled my messages reporting the incident, then I sent Bengough a very rude signal asking him why the hell his so-and-so missionary was unconsciously spreading alarm and despondency on our coast. I also signaled Forster that he could now let Bengough's launch, *Gizo,* carry on with her return trip.

My relief that we had not been caught napping was tremendous, but it was important to find out how the alarm had come about. Sending Eroni's messenger off to fetch the scouts and persons concerned, I followed more slowly the next morning. Everything at Aola appeared to be in order, and the scouts alert and smartly on the job. Eroni was distressed at passing on the message, but it was not his fault. As a test, I sent a message to be passed from one Home Guard section to the next as far as Rere; the answer came back speedily, so there was little doubt my chaps were on the job.

The missionary had, of course, returned to Malaita, unaware of the scare he had caused. He had never thought of telling anyone he was coming, and I could not discover what he had been doing at Rere, unless he was returning the mission's local residents to their homes. His boat's crew had been scared stiff the whole time; as they returned to Rere after dark after visiting the nearby village, they had imagined that they saw the missionary talking to some armed men, and had rushed off and alarmed the whole neighborhood. Returning in the morning, they found that all was well, so they got on board without thinking to correct their false news. I checked every post and NCO, and made them understand clearly what their duties were. We could ill afford similar scares: another such panic might scuttle the whole show.

I felt much relieved next morning. The district headman, Vakalea, had brought in two good bushmen volunteers, whom I gratefully signed on as scouts. They looked pretty fit, but they would require much training, discipline, and practice in accurate observation before they could be relied upon to carry on our dangerous trade. I intended to use them at first as messengers between my different coastwatching sections, until I had some idea how they were shaping. I also besought Vakalea to get as many villagers as he could to plant more vegetables: they were badly needed, and we could still pay for them with ration tobacco.[1]

Hark! to the glad sound

About 1225 a very large plane went over; unfortunately it was obscured by clouds most of the time. The sound of its engines was new to us; we began to hope that it was a B-17—a Flying Fortress. It had our good wishes. We heard bombs being dropped in Tulagi, and then the plane, in the distance, returning to the south.

The next day, Sunday, was quiet. I spent most of the time charging up the batteries: in addition to the morning schedule, we were now keeping listening watches at four times during the day. It was essential for everyone to know what was going on, especially for us on Guadalcanal. I couldn't help speculating whether the Japanese would investigate Aola by boat, and, if so, when. On reflection, given everything that had happened, it was really incredible that they had not been there already.

Bingiti let me know that George Bogese, about whom we had worried so much, had not been seen in Tulagi or Nggela for some weeks. The reason for this was soon explained in a message from Rhoades. Two Japanese officers and sixty-five men had called at Savo Island the week before, reportedly on their way to Visale; they had distributed pamphlets in the Nggelese language stating that there was no British rule and that the Japanese military forces were the only good friends of the people. Another pamphlet instructed islanders to hand over their arms and ammunition and tell the soldiers where the white men were hiding. (The Japs had told them that Bogese and an Nggela man, Kuini, had been taken to Rabaul, where presumably the printing was done; the pamphlets had come off a destroyer dispatched from there. There was little doubt who had made the translations.) The craft that had brought the Japanese had a two-way radio, for the party was recalled by wireless to Tulagi. I felt glad that they did not go to Visale.

Monday, 15 June, was the King's birthday; everything was quiet on the

Tulagi front, so I attended to administrative matters. A lot of resentment had arisen over Vakalea's effort to get the locals to plant more vegetables. The villagers had as usual misunderstood, and thought he would be taking the produce without paying for it. Then I had a letter from Rhoades: he was very worried that the Catholic printing press at Visale would be used to print anti-British propaganda. I told him that it should have been dispersed some months ago and that if the type was removed, as at Maravovo, the press could hardly be used. Snowy's charging engine, like mine, had packed up; I arranged for him to requisition the mission lighting plant engine from Maravovo.

On Tuesday there was great excitement. At 1100 a Flying Fortress, returning from Tulagi, flew directly over the station. She appeared to be flying quite slowly, and the powerful purr of her engines was extremely satisfying. I was not able to make out under what colors, Australian or American, the plane was flying, but she really impressed the locals, who all turned up to watch. Forty minutes later she was still majestically cruising about, toward the southeast, when the hum of a Kawanisi was heard. Excitement grew at the prospect of an aerial battle.

When it was opposite Ruavatu, the Kawanisi suddenly banked to port, turned through almost 120 degrees, and shot upward into the clouds at great speed. "Our" plane appeared to see it; she came roaring in from the seaward and, turning in a wide curve, sailed over Paripao, only just clearing the trees. At such close range the Fortress appeared tremendous, and as she swung back out to sea the air was filled with leaves sucked off the top of the trees. Then she flew round several times in a wide circle; while she was over Nggela we could hear the Kawanisi, gaining height but "treading air" in the cloud. Just after 1200 the B-17 gave up the game and flew off: she probably needed all her fuel to get home. About five minutes later the Kawanisi sneaked out of the cloud and, after a cautious look around, chuffed off sheepishly toward Tulagi; he must have been quite scared. If the wishful thinking of my scouts had come true, the Kawanisi would have utterly disintegrated, for the Fortress was cheered to the echo every time she went over the station. When it was all over, we were left grinning like fools and shedding a sentimental tear. I began to wonder whether we had all gone mad, and ordered them back to work.

Battery charging soon brought me back to earth, as did a case I had to try. We had had another nasty alarm, this time caused by a half-wit's stealing a rifle. Andrew brought up a man from Gorabusu, or Ruavatu—I cannot remember which village. His name was Bolikeli, and he was well known for having more than the normal ration of "bats in the belfry." Bolikeli had followed one of my scouts on patrol, and waited until he went into the bush to perform a natural function; then he had nipped the man's rifle and run off down the trail. The scout followed Bolikeli's tracks with little difficulty but didn't catch him until he had got to Ruavatu plantation, where the blighter told the two islanders he saw that he had orders from the "government" to shoot a bullock. Two whole villages evacuated when they heard the rifle shot, to cries of "Japan 'e come!" It should not have happened. Bolikeli was detained, and the scout was reprimanded severely for his negligence; all the others were gravely warned. It was a good example of the widespread effect of one man's thoughtlessness.

It was about time for Bingiti to report again in person and tell me about Japanese activity in the Nggela area. He used to come over in a tiny two-man canoe, which took up to ten hours and was an ordeal even in daylight. I had tried to insist that he send his messengers by night, but Bingiti had told me that it was not safe to cross open sea in the dark in small canoes, as waves could not be seen and the boat was likely to be swamped. He also had said the Japs were not bothering much about isolated canoes.

There was no doubt that the Japs in Tulagi were hampered by the increasing pressure of our air raids. They had confessed to the islanders that they were very much afraid of being bombed. Their launches were often seen taking parties out of Tulagi or Tanambogo early in the morning, and the commanding officer had now moved his flag from the resident commissioner's office in Tulagi to Makambo. There were four Kawanisis in the harbor, which could not fly because they had been damaged in air raids. The Japs had also spent some time on Nagotana Island, Schroeder's old retreat, dismantling and removing guns from one of the sunken minesweepers, whose superstructure was still above water. (I assumed that they were antiaircraft guns.) This annoyed Rhoades, as Schroeder had left a large supply of food there, and Snowy was itching to send him across to remove or destroy it. There was also some evidence of the presence in Tulagi of a political officer, who walked about in a white starched uniform and who knew pidgin English very well.

There was not enough room for large forces in Tulagi Harbor. Everything pointed to the fact that the Japanese had established their base in Tulagi and were now awaiting reinforcements before landing on Guadalcanal. It was now the seventeenth of June.

Vouza Returns

That afternoon, the sound of a loud but obsequious welcome at the guard room announced that Vouza had reported for duty at last.

Vouza said that he had carried out my orders and told all his people that if the Japs asked where the district officer was they were merely to say that he had gone—full stop; not gone bush or gone south or gone anywhere else, just gone! He was very angry because several visiting Nggelese had unfortunately managed to slip off home before they had been rehearsed in the act. Nothing could be done, however, as they might have spoken to the Japanese already. Vouza thought he could answer for the trustworthiness of his relatives, but not for the rest.

We had a long discussion as to what was likely to happen if the Japanese landed in the Tasimboko area. Clearly, Vouza had taken the trouble to work out various courses of action, so it was not difficult to persuade him that his duty lay in keeping the coast quiet from Koli Point to Berande. There was no doubt that the best thing he could do was to run the coast watch in the Tasimboko area, pass the information to the scouts for collection, and try to prevent the mad "Tasimbokoes" from doing anything suicidal, against either their own interests or ours. The Tasimboko headman, Luvena, would have to be kept really busy: his coastwatching organization was not nearly as efficient as some of the others, and they had not been keeping a good lookout.

The low morale of some of the police and scouts had begun to worry me. Vouza's cheerful spirit and loyalty would help whenever he was about, but the men were not working in a large unit, which might have given them a measure of encouragement. They had all done extremely well to date, but I had to consider whether any of them was likely to desert, for if even one man did the news would go around like wildfire, and then we would all be in the soup.

Vouza took Chimi, one of the two new bushmen scouts, to hang around near Lunga. He was an extremely fast walker, who could keep direction through the densest bush, and he could act in an emergency quicker than anyone. No sooner had they gone off the next day than things began to happen. From the reports of Rhoades and Macfarlan it was clear that a destroyer and two smaller warships, together with eight submarines, were now using Tulagi as a base. The destroyer had also been seen anchored off Lunga. It seemed that Vouza would only just be in time to stop the rot.

Rhoades also reported that the Japs were continuing to put over their propaganda on Savo, where they had now told the people that there would be no taxes and that those inhabitants wishing to be friendly would be given badges. This propaganda was being spread by the political officer, who had also told the Savo people that the whole of the British and American fleets had been sunk.

Snowy claimed that several Savo people had been spreading Japanese propaganda and that a party of them was shortly expected on Guadalcanal to spread the gospel. Bogese would be the leading propagandist. Rhoades rightly asked that Lafe Schroeder, who was going to sneak in behind Lunga from across the hills, be given some sort of status. He also inquired whether members of the pro-Jap propaganda team should be shot on setting foot on Guadalcanal. I doubted the proposal would receive official blessing, but I lost no time in passing instructions round the island that if Bogese or his assistants did land on Guadalcanal they were to be tripped up, tied up, and taken to a safe place without further ado.

Rhoades gloomily reported also that the Japs had told one or two of the locals that they knew there were three teleradios on Guadalcanal, one at each end and one in the middle. They were also aware that there were sets on Ysabel, Malaita, and San Cristobal; however, they proposed to deal with Guadalcanal first. He also advised that they had several large dogs, possibly bloodhounds, for use in tracking us down. That *was* cheerful news.

From Macfarlan's direct observation and scouting reports coming back to Rhoades and me, it was clear that the destroyer had landed a large party at Kukum and Lunga, and that they were busy reconnoitering or surveying the area. There were several landing craft in company with the destroyer, and they had landed men at different points. The Japs had set up some water tanks at Lunga, and had fired the grass plains in the vicinity; that might be an indication that they were going to build an airfield, or perhaps it was done to prevent snoopers from having cover.

I carefully checked our secret caches, inspected our weapons and posts, and waited for information to come in. The destroyer, I knew, had come down as far as Makile, and a landing party had questioned the locals; I hadn't yet heard what they had told the Japanese. Ten bullocks had been killed at Lunga, and gasoline had been used to start the grass fires. Jap patrols had fanned out for several miles behind the plains; it was not known whether they were merely putting out the usual security or actually looking to see if we were skulking in the undergrowth. The description of the Jap soldiery, wearing khaki uniforms with cloven-toed boots and carrying long rifles, sent a chill down my spine.

While I was waiting, I became very worried over another problem. Although I had persuaded all villages to evacuate the coast, curiosity usually overcame fear, and there was not much I could do to prevent uninformed locals from talking to the Japs or from knowing where I was. It had been hard enough training the number of lads I had; it would be just as difficult to increase the number, and to have even one trained scout resident in every coastal village was quite out of the question. Any landing party from a destroyer would be far too strong for us to repel, and they would be bound to get some sort of clue at Aola. Our only defense appeared to be depth, and elusiveness, and I very much feared that I might have to move farther into the bush. Kennedy had reported that Gizo was devoid of Japanese; that made it almost certain that Guadalcanal was the best island from the strategic point of view. Tulagi would be the port, Lunga the air station, and the army would ensure there were no snoopers.

From Paripao, the destroyer could be seen steaming peripatetically between Lunga and Tulagi. I wondered whether we had any submarines in the area, for she would have made a good target. Chimi arrived; damned good bushman that he was, he had traveled from Lunga across country direct within forty-eight hours of his departure. He had bags of information. The wretched Tasimboko crowd had gone down to see the Japs out of curiosity. The soldiers, brandishing fixed bayonets, had warned them off, and forced some of them to get coconuts from the trees. They had told the natives that they were going to use Lunga permanently, and asked them who had made the coastal road. They also had searched most of the people, and had kept them well away from the main Jap party. Chimi managed to evade the outer ring, but he could not get close enough to count them all. He was able, however, to ascertain that they were all in khaki, with packs and ammunition belts, and were, in all probability, army rather than navy.

Sending Chimi back hot foot to keep an eye on the situation, I spent an hour trying to identify the destroyer, which was still steaming about. It was really a waste of time, as no one had ever provided us with silhouettes of the different classes; in any case, the three of us on Guadalcanal had described her in full, which should have made her identification down south fairly easy.

The next problem to be solved was how to get ready to move. I reduced our belongings to even more of an absolute minimum than before. What I could not take, which included all my current records, Treasury documents, and safe, would have to be removed from Paripao and safely cached. I walked several miles up and down the mountain road leading farther inland; after a long search, I found a clifflike sandstone ridge in the center of a copse, a few hundred yards off the track and some miles on from Paripao. Straightaway I got a score of chaps started on digging out a cave. The difficult thing to decide was whether to get off the road and get stuck in one place, or to stay on the road and trust to being able to flit immediately if there was any sign of our being disturbed. I was inclined to do the latter.

Most of the road from Aola to the river had been obliterated by the planting of vegetables, but I told them to do even more. I had given up wearing shoes as far as possible, although my feet were much larger than the scouts'; I had also practiced scouts in combing a village for shoe prints, over which they would then walk. This drill would take place after I evacuated from Paripao.

I wrote a note to F. M. Campbell, telling him that he might have to move out soon, and another for Michael Forster on San Cristobal, hoping that a canoe would be able to slip over from Marau and pass the word that we could not use the teleradio for anything except sending out information. At nightfall Chimi, with beads of sweat on his brow, arrived hot foot from the coast, to say that the Japs had told the people that a large warship was expected at Lunga very shortly with troops and that the manhunt would then start in earnest. As Chimi put it, "Altogether Jap-an 'e wait'm onefella war [warship] 'long Lunga. Closeup 'im 'e come. 'im 'e full up altogether 'long soldiers. Bymbye altogether come look'm youmefella. 'im 'e no blurry good tumas! No blurry good tumas."

Chimi was right. It was a lovely end to a very agonizing day. The night was not much better.

13

"Devil b'long Chimi sing out!"

A T PARIPAO it became intensely quiet after nightfall. The wind dropped completely, and the silence could almost be felt. Sitting alone in the darkness, I was often conscious of a feeling of impending fate —as if something awful was about to happen.

How that feeling was connected with an incident that happened one night, I cannot say, but I have no doubt that happen it did. The pagan islanders believed that departed spirits, especially family spirits or "devils," could communicate with the living. Thus, when during the night someone suffered what at first sight appeared to be an epileptic seizure, it was not thought extraordinary, for it was his "devil" speaking to him. The man would appear to be possessed, and shout at the top of his voice.

That night, I was standing outside my hut having a smoke before turning in. Everyone in the village, except the various guards, was asleep. It was unbearably still and very close. The path past my hut, which led up the mountain, could hardly have been more that two feet wide; as it had rained all day, the mud surface was fairly soft and slippery. The ground sloped away very steeply on both sides, and there was little or no foothold off the path, for the slope was covered with trees. It would have been impossible for anyone to pass without bumping into me.

Suddenly I felt the hair rise on the back of my head. As I took the pipe out of my mouth, wondering what was going on, I felt a disturbance of the air, as if someone had passed very close. I dashed back into the hut and grabbed my gun. Before I picked it up, there was a horrible scream, which seemed to come from the guard room. I doubled down there; by the time I arrived, four of the lads were holding Chimi down on his bunk.

His eyes were only half open, and rolling, as if he were asleep, but he seemed to be possessed with extraordinary powers. Chimi was trying to get up, and it was taking the four of them all their strength to hold him down. He was sweating profusely and screaming at the top of his voice. We could not understand what he was shouting, but someone recognized it as one of the more remote bush dialects. Chimi himself did not normally speak it: it was the dialect of his birthplace, which he had left when he was very young. After about ten minutes he collapsed and fell into a deep sleep. We left him to sleep; none of us could.

In the morning, Chimi would say very little about what had happened: "Devil b'long me 'e sing out 'long me, 'long night." He was a frightened man. He was obviously quite sincere about it, and I did not push him any further. What worried me was whether there was any connection between what I had felt brush past me and Chimi's "devil." Of one thing there was no doubt: as it had rained all day, the path above my hut was innocent of foot marks at dusk. There were none in the morning either, but I could swear that something passed me. It was an unnerving experience.

I got a signal from Macfarlan. He wanted another police post established between Koilo and Gold Ridge. Mac said that if I provided one policeman he would arrange to have one of Hay's men also detailed for the job. "Yes," I replied, "good idea."

I also received a signal from Snowy Rhoades. Snowy was as worried as I was about the Japs' tracking dogs. This time he proposed that when we did our "final flit" we put citronella oil or vanilla or some other strong scent on our feet. In addition, we were to sprinkle the feet of several policemen and have them make false trails. We should walk up rivers as much as possible; he also affirmed that a good shower would destroy all the scent. Rhoades also reported that one of his police had fired over the heads of a canoe full of Savo people, in order to make them come ashore and report their business. They raced out to sea and went straight to Visale, where they announced that they would go and tell their Nippon friends. Had they stated their intentions, Snowy said, they would never have been allowed to leave! And so it went on, with confidence and good order declining all the time.

It had to be accepted that the Japanese intended to settle in at Lunga for good. They had occupied Tulagi, but I knew that they found it most uncomfortable. It was painfully clear that we would be relieved only if our own people recaptured the islands.

On 23 June the long-awaited Bingiti arrived at last, with lots of good information and his usual cheerful grin. His detailed report on the movements of ships and planes in and out of Tulagi read like Bradshaw's British railway guide! Some of Bingiti's news conflicted with Rhoades's reports, and I treated as gospel only what he claimed actually to have seen himself.

Bingiti had seen two barges sunk by our bombers off a promontory near Gavutu. As the occupants of one were on a reef fishing, there were only twenty casualties. The Japs had started to take parties over to Nggela, where they had dug up vegetables from the village gardens; Bingiti confirmed that most of the Nggelese were now thoroughly anti-Jap. He had met some rough weather coming across from Nggela in his canoe, which had nearly broken up in mid-channel. This forced him to return, get another canoe, and come over the next night. I decided I could spare a certain amount of native tobacco, which he could take back to keep the Nggelese anti-Jap. "My word!" he said, "it would."

Later, I went up the road to check on the digging of the secret cave. It was going on apace. The material to be dug out was hardly more than compressed earth, and the prisoners had worked well. The idea was to stack everything up in the middle, cover it with tarpaulins, and fill in the entrance completely. It would then be jolly hard to find. I returned to Paripao to find the warder, Anea, arrived with a gang of prisoners, carrying vegetables from Aola. He was in the last stage of jitters and claimed that he was very frightened about his wife and child. They were in no danger, as they were on the weather coast; from the expression on his face, however, I was convinced that he had been dreaming of samurai swords whistling through the air.

While I was doing my best to reassure him I had rather a puzzling note from Father Engberink, which threw sand into the works of the intelligence machine. He reported that he had come back from Visale in his tiny launch by night, and that he had found no Japanese when he called at Makile. (They had probably all collected at Lunga, and did not hear the feeble exhaust of his engine as he passed far out. His message would be checked.) I admired the man's bravery, but considered him extremely foolhardy. It was lucky that the destroyer had gone back to Tulagi the night before. I still could not see how the Catholics would be accepted as neutrals by the Japanese. From what I heard on the wireless news, it was not an idea that their troops were likely to share.

When I received the circular about denying resources to the enemy I had thought that it concerned merely the derelict plantations. Now I got a signal from the resident commissioner asking whether Hay, Rhoades, and Hart had destroyed their "plant" before going bush. All three had, of course, long ago removed the vital parts of their installations, and the replies that I got back from them were hardly to be repeated. I sent one or two delaying messages, and finally managed to convince higher authority that all had been done that could be done.

I also received a message full of queries about the advances for which Ken Hay had asked. I had given him over four hundred pounds, which came from Burns Philp in Australia. BP was a very large concern, consisting of over a dozen different companies, and it was rather tedious having to explain on Hay's behalf that he had been doing his best to settle up the affairs of all the different subsidiaries. Most of the plantations that Ken was nominally looking after had been left suddenly by the managers, and there were bills and labor unpaid; there was very good reason for his getting matters straightened out. Besides, I represented that what he was doing was also in the interest of the government!

First Casualty

On 25 June, one day after I had sent Chimi down to Lunga, a report came back that he had been bitten by a centipede and was out of action. It could not have happened at a worse moment. I sent Beato down to find out what had happened, but he soon came back to say that Chimi had gone on. In the early morning it was common to find that spiders had woven their webs across the narrow bush trails. When I first went bush walking I found this out to my cost, and soon allowed one of the shorter constables to go first. The centipedes used to crawl about in the trees, and if the branches were shaken, as by the breaking of spiders' webs, there was no knowing when a centipede might drop on an unfortunate bush walker's head. This was what had happened to Chimi, and the brute had nestled on top of his hair until he lay down beside the track for a rest. When it dropped off, he was bitten very badly on his thigh. This rendered him a comparative cripple for some time. It really was most exasperating, because if Chimi had got to Lunga we would probably have known much sooner whether or not Father Engberink's report was true.

Another message of congratulations came from the resident commissioner "on our valuable intelligence work." I had to laugh when I told the men: without batting an eyelid, they one and all said that reinforcements would be far more welcome. "Youmefella do'm job numba one, but more better send'm war[ship], youme kaikai'm [eat up] Jap-an altogether!" Congratulations were all very well, but there wasn't much of a future in our present game.

Next day a scout from Rhoades's area brought a long letter of protest from Bishop Aubin, who was gravely concerned about rumors, circulating amongst the islanders, that he was pro-Japanese. I had done my best to tell him how difficult it was going to be to remain neutral, and it took me a long time composing a reply. There was no doubt that Rhoades felt himself embarrassed by the bishop's "neutrality," and Snowy could hardly be expected to be responsible for him and his party if the neutral attitude proved of no avail with the Japanese. Yet, short of detaining the bishop, there was not very much that I could do about it.

My reply was unfortunately never received. I sent it with Chimi, who in order to spy on the Japs passed as close as he dared to Lunga on the way. I had told him to destroy the letter and one to Rhoades if he were in danger of capture. When he got there it was pouring rain, and under its cover he went right down to the beach, where the Japs were busy unloading stores. Unfortunately, the rain cleared for a few minutes, and Chimi was seen dodging between the coconut palms. They chased after him in a truck, but he had enough sense to go to earth in a swamp, where he slipped off his lavalava and, throwing it on top of the letters, jumped on them until the whole lot disappeared in the mud. He then darted naked into the jungle and got back safely to where he had secreted his uniform and rifle. I could not risk Chimi, or another scout, to split hairs with the bishop about his neutrality, so I had to leave His Reverence uncomforted. Chimi reported that all the people who had been asked, at bayonet point, where the whites had gone to had replied, "Me, no savvy," or "Altogether go finish." This had been carefully cross-checked. I was much relieved.

During the next few days it was pretty quiet during the day, but our bombers were doing a lot of night raiding, most of which caught Tulagi unawares. The Japs continued to make recces to Lunga, Kukum, or Tenaru; they did not stay there for more than a day or two at a time, and it was not clear what they intended. They had pulled down one of the plantation houses at Kukum and used the timber, together with coconut logs, for the erection of a sixty-foot jetty. Surely this meant that they were going to settle? They had ripped timber out of most of the buildings and, much to the disgust of my scouts, who were very clean people, had defecated all over the verandahs. All this worried me.

What worried Macfarlan, Father Engberink's report notwithstanding, was contact between the Makile people and the Japanese. Mac asked me whether we could not get them all off the beach. I wearily replied that they *were* off the beach and that it was the coast watch who had spoken to the Japs: an enemy party had walked along the coast and surprised them, instead of coming by launch as previous parties had done.

Rhoades's worry about this time was that he was getting a little involved in his efforts to settle native affairs. Snowy was doing an excellent job, but he was not always sure of the customs involved. On this occasion he had awarded damages up to the value of six pounds in native shell money; the loser in the case had paid over half the amount, and promised to pay the rest during the next month. The payment was accepted, but the complainant had since brought the money back, saying he wanted the full amount or nothing. There was, of course, no right answer. I told Rhoades to rehear the case and make the damages three pounds. Hearing nothing further, I assumed both sides were satisfied.

By the end of June, reports were coming in from six main collection centers along the coast, and all my real "trustys" were down there at the perimeter, either "coaching" volunteer coast watch sections or collating the information and operating the communication parties that continuously brought it back to me. My inner defenses round Paripao were manned entirely by our newest recruits. I had precious little time to train them, so it was just as well that some of the men had had prior experience.

One of those who signed on at that time was Gumu, who had once done five years with the police. He had a thin face and a rather saturnine expression, and he rarely smiled; but he was a good bushman, and a steady sort of chap, and he knew his arms drill perfectly. I kept Gumu at Paripao until I got to know him, and in order to help me train the other volunteers.

The only snag was that I did not have rifles for everyone. I laugh now when I think of the recruits' equipment, which was scanty in the extreme. Some men insisted on retaining their own spears; if they were happier with them, I felt, they should have them, at least until we were able to "win" more rifles from the Japanese. That was a policy that I did not want to adopt until we were sure that help was on its way: to go on the offensive now would only draw reprisals, and lead nowhere.

The only items of which we had plenty were bush knives or machetes, which all the men knew how to use. They had been part of the road-clearing equipment at Aola, and Andrew was busy making scabbards for them from some untanned hides.[1] Very few of the men had more than the scantiest G-string in the way of clothing.

I used to start off by giving them a drill to wake them up; then I concentrated on rifle handling and cleaning. This latter problem was getting a little desperate, as Guadalcanal had a great deal of rain[2] and in the tropical jungle rifles would not stay unrusty for very long. We had more or less run out of issue rifle oil, and we no longer had any emery paper. Lubricating oil was a good substitute, but I needed all I had for the charging engine. We started to use coconut oil, but we had no idea how long it would last without decomposing. It was well nigh impossible to keep rifles in good condition in that appalling climate.

Once the recruits could stand up and point their rifles in the right direction, I developed their observation through "Kim's game," that well-tried exercise. As a rule, the Solomon Islander was quite observant, but what he was now being asked to observe—machine guns, mortars, construction machinery—was alien to his environment, and he had to learn to describe something even if he had never seen it before. Neither could I describe any of the things that I was asking him to go and observe.

The hardest thing of all was to make them stick to facts. Take weapons, for example. A scout would say he had seen a "gun, bigfella tumas." No doubt, but what was important was whether its caliber was bigger or smaller than, or the same as, any of the sample pieces of wood I kept handy for such interrogations. After trying one or two, the scout would find the right size, and then a look of delight would break out on his face.

"'im, no more, Sah," he would say with emphasis, and I would know that we had the right answer. That type of comparison and detail was what was required.

On looking back, I am sure that our accumulated reports must have given a fairly good idea of what the Japs were doing during the latter part of June. They had set up some sort of radio director station on Nagotana Island, and new large landing craft had been reported from Tulagi. (They bristled with guns and held about a hundred men; I smiled when I thought of our anti-invasion practice of last February.) As for our bombing, it certainly had been successful, and it had hampered their naval activities: at least three destroyers had been sunk in Tulagi Harbor, several landing craft had been put out of action, and a large number of fatal casualties had been inflicted. Kennedy had reported the sinking of a light cruiser, and the Japanese medical facilities in Tulagi were always stretched to the limit. Enemy activity on Guadalcanal had, as far as we could see, not yet produced positive results; it too had been considerably delayed by our bombing.

By 30 June the secret cache was nearing completion, and I immediately started packing away office records and other impedimenta. I sent out pay for everyone, including pay for district headmen for the next quarter, then I made up and balanced the accounts and closed the books for good. There was nowhere for the locals to spend the silver, but it was good for morale. Deke, who was sent off to Koilo with the pay for the men there, also took letters and some "buttons, fly" for Macfarlan. I told Mac not to worry about his dress, as he would not be making any personal appearances, but we were all getting pretty ragged. Deke also had instructions to take a complete inventory at Koilo and have everything that was not being used hidden away.

"Altogether Japan 'e come!"

The situation clarified a bit on 1 July. Macfarlan reported that a cruiser of about eight thousand tons was operating between Lunga and Tulagi, and Rhoades reported another farther west. At noon Dovu arrived to say that one thousand men had come ashore at Lunga on Monday. The Japs had told the islanders they would be at Lunga in force on 29 June; it looked as if they had been as good as their word. Dovu, and one or two others, had watched them come ashore from landing craft at some distance, but with ten stones in one hand each had counted the enemy with reasonable accuracy.

After heavy cross-examination, Dovu had to admit that he should have been there the night before. I reminded him in no uncertain terms how important it was now to get such news passed along. He said that he was sick—"Me get'm sore leg 'long belly b'long me"—but I soon disabused him of the idea: "Dovu, you numba wan blurry larrikin, time you work, you work, time you spell, 'e alright for sick. Now you double up quick-time tumas, or bigfella trouble 'e catch'm you!" He left the house very fit!

It rained heavily that night, which was good for the garden but bad for observation. To complete the misery a wind blew up at dawn and the thatched roof over the lookout was blown to bits. Another unfortunate incident was reported the following afternoon. As the Catholic fathers had not been prepared to destroy the copra at Ruavatu plantation, a patrol from Aola was stupidly burning it on the beach. They had a huge fire going, and a Kawanisi circled a couple of times to see what they were doing. He wasted no bombs on the luckless fellows, but they certainly got a "hurry up."

Lots of information was coming in, but I was beginning to realize that we were not getting as much as we should from Makile, between Vouza's mob at Koli Point and Tasimboko village. It was not properly organized; Macfarlan had been quite right to worry about it. I decided that as I had now packed up all my office work I could dispense with the services of Daniel Pule at Paripao, or wherever I was going to go next. He had been helping to sort out information, and he knew what was wanted. Daniel also had a pretty good idea of what I felt about the Makile people and their lack of alertness. I therefore sent him down to take charge of that area and send me up quicker and more accurate reports.

Bingiti's information was not quite so interesting as it had been. There were more Japanese about, and he was finding it more difficult to get in close enough for accurate observation. On the other hand, enemy popularity on Savo had reached a low ebb, and people from there had no difficulty in getting over to report to Schroeder or Rhoades. Lafe Schroeder had managed to get two Savo men to accept Jap friendship badges, in the hope that they would be allowed into Tulagi. The minesweeper that had been sunk at Nagotana had been bombed again; a thirty-six-man salvage party had been caught napping there, and all of them had been killed.

While decoding a signal from Rhoades one morning, I came to the word "YUAMA." My heart missed a beat. It was the name of the captain of a Jap pearling lugger, whom I had helped arrest on Malaita and who was convicted of illegal pearl shelling. The message went on to say that Yuama and four of his crew had arrived in Tulagi in Japanese naval uniform, together with sixteen others who had been arrested for illegal pearl fishing on other luggers before the war. I did not like the sound of it at all, especially when it was reported that three Jap schooners had arrived in the Cape Esperance area and two others were reported coming eastward down the coast. They were making leisurely visits ashore, searching houses, taking away anything of value, and questioning people closely as to our whereabouts. With the two cruisers dodging backward and forward and the flying boats cruising up and down the coast, the Japs were getting far too close for comfort; now, as a last straw, here was Yuama, who knew who I was and who would probably consider that he had a grudge against me.

Andrew arrived to say that all was well at Aola and there had been no visitors. This was reassuring, but after lunch Garimani, one of my most reliable scouts, came in from the western side, stained with sweat and mud, with his eyes popping out of his head. At 1000 a Jap schooner had passed Talaura, a small settlement near Berande, and was sailing on down the coast, toward me.

The Japs were on the move at last, and it seemed as if they were moving in my direction. I turned things over in my mind, wondering what to do. After dark, Dovu arrived, looking thin and haggard. He had walked up straight through the bush to tell me that a Jap schooner had landed a party at Taivu Point. The Tasimboko mugginses, in spite of all they had been told, had met the Japanese at the water's edge and carried their gear ashore. The two cruisers, together with five Kawanisis, had anchored off the coast somewhere between Tenaru and Makile.

Distances suddenly seemed to shrink, and I began to realize just how insecure my present position really was. I doubled the sentries on all approaches and passed the word to all the village headmen together with their pay for the next quarter. It was then that I decided to shift back farther into the mountains, as quickly as possible. I sent news to Andrew and Daniel to tell them what I intended to do. As for Vouza, I hadn't heard a word from him. I wondered what he was doing.

After arranging for carriers to be ready in the morning, I threw myself onto my camp bed and endeavored to get some rest, but I remained awake for most of the night. My God, I was afraid. I dared not go to sleep, not merely because I thought they might come and catch me unawares but also because I knew I would dream that they had, and the one state was worse than the other.

Tulagi Harbor, looking east toward Gavutu and Tanambogo. *Middle right:* resident commissioner's office. *Hall photo postcard*

Aola government station from the sea. The cadet's house is farthest back on the hill. *Author's photograph*

Mbangai Island from near the Residency, Tulagi. *Hall photo postcard*

Auxiliary schooner *Tulagi* at anchor in Tulagi Harbor. *Author's photograph*

SS *Morinda* in the Shortland Islands before the war. *Photo courtesy Stanley C. Jersey*

District officer's house, Kira Kira, San Cristobal. *Author's photograph*

Clemens's dog Suinao. *Author's photograph*

Lunga Point from the air. *Photo captured by D-2 at Kukum, 7 August 1942.*

Capt. Hank Adams, *left,* and Lt. Fred Kidde with Japanese ensign that flew over Lunga. *Photo courtesy Robert Howard*

The author being debriefed by D-2 after his arrival at the Lunga perimeter, 15 August 1942. Others, *left to right:* Lt. Col. Edmund J. Buckley; Lt. Fred Kidde; Fl. Lt. Charles V. Widdy, RAAF. *Photo courtesy Robert Howard*

Some of the D-2 crew. *Photo courtesy Robert Howard*

The author with scouts. *Standing, left to right:* Daniel Pule, Andrew Langabaea.
Sitting, left to right: Olorere, Gumu, Chaparuka, Chaku. *USMC photo*

Sgt. Maj. Jacob Vouza, scouting in the Volonavua area. Taken before the Battle of the Tenaru. *USMC photo*

Capt. "Pappy" Moran, the 1st Marine Division's Japanese language expert, escorts a wounded enemy pilot back to the prison cage after interrogation. On the right is an example of the Marines' excellent ad hoc plumbing. *USMC photo*

". . . and to bring back a prisoner." At right, Capt. Hank (Henry J.) Adams, intelligence officer of the 5th Marines. *Henry J. Adams*

Brig. Gen. William H. Rupertus, assistant commander of the 1st Marine Division, and Col. Robert C. Kilmartin Jr., then the D-1, with scouts at Tulagi, late August 1942. *USMC photo*

Butch Morgan. *USMC photo*

Jeep road to Raiders' Ridge. Edson's men defended the long ridge in the center of the picture. Taken a week after the battle, when nothing but scars in the ground, from the intense volume of fire, remained. *USMC photo*

The author giving instructions to Selea prior to the scout's departure on an armed reconnaissance with the 1st Raider Battalion on the Matanikau front, 26 September 1942. *USMC photo*

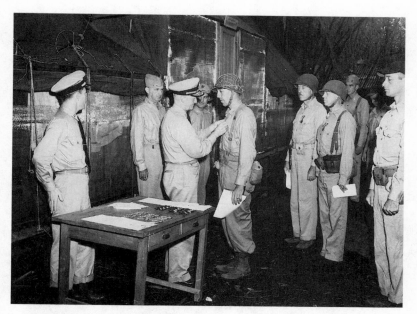

Admiral Nimitz presents the Navy Cross to Lt. Col. Edwin A. Pollock as Major General Vandegrift looks on. *At right,* Brigadier General Rupertus, Colonel Edson, Lieutenant Colonel Carlson (in garrison cap). *USMC photo*

The fighter boys after being awarded the Navy Cross. *Left to right:* Major Smith, Major Galer, Captain Carl. *USMC photo*

AV (auxiliary vessel) *Ramada* returning from Tangarare after Dick Horton's daring daylight rescue operation on 4 October 1942. *USMC photo*

"Macfarlan of the Glens" (Don Macfarlan) after his trek to Lunga, 5 October 1942. In khaki at last, but still with a white cap cover, he vowed, "I'll keep that beard till we push the Japs off the island!" *USMC photo*

Cpl. Ralph E. "Wimpy" Wendling (smoking pipe) and Pfc. Warner with scouts Bingiti, Daniel Pule, and Gumu. At rear, Coast Guard coxswain Ray Evans and the author. Taken at Aola, 7 October 1942. *R. J. Evans, U.S.C.G.*

Lieutenant Colonel Hill's men assemble at Aola government station prior to the attack on Gorabusu, 10 October 1942. *Center,* scout Selea; *right,* ammunition carriers. *USMC photo*

Some of the recce party at Aola, 27 October 1942. *Front row:* Clemens's dog Suinao, and Hartmann and Russo (Coast Guard coxswains). *Back row:* Banco, the author, Daniel Pule, Longley, Pratt. *R. J. Evans, U.S.C.G.*

Corporal "Wimpy" Wendling poses with a group of Solomon Islanders. *Left,* scout Olorere; *center,* Andrew Langabaea's son, Wilson, held by his mother; *top step,* Michael, the cook; *far right,* Tabasui, the digger of shelters. The others are relatives of Andrew's and of Daniel Pule. *USMC photo*

Scouts Vura, Tabasui, and Kimbo bring in volunteers for unloading on the beach, October 1942. They have just come through Japanese lines on the Tenaru. *USMC photo*

Corporal Wendling with scouts at Aola on their return from Operation Recalcitrant, 6 November 1942. *USMC photo*

Assisted by Sergeant Major Vouza, Maj. John V. Mather, AIF, pays a Solomon Islander his monthly wage for work as a stevedore on Guadalcanal. *USMC photo*

The schooners sail again. *G. F. Jones* and *Ramada* at anchor off Tenaru. *Author's photograph*

Scout Chaparuka guiding a patrol from the 2d Raider Battalion (Carlson's Raiders). *USMC photo*

Lieutenant Colonel Carlson's supply train winds across the grass plains on their return from a month-long expedition against the Japanese. *USMC photo*

RNZAF Hudson crew from No. 3 Squadron in front of their aircraft on Guadalcanal. *USMC photo*

The author after the conclusion of the Guadalcanal campaign. *Author's photograph*

14

Retreat to Vungana

O N 5 JULY we put our evacuation plan into operation. Everything spare or nonessential was bundled into its container, which had been prepared for it some weeks before according to a prearranged plan and stacked in the secret cache up the road. After the morning schedule the teleradio was dismantled, and at 0930 off went my best carriers with it. They had to go very slowly and carefully up the slippery bush track: if the battery carriers lost their footing, they could spill the irreplaceable acid, and then we would be sunk.

By noon we had the mouth of the cache filled in and all foot marks carefully brushed away, and quick-growing creepers were planted at the entrance. After some rain it would, I hoped, look natural. All used tins had been buried, and every trace of our occupation removed. About 1245, after a last nostalgic look round, I started up the trail. It was a sorry procession, compared with the hundred or so who had brought us to Paripao: two scouts with rifles in the lead; Michael, the cook, and Peter, his understrapper, who managed our scanty kitchen; a half dozen carriers with the rest of my equipment; and Suinao and me. I did not know where I was heading. Perhaps it was just as well.

Everything went smoothly, and all hands worked with a will. When there was action, my lads were all right, but they were not used to waiting for the worst to happen—it tried their nerves. As I trudged up the track, mile after weary mile, I had that "end of term" feeling again, as if everything had finished and there was nothing more beyond; but there was no elation, no relief.

The climb up the mountain ridge was fairly steep, and the land fell away sharply on either side. About three miles from the village of Bumbugoro, however, it began to level off into a sort of plateau. This was rather frustrating, as I had hoped to have a peep at Tulagi before nightfall. I climbed a tall tree, but there was no chance of my seeing the coast even from the top, for the land was level for several miles around.

Bumbugoro was our overnight stop, and we were tired out. The rest house, on the far side of the village, was a miserable shack, in bad repair. Depressed, I assembled the teleradio on the uneven floor and strung the aerial between two trees. There had not been much time to charge up the batteries before leaving, but even allowing for that the reception was pretty poor, and I could not contact anyone. I had thought that the village might be our next observation post, but it was quite hopeless. I could have kicked myself for being unable to spare the time to recce possible places to which to retire. Instead, I had had to rely on my scouts, who reported that Vungana, the next village in from Bumbugoro, was ideal for observation. I feared that it might be too far from the coast for quick communication with my sources of information; but I couldn't have it both ways, with security as well.

At daybreak, as the smoke from the morning fires curled up into the green shadows, I woke from a fitful sleep to find that a scout had arrived from Paripao. He said that there had been no air activity during the night and that nothing had been heard about the Jap party at Taivu. I was uncomfortably stiff from the previous day's walk, but there was nothing for breakfast, so we picked up our loads and straggled off gloomily up the hill. After the village of Kerembuta, the road became the merest of rough tracks, rambling up and down a lot of hog-backed ridges in a most improbable manner. Sometimes the slope was so steep that the ground was devoid of trees, and one looked down into space. It was worse than anything I had ever seen.

Poor Michael didn't like this bush scrambling at all. "Me b'long cook,"

he protested, "me no b'long walkabout. Lunga 'e fullup 'long Jap-an soldier, bymbye altogether look'm youme. Whichway youme stop nothing
'long sickerup [scrub] and no got'm kaikai. 'im 'e no blurry good tumas."
I had no answer for him except "Bymbye," and that was wearing rather
thin.

The track still contrived to be slippery earth, and I died a thousand
deaths as I watched the battery carriers, who had had to give up pole and
sling, holding a heavy battery on their shoulder with one hand while trying to stop themselves from falling with the other. I wondered how far a
battery would bounce before it smashed to pieces on the rocks below. The
track got steeper and steeper, and we had to break down the loads and pass
the teleradio cases from hand to hand up some of the more impossible
places. On we went until we seemed to be near the top of the world, and
the clouds were only treetop high. Suddenly, through the thinning, lichen-
covered trees, I saw a small row of houses quite close at hand. Thank goodness, I thought: I was utterly exhausted.

It took us another mile to get there. A yawning chasm lay between, and
we had to walk halfway round before we came to a knife-edged connection only four feet wide, with a sheer drop on both sides. This saddle merely
led onto the toothlike pinnacle on which the village rested; the final ascent
was nearly vertical solid rock, into which hand- and footholds had been
cut. I staggered and crawled my way up to the citadel, keeping my fingers
crossed while the teleradio and other equipment were being handed up.
Vungana was a miserable place, but as long as no artillery was brought up
it could be defended with very few men: you could walk only forty or fifty
yards in any direction from edge to edge of the precipice, which continued
all round, except where the tiny saddle of rock spanned the chasm. The
river that ran at the bottom had worn its way down three or four hundred
feet through the ages into an exaggerated oxbow. There were not more
than ten houses, and a handful of naked, dirty people living in them.

I took over the headman's house; actually it was a one-room shack,
which had only recently been built and was therefore fairly clean. The very
uneven split-palm floor was raised about two feet off the ground, so the
wind whistled remorselessly through the slatted floor and walls. It had a
small verandah, but there was no furniture, not even a table or a chair. The
headman was an angular, bony individual of miserable aspect; although
honored by my selecting his great mansion, he could not understand why

I had picked his village as a refuge. Vungana was like a miniature Edinburgh castle, but it was neither pleasant nor impregnable.

Life would not be very comfortable, but I had to admit that the view was simply superb. My field of view extended more than twenty miles in all important directions: to the east I could see the reefs of Rua Sura, while to the west I could see right across to Savo and to Cape Esperance, and clear into Tulagi Harbor as far as Makambo Island. The plantations in the center, especially Lunga, were easy to pick out: the level tops of the coconut palms were a darker green. Most of the grass plains were hidden by the foothills, but the coast was in full view as far as Berande, and I would be able to report Japanese naval movements straightaway.

I set up the teleradio, but there were very few high trees in the village, and I had great difficulty in erecting an aerial. I finally managed by connecting the two ends of the aerial to two very large green bamboos, which were then loosely bound to two betel nut palms that were not really high enough by themselves. When the set was in use, the bamboos were raised and tied firmly to the betel nut palms; at other times, the bamboos were retracted and the aerial hung slackly between the crowns of the two palms.

Shortly after I arrived, I was twiddling with the teleradio, which would not work, when a scout arrived with a gloomy letter from Macfarlan. Mac made more than tentative inquiries about the schooners at Marau Sound; obviously he was thinking about pulling out, a prospect that only added to my insecurity. While I was reading his letter, Daniel Pule came in with a splendid account of what the Japanese had been doing on the coast. Unfortunately, the batteries had run right down, and I couldn't send out a report.

Then, at 1515, I spotted a convoy of five large warships approaching Lunga from the west; one or two looked like cruisers. The rain started up again, preventing any further observation, but about fifteen minutes later we could hear the sound of bombing at Kukum or Lunga. Naturally, the charging engine picked this time to go temperamental again—it appeared to resent working at high altitudes—and after one or two code groups the batteries gave up.

Fed up, I decided to forward Daniel's report and the news about the cruisers to Macfarlan, so that he could send them out; as I was writing it out for him, however, my typewriter broke down. It took more than a day to get the charging engine going.

That night I found out that it was much colder at Vungana than at

Paripao. My two lightweight blankets were quite ineffective, and I was up very early the next morning pacing up and down, trying to get some warmth into my frigid limbs. Keeping clean was also a problem. It took well over an hour to go down to the river at the bottom of the chasm. That was the only source of water, but it all had to be carried up in lengths of bamboo stems, and the amount brought up was far too small for washing. Standing starkers out in the rain was an effective way to have a bath, but one had to keep a weather eye open for village women.

On 7 July the Japanese Navy was around pretty early. Three large vessels were anchored off Lunga by 0630, and a smaller one, accompanied by a landing craft, was steaming toward Tulagi. I heard, quite distinctly, the Kawanisis warming up in Tulagi Harbor before going off south and southeast, while three or four others patrolled up and down the coast between Kukum and Aola until about 0800. In spite of their efforts, friendly bombers dropped their loads on Kukum both morning and afternoon, and at noon, through the mist, we caught a fleeting glimpse of two of our planes as heavy detonations were heard from Tulagi.

As for me, I spent most of the day tinkering with the charging engine. At last I got it to work, just enough to get sufficient juice into the batteries to make the set transmit a decent signal and pass some of Daniel's latest dope to ZGJ.

The Japs appeared to have settled in on Guadalcanal. At least seven hundred were reported to be bivouacked in tents between Kukum and Tenaru. They had trained dogs posted along the Tenaru boundary to keep us out. They also had set up three small posts—at Sapuru, near Cape Esperance; at Taivu Point; and at Berande—and a party of five hundred had been reported en route for the weather coast, where Talisi, the one safe anchorage, was our only possible escape route. The Japanese had told the Tasimboko people that they had come to Guadalcanal for the express purpose of looking for government officers and all other whites.

The small outlying posts had between seven and twenty men, some of whom did not wear a uniform all the time, and, worse luck, a radio. I began to wonder who was watching whose coast. The men told the islanders that they were naval auxiliaries and that they had worked before the war near Thursday Island. They took pigs, fowls, and native vegetables from the village gardens.

In spite of the sentry dogs, we managed to find out all the positions of the ack-ack guns at Lunga, the number of trucks working to level an airfield behind the plantation, and many other interesting details. Vast dumps of stores had been landed all the way along the coast from Kukum to Tenaru, a distance of several miles, and the Japs were working night and day to disperse them. Their luggers were busily going up and down the coast and to and fro from Tulagi. The "schooners" that had been reported were probably former pearling luggers; they were very slow.

To Stay or Not to Stay

Our bombing continued fairly regularly, but we were all disappointed that it did not grow in intensity and that there was no news of anyone's retaking the Solomons. We had long got past the depression stage, but, even so, the general state of gloominess continued to increase. Mac had decided to move back from Gold Ridge and was, in fact, contemplating leaving the island altogether. With the people on the coast bewitched by the Japanese and doing their bidding, however, it would be extremely difficult for us to muster enough carriers to get even Macfarlan and Hay, let alone the gold miners or me, down to the weather coast for evacuation. I knew I couldn't go until the last, so I offered to assist Mac by collecting carriers for him and covering his evacuation. The whole position looked very black, and to cap it all my miserable charging engine was out of action again.

One of the problems at Vungana was the frequency with which it became enveloped in cloud. Apart from hindering observation, the condensation interfered with the teleradio, which got very damp in the morning. I had to keep a small hurricane lamp burning underneath its table all night. Had the charger been in good shape, I could have kept the sets turned on for longer periods.

With the colder nights everyone began to miss the sustaining cup of tea at nightfall: we had run out of sugar before leaving Paripao, and tea without sugar was not much of a drink. Li-oa, my gardener from San Cristobal, said that he knew how the Polynesians made sugar from the coconut palm; I told him to have a try. What the Polynesians produced was, in fact, molasses, which was made from the sap of the growing terminal shoot of the coconut palm. The nearest coconut palm was not much of a specimen, and it was several miles downhill; but Li-oa went down there, and after a few days of laborious work he turned up with a smile on his normally sad face, brandishing two gin bottles full of his treacle-like brew. It wasn't as sweet as the store product, but, when well stirred into a cup of tea, it was just what was required.

The Kawanisi flying boats, or "usuals" as we now called them for briefness in coding, quartered the bush most mornings, singly or in pairs. They were frequently overhead, and pretty low. Decent of them, I thought, to give us so much attention.

My charging engine was giving me more trouble. It would run for three minutes and then have to be cranked again. By dint of persevering with the three-minute bursts, however, I managed to get enough kick into the batteries to send out my messages.

After several days of miserable existence a signal came that Macfarlan had planned his move from Gold Ridge. He intended, in the first place, to shift to Bambatana, one of the prospecting camps, which was far up the Sutakama River and did not appear on the map. As I did not think that the miners realized how desperate our position had become, and I did not know what or whether Macfarlan had told them, I wrote and advised them to get going before the rush came. Being private citizens they would, of course, want to take all their worldly goods with them, but for them the carrier problem would be appalling: there were no trucks, no roads or tracks, and, worst of all, no carriers.

The more I looked, the more impossible the situation seemed to be. With my charging engine working only intermittently, it was a struggle just to get out the traffic, let alone consult others as to what should be done. The Japs were all around us, on both land and sea, and their flying boats had the coast so well patrolled that even if we did manage to set sail from Talisi it would be almost impossible to escape them. Things seemed so bad, and so inevitable, that I felt I needed further instructions, so on 8 July I sent the resident commissioner a long signal: "Coastal natives no longer amenable—Japs intend infiltrating weather coast—looks like search for us will be on both coasts—can trust very few natives—administration almost impossible—cannot do very much good for much longer. Stop. Have you any instructions? Position at present merely a matter of time unless relief comes within week or so. Clemens." It wouldn't help much, but it might, I hoped, stop me from feeling so alone and deserted.

After all these years, and even though I know what subsequently happened, that gloomy message remains a fairly good, unexaggerated summary of the position. Having sent it, I then put the hard word on Macfarlan, asking him point blank whether he intended to scuttle. His reply, which was confirmed by letter, was brief and in the affirmative; it went something like this:

> We are moving Monday morning and hope to see you. I don't think we will have any trouble for a few days but after that, well, who knows. Anyway if I can get off the island I intend to. There are cruisers, destroyers and floatplanes everywhere. A transport is still at Kookoom.
>
> Your police boy wanted a fry pan [from Ken Hay's stores], but had no money and said he had no pay coming to him, so I declined to sell!
>
> Regards and all the best. Two letters for Snowy in case you have contacted him.
>
> Yours,
Mac.

Rhoades was in just as bad a pickle as anyone else, and the terrain between him and Macfarlan was mostly steep mountaintops. To get away he would have to sneak round to the weather coast by cutter or canoe. A few days before, Snowy had heard a shot in the bush only fifty yards away from his hideout; he had not discovered what it was, but he had wisely moved his camp forthwith.

The RC's reply to my signal made me furious: his only advice was to go deep into the bush, transmit as little as possible, and keep in touch with Macfarlan. Some help, I thought—I had already done everything he suggested! If I went much farther into the bush I would be going down nearer to the other side, and a fat lot of good it would do keeping in touch with Macfarlan if he was going to evacuate in the near future. As for keeping off the air, my charging engine was managing to do that for me pretty successfully. I angrily dashed off a most insubordinate reply, and only later tore it up. Ironically, the message from Malaita had the result of putting me on my mettle; I shook off some of the gloom, and felt a little happier about facing the situation.

After I moaned in a letter to Hay about the inefficiency of my charging machine, he replied jokingly that there was an old one at Berande, and that I could have it if the Japanese didn't want it! They had occupied the plantation house, but I was determined to get it anyway. I sent one of my scouts, the poker-faced Gumu, down to Berande; he worked as batman to a Japanese officer for a few days until he had discovered the charging motor. Then, one night, he decamped with it. After several days of impatient waiting I was really pleased when Gumu arrived, with the motor slung on a pole between two carriers. I soon had both motors in pieces, and after about five hours' fiddling and tinkering I had finally assembled a combination of parts that almost worked. It was now dark, and it required perseverance.

We all took turns at cranking the engine. There were blistered hands, and horrid language, but I was determined that it was going to work, and work it did: after more than a hundred pulls on the cord, the wretched thing started at last, then ran like a bird. It was midnight, but I didn't dare stop—it had to run all night. Ken Hay and his jokes. I'd bloody well teach him!

15

"Oh! Lord, how long?"

I THOUGHT I HAD FACED the worst when the old *Morinda* was bombed, while defenseless, in Mboli Passage. And then, again, on the night the Japs arrived in Tulagi. Then, however, there had been a ray of hope; now there seemed none. This was a strange kind of war: it played on one's nerves. That awful hard feeling in the gut worsened with every new catastrophe.

Our bombing was at a low ebb, and the Japanese did what they pleased. There was little activity at night, but during the day they bustled about all over the northern plain, probably building airfields and roads. The smoke from the grass burnings hindered observation, and you could hear their vehicles all day long.

It was strongly rumored that the Japs had started to compile a census of everyone on Guadalcanal and that to a man the people of Tasimboko and Matanikau had gone down and cooperated with them. Certainly the garrison at Taivu Point had some Matanikau men working for them, whether by choice, fear, or force I could not determine. I doubted that anyone had as yet given us away, but it could happen at any moment. Even the most loyal of the district headmen had little influence over their people any longer, and that meant that effective administration was at an end. We were sitting waiting, waiting for something to happen—but for what? Would it be anything good? Or would it be better to rush out and finish it all? Every minute of waiting was an age.

One of my men no longer wanted to wait. Eroni, whom I had not thought impetuous or aggressive, sent me a message asking for general permission to fire on the Japanese. I told him to be very careful and not fire unless he had to in order to escape capture. If he was reckless he would only draw the crabs, and our game would be up. At least that was how it looked at the time.

Rhoades, who appeared to have become the Cassandra of our outfit, gloomily announced that he had it on good authority that the Japs intended to drop paratroops, fifty apiece, on Macfarlan and me. Kennedy, on Ysabel, already had the enemy nosing about, and the *Wai-ai,* his schooner, was gone. She had been hidden in the middle of a mangrove swamp, but a local man, whom Kennedy later captured, had shown the Japanese where she was, and they had burned her to the waterline. It had nearly cooked his bosun, who was by some mischance asleep below. What a nice war it was becoming!

Then, very slowly but perceptibly, things began to improve. More interesting messages started to come in from the coast. The scouts reported that two Flying Fortresses had raided Kukum on several occasions in the early morning. Enemy aerial activity noticeably increased, and on several nights a peculiar long, straight beam of light, perhaps an air beacon, could be seen.

When not actually observing, I spent most of the day charging the batteries. It was rather annoying having to stop the charging engine every time the lookout sounded a warning, so I could check the plane in. The batteries were being worked very hard, and did not seem able to hold a good charge any longer. We had no spares.

The morning of 10 July was fine and clear. Work went on apace on the airfield. There were three small vessels anchored off Lunga, and just after noon I watched a cruiser come out of Tulagi and head straight across the channel toward Makile. She had one very large funnel and was bulging with armament—probably one of those London Naval Treaty light cruisers that in the end turned up with eight-inch guns. I sent a short message about her in my version of an American voice: if the Japs had not yet got direction-finding gear ashore, by now their ships must have got it, so I went very carefully on the transmitting.

That afternoon, Beato, Tabasui, two prisoners, and several carriers brought up the last lot of our gear from Paripao. It consisted mainly of bags of sweet potatoes, which were now our staple diet. My tiny stock of flour had been ruined when a carrier slipped and fell into a river, and so I had no bread. Butter was finished, and cooking fat very nearly so.

Up the Creek

The next day, I was watching the Kawanisis coming home as usual just after 1600, thinking that aerial reconnaissance must be a dull game, when my reverie was disturbed by one of my scouts, Selea, who arrived, out of breath, with a letter from Macfarlan. Selea was even more solemn than usual, for the news was not good. Mac was terse and grim: "We're now at the Suta, and all buggered." After an awful trek his party had withdrawn to the pass of the Suta River, as far as one could go before coming down on the far side from the hills. Before they left Gold Ridge a floatplane had roared over at one hundred feet, and the day after it had returned and dropped three bombs. "They were well on the job, the bastards," Mac said. Most of the local carriers had fled; the party had got away, luckily, because of the timely arrival of my emergency squad, which I had reluctantly sent over to help. Hay was with Macfarlan, and I wondered how his 1916 leg was behaving. I was a little relieved to hear that the miners were there too. It had been one hell of a way to celebrate F. M. Campbell's sixty-fourth birthday.

Now, Mac wrote, they were getting all their gear up there, to prepare for a dash to the weather coast and then off the island. Talisi Bay was the only decent all-weather anchorage on that side that was reasonably safe, and probably the only one that he could use for evacuation. I thought that Mac had postponed it when we got the news that five hundred Japs were making for the south coast; we were still anxiously awaiting news of them. After Rhoades's scare it sounded very risky to move just then.

I really didn't know what to do. The weather coast didn't sound any safer than the northern coast, where the Japanese now had posts at Taivu and Berande as well as at Lunga, and patrolled all the areas regularly. I had never been round to the south coast and didn't know its people, and they hardly knew me; yet, if Macfarlan was definitely going, I would be on my own. And then what? I don't mind admitting that I was very much afraid, perhaps as much of making the wrong decision as of the enemy.

At 1000 on 12 July, two aircraft, one a Kawanisi, the other a reconnaissance plane with floats, attacked Gold Ridge again. They had been flying around all morning. I hoped Macfarlan hadn't gone back to fetch anything, as two of the scouts said they could hear guns strafing. I sent someone off immediately to investigate. This was the third call at Gold Ridge. Who would be next?

A Roast Duck

I was getting tired of the interminable sweet potatoes, tinned meat, and jam, so I sent down an urgent appeal to Andrew to send up something fresh to eat. On 13 July, after two days' eager anticipation, a basket of tomatoes and a good fat duck, plucked and wrapped in pawpaw leaves, arrived from Aola by special messenger. I had forgotten the ducks we had left on the station. It was extremely welcome, but I realized that we had no stove at Vungana, and I wondered how on earth I was going to cook it.

As visibility was then rather poor, there was nothing for observers to do, so I started the charging engine and concentrated on the duck. With a lot of free advice from the interested audience of scouts and villagers, we finally devised a method of cooking it. Amongst our paltry belongings, Michael, a brilliant improviser as always, found a smallish biscuit tin. We dug a hole slightly larger than the tin, and in it we lit a fire. When the hole was nearly full of red-hot ashes, they were shoveled out and the duck was popped into the biscuit tin. This, with its lid fitting as tightly as possible, was then placed in the hole, with the ashes on top. Then it was a case of watch and pray.

I became impatient; I could have eaten half a dozen ducks. Michael, expert cook that he was, kept on saying, "'im 'e no ready," with a smile on his face. He added, "Me savvy you hungry tumas allsame me, but thisfella oven, open 'im one time no more." After this had happened several times, Michael burst out laughing at the look of disappointment on my face, so I chased him round the village. This delighted everyone. At last he was satisfied, and I tucked into my first square meal in weeks. There wasn't much left over, but Michael and the villagers had a pick, and Suinao could be heard all night long, cracking the bones.

In the Mess

There was always something going wrong. The next thing that happened was that the lead-in dropped off the aerial; luckily I had remembered to bring up the tools with which to resolder it. We had a primus stove, which Michael had religiously carried up to Vungana from Paripao; but the damp air had corroded it, and it did not get properly hot. It also smoked abominably. Not being much good at soldering, I made several unsuccessful attempts; at last, after I had used it all up, the solder finally held. It was just as well that I had pulled the aerial down, for the halyards had rotted. The new ones, of linen fish line, were shining white; taking advantage of the smoky primus, we smeared them black, and coated the porcelain insulators with mud to stop them from glistening in the sun. The set worked, and I was much relieved.

The weather was terrible. About lunchtime the mist settled into a steady rain, which kept up the rest of the day. I had rarely felt so sodden. There was nothing to see, but I was able to get a large amount of traffic sent out; I replied delightedly to requests for detailed descriptions of enemy establishments on Guadalcanal and Tulagi, and sent down for more information.

Our bombers had gradually intensified their midnight raids. I hoped that this positive request for targets heralded some new offensive action on our part; we certainly had sent them plenty of information. I always lived in hope, but it was hard to keep going. Life had become rather formless: with so little to eat, it didn't really matter when I ate, and my working hours depended on what there was to see and when reports came up from the coast.

The Japanese were steadily gaining control, and despite the increased counterbombing our chances of dislodging them seemed pretty slim. My anxiety was heightened by hearing the Jap trucks moving about on the grass plains all the time. I knew that sound traveled uphill quite easily, but they sounded very near, and with the Kawanisis flying overhead every day I felt absolutely hemmed in. They had begun flying lower and lower, sometimes only two or three hundred feet up, and we had to be careful to get the aerial down and any washing taken off the line. I was getting fed up with the miserable swine, patrolling up and down interminably.

On 14 July there were even more Kawanisis about than usual. I wondered whether the squadron had increased its strength—they kept it up all day long. "Down South" inquired into the clearing work on the grass plains. From what the scouts had observed it was clear that an airfield was being constructed behind Lunga plantation, while another strip possibly was being laid out at Tetere, farther east. Once the Japs could fly planes from Lunga, it would be extremely difficult for the island to be relieved.

Late that day I received a long report from Snowy Rhoades. Rhoades, with his gloomy logic, reckoned that it was equally dangerous whether we went or stayed. He himself had started out for the weather coast in his cutter, but had nearly run into two Jap luggers, which he avoided only because he was sailing and was able to hear the sound of their engines before they could catch sight of him. Snowy had only just managed to duck back round the point and into his mangrove hideout without being discovered. Then he had moved to a new camp, well away from his last one.

Till then we still had heard nothing definite about the activities of the Japanese on the weather coast. Rhoades reported that the two Jap vessels that he had narrowly avoided meeting had called at each mission station and asked the fathers to translate into the various native dialects certain orders that they wished to issue to the islanders. He was trying to get copies.

Rhoades had had a canoe visitor from New Georgia, who had reported that though the south of Ysabel was free there was strong disaffection in the northern part of that island. He advised that a soldier at Lunga had told the people that the Japanese had been bombed out of Rabaul in New Britain, and so they were busy shifting large numbers of men and material to the Lunga area, for an attack on Vila. I suppose we should have read this as a hopeful sign, indicating that our bombing was at last having a real effect; but all we could see was that we would be completely cut off by an attack on the New Hebrides. Snowy confirmed what we had long suspected, that the Japs hated Tulagi because they had had such high casualties, in men, ships, and aircraft. It was very convenient for us that they bragged such a lot.

From Rhoades also came news that the Japanese had established another coast watch post, guarded by two machine guns, at Cape Hunter, to the south. All my scouts had no doubt about the feverish activity of the Japs at Lunga, who hadn't been idle for a moment. They were trying to conscript a large number of villagers as a labor force, and I was very much afraid that my men would not be able to refuse to go and work there. The airfield runway was progressing fast: at sea between Savo and Lunga a Flying Fortress sank a seaplane tender and shot down a single-engined aircraft that both Rhoades and I thought was a fighter plane, although there was no proof that these had yet landed ashore.

I myself felt extremely reluctant to evacuate after all the trouble we had gone to in organizing our little show, and after the success that it seemed to be having. Finally, after weighing it all again, I concluded that we might just, but only *just,* be safer staying put and continuing to pump out the information. "Oh! Lord, how long?" was the biblical entry in my diary that day.

With the perishing weather, and no proper clothes, by daybreak everyone was usually half dead with saturation and cold. It was muddy underfoot and still raining, so the only thing I could do was turn out all hands and hold PT drill. That soon warmed them up, and restored their flagging spirits—a few slips in the mud were always good for a laugh. It cheered them up to finish with leapfrog, which could be very nearly fatal owing to the slippery ground: once a lad almost slid over the precipice.

When it rained like that, and I could not see anything, I would get very depressed, for the miserable weather always seemed to coincide with comparative silence on the air. I had not heard from Macfarlan for four or five days, and I desperately wanted to know what had happened to him. I would miss his amusing letters if he went, and his strong, definite manner on the radio.

Writing up my diary stopped my talking to myself, but I couldn't do that all day long. What exercise I could get on Vungana, that benighted pinpoint, was negligible: the village was level for about forty paces in one direction and about thirty in the other. As I walked up and down my thoughts used to wander back, sometimes to the good old days, sometimes to the more recent bad old days. But it was little good summoning back the past—it only brought into sharper focus the uncertainty of the future.

Evacuation Fever

As so few headmen had control over their people, we stood a grave risk of being unable to move. The lack of carriers could immobilize us completely. There were no large villages to call on in Macfarlan's area, and it had taken some days to collect the number of men for which Hay had asked. Although there were still no Japs ashore at Talisi, no locals would be available for a week or so, as everyone had gone to Avu Avu to hold a feast over someone's moribund uncle. I could see, therefore, that I had no choice: I would just have to stay put and hope for the best.

By now, aerial activity over the island had become almost continuous, and the airfield at Lunga was nearly completed. The BBC told us that Rabaul had been badly bombed, which would push the enemy onto us at Guadalcanal, as the Japs themselves had said. At sea there were frequent reports of submarines, and an aircraft carrier, as well as the cruisers and transports that called daily at Lunga. At Vungana the afternoon drizzle turned into solid rain, which, accompanied by claps of thunder, continued all night long. Everything got wet, and my flimsy hut reeled and rattled.

At long last, on 16 July, I got word from Macfarlan. He had got the carriers to work, but had had to pay them 25 percent more than usual. That made me very angry, for it would probably cause carrier strikes at some later and more critical moment; but he had had no choice—the situation was pretty grave. All of Mac's own carriers had deserted, and the local headman had the willies. The old men of the villages nearby had held a meeting, after which they had pointed out to Macfarlan and Hay that they had paid taxes for years; now that the government was running away, they said, why should they help carry our food? They also said our money was now no good and only Jap occupation currency or New Guinea money was of any use. Mac tried to reassure them, saying that we were going to bring soldiers and ships. They replied that we were taking a devil of a long time doing it. To that he had no answer.

Mac also believed that the Gold Ridge location had been disclosed to the Japanese. I had been under the impression that Rhoades was in touch with Macfarlan and hoped to join him; but now Mac was asking me what Snowy was doing. S'truth! Had I to get *him* out of the soup too? He added in a postscript that even if Hay and Campbell managed to get out, which would be most difficult, he would probably join up with me. There we were!

The situation could not have looked blacker, but I had to laugh at the messenger's description of Mac and company beating a hasty retreat from Gold Ridge, strafed by Japanese planes. They were all going up the track as fast as they could, with the exception of Ken Hay, who had decided, *au moment critique,* to pay a visit to the rather decrepit one-holer. This had been constructed of old packing cases poised over a deep pit, and the ravages of white ants had rendered it fairly fragile. Hay was apparently taking his ease when the strafing started, and in his valiant effort to rush out the throne had collapsed under his immense weight and left him suspended. Impassioned shouts and blue oaths had raised a messenger, who overtook Macfarlan and breathlessly urged him, "Stop, stop, Mr. Hay is in the shit!" "Never mind Mr. Hay," Mac replied, increasing his speed, "we're all in the shit!" Having told me this merry story, with a long, serious face, the scout who brought Mac's letter asked if he could hand in his papers and go home! He hadn't been with me very long. Oh, dear, I thought, what would happen next? "Me sorry tumas," I said, "me savvy do'm, closeup youme alright." He stayed.

Then a scout came in from Paripao with terrible news. The locals there had uprooted all our new vegetable gardens. That made me really angry: they could easily have waited until the Japs got closer. Part of the crop would have been ready in another week. It was a great loss.

The final touch to a depressing day was a message from Rhoades alleging that Father de Klerk at Tangarare had supplied the Japanese a list of all baptized Catholics in his parish. The Japs had then announced that all fit men would have to muster for conscription. Snowy said they were prepared to dodge it only if help really was at hand.

Next morning, things started out a little more cheerful. First came a message cryptically indicating that, at long last, "things will happen for the best." All that meant, I supposed, was decent air attacks, and mused rather skeptically that seeing was believing. Then I received a long report from Daniel Pule about the activities of one of the Jap lugger parties. They had called at the Ruavatu mission station, where they had questioned Father Engberink for a long time; after destroying some of the school huts, presumably in case we used them for ambush, they had smashed the radio receiver and taken away the only shotgun.

The leader of the party, who appeared to be a naval warrant officer, reportedly had worked for Carpenter's in the Solomons as a second mate before the war, and knew pidgin English very well. His name was given variously as Ishimoto, Yishimoto, or Yashimoto. Whether this was his proper name, or a nickname acquired before the war, I could not then, or afterward, discover.[1] In any case, we could have done without him. It gave me gooseflesh when I read that he also knew a great number of islanders and, worse luck, the geography of Guadalcanal. It was not difficult to deduce what his mission was. No one had heard what he had asked the father.

When they called at Aola, Sergeant Andrew was coming from the gardens. Luckily he had no arms and wore only an old pair of shorts, for Ishimoto immediately recognized him and, though Andrew had not been in the police in his day, put him through a pretty searching questionnaire. Andrew kept his head and spun them some yarn, posing as a local yokel; but he could not prevent them from roaming about and discovering our crop of potatoes, which was all ready for harvesting. The blighters brought sacks from the lugger, and Andrew could hardly contain himself as load after load of our precious rations was dug up and carried away. I hoped that the prisoners had had a good dig first, as this was our last crop and we were all very hungry. When they left, the Japs calmly announced that they would return on Saturday for more; this proved our salvation, as Andrew got every man jack available to dig feverishly the next day, and saved what he could from the rape.

I had come to the end of my tinned food, and my diet became as monotonous as that of the scouts. It had not been helped by an infuriating discovery made when I sent down for what I thought was my last case of meat. In those days that was a fairly substantial ration: a case contained forty-eight twelve-ounce tins, which would last more than two months if used sparingly. The case duly arrived, and Michael opened a tin for me to look at. It was a horrid-looking mess, swilling about in what looked like water. "Me no savvy 'long this kind," he said. "Which way me do 'long 'im?"

I was not too sure. It wasn't meat at all; it was Tasmanian scallops. The Tasmanian scallop is a shellfish, which, under normal circumstances, is quite tasty, and is regarded as a delicacy. I quite enjoyed the first tin. My suspicions, however, were aroused, and I soon found to my horror that the case was not of "assorted meats" at all: every tin contained Tasmanian scallops! I was completely thwarted. They were neither filling nor nourishing; after I had eaten them cold, hot, fried, curried, and even chopped up with rice, they had begun to pall, and by the time the end of the case came I could hardly face them. Assorted meats? Pah! I shall never be able to face another scallop again!

No Way Out

On 18 July there was more news from Daniel Pule. He confirmed that the Japs had told the local people that the lugger would return to Aola the following Saturday, accompanied by a coastal patrol. My scouts hung onto them like clams, but the Japs stopped every villager they saw and asked him where he was going. That could become a great hindrance to our operations.

The last straw was the issuing of the following orders, typed in English and distributed to all the coastal villages:

> JAPANESE OFFICIAL issued in 16th July 1942 to inhabitants of Guadalcanal.
>
> *Notice No. 1.* All of the inhabitants on this island must be ordered by Japanese Government to co-operate for Japan. Any inhabitants against it should be severely punished by Japanese martial law.
>
> *Order No. 1.* Men only of 14 years old or less than fifty years have to work for Japanese troops at some places on this island. After a month's labour they will be given the identity as a civilian on this island. During work for Japanese troops they will be given meals et cetera.
>
> [No signature.]

Who *was* the district officer, anyway? And what awful grammar! I would not have minded a nice drop of "et cetera" to vary my diet, but I expect that it meant an inch of cold steel.

A later report from Daniel gave the lugger's program for the next few days. They were to go southeast, to Kau Kau and Rere, and then round to Marau to meet the phantom weather coast party. They might find the boats if we didn't get to Marau first, and even if we did we would probably be seen going out. Worse, every area would be covered except the southwest coast, a wild, inaccessible, unnavigable place swept by a thunderous surf that made landing from a dinghy a suicidal business and anchoring impossible. There were few carriers available down there, anyhow.

It was patent that Macfarlan and I just could not get off the island.

Even if Mac got started, his lads might desert, except for my scouts who were attached to him, since they had sworn to carry on as long as I did. I decided that the civilian party would have to make the first attempt, with all our resources and influence. If they got away safely, Mac and I could join up; without the others and their paraphernalia, we would probably be freer to move around. If things got even worse, Mac could perhaps still have a go.

It would have to be carefully organized, for if the party were seen pulling out the Japs would no doubt try to look for any other Europeans who might be left behind. They had repeatedly asked all the locals where the district officer was; getting no reply, they had threatened to bomb the smoke from any fires in the bush on a certain day. On that day I had replied by having dozens of smoky fires lit from one end of the island to the other.

While drafting a letter to Macfarlan on my plans, I received a short radio message that he had been told to stay put, and that "it will not be long now." I felt no relief at the time: after thinking everything over so carefully and working out the right answer, it all appeared to add up to the same thing. In a mood of rather rebellious forced humor, I signaled back sarcastically, "Days or weeks?" It all seemed so very important.

Whatever happened, we were committed to getting the miners out. I sent an extra scout down to the weather coast to reinforce the watch at Talisi, and told Jack Sua, the loyal district headman from Vololo, to send every available carrier he had across to the Suta. Then I signaled that I would be off the air next day.

As I had no carriers, nor would have any for a week or so, my position was untenable. The scouts were doing magnificent work and bringing in grand information. It was far more useful than my direct observation; I had to get it sent off. I decided to move even farther into the bush, where, I hoped, I would not be interrupted until the rest were safely away. It made me tired thinking of it, and I slept that night.

16

Watch and Pray

A ND SO, on 19 July, I prepared to set off again. The weather continued miserable: it was so damp that I could get nothing out of the wireless. Finally, I was able to thaw out the wretched thing with the kerosene lamp and see to the morning teleradio schedule. Then I packed up the barest necessities and, with a few faithful retainers, clambered down to Matanga, the next village.

Benighted at Vuchicoro

Although the way was straight downhill, it took us an hour and a half to get there, on the roughest track imaginable. It consisted mostly of the edges of broken rock. My practically nonexistent foot gear was useless; I had many falls, and my feet were badly bruised on the slippery rocks. Suinao had to be passed by hand down some of the passages, and three times we nearly lost the batteries, and their carriers, over the precipice.

At last, after crossing a swiftly flowing river at the bottom of the gorge, we reached the village. Matanga proved to be merely a collection of miserable huts and a leaf-built church. Jack Sua, who had come with us, departed for Vololo to take my letter to Mac and raise carriers for the party at the Suta. There was nothing to eat or drink, and I was far too exhausted to set up the teleradio; so, once Michael had selected me a hut, I curled up in my damp bedroll and subsided into a sort of coma, half awake, half asleep, too tired to pull myself together and do either properly. Suinao curled up beside me, shivering with cold.

In the morning, by the light of a pale sun that came out as if to mock us, we went through the back of beyond. This was the roughest country I had ever seen. It was wilder, I thought, than Kintail in the west of Scotland, and as it put me in mind of Kintail I had the most awful pangs of homesickness. There was no track this time: the river lay at the bottom of a wild gorge, and we had to make our way upstream, waist deep, against a strong current, slipping from one round, smooth stone to another and catching at the banks—craggy rocks, really—to keep ourselves from being washed away.

My very last pair of shoes split soon after we started out, and later the soles just floated off. (I can vividly remember the odd feeling, as I lifted my feet, of the soles being pulled away by the current.) By then my feet were so bruised that I could hardly walk. Beato, the scout in charge of the convoy, fashioned me a pair of "John the Baptist" sandals out of the canvas inner lining of a mailbag, lashed together with loia cane. "Mine t'ink thisfella river no good 'long boot b'long you," he said. "Me savvy goodfella, Beato," I replied, "but you want'm kaikai, or you want'm Japan 'e kaikai'm youme?" I vaguely recalled a Protectorate regulation about injuring mailbags, but one did not bother about such things now.

It took us all day to do a few miles: it was a terrible struggle. Some irreverent impulse made me think of the Israelites carrying the Ark of the Covenant. We all felt the effect of having had so little food over the last few days. Though there was little to carry, every step up the river was an effort, and I reached such a pitch of exhaustion that I did not really care what happened. Surely, I thought, the Japs would never get this far.

Finally, we scrambled out of the river onto a rocky ridge resembling nothing so much as the breastbone of a fowl. It was the edge of an almost perpendicular ridge of solid rock, thrust up in some volcanic age, long before man ever reached that benighted spot. The forest around was sparse and scrubby, and all the trees were covered with hairy lichen. At the top, amidst the craggy peaks, were four filthy huts on an inaccessible pinnacle, reached after a difficult rock-face climb. It was called Vuchicoro.

We had to use ropes to haul up the gear. It was hardly a village. The two or three inhabitants were poor creatures, numbed into silence by the perpetual cold and damp and the awful roar of the river below.[1] They had nothing to offer us, and it soon struck me that, as so few people were living here and the conditions were so primitive, it would be even harder to get food. The huts were in wicked shape, and would have to be repaired.

Well, there we were, on the rock. The teleradio had escaped serious injury; I got the charging engine started, but it was so clogged that it made little difference to the batteries, and I had no luck in contacting anyone. This really was, I thought, rock bottom. From dusk, rain thundered down incessantly and leaked over everything. All I could do was lie on my damp bedroll and think. Would it not be better to leave everything and sally forth for a final scrap with the Japanese? Then I wondered if I could manage it without any boots. "A kingdom for my boots," the old duke had said, somewhere in Shakespeare. Apart from my file of signals, I had thrown away all my reading matter except three pocket volumes of Shakespeare. They were my last remaining literature and my last touch with civilization: of late, I had read all the plays a dozen times. What, I wondered, did the Japs think of Shakespeare? Take our present situation: was it comedy? It felt more like tragedy. Did they know about Birnam Wood?

It was suppertime, so I made up a menu for the meal I would have if I ever got out. I had a lot of trouble with the soup, but, as we were in the Pacific, I finally plumped for Toheroa, New Zealand's national masterpiece, made from little shellfish. Then I munched on a sodden ship's biscuit and rolled over, still wet.

I woke to the thunder of brown flood waters boiling and rushing down the gorge. The river had risen ten feet. My only satisfaction was that it would be humanly impossible to reach Vuchicoro. I was so cold, damp, and hungry that I felt detached—it took time to decide to do anything. After putting it off as long as possible, I reluctantly got down to the good old sport of cleaning the charging engine. The correct spanner had been forgotten—I might have expected that—but finally I got the head off and decarbonized the filthy thing. At last, having pulled a finger muscle and split the finger as well, I got it all put back together again; and then the horror wouldn't start. I only just restrained myself from heaving it in the river. In despair, I eventually got it going with a long-discarded plug. Then there was three hours' hard work soldering, and a complete overhaul of the receiver, before I got the sets working. I was so exasperated that when schedule time came round I found that I had forgotten to put up the aerial. Hell's bells! At length, very tired and worn, I managed to make contact, but even then reception was very bad, owing to the enclosing hills. We blamed the teleradios all the time, but it was a miracle how they went on and on without spares.

Toward nightfall the river went down, and two of the scouts, Chaku[2] and Deke, arrived, looking like drowned rats. They were completely exhausted, but they had the latest details from Kukum and Lunga. One of them had seen one of Macfarlan's lads, who had left the Suta that morning; the messenger must have avoided the floods by hanging on by his eyebrows. Mac was distinctly cheerful: he reckoned there would be a big show within two weeks. I was still in a sort of coma, and so doubted this; nonetheless, I was consumed with curiosity. Doing nothing at Vuchicoro was useless. I felt I ought to go over and see Mac; if his newfound confidence was justified, I might risk returning to Vungana. I doubted, however, whether I could face the trip in my condition.

On 22 July, the teleradio reception continued as bad as ever. I sent Londoviko to Marau to scout down the weather side and see if it was clear, patrolled, or occupied.[3] Chaku was dispatched to Joe Love, the headman at Talisi, to recruit carriers if possible.

Then, just to balance Mac's good humor, everything seemed to go from bad to worse. First, three prisoners arrived from Aola: the miserable warder, Anea, had panicked when the Japs disturbed his vegetable digging and deserted to his home on the south coast with the remaining long-sentence prisoners, all from Malaita. The net result was three more to feed up here, and less food brought to do it. I would have to investigate the matter when I had time.

Next, Chaparuka came in from Snowy Rhoades. All was well in the northwest, but he complained of a lack of food and of the difficulty of walking fast on an empty stomach, which had cramped up on him. No sooner had I taken care of him than Gumu, even more pokerfaced than usual, arrived post haste from Aola, bringing Dovu under open arrest: Dovu was accused of disclosing to the Japanese where *Hing-Li*'s gear was hidden at Balo village. It was rather a confused story: apparently, all the men save the stalwart Andrew had panicked when the enemy arrived at Aola before they could get out. Far more serious was the news that the Japanese now had working for them some Catholic islanders from Visale, who were to comb the bush to recruit labor and look for me. The situation was impossible: if even one local dropped a careless word they would have little difficulty in discovering us, and if we detained such renegades the Japanese would smell a rat. I decided that if they reached our outposts they would simply be "stopped"—that was all. Then Selea reported in sick—what a time of it were we having!

Finally, Londoviko's offsider, immobilized with a swollen hip, sent on a message from Tasimboko. In spite of Vouza's presence, Luvena, the troublesome headman, had looted Ken Hay's last hope, a cache of food hidden behind Berande. Hay was livid. It was all a madhouse, and I was nearly at the end of my tether.

Back to Matanga

That night I went to bed early with a temperature, probably the result of a lack of sleep and food. Fortunately, I had not had a fever so far; if I did it would put paid to everything. I did not think it was malaria, which I had miraculously escaped; there was no quinine left now,[4] so that was just as well.

From Tasimboko had also come the cheering news that an enemy party was ready to have a look at Gold Ridge. That would keep Mac well up the Suta; it didn't sound nice at all. After weighing all the reports and rumors, and studying the geography, I concluded that, with the Japs about everywhere, we could be surprised as easily from the weather coast as from the north, and probably with less warning. Vuchicoro, though inaccessible from the northeast, was far too close to Talisi; I had been there only five days, but that was enough. Much to the relief of the scouts, I decided to return to Vungana, where observation and communication were best and there was some security. Beato, shaking his head sadly about my bruised feet, told me that I was the first white man ever to reach Vuchicoro. I felt I would probably be the last.

As soon as the morning Kawanisi had passed over on his usual search, we set off for Matanga. (I wondered, as it was 23 July, whether they would hold the Bedford Regatta that year; I would not have minded walking along the river there.) The downstream journey was no easier than the upstream one had been: we did not reach the village till 1330. My feet were in terrible shape, I was staggering from my temperature, and I had a blinding headache from lack of food. The scouts and the few carriers were not much better off, and it took them several trips to get everything down to Matanga. I cursed and swore and got furious with the carriers for stumbling, but managed to check myself before I lost control. Everyone was pretty jumpy, but they still thought I was not. To have lost control then would have been the end of everything.

At Matanga I wearily waved Gumu and Chaparuka off to catch the Catholic recruiting agents and any Japs with them. A great deal depended on those two lads, but I felt I could trust them. I reflected on how lucky I was to have men like these: they could have faded into the bush, and returned home safe and sound, but instead they had gone through almost intolerable hardship with me.

Suinao shook himself dry and went off to lay down the law to the few decrepit dogs of the village. I could only sit gloomily in a towel: my only clothes were dripping wet, and there was no sun to dry them. There was absolutely nothing to eat, and I still had a splitting headache. I had no shoes, the teleradio was not assembled, and with the bed broken there was only a sodden bedroll to lie on. It was a miserable night—I felt almost past caring.

The next morning I looked out and shuddered. It was no good going on to Vungana: the fine drizzle might be good for cover, but it would make the track and rocks practically impossible to traverse. One scout nearly fell out of a tree, and we had to suspend operations until the patrolling Kawanisi had departed. I also had to send back the three prisoners to bring the last gear from Vuchicoro: I had rewarded their loyalty, and they were now willing "volunteers," even if they could not pronounce the name. The leader, full of character, was a rogue named Bili Isihanua.

I settled down to coding and sending out all the information that had been brought in. When the volunteer carrier party returned, I found that they had broken up all the loads in order to carry them in local baskets. As a result, everything was sopping wet, but I did not have the heart to be angry when I saw whom they had brought back with them.

It was the wretched, miserable, cringing Anea, the warder who had deserted. He had come straight up from the weather coast, which rather shook me, and had turned up the night before, with one of the prisoners, at Vuchicoro. Shaking like a leaf, with tears running down his face, Anea stood there, trying to explain what had made him lose his nerve at Aola. To add to the agony, he had allowed two of the Malaita prisoners to escape. Both were skilled murderers; I hoped they would not start headhunting.

Before he became utterly incoherent Anea was down on his knees, quivering with fear, telling me that the Aola headman was conducting the Japs around and that I was in great danger. It was kind of him to let me know. All the scouts seemed strangely moved by that sorry spectacle. I was almost unnerved myself. What was the use of all this, which reduced a man to a crawling thing?

A scout sent to Vungana mercifully returned with a few potatoes, and we had our first meal in three days. He further raised our flagging spirits with a description of two Flying Fortresses over Lunga, cruising about without opposition and dropping nine loads of bombs. There was reliable news from Londoviko that an enemy party would arrive that day at Avu Avu on the south coast, where old Father Boudard, the Catholic missionary, still hung on. The Japanese had sent ahead an order to have meat killed for them. Father Boudard had delayed the scouts' departure so the Japanese would not suspect anything; I wrote him a letter of encouragement in French, the only language he knew. Another report informed us that the Japanese outpost at Vioru, at Cape Hunter, had landed supplies to enable a bush patrol to start from there the next day. It looked as if Rhoades would have to stay where he was and we would all have to keep a sharp lookout.

I had to admit that during the last few days our bombing had become much more effective. When the seaplane tender had been sunk on 14 July, the enemy had sustained four hundred casualties. Few men were observed to come ashore, and not one boat was sent out from Lunga to pick up survivors. This callousness was, no doubt, typically Japanese, but nevertheless it rather amazed me.

Over the next few days Allied bombing continued to increase in intensity, and the number of reports coming in from the coast increased correspondingly. Not only were we calling targets, but we had begun to report damage done fairly accurately. Did it presage a new stage? Where was

Macfarlan's "big show"? It would need to be big, judging from the way the Japs were settling in.

The increased bombing had not disturbed the daily routine of the Kawanisis, though they sometimes flew in odd directions. On 26 July, just after 0900, I was surprised by one while bathing in a pool above the village. It shot over the Vungana summit at only a few hundred feet, and came straight on overhead. I had just about beaten the record to the nearest hut when the blighter banked steeply and came over again. He probably was paying attention to Gold Ridge, but a white figure on black rocks was almost as inconspicuous as a banana skin in a coal scuttle!

My turn nearly came again the next day. A mob of villagers from near Berande suddenly arrived: they had been press-ganged into acting as guides for a patrol of ten enemy troops, who had followed the Berande River to where it forked with the Givunaga. (One branch of the latter led up a gorge very close to Matanga, although well below.) Some of my scouts, who had joined them as guides, had conveniently disappeared at nightfall and rushed hot foot to report, leaving an angry lot of Japs, minus a rifle and some ammunition, to find their way back to the coast as best they could. I was so busy on the air,[5] and my feet were in such poor shape, that for the moment there was no question of moving up to Vungana. In any case, the Jap luggers were making life very difficult for the coastal patrols: we never knew where they would call next, or land another party to strike inland. Was anywhere safe? The Japanese, a hundred of them, were in force at Aola, and this had prevented Andrew and his men from sending us anything. It would not be much good "stopping" a few of them now.

The food problem was getting desperate. The potato stock at Vungana seemed to have run out very suddenly. There were very few local villages, and none had any surplus for hungry souls like us; in fact, the inhabitants appeared to be half starved themselves most of the time. After a whole day, a bargaining party would return with forty pounds or so of taro or sweet potatoes. As two and a half pounds per man was needed for a decent meal, it did not go very far. (I noted in my diary for better days that the bush villages needed an agricultural officer.) The scouts who did the long patrols to the coast most needed feeding properly, especially since they were frequently chased by the Japanese. Bush walking was killing work, and they were all becoming skin and bone.

On 27 July, Jack Sua and one of my scouts, Olorere, turned up. They had come through Vuchicoro; it was comforting to know that that road was still open. The men reported that all of Hay's gear had at last been carried down to Talisi. This was splendid news. Legu Legu, a former policeman and a recent recruit of mine, returned from Macfarlan; he was still holding out on the Suta, and Campbell and the other miners were up in the mountains close by.

My Fourth Anniversary

My diary entry for 28 July noted that I had left England four years before —a hopeful cadet! What fun the voyage out had been, and what a great time we had had in Sydney. It was spoiled only by my first view, from the deck of our large liner, of the little *Malaita*. A friend pointed down, away down, to a tiny white vessel with a black funnel in a neighboring dock: "There's the *Malaita,* that's what you'll be going in to the Solomons." I hardly believed him. Goodness me, she did look small, almost too small to go all that way by herself! Little did I realize that, a few years later, after being tossed about in tiny cutters and schooners, I would think the *Malaita* quite a large ship indeed.

Four years ago! I wouldn't see her again if I wasn't jolly careful. And careful I had to be: the game was getting tricky. The sky was full of planes of all kinds—Kawanisis; Zeros; other single-engined planes, probably Allied; Flying Fortresses—and the Japanese Navy moved around and about like a lot of busy beetles. Their patrols were everywhere.

I reorganized the whole of my inner guard network. A new patrol, under the trustworthy Tabasui, would cover the approach to the Berande River, in case we were surprised from that direction. I sent Jack Sua to find an emergency bolt hole in case we got jumped at Vungana. Then I reduced all guards to a minimum, which enabled me to send the spare chaps off in all directions to get food. The work of sending out information went on full blast.

Bingiti turned up that morning, having been unable to get back to Nggela. The sea had been so rough that it had smashed his canoe. (As he put it so expressively, "Me no catch'm Nggela, canoe 'e smash finish 'long big sea.") One of his lads had got across, however, with an interesting story about the Jap seaplane base at Halavo.[6] He also brought many heartrending letters from the Nggela headmen, asking for help. Alas, I could give them none. Even so, no Nggelese were helping the enemy, except the old rascal Kuini, who had gone with the Japs to Rabaul together with George Bogese. I wished the two of them a long holiday.

According to a letter from Daniel Pule, the Japs had declared their intention of looking for the "Government road" at Aola. They had found an old map of bush tracks at Berande, and Botu, a cross-eyed traitor from Berande village, was going to guide them. There was no future in that. On the other hand, Luvena and his cohorts from Tasimboko had been rebuked by the Japs for removing the galvanized water tanks when they looted Hay's homestead at Berande. A white-uniformed Jap official had lectured an assembly of locals about work at Kukum, and when they had bragged of their looting they had been smartly told to replace the stolen goods. Several scouts were standing in the front row in ordinary clothes, and, like everyone else, they promised ready obedience when the Jap "commissioner" exhorted all present to capture the district officer's police constables and deliver them to the Japanese! The Jap affirmed that he knew where the district officer was, but that they had decided to leave the DO to starve in the bush. Ha, ha!

Even the weather was against us. It continued very rainy away from the coast, and most of the rivers were flooded enough to make it very difficult for scouts and ration parties to get up and down the tracks. But I could not complain, for during the last two days of the month the Japs were raided continuously.

At 1700 on 31 July, Beato arrived from Vungana, sopping wet. "My word," he said, "plenty bombing tumas this time." He was right: for about four hours, starting at 1030, several flights or squadrons of planes had carried out heavy attacks on Tulagi and Kukum.[7] Beato reported that the fires were still burning at Kukum and flames were visible on the foreshore. There was a stiff night raid, too, at 2200. I wondered where the planes were based; they must have come a long way. It was exciting to hear the BBC news talking the following afternoon about "direct hits on a supply vessel and on a supply dump, at Kukum, Guadalcanal." The announcer was not at all happy with the pronunciation, and I wondered how many people in England even knew where it was.

On 1 August Corporal Koimate came in. He reported that when he had come through Gold Ridge, taking some information up to Macfarlan, he had found that all the houses there had been well and truly looted. Anything remaining there, even empty rice bags, had been ripped open, and things like typewriters taken out and smashed. Tasimboko, I thought; I couldn't have been far wrong.

Then Londoviko arrived with a letter from Macfarlan. Mac's opening words, "We are now living in hope," told me that the situation was desperate: if nothing happened before the weekend, he intended to flit. He suggested I do likewise. Mac was sure that the Japs knew his whereabouts, from locals who had deserted, but reckoned that they would have to go hard to catch him. He still thought that everything pointed to a big stunt, but he wanted to be prepared in case of failure. With Jap patrols so near, and the islanders gradually deserting, he believed that without immediate action our position was untenable. Poor old Mac, I thought—he dare not admit it, but he's beat.

Well, the end of the week had come, and I certainly could not see myself moving out. I suddenly felt very weak. My scouts and I were all living on our nerves, and we couldn't carry on much longer, whatever we decided to do. I still had not been able to get to Vungana: the river was in full flood again, and we hadn't yet got anything to eat to strengthen us for the trip. The three-day fast had pulled me down badly.

On Monday, 3 August, I pulled myself together and tried to deal with young Dovu, who was still under close arrest for alleged dereliction of duty at Aola. I spent most of the morning cross-examining him and trying to find out the truth. There was no doubt that he had been a damn fool, but whether intentionally or not was not at all clear. Had I dismissed him, with a chip on his shoulder, he would no doubt have gone straight to the Japanese.

In the end I found the right solution. (At least it seemed so later.) When some of the scouts came in, I paraded them all. In front of them stood Dovu, the young pagan, with a defiant air and his round eyes popping. What was the most serious oath, I asked him, in his clan? I then told him, in accordance with their custom, to swear it solemnly on the village drum. It was on the head of his grandmother that Dovu swore that he would never fail to do his duty. He seemed much impressed and relieved: I believe he really thought I'd have him shot. Dovu had plenty of courage, but at that time he had not enough sense. I packed him off to work, and when he departed I thought I detected, curling round his mouth, a ghost of a little smile. He never let me down again.

That was only one problem. Now I turned to another. Owing to the lack of rifles, I had a considerable number of unarmed guards, who had formed the inner ring of sentries. With the possibility of the Japs' jumping us suddenly from any of several directions, I reversed the position, moving the armed guards to the inner circle and reassigning the unarmed ones to the perimeter tracks, where they could withdraw if surprised without raising the enemy's suspicions. I felt much happier, and spent most of the afternoon watching two scouts trying to swim the flooded river to get to Vungana, and two from there trying to reach me with news from the coast. Both pairs made the grade after a couple of hours. One of the reports, another letter from Daniel Pule, included a splendid map showing all the Jap installations in the Kukum-Lunga area. Daniel also reported that all the Tasimboko conscripts had run back to their villages! Several more enemy ships had been sunk, or were still on fire, while ashore three trucks had been done in, and ninety Japs killed. It took me some hours to get all this information turned into a suitable message.

Another letter from Macfarlan indicated he was in a terrific dither again. I had written to tell him that I was stuck, and suggested that he also hang on for another few days. He had agreed to do this, but, although he had spoken in no uncertain terms, all his efforts to get the others to move had apparently failed. He also complained that his food supplies, like mine, were practically at an end, and that he could move only if I sent him carriers. What a hope! There we were—no joy anywhere.

In no time at all there was no food in Matanga for anyone, not even for the villagers who had shared with us their almost nonexistent supplies. On 4 August a deputation waited on me, to say they could not work without food. I told them that I was quite prepared to buy food for everybody, if only we could get it: the locals would sell none, or, what was probably nearer the truth, had none. Some of them had thought, wrongly, that we wanted the stuff for nothing, and had refused to part with it.

With the floods we were cut off in three directions; the fourth was toward the enemy, and there was no food that way. I sent a party of the least hungry, who could ill be spared, across country to the last remaining village in the vicinity where food might be obtained, and surrendered the last twenty-five pounds of rice from my personal stores to make a feed for my famished scouts. It was the end of my very last reserves. The scrounging party returned in the evening with seventy-five pounds of stringy roots, fifteen pounds of taro, and two pumpkins. There were at least twenty-five to feed, and the food all disappeared in one go.

Campbell, who was also desperate for food, sent over twenty ounces of gold, hoping to exchange it for silver shillings with which to barter. I had to take his word as to its value, but F. M. had always been a man of his word, and I "allowed" him 150 pounds on it. He had the goodness to say, "We don't want you to worry about us in the least, we will make our own getaway, somehow, if the need arises. All this, of course, if the Japs are not at Marau before us. Rumours are so fast and so frequent that one doesn't know what to believe."

He was quite right there. When Eroni nearly had run into the Japs at Marau, they had been nosing around during the several days they spent there. It was with difficulty that Londoviko, who was trailing them, had managed to keep them from prying into the mangroves and discovering the precious schooners, our only means of escape. Wily old Laena, bosun of the cutter *Lofung,* had taken the great trouble to cut holes in the mangroves for each vessel. The awnings and the masts had been covered with creeper, so they would have been difficult to discover, even from the air. Even if they were safe, Campbell could not possibly have got to Marau.

Campbell's last paragraph corroborated the looting at Gold Ridge:

I guess Mac has told you of all the River looting. Very complete. When we got settled up here I sent back to Tin o' Meat camp for things—nothing left—beds, mattresses, food, small tools, all gone. My boys even saw the Reverend Ini take some things from another camp. He, by the way, was the originator of the Christian Bush Brotherhood and is now said to be the chief propagandist for the Japs, or in their employ.

In spite of some nasty thunderstorms, the rain slackened off and the river fell to only a few inches above its normal level. I scraped up a party of spare men and sent them to Macfarlan, so he could join up with me. This left me without a single spare body, but the risk had to be taken. I returned to my radio.

As the weather cleared up, an almost continuous rumble began to be heard from Lunga. A new note, heavy ack-ack, had crept in: clearly, the Japs were getting it hot and strong. In addition, many enemy planes were being shot down. There were many inquiries from "Down South" on matters of detail, to most of which, I am glad to say, we were able to supply an answer. A destroyer, another large ship, and several smaller vessels had been reported sunk, and there were several fires on the grass plains. There was no letup with the teleradio.

I could not help feeling that something was about to break. Each day brought the thought, "Would it be today?" There was no elation in it.

On 5 August, Koimate's patrol confirmed that the runway at Lunga was ready to land planes; it was made of red clay and gravel. I rushed out an urgent message: surely the Japs would not be allowed to use it? The following day our expectations still had not been realized, and my incipient mood of pale pink optimism began to fade. Was nothing going to happen after all? If the Japs used their airfield, they could bomb the New Hebrides, and we should be too far away to be of any further use. I felt fed up at the situation, and hungry and depressed—in fact, quite "gray."

Michael gently put a large plate of steaming mashed sweet potatoes in front of me. I could not eat them. "Me look'm you sick tumas," he said, "more better you eat'm kaikai." So near was I to breaking down altogether that I could hardly face him. "Which way me eat'm kaikai, Michael?" I replied. "Belly b'long me buggerup."

All I could taste was the bitterness of defeat. We were cut off. I would never see home again. I couldn't stand it. Turning face down on my bedroll, I lay there, listening to the water roaring down the river, till my ears hurt.

17

The Marines Have Landed

O, do but think
You stand upon the rivage and behold
A city on the inconstant billows dancing;
For so appears this fleet majestical.

—*Shakespeare, King Henry V, act 3, prologue*

HAVING GONE to bed with no dinner on 6 August, I slept pretty solidly, and it was not the dawn that awakened me. Starting about 0610, very heavy detonations, at very short intervals, were heard from Lunga and Tulagi. There was no doubt what they meant. I was up in a flash, tired no longer. I could hardly comprehend that help had finally come, and yet, instinctively, I knew that it had.

"Calloo, callay, oh, what a day!!!" Help Arrives at Last

A panting scout from Vungana rushed in to report that the whole Japanese fleet was at anchor between Lunga and Tulagi. I couldn't believe it—for a moment my heart stood still. Luckily I had just turned on the radio, and after swinging the dial madly for a few seconds I picked up the wavelength of the invaders. From the intercommunication of ships and planes it was clear that not only Lunga and Kukum, but also Tulagi and Gavutu, were being attacked by Allied landing forces. They sounded as if they were mainly American. It was dies irae for the Japs at last.

We heard "Orange Base," "Red Base," "Black Base," and "Purple Base" calling their aircraft; it did not take long to deduce that there were three carriers supporting the landings. Planes were assigned targets, and look-outs came in with reports of their pet objectives at Lunga going off with a bang and a cloud of smoke. The fuel dump, the ammo dump, and the power station on the river, which we had been at pains to describe, went up beautifully.

More than fifty ships, including two Australian cruisers, were counted in the channel. Twenty of them plastered the shore that morning, from Kukum to Tasimboko; we all hoped that they had given the Tasimboko boys a good pasting. The radio reported that several guns had been knocked out and the Japanese were running madly in all directions. At 1205 I picked up a message that U.S. Marines had landed on Gavutu. I had heard of the Marines, but had never met them at close quarters. "Wizard!!!" I wrote in my diary. "Calloo, callay, oh, what a day!!!"

Our planes passed overhead all day long. It was a nice change. We could not resist waving madly and giving the chaps in the air a cheer. At 1245 a two-engined job, probably a Hudson, went past fairly low, heading due south with a damaged tail. We heard over the air, "I see a truck, I see two trucks, I see a hell of a lot of trucks. Swoop in low and you'll get a good haul."

In the middle of all this jubilation and excitement came a message that sounded a more serious note, at least as far as I was concerned. It was from Macfarlan's boss, Hugh Mackenzie, warning that we might be in danger from Japanese soldiers retreating into the bush. The lads' morale was so high, however, that it raised a laugh: that day we would have walked through a whole division. The "powers that be" would also try to let us know when to come down. I wished they would send me some shoes instead.

At 1600 Gavutu was reported secured, but the Japs still held out on Tanambogo. Some dive bombers were told off to attack them. At 1645 Tulagi was declared under control, except for the hospital (southeastern) end of the island. One pilot asked permission to down a Japanese flag on Makambo; "Permission granted" came the reply, and then, shortly afterward, "Assignment achieved."

From Vungana came a continuous glowing account of din and destruction. Man and boy, they were all watching in wonder. I couldn't stand it—

the wireless's reception was fading badly, I had to see what was going on, and Vungana had the best view. Earlier I had sent there for a few carriers, as there were hardly sufficient people at Matanga who were strong enough for the task. Macfarlan had signaled that floods had held him up, and in any case there was not much point in his making the journey across to Matanga now that the situation had so changed.

Moving off at 1915, I walked the river with bare feet, of necessity, then painfully traversed the rest of the rocky track to Vungana. Had it not been for all the excitement, I doubt I would have completed the journey; at last, however, I made it, and so did the carriers, without dropping a battery. It was a clear, starry night; Lunga was quiet, though Tulagi flared up from time to time. It would have to keep till morning. And so to bed.

I awakened to behold an amazing panorama, spread out as far as the eye could see. In clear weather, on a calm sea, there were ships everywhere —from Savo to Rua Sura, from Lunga to Tulagi. I could make out about fifteen transports and cargo vessels, as well as eighteen cruisers and destroyers, lying off Makile. The latter were the escorts, laid like flags round a football field. The destroyers cruised up and down, running all about and across the channel. One of them put on a lovely burst of speed, which left my lads pop-eyed. "Allasame motorcar," they said.

Unloading was by fast motor launches of some sort or other. One could see more of the wake caused by their speed than of the boats themselves; they certainly were not wasting any time. They operated in groups: through the binoculars I counted more than twenty-five of them, all going for the shore together. Another large group of ships stood over toward Tulagi, which was shrouded in smoke and still reverberated with heavy explosions.

Assault by Air and Sea

About noon, in spite of the smoke and mist and the gathering low clouds, we witnessed a heavy air raid on the fleet. Over the WT came "Orange Base standing by for air attack." I heard the drone of planes, and then all hell broke loose. It appeared to be twenty or thirty two-engined bombers. A tremendous barrage of ack-ack was put up as every ship went into action. Goodness knows how many guns opened up—it was a mechanical concerto, of pops and bangs, cracks and thuds, every conceivable noise from "boom" to "ping." Flashes, flare-ups, founts of water as bombs dropped, orange smoke, black smoke, a line of gray mushrooms where shells were bursting just below cloud level, planes roaring in and out. What a game! It went on for over half an hour; all the while my lads were jumping up and down, cheering on the fleet and shrieking imprecations at the enemy. There were hurrahs as our fighters swept over, and bigger cheers when a plane smacked down onto the water near Rua Sura; we hoped it was Japanese. The fighters could hardly be heard above the din or be seen much as they dodged about amongst the clouds. I wondered if the Japs were enjoying it; they had dived right into the middle and flown low across the water, presumably to evade the antiaircraft fire. We couldn't see a thing for an hour or two afterward. When the smoke had cleared, it looked as though three ships had been hit, but only one, which was on fire, appeared to be in a bad way.[1] Later, Jack Read, in northern Bougainville, reported that of the twenty-seven Bettys that had passed him that morning only nine had come home.[2]

Three scouts came in. They had left Lunga on the night of 6 August after managing to get a fairly senior Japanese officer to confirm that the enemy definitely expected their own land planes there in a matter of a few days. The scouts soon learned, to our merriment, that their report was rather late! It was not until they arrived, clamoring for food, that we realized that we had eaten nothing all day for excitement. We attacked our sweet potatoes with zest, and so ended another splendid day.

Sometime after 0100 on 9 August we were awakened by the rumble of gunfire and heavy explosions; it sounded as if a naval battle was raging off Savo Island. The rest of the morning, however, was fairly peaceful. Off Tenaru, fourteen combatants and a like number of auxiliaries were identified; they all dispersed about 1000, leaving some fifty small landing craft scattered in all directions. The burning vessel exploded, and by lunchtime had sunk. Smoke still floated over Tulagi; there must have been some stiff fighting there. At 1500 the convoy departed, with what was unmistakably an RAN County-class cruiser in the rear guard; it must, I thought, have been either the *Canberra* or the *Australia*.[3] The fleet looked a bit smaller, but I surmised that some of the escorts had left under cover of darkness. I sat down and started to speculate as to what would happen next; before long, however, I was back to wishing that I had something civilized to eat.

I woke to a clear and peaceful morning with nothing in view. After half an hour's search I could not discern any vessels at either Kukum or Tulagi, nor was there any activity in the air. Although Macfarlan was not coming over—he said the Sutakama was in flood—I sent him a message insisting that he send back the prison gang of carriers: they would be empty-handed, and could swim the flooded river. Then I sent word to Father Engberink and Clarry Hart, to tell them what had happened and to keep out of the way, and passed the word to Andrew and Daniel to take offensive action against any stray Japanese and reconnoiter the small enemy party at Taivu Point, as we had lots of captured ammo and might be able to knock them off. They could enlist all volunteers who could "obtain" a rifle and fifty rounds—by stealth, if possible.

Vakalea, the district headman from Belaga, arrived, very excited at the big show. He had come, he said, to assure me of the loyalty of his people. It would, I thought ruefully, have been much more valuable a week ago, but the oranges he brought were very welcome indeed, as were 120 pounds of sweet potatoes that he had convoyed up from our gardens at Aola. A lot of growling arose over the issue of the potatoes, as everyone was hungry. I finally shared out the ration myself, fair do's all round and the same for me; I had to put a guard on the remainder.

It continued peaceful and quiet all day. Having got the batteries, at long last, fully charged, I sat in the sun listening to soft music. (I went without a shirt, something I had not been able to do for a long time; the browner I got, the less likely I would be to get scorched if I had to cross the grass plains to get to Lunga.) It was absolutely clear, with not a breath of wind, and I took in all the different smells of primeval forest and clear mountain air as I looked down on what last Friday had been a raging inferno. For a moment, at least, one could forget that war had ever touched these beautiful islands. Fighting laziness, I packed up as much gear as possible and sent it down to Paripao.

Vakalea was very proud that, although Japanese agents had spent a long time trying to coax his people to work at Lunga, none of them had gone. Vouza had run into the Japs three times at Koli Point, but he too had managed to keep his people from going to work for the enemy. I felt the other headmen could have done the same; many of them, I suppose, had been too frightened to do so. (In actual fact, the Guadalcanal people did not contribute in large measure to the construction of the Japanese airfield. En route to Lunga, the first contingent—they had been bribed with a large feed of rice—had been warned by one of my scouts that if they worked for the Japs they would be bombed. As luck would have it, two Flying Fortresses bombed the runway that very afternoon, and most of the islanders were home by nightfall! After that, few of them risked their necks, and the Japanese worked alone.)

Ready to Go

The most pressing questions were what to do next, and when. It was obvious that a new phase had begun, but I had not received further instructions, and was fretting that we could not yet move down to the beach because of Mackenzie's warning. Clearly, if enemy parties could be avoided we ought to go down to Lunga and assist the forces there with all the information at our disposal and the intelligence net we had spread all over the island. The BBC was quite sure that there was a naval and air battle raging from Timor to Ontong Java to the southeast of Guadalcanal, but everything appeared to be very quiet. One thing was certain: to cross the grass plains with the Japanese scattered about, I should have to travel light. So, when the carrier gang returned from Macfarlan, undrowned, I packed up more of my scanty gear and sent it down to Paripao. After all its adventures it was a miracle that the teleradio was still working, and I was determined to keep it going right to the end. The last bottle of "real" distilled water for the batteries had been smashed on the way to Vuchicoro; to replace it, I caught some rainwater in a clean piece of stretched-out canvas and topped up my failing batteries with that.

Messages began to come in from all the headmen and from the scouts along the coast. Many of the smaller Jap parties had been very lucky in avoiding death and destruction from the air during the landings. Daniel reported that at Taivu Point bombs had been dropped right on the given target, but that the lugger had slipped away on 5 August and the remaining Japs had moved to a new camp across the creek, near Bokoagau. (He sent an interesting account of their household habits: it would be useful if we had to attack them.) Our bombers had missed the outpost at Sapuru, near Cape Esperance, and instead had unloaded on the edge of the mission station at Visale Island and machine-gunned the bishop's house. Father McMahon must have had some choice words for the Americans.

The morning of 12 August was glorious, not a cloud in the sky nor an enemy plane to be seen. As I noted in my diary, this was, appropriately, "the glorious Twelfth," the day the grouse season opened in Scotland. Although the Japs didn't have feathers, there was no harm in telling the headmen that an open season had been declared on them! Just after noon I sat outside in a deck chair quartering the skies with the binoculars, as three of our planes did a recce of the straits. Listening to their conversations, I longed to speak with them; I tried flashing Morse code with a mirror, but it was too far away. We hoped they would come a bit closer, as I had hoisted my Union Jack conspicuously to the top of the highest tree. I wondered what had happened to the Kawanisis.

There was very little traffic on the teleradio. Rhoades reported an enemy party dangerously close to him, on the Hylavo River; they could have been from Vioru, or runaways from Kukum. The only section of scouts that had not reported in twenty-four hours belonged to Corporal Koimate, who was holding the fort between Gold Ridge and Lunga. I thought that he had probably gone into Lunga to contact the landing forces, or, what was most unlikely, that he had been caught by retiring Japanese. We still had no instructions except to keep a strict watch for enemy counterattacks, which was exactly what we were doing.

A huge party of locals arrived; they appeared prepared to carry anything anywhere. It was infuriating that they had turned up when there was no longer any real need for them, but I took the opportunity to send the spare charging engine, the field safe, and some useless supplies to Paripao. I was dying with impatience, and as there were still no instructions I decided to test out the route to Lunga by sending a scout to the officer commanding there. For good measure I provided a full written report on the Japs at Bokoagau, with a map, and complete details of other enemy parties. I also offered to deal with the Bokoagau mob if necessary. Daniel Pule had advised that there were now two hundred Japanese at Marau Sound but that the lugger that had brought them there from Taivu Point had since been bombed and sunk. It struck me how lucky we were that we had not chosen to evacuate via Marau.

Next day, more locals turned up offering to act as carriers. Just to teach them a lesson, Beato paraded all forty of them and gave them an hour's tough physical training. They looked really disappointed—the local headman, Nelea, and his villagers were paralytic with laughter—but when they had finished we hired them too, and sent them off down the hill at the double to bring up more rations. Potatoes suddenly seemed to have become plentiful.

That afternoon I got an amusing letter from Andresen. He had been up to see Macfarlan, Hay, and Campbell, whom he called the "Boys of Bombadeha," after their hideout on the Sutakiki. "Some Boys," he said, "with their various coloured whiskers one could easily imagine he had walked into a Mormon Camp"; I had forgotten that they had all grown beards! Andy had heard the "bomb to bomb running commentary" on 7 and 8 August: "Say, Brother, wasn't it sweet music. The Yanks seemed to conduct it more like a Ball Game than a battle." It took a lot to perturb him, and I was not at all surprised to hear that, while Mac and I were trying to make up our minds whether to go up or down like the good old Duke of York, Andy was improving the shining hour by "trying to rake some elusive out of the Sutakiki." He had found that "she's a poor show," however, his workers having won only eight pennyweights in two weeks. Perhaps for that reason, and as he had heard me ask Mac to send back the carrier gang, he had taken the liberty (for which he apologized) of asking permission from the constable in charge for the prisoners to haul some of his stuff to Nuhu on their way back.

Off at Last

Finally, I got "the word." At 1700 on 12 August Macfarlan signaled that one of Koimate's scouts had arrived from Lunga with a message giving the route for going down. It was from Charles Widdy, who had been Lever's manager at Gavutu. Mac was sending the man straight over. Well done, Koimate; I was very pleased.

I so longed to be away that had the scout flown with winged heels I would have cursed him for being late! To try my patience, a confident note came in from Daniel Pule: he was sure that, with my assistance, he could handle the Japs at Bokoagau. Vouza had done well too: he had invited three Japs into a house at Koli Point, promising refreshments; as soon as the door was closed, they were subdued, neatly trussed, and taken down to Lunga. In addition, Daniel had heard from Koimate that Horton and Waddell, or some other district officers, were with the invading forces.

At last, late on 13 August, the long-expected messenger came, with a printed yellow envelope headed "U.S. MARINE CORPS FIELD MESSAGE." and "Native runner" written in the space for the messenger's name. I feverishly opened it and read the terse note inside. It was from Widdy, all right, now styled "Pilot Officer, R.A.A.F.": "American Marines have landed successfully in force. Come in via Volanavua and along beach to Ilu during daylight—repeat—daylight. Ask outpost to direct you to me at 1st Reg. C. P. at Lunga. Congratulations and regards. C. V. Widdy." The scout told me that Viv Hodgess, the owner of Paruru plantation at Marau Sound, was also with the Marines, and that most of the remaining enemy forces had moved off westward toward Matanikau. I was really excited to have the chance to be on the move at last.

Although I had received no specific instructions, I decided to come down in the morning, for I knew I could be far more use with the Marines than on a mountaintop. For the last time, I hoped, I packed up the wireless set, which, as a parting shot, suddenly revived. Two of the switches had gone, the ball bearings having rusted; after considerable experiment, I used a lemon to clean the bearings, and the set worked all right. I almost hugged that teleradio: it had been my constant companion for over five months. In spite of its travels it had really worked jolly well, and I would miss the friendliness of the morning "sessions."

Leaving my last stronghold aroused mixed feelings, and before I went I walked round Vungana, giving one last look at each old familiar. Some of the children received small trifles, such as colored handkerchiefs, and I formally presented Nelea's aged father with an ancient pair of corduroy shorts, now bright yellow. He was delighted, and donned them immediately; although the shorts went about twice round his waist, they looked very good against his black shirt, which had formerly been his only garment.

My plan was to head straight across country by the shortest route, as fast as I could go. (The enemy parties seemed to stick to the tracks.) We traveled very light: our surplus gear and the teleradio went down to Paripao for safekeeping. I had to leave a pretty dead beat pair in charge there: Anea, the warder, now over his jitters, and Chaku, the suspected killer in the Wilmot case.[4] They had orders to defend Paripao to the last man, if need be.

At 0735 on 14 August, we began our trek down from the hills. In order to maintain all posts I could spare myself only five rifles. Two scouts led the way, well ahead of the bare-bottomed carriers. There were but ten of them, carrying only bedding, cooking apparatus, and the inevitable basket or two of sweet potatoes; Michael, the cook, and Peter, my orderly, saw that they didn't drop or ruin the loads. Young Peter was very proud of himself as he carried my .22 rifle; it was more for morale than anything else. Two more scouts brought up the rear. The most senior scout, Chaparuka, stayed with me; we kept well up to the front. I had a compass, and a tiny .32 pistol, with eight rounds.

We followed as direct a route as the hills and gorges would allow, trying to keep on earthy ground rather than rock in order to save my feet, for which I had little or no covering other than several pairs of miner's woollen socks.[5] Once we had dropped down from the ridges, which were pretty steep and showed signs of ancient fortified villages, we followed the Givunaga River a few miles to Tanekea, then headed northwestward onto the undulating savannah just behind the grass plains. (According to my diary, we ate sandwiches before we left the riverbed, but as I had no bread and no butter I can't imagine what kind they were!) We heard planes, and scattered several times, but nothing was seen as we were immediately deluged by torrents of rain; it was just our luck that it came while we were scrambling, two paces forward and one back, up the muddiest and steepest of hills. In the middle of the afternoon we reached a deserted village, Luvenibuli, with a few weedy coconut palms and some orange trees. I had not seen oranges or coconuts for over two months, and we gorged ourselves on them.

By the greatest of good luck I ran into Vouza, on his way back from taking in an American pilot who had crashed. He told me that he had met a Marine patrol to the east of Volonavua that morning. As far as he knew the way in was clear, but he warned about a large number of dud shells behind Gaimale. Vouza had lots of information, and I told him to pass the word to his people that I would be at Lunga, and to send all reports to me there.

I decided to spend the night at Teatupa: we were all very tired—we had done a pretty hard fifteen miles straight through the bush—and we wanted to be in reasonably good condition for the last stretch across the open. My cut and blistered feet were in shocking shape. Fortunately, there were no alarms, and at first light I had two of the scouts out on a recce. They gave us the all clear signal from a very high tree at Bamboo Creek, and soon we were pushing on as fast as we could go, in single file across the grass. It was quite good going for bare feet.

My ears pricked up as I heard bombing from Lunga, and when a trio of Bettys flew low over us from the northwest we stupidly stood our ground and waved. They waggled their wings in recognition and banked round steeply. I had got out my field glasses; the first thing I saw was the large red blobs on the side and tail. Japs! What a terrible mistake! Snatching up two wickerwork containers that they had dropped on parachutes, we moved off at a very fast double, in case they had men out looking for them. Luckily we saw none. What we had heard was probably ack-ack fire, and not our planes dropping bombs on the Japanese.

I Join the Marines

We made very good time, and soon reached the coast. Once on the beach, I forced Macfarlan's fancy shoes onto my swollen feet and generally smartened up. We closed column, and marched along in two ranks with rifles at the slope; I figured no Japanese would march in this stupid manner, and we would therefore be regarded as peculiar, rather than hostile! As we came round a bend in the coast after leaving Volonavua, we suddenly saw hosts of green-clad Marines hauling trucks on the beach.

The outpost guard stood fast, with his rifle cocked. Thank goodness he did not fire. Suddenly a peculiar feeling welled up inside me, and I felt a queer lump in my throat. As I walked the last hundred yards, with my ragged mob behind me, I wondered what it would be like to speak to someone, face to face, in my own tongue again. I had tried to rehearse what I was going to say, but when the awful moment came all I could do was whisper my name.

Happily, the guard seemed to know who I was, and he gave me a cigarette and a piece of chocolate. We were surrounded by an inquiring mob, all talking at once; then I was taken to a Captain Allison, who had had "the word" from Widdy. After shaking several dozen hands I clambered into a jeep and was whisked off to the regimental headquarters of the 1st Marines, the carriers following on foot. The beach, all the way to Tenaru, was piled high with equipment, and the whole place was bristling with machine guns.

At headquarters I was introduced to the regimental commander, Col. Clifton B. Cates, whom I was frightfully glad to see; then, out of his own coconut trees, came Charles Widdy, who was attached to Cates's HQ as a guide. We slapped each other on the back for some little time; he told me later that tears of excitement had streamed down my face. I didn't get a chance to ask many questions, as everyone was mad keen to know where the remaining Japs had got to and what they were doing.

In the afternoon I was taken over to 1st Marine Division headquarters, where at D-2 (Intelligence) Lt. Col. Edmund J. Buckley and his merry men pumped me dry of all I knew about the situation, including geography. Later, Colonel Cates gave Widdy and me each a two-ounce brandy ration, which, with some sake that Widdy had recently acquired, kept us both nervously talking most of the night, much to the colonel's annoyance.[6]

After all the excitement had died down, however, I felt empty and alone. I was enormously thankful that I had joined up with the Marines; yet I was horribly disappointed that, after everything, I had to turn in, hot and sweaty, in a foxhole with Charles Widdy. I would have given anything for a hot bath and a soak for my feet.[7] Widdy was very kind, and gave some spare clothing to me; but his last remark, before we turned in, was, "If you'd told me that one day I would be sleeping in a hole in the middle of one of my plantations, I'd h've eaten my fucking hat!"

I spent most of the next day, after I had been fitted with a pair of shoes,[8] driving around learning what had happened at Lunga and familiarizing myself as rapidly as I could with the Marines' layout and organization. I viewed with rather academic interest the smashed remains of the Jap installations. Although I had never seen them as going concerns, I was quite pleased that their locations well fitted our descriptions of them.

Then I was taken to call on the divisional commander, Maj. Gen. Alexander Archer Vandegrift. He had a modest tent under some trees behind a slight rise near the Lunga River. The general was clean shaven and had a pink complexion, but his jaw was set and he had an air of quiet determination. After he had heard "the story" and learned that the resident commissioner had instructed me to offer my services, General Vandegrift summed up the Marines' situation in a few words and told me to take complete charge of all matters of native administration and of intelligence outside the perimeter. I was to attach myself to Colonel Buckley, of D-2, collecting information, through my scouts, on the whole island and supplying guides as required, if possible.

Information on matters outside the perimeter was of vital importance, as the enemy situation was very obscure. Three days before, Lieutenant Colonel Goettge,[9] the division's intelligence officer, had been ambushed with twenty-five men somewhere on the far side of the Matanikau River. During interrogation a Japanese prisoner had suggested that his comrades might be willing to surrender. They took him back there by boat, and walked right into it. Goettge and all his patrol were killed, bar three, who made the beach and swam back through the shark-infested sea.

Viv Hodgess, now an AIF captain, was attached to the 5th Marines, the regiment defending the west flank. He had come in on the transport to guide them to the correct landfall. As befitted an old Digger, Hodgess had settled in well. He had "acquired," probably from the plantation house at Kukum, a working Electrolux refrigerator, and I gratefully accepted a cold bottle of Japanese beer that had also somehow found its way into his possession.

18

Out of the Frying Pan and into the Fire:

The Battle of the Tenaru

B Y COMPARISON with my shadow army, the 1st Marine Division was gigantic: it was spread over the three Lever's plantations, Kukum, Lunga, and Tenaru. At that time, the area within the perimeter—roughly a semicircle, bounded by the sea on the east and west—was almost entirely under regularly planted coconut palms, whose canopy of stately fronds gave a measure of protection from air observation. Into it the tangled jungle stretched green fingers at different points, especially along the Lunga and Ilu Rivers and on the western boundary beyond Kukum. The soil was a fine black alluvial deposit, and even when the sun was drying up a shower of rain, with the water still lying in puddles, there would be dust flying. After a jeep ride, everyone would be black behind the ears and round his glasses, and sweat would streak his face.

A New Life

With the Marines had come a convoy of newsmen. One of these, Richard Tregaskis, seemed to get his front-line stories firsthand; a very tall chap, he took size 13 in shoes, which I was told he found a great handicap when taking shelter in the normal-sized foxhole. Bob Miller, another correspondent, came in for a chat about dusk. He wore a baseball cap and large horn-rimmed glasses, and had nervous trick of turning over two or three silver dollars in his hand. Miller asked a fantastic number of questions about life in England, at Cambridge, and especially in the Solomons. He was astonished at what he considered a lack of normal amenities in the bush, and found it hard to believe that I had managed to cope for so long without them. The local tobacco fascinated him, and in return he pressed a tin of American tobacco on me. It was different from my favorite brand, but a treat after the stuff I'd been smoking and the filthy Japanese cigarettes I had tried.

On 17 August, Mike Winter, the section driver, took me, Michael, and Suinao and our scanty belongings over to D-2, which was destined, for the next few months, to be our home. Our headquarters was in some scrubby trees at the airstrip end of the slight ridge of jungle-covered ground that reached into the grass plain behind Lunga from the Lunga River; the airfield was only 150 yards away. It was hardly elegant: an old pyramidal tent was our map room and office, while the living quarters for both officers and enlisted were in a brown Japanese marquee, whose roof had been liberally holed by our bombers. (The holes were so placed that we got all the rain.) Apart from a few Japanese air raid shelters, that was all there was. We slept on wooden bed boards left by the former occupants; they seemed to attract dust when it was dry and mud when it was wet. As we were packed in like sardines, there was always much growling as the midnight watch groped its way out.

Colonel Buckley, the new intelligence officer, was of medium height and cheerful disposition. His hair had gone prematurely gray, and the sun had turned his skin a bright pink. A reserve artilleryman from the 11th Marines, he was a sensible, well-educated, adaptable man who had been well up in Bethlehem Steel in peacetime. The other senior officers usually referred to him as "Old Buck" or "Ed." The king interpreter, Capt. Sherwood F. Moran, was a rather frail fifty-six-year-old Quaker who for many years had been headmaster of a school in Japan. We should have called him "the Mikado"; owing to his comparatively venerable appearance, however, he had earned the sobriquet "Pappy" from the younger members of the section. We had two majors: Dick Evans, a regular, was a quiet man who kept the machinery of D-2 running smoothly; Jim Whitehead, a reserve officer, had worked for Schick Razors before the war. The lieutenants were all reservists from Ivy League universities; their officer training course was similar to what we had had at Cambridge. Fred Kidde, a bright chap, had been a businessman, while Art Claffey, from Philadelphia, had worked for American Telephone and Telegraph and been music critic for a big newspaper. Karl Soule, our photographic officer, had a habit of sleeping with his mouth open; this made him the object of many practical jokes, as people would come by and drop things in! These were my tent mates, and a good lot they were.

The big "buzz" was that heavy enemy attacks were expected. As everyone at D-2 had been so busy, the foxhole situation was pretty poor, and although the engineers were working hard to improve the airfield we had no planes yet for our defense. Whenever we had a spare moment, therefore, we all sweated away, officers and enlisted alike, hacking a more secure air raid shelter out of the coral rock of our protecting ridge. For sandbags we used Japanese rice bags, of woven rice straw, filled with coral rubble. It was hard work swinging a pick in that heat.

On the ground there was still very little information about the Japs to the west, my scouts having reported back that they had seen nothing as far as Point Cruz, which was somewhat over two miles from our front line. The number of questions that I could usefully answer appeared to be endless, and during the next few days I was subjected to a barrage from practically everyone at headquarters, from the general downward. Americans seemed to love information. I gathered that I was "indoctrinating" them.

I also met Hugh Mackenzie, the DSIO, for the first time. He had come on 15 August to establish a coastwatching headquarters in the Solomons, with a teleradio setup so that messages could be passed to our forces on the spot. Mackenzie had left the RAN and become a planter in New Britain between the wars. An obstinate individualist, he often seemed to have a chip on his shoulder, but he was a great improviser, and a man of dogged perseverance. He was concerned about Macfarlan, who had signaled several times that he was very hungry. (That made us laugh: we were pretty hungry too, on two meals a day. It was all that could be spared from our meager supply of rations, and at that point none could be shipped in.)

Mackenzie had with him Gordon Train, who had been with the Treasury in Tulagi; they operated out of a Japanese dugout amongst the coconut plans on the northwest edge of the airfield.

A message from the resident commissioner told me to continue on as district officer, Guadalcanal, for the time being. Being the only Britisher amongst so many Americans made me feel quite alone, but in a rather different way from the preceding months. We were all doing the same job, and we were becoming good friends, but after being tucked away in the bush for so long it took me time to adjust to such sudden changes.

Having just got back from the aid station, where my badly blistered feet were bandaged every day, I was standing talking to Colonel Buckley outside our map tent when our first aerial visitor arrived. It was a Japanese floatplane, zooming over for a look-see. The plane looked like a cruiser type, which probably meant that there were more Japs on the way. It got a hot reception from our ack-ack, and sheered off with a smoky tail.

Captain Moran showed us translated extracts from the *Tokyo Times,* a copy of which had been found in one of the parachute containers dropped on 15 August. It hailed the American landings as a Japanese victory, and threatened with annihilation the few of us who they thought remained. The paper made amusing reading; it was just as well that we did not know what was to come.

Although we couldn't find out what the Japs were doing across the Matanikau, we had accurate details from my scouts of the other enemy parties on the island, and these we plotted on all the maps. The information was, of course, several days old.

Our next visitors, at 1100 on 18 August, were eight Bettys, which came over parallel to, but on our side of, the airstrip. As our radar was not yet tuned, there was no warning, and we were stupidly standing in groups, watching, as the first bombs dropped about seventy yards away. Then there was a scurrying! The bombing was quite good: three direct hits on the runway, and others all round the ack-ack positions. One of the bombs that dropped in our vicinity fell between two antiaircraft guns and plowed deep into the ground without exploding; it was marked with a white flag. Two hours later it went off with a terrific thump, covering the gunners with earth and stones.

We had no rest that night either, as we were shelled from the sea. Confusing information came in all night, reports of vessels varying from armed

Sheet #1

TIME FILED   MSG CEN No   HOW SENT **PHONED**

_____ SHEET #1   **MESSAGE**
(CLASSIFICATION)   (SUBMIT TO MESSAGE CENTER IN DUPLICATE)

No **NR36/074526AU** DATE 25 Aug 42

TO DSIO v D2/074526/BT/Commandg General appreciates the services provided by the
Coast Watching system X Your Timely warning
enabled us to bag 2d planes yesterday x Today
however due to the short warning we were unable to get fighters on station in sufficient time
to contact the enemy aircraft. X Would it be
possible for STO and JER to give plain
language warning direct HUG immediately

: CONTINUED :

OFFICIAL DESIGNATION OF SENDER   TIME SIGNED

IF SENT BY RADIO. OR OTHER   **ENCODE**
MEANS WHEN DANGER OF
INTERCEPTION   EXISTS. **SEND IN CLEAR**   SIGNATURE AND GRADE OF WRITER

ALLSET

Sheet #2

TIME FILED   MSG CEN No   HOW SENT **PHONED**

_____ SHEET #2   **MESSAGE**
(CLASSIFICATION)   (SUBMIT TO MESSAGE CENTER IN DUPLICATE)

No **NR36/074526AU** DATE 25 AUG 42

TO DSIO v D2/074526/CONTINUED BT/
Enemy planes are sighted which appear
likely to be proceedg to attack This area X It
is believed that the enemy aircraft which
attacked yesterday came from Rabaul /X

OFFICIAL DESIGNATION OF SENDER **D-2**   **0745/26**
    TIME SIGNED

IF SENT BY RADIO. OR OTHER   **ENCODE** S/S **CLEMENS, CAPT.**
MEANS WHEN DANGER OF
INTERCEPTION   EXISTS. **SEND IN CLEAR**   SIGNATURE AND GRADE OF WRITER

ALLSET

Adapting to circumstances to improve the service.

barges to cruisers. The intermittent shelling continued until 0300; quite a few casualties resulted, but most of the barrage fell between Kukum and the Matanikau. Our artillery replied, but its range was too limited, since the Marines had left their heavy stuff behind. We just had to sit and take it.

Patrol Activity

General Vandegrift was greatly concerned over the wretched performance of Marine patrols. This was due to the general lack of liaison between units, which was complicated by the total inability of their fishpole aerials to transmit in the jungle. My scouts had been stalking the enemy for some months, so I was able to show the Marines a thing or two. I taught them how to rig a reliable alternative aerial, something I had learned by bitter experience. Soon I was in charge of extended patrolling.

Our information was confused, but everything pointed to the fact that the Japs had been trying to land reinforcements. It was vital to find out what success they had had. On 19 August I sent Vouza to gather some men for a patrol round the rear of our perimeter from the eastern side, to identify suspected enemy positions spotted in the bush, while Daniel Pule and three other scouts went out as guides with an offensive force of about sixty men under Capt. Charles H. Brush, Jr., to see what could be found to the east along the coast. By that time it was noon; there was no hope of getting back to D-2 for lunch, so we sat and had a bar of chocolate on the beach, at the mouth of a sluggish stream that on the Marine maps was marked "Tenaru River" but in peacetime had been known as Alligator Creek. There was definitely something in the air, and as I looked out over the channel I felt a cold shiver down my spine. There, in broad daylight, Japanese destroyers were shelling Tulagi. We got ready to move as one started to come across to Guadalcanal. Suddenly, however, three Flying Fortresses appeared; they scored a direct hit, and we were greatly relieved to see her hobbling off to the west, burning merrily.

When we got back to D-2 things really started to happen. "Info" poured in from all directions. Judging by coastwatchers' reports, enemy planes were everywhere, and one of the destroyers I saw had stood in close to shore and signaled the Japanese beyond the Matanikau. Daniel and Vura, one of the scouts, came back with Captain Brush: near Volonavua they had run smack into twenty-five enemy soldiers, who had just landed in small boats, evidently from the destroyers. The patrol had dispatched eighteen of them, but the other two scouts and one Marine, who were on the flank, were missing.[1] Daniel was scared stiff, but he had been remarkably observant in noting Japanese equipment. The ambushed patrol had lots of radio gear; Captain Brush thought it was but one platoon from a much larger unit, sent down to retake the airfield.

Now the situation had become precarious, and the division was immediately put on standby. If the Japanese could land troops at will, we should have a fair war on our hands at any minute. Out of the frying pan and into the fire, I thought sadly; I had exchanged my little pistol for a Colt .45, and intended to give a good account of myself, if need be. I hoped none of my scouts would be caught unawares. As we waited for something definite to happen, everyone was very much on edge.

I had my hands full laying out the coastwatching setup and call signs for the Marines on watch at D-2, so they could properly interpret and enter on the maps the information coming in through Mackenzie's center. The only snag was that Macfarlan and the rest took it for granted that the Americans knew the local place-names. The Marine maps, at this stage, were little more than charts, and I was constantly being called in to identify new names. I also had to go down to the perimeter when scouts arrived, to identify my men and get the information as quickly as possible. This took time, bounding across country from one shell hole to another.

Next morning, in addition to several false air raid alarms, we suffered the indignity of having two Japanese cruisers steam up and down the channel, quite close in, and throw in the odd shell from time to time. Vouza went off on his patrol, while Daniel prepared to go out again with Brush and his commanding officer, Lt. Col. Lenard B. Cresswell, whose whole battalion was moving out to the attack.[2] The sharpness of six samurai swords that had been brought in led me to reflect how lucky I had been—up till then.

The afternoon was spent down at the prison compound. Our prisoners, mostly from construction units, were scruffy-looking but sturdy little men; I helped Captain Moran to interrogate them and to decipher the Japanese operations maps. Seeing Viv Hodgess on my way back, I complained that since I had joined the Marines I hadn't been able to take off my boots at night. He then told me of an amazing episode on the previous day, in which he had escaped death or serious injury only because he did not have his boots on. When the shelling started in the early hours of the morning he had darted for his foxhole, only to stub his toe on a tent peg and measure his length on the ground. While he lay there, swearing, there was a tremendous explosion, and an incoming shell sheared off a coconut tree directly above his head. The men who had been sleeping on either side of Hodgess had kept their boots on; one was gravely wounded, the other killed. They had got twice as far as he had, but they were erect and running as the shell exploded.

About 1600, while returning from the prisoners' cage, I heard a distant sound. It became a drone, and then the drone became a roar as a squadron of dive bombers and another of fighters swept over, circled, and landed.[3] Our own planes at last! When I got back to D-2, Michael, who had not felt too happy during the night shelling, was wreathed in smiles. Through my binoculars I could see Marines in their bedraggled "dungreens" rushing out to welcome the pilots; it was indeed a gladsome sight, and gave me a tingle right down the spine. This was but a momentary relief, and I still had that queer feeling that something was about to happen; but now, at least, we were in a position to hit back for a change.

Battle Joined

We turned in uneasily that night. No one seemed to think we would get much sleep. Sure enough, after several alarms, Colonel Cates received word about 0215 that his outposts had been withdrawn in the face of large numbers of the enemy. Coming as it did from the east, this attack meant that the Japanese had landed a large enough force to give them sufficient confidence of success in assaulting our positions. Everyone was soon on the alert, and about 0230 heavy machine-gun fire broke out on Cates's line. I turned uneasily and looked toward the Matanikau, wondering what the Japs were doing there, but all was quiet in that vicinity.

As the enemy attacked across the Tenaru River, the staccato of the machine guns increased, and became interspersed with rifle fire. The firing grew so intense that one could almost distinguish chords in the weird, horrible music of battle. Contact reports kept coming in, and at 0350 Cates reported that he was committed all along his front. New sounds were heard, the thud of mortars and then, about 0430, our artillery. There were also enemy support weapons, which were as yet unknown to us. Tracers ricocheted up into the sky, together with red and white flares as Japanese columns came into the attack. We could see the coconut palms silhouetted in pink flashes and, in that strange light, debris being thrown heavenward. Everything appeared to be going all right, but it all seemed dangerously near, and as the din increased I had the eerie feeling that the battle was creeping closer. The tracers seemed to dart right across the airfield.

The Ordeal of Sergeant Major Vouza

Dawn broke; then, just before 0700, when the coconut palms became green again above the holocaust below, I got an urgent telephone call that a native, mortally wounded, had staggered through the enemy lines and was repeatedly asking for me. They couldn't get much information from him, as he was wounded all over the front of his body and his throat was full of blood.

Grimly I grabbed the jeep and rushed down to the front with Daniel Pule. The noise got louder and louder, and I heard bullets thwacking into the coconut trees. We managed to get to Colonel Pollock's command post,[4] which was but a hundred yards from the raging battle at the river line. Here we found the dying native.

It was Vouza. He was an awful mess, and unable to sit up. I could hardly bear to look at him. We dragged him behind the jeep, and there, in spite of a gaping wound in his throat, he told me his story as best he could.

On his patrol Vouza had taken a miniature American flag given him as a souvenir. He tried to hide it at Volonavua, but the area was thick with enemy troops and he barely got away. Near Makile, Vouza approached what he thought was Captain Brush's patrol, only to find that it was the Japanese patrol later ambushed by Brush's Marines. Caught red-handed, he was hauled before the regimental commanding officer, Colonel Ichiki; Ishimoto, who interpreted, recognized him. He was brought to Gaimale and left in the sun, tied by straw ropes to a tree; but he would not divulge our dispositions. The soldiers smashed his face with rifle butts, slashed him with a sword, and made him lie on a nest of red ants; still he did not answer. They then hung him in a tree until he passed out from wounds and exposure. At dusk they took him down, tied his wrists, and moved into position for the attack, taking him with them.

When the assault began, Vouza's guards were ordered to dispatch him. Since shooting would give away their position, they bayoneted him repeatedly and left him for dead. Vouza received seven wounds in his chest and another, the biggest of all, in his throat. As the battle unfolded, he staggered away and managed to bite through the cords that bound him. He must have walked or crawled nearly three miles, right through the battlefield. At the Marine outpost, Pvt. Wilbur F. Bewley, of Company G, 2d Battalion, 1st Marines, saw that he was not a Jap, but on our side.[5]

As if that weren't enough, Vouza insisted on spluttering out to me a very valuable description of the Japanese force, its numbers and weapons. This was passed on immediately; a bullet hit the jeep as I lay behind a tree telephoning it in.

Vouza, who had lost pints of blood, was in terrible shape. He fully expected to die, and before he passed out again he gave me a long last message for his wife and children. I wrote with one hand and held his hand with the other. Once he had done his duty, the terrific strain told, and he collapsed. We carried him back and got the doctors operating on him. They pumped Vouza full of new blood, and amazingly it was expected that he would live—if, that was, the hospital was not disturbed by air raids. What loyalty the man had! I felt immensely proud.

Shortly afterward, Bili, one of Vouza's patrol, came in with a bayonet wound in his arm. A lad of fourteen, he too had been tied up by the Japanese, but Vouza told them he had not been to the Marine lines, and he was let go. The boy was so scared that I got very little out of him, but he did corroborate Vouza's story. Bili had counted three or four hundred Japs at Makile, some, with twigs and leaves on helmets and uniforms, in battle camouflage.

By the time I got Vouza squared away and attended to, and dealt with a multitude of other problems, it was about noon. The battle was still in full swing, and our newly arrived fighters drove off some Zeros that had come in to support their infantry. A prisoner from the Tenaru front, interrogated by Captain Moran, said that he had walked up the coast for two nights in a party of two hundred. This added to our knowledge of the enemy landings.

I called on Colonel Cates, whom I found very direct but easy to talk to.

Cates had the air of an experienced soldier, cool, calm, and collected; he wore breeches and knee-length campaign boots and nonchalantly smoked cigarettes from a long black holder. When I had first met him he had seemed nervous and fidgety and apt to imagine snipers in every tree; when the heat was on, however, he was really at home, and quite a different man. There was no doubt he was a bonny fighter. The colonel was quite pleased with the operation; he was about to swing Cresswell's battalion on his right flank and cut Ichiki off to the sea.

About 1630, just as some of our planes flew back in, the din suddenly stopped and the fight was over. Afterward I went down to the shore with our photographers and equipment experts to glean what we could about the Japanese. This was my first view of a real battle, and I must say I was appalled. Never had I seen such terrible destruction occur in such a short space of time. There were seven or eight hundred dead strewn in bits over about three acres. The fighting had been at very close quarters, and our 37-mm guns, firing canister shot, had done ghastly work. One of Lever's cows had unfortunately wandered into the scene and, in the confusion of the night fighting, had been eliminated by a Japanese flamethrower. On the beach, close to where so recently we had sat and eaten chocolate, those who had attempted to creep behind our lines were being covered up by sand carried in by the sea.

I found the sweet smell of death quite revolting, but Michael and my scouts were frightfully pleased: they understood this sort of thing. We had great difficulty with Marine souvenir hunters as we searched for maps, orders, and the like, and had to clear the area of sightseers. Some of the enemy, shamming death, turned over slyly and lobbed hand grenades. They were soon dealt with. The Japs were extremely well equipped, especially with wireless, signal gear, even bicycles, and we brought back plenty of work for Captain Moran and his interpreter team. It had been an eventful day, and even if an ammo dump had not exploded that night I would not have slept for thinking of those ghastly bodies.

The next day we all worked like beavers getting the "museum" sorted out and testing some of the Jap apparatus. Wireless sets, mortars, machine guns, even intact flamethrowers were captured. Betweentimes I managed to go down to see Vouza. His condition was improving, but he was still very weak; he could hardly be seen for the bandages. I was also pleased to get a message from Macfarlan that Gumu and Beato, the scouts who had gone missing on the Brush patrol, had turned up safe. So much for the Battle of the Tenaru. Our own casualties were small compared to those of the Japanese.

I was sent to take some Japanese equipment to show to Colonel Hunt[6] and to bring back a prisoner from his sector. As a result I missed the afternoon meal again. (Somehow I never seemed to be near the kitchens at chow time, but I was so used to going hungry that I didn't worry much about missing meals, which in any case were pretty scanty.) I managed to do a little trade, however, and returned triumphant with a case of Japanese beer for the thirsty souls at D-2.[7] I was still worried about Vouza, and about Ishimoto—I felt that as long as he was loose all my scouts were in danger. During the day three scouts who could identify him had combed the battlefield for Ishimoto, but there was no sign of the man amongst the dead. We should have to look for him at Taivu.

No Rest for the Wicked

Until the end of the month, the Japanese kept up their air and sea offensive. For now, they did not make another large-scale effort on land—they just worried our perimeter and kept us all awake. Their air raids increased in number and size, and though our air force was gradually reinforced it did not make very much difference in the number of bombs that were dropped on us.

On 23 August, following several raids, eight Zero fighters zoomed in to strafe the airstrip at about two hundred feet. One came straight at us, diving down a gully between the ack-ack pits. As the bullets hit the ground, a line of dust slewed past our shelter. Colonel Buckley, who was still outside, carried out a wonderful acrobatic wriggle apparently without using his arms or his legs. He only just beat the bullets inside. Though partially under cover, I was so fascinated by his evolution that I remained rooted to the spot, and was covered by small stones.

Most evenings a cruiser or destroyer would play "lights out" with a dozen or so salvoes clanging onto the airstrip—or, as it had been renamed, Henderson Field, after a gallant Marine dive-bombing squadron leader, Maj. Lofton R. Henderson, who had been lost at Midway. For the most part the shells were aimed at the airfield, but sometimes the Japs waggled the spout a bit too much and they fell about our ears in D-2. The Seabees were kept pretty busy maintaining Henderson Field, as there were two or three new holes on the runway practically every morning. I felt sorry for our pilots, who had flown in from carriers and had no bedding or equipment; they were handed a rifle and a spade, and in many cases they had to sleep in foxholes that they dug near their planes. Our dive bombers began to get their eye in, and over the next few days managed to damage or sink several destroyers and cruisers. The pilots soon realized that every one sunk meant a better chance of a night's rest, and more planes to fly the next morning.

More fighters had arrived, including some queer things called Airacobras. They looked quite flimsy next to the sturdy "soapbox" Grumman Wildcats. Fourteen Flying Fortresses had also landed, but our ground staff was very browned off with these birds of passage because they used such a lot of fuel in return for their alleged accomplishments. All our fuel, then and for months afterward, came in fifty-gallon drums, which had to be manhandled ashore.

One air raid that I shall never forget occurred on 25 August, under a cloudless sky. I was sitting down at the "pen," listening to Colonel Buckley and Captain Moran questioning prisoners, when suddenly, for no reason at all, I looked up and there, floating in the blue haze, were twenty-one Bettys in a perfect "V," like moths flickering in candlelight. The Japs had come over at twenty-eight thousand feet to evade our antiaircraft guns. We ducked off our camp stools and threw ourselves into a wide-open ditch—only a little faster than the prisoners. We had just hit the dust when the ground shook and swayed under the weight of heavy bombs. They fell all round the airfield, and round where we were crouching; though not much damage was done, several men were killed or wounded.

The next day, Japanese bombs became almost a personal matter at D-2, three men being killed within a few yards of us and some ammunition blowing up close by, touched off by a delayed-action bomb. The bomb flung a piece of iron through the stove of the general's cook, Sgt. "Butch" Morgan.[8] Butch, who was of Welsh extraction, was furious: the air was blue for miles around with his expressions of love for the Japanese. This time, however, the Grummans blew a number of Bettys and Zeros to pieces, and several others were barely able to limp home to their base at Rabaul.

In between interrogating scouts, sending out patrols, elucidating other coastwatchers' messages, and trying to identify place-names from prisoners, I managed to fit in a daily visit to Vouza. The hospital must originally have been one of the Japs' administrative buildings. It was raised off the ground and built of the very same bed boards we slept on, with a roof of native palm leaves; but it had little or no protection from the air, and the original Signal Headquarters, at one end, had been smashed to smithereens, Mackenzie having a lucky escape. Some wag had put a notice outside: "3,666 or was it 3,686 miles to Tokyo."

Vouza's vitality was amazing. By now he was sitting up in his cot, swathed in bandages and usually smoking a large cigar. He had become the center of attention at the hospital, and would tell his story to each admiring visitor. The doctors, with great modesty, said he had the constitution of an ox, but I think they did him proud. A layman, at any rate, would hardly believe that he had nearly been dead a few days before. At the worst, his rich copper color had faded to a deathly pale green, and although he had lost a lot of weight he had begun to regain a healthy flush.

Feeding the Hungry

My scouts were busy trying to find out what had happened to any enemy survivors after the Battle of the Tenaru and what went on across the Matanikau. Macfarlan had reported that some of the lads were afraid to bring in reports, as the Japs had blocked the roads; I couldn't really blame them. On 27 August, however, Vura and Tabasui came in, with letters from Mac and several civilians.

Macfarlan had suggested to Mackenzie that the latter send him "a few tins of meat or other tinned stuff, suitable for the high living standard to which I have been accustomed for the past few months." ("In fact," he joked in a later signal, "the house cats do not realise the danger they are in.") The story was the same all over; in a cheery letter, Campbell wrote:

Well here we are again, all the happy party, after 6 weeks sojourn at the health resort on the Suta! . . . I put in one of the weeks there, on my back, with a poisoned leg, and was only two days up when I made the trip back.

I think Mac and Ken have both written you about our kaikai position and have asked you if you can do anything for us in that line with the "powers that be" down there. We are really down to pretty short commons in all lines for ourselves, and my Makira [San Cristobal] and Ulawa labour are causing me quite a lot of worry of how to feed them.

He also mentioned that Andresen and Freshwater had opened their last tin of meat.

Mackenzie made a tremendous fuss about the food shortage. Apart from the fact that Macfarlan now had Hay and Campbell at Bombadeha with him, they'd all lost so much every time they had moved that they really were pretty hungry. It took a lot of persuasion and complicated arrangement, but I managed to organize and deliver, that same day, the first air drop of the campaign. There were no proper containers or parachutes for dropping supplies, so we wrapped up tins of C-ration stew, cigarettes, and atabrine and stowed them in Japanese straw bags. I could not make the parcels too big, nor could I take very much, as I had to get all of it, and myself, into the rear cockpit of a dive bomber.

For a start, I was scared stiff: apart from the fact that it was the first time I'd ever flown, I could not hear a word of what Major Mangrum, the pilot, said through the intercom. (I hoped we would not meet any hostile aircraft, as I had not really mastered the tail gun!) I was quite astonished when we found Gold Ridge: it looked very small, and Mount Tatuve, a neighboring peak, got in the way for low flying. Against the green grass and surrounding bush, however, I soon picked up "Macfarlan of the Glens," in gleaming Navy whites set off by his black beard. As we zoomed over on each of our three runs, I stood up, facing backward, and dropped a bag; I very nearly followed the first one out. Bump, down went each bag, slowly turning over and over until it hit the ground and bounced. One of them burst, and another narrowly missed Mac, but the shooting wasn't too bad, and it was jolly funny watching him dodging his dinner. We got home without enemy interference. Mac wired that he had collected the bags, but quite a lot was mangled: he was busy scraping stew off the cigarettes and his uniform!

I also heard from Father Engberink at Ruavatu. He had got the impression that I had accused him of collaborating with the enemy. He protested that in fact the Japanese had ordered the local people to work for them for one month and had threatened to shoot them if they refused. How, he wrote, could he tell them not to go? (What I had blamed him for was lack of common sense in not letting the islanders at his settlement disappear into the bush, where they would have had no opportunity to either obey or disobey the Japanese.) Enemy soldiers had called at his station three times and subjected him to questioning. I was relieved when he noted that the troops had been very polite and had never asked the missionaries or the locals where I was. All they took was his shotgun, his wireless receiving set, and his camera.

The Marau Party

Clarry Hart, at Kau Kau, had not realized that anything more than a heavy bombing attack had taken place. In a letter he described in detail the adventures of the Japs at Marau, and how they had tied up and questioned the fathers and brothers at Makina. What worried him most was the way in which the local people—together with, so he claimed, two of my policemen—had looted his belongings and stores while he was in the bush. Hart had hardly had time to digest my letter, but he was wildly excited about it, and wished that he had someone and something with whom and which to get drunk. Good old "Concrete Clarry."

As regards the incident at Makina, I eventually got the full story in a letter from Father Boudard, who happened to be at Marau at the time. Some Japanese barges from Bokoagau had been bombed when they were near Marau on 8 August. A Jap shore party then had called at Makina and accused the missionaries of being in league with the Allied forces. Father Boudard's charmingly vivid account reads best in its original French, but this English translation by Brother James Thrift conveys some of the flavor of his recounting of this episode:

> My Dear Mr. Clemens,
> I am taking the liberty of writing to tell you what happened at Marau. You no doubt already know the main outline but not perhaps the full details of the story.
> The Japs first appeared on Wednesday the 5th immediately after their visit to Makina. Their visit to us was much the same as previous ones to other stations: our arms and radios etc. were seized, but otherwise nothing unusual happened.

At about 5 o'clock on the morning of Saturday the 8th some 30 fully-equipped soldiers commanded by Captain I. [Ishimoto] again climbed the hill. Old Father Jean Coicaud, who is 68, went out to meet them. Some of the soldiers immediately bound his hands behind his back whilst others entered the house. They found the other Father [i.e., Van Mechelin] dressing and bound him in the same way. Then they led the 2 venerable prisoners like that to the Brethren, who were taken by surprise as they were getting out of bed. They too were seized and bound like the Fathers. Then they were all taken out and tied to pillars on the verandah.

The Japs then threatened us fiercely, pointed their revolvers at us, banged their swords on the table and finally started their questioning:

1. "You have a secret wireless & transmitter and have revealed our position to the Americans."

Then followed a minute search everywhere. One of the Brothers said very politely: "Yes, we have a wireless, but it doesn't work. You could have taken it the first time you came, but you didn't ask for it then. And we haven't hidden it either. Open this cupboard and see for yourselves what condition it's in. But we certainly have no transmitter."

2. "You sent out signals one night with Very lights?"

The Brothers pleaded "not guilty."

3. "You looted Paruru after the White Man left?"

The Brethren asked permission to look in a drawer and produced a letter written by Mr. Hodges[s] proving that the things he left behind had been bought by them.

So these gentlemen could find no incriminating evidence though they declared that accusations had been made by the natives.

And then began another drama: American planes flew very low over the station and were no doubt surprised at not seeing either the Brethren or their pupils (the pupils were detained in their rooms).[9]

The Japs then untied the prisoners and led them into a room where they were forced to sit absolutely still on the floor; they remained in that position until 11.30 a.m.

The American planes circled round the houses all morning and the Japs were probably even more terrified than their prisoners.

It was obvious that the Americans had seen the Japs in the Brethren's house, had realised the situation and so did not want to drop their bombs.[10]

At about 11 a.m. the Captain ordered one of the Brethren to cook a meal and Brother Ephraim [Ephrem] was led to the kitchen with great ceremony. I don't know what the menu consisted of but I do know that everyone was much strengthened by the meal.

After the Americans stopped flying around the Japs gave their orders to the Fathers and Brethren:

"Do not leave the station:

"Do not even go into the grounds:

"Only the pupils may go into the grounds" etc.

Then they departed with polite farewells.

The next morning—Sunday—the American planes returned and destroyed both the Jap boats.

Apparently the Japs—about 40 or 50 of them—are now on the height overlooking Makina between Paruru and Makina.

Yesterday, the 24th, 2 American planes flew over here at great speed coming, apparently, from Marau and travelling westward—probably making for Veuru [Vioru].

Ishimoto Again

Also on 27 August, Gumu returned. Separated from the Brush patrol during the firefight, he found that three survivors of the ambushed Japanese party were leading their battalion to the Tenaru, so he hid beside the track, using ten stones to count the troops as they went by. When the main body had passed, Gumu crept up on a straggler, who was washing his feet in a stream; after disposing of the soldier, he departed with his boots and papers. On account of the battle, Gumu could not get through to Lunga, so he decided to find out what the Japs were up to; unfortunately, he ran into Ishimoto. Ishimoto had four soldiers with him, together with the two fathers and two of the sisters from Ruavatu. He tried to make Gumu carry his pack; when the scout said he was sick, and couldn't do it, Ishimoto angrily hit him across the face. Knowing that he could not hit back, Gumu alertly suggested that the three Catholic natives who were with them could carry the packs; Ishimoto then let him go. At Makile he met the survivor of five Solomon Islanders who had carried a wounded Marine back to the lines; the man had escaped, but Ishimoto and his squad had killed the other four with the bayonet. (I gathered that Ishimoto took the missionaries back to Makile and then returned to join the main force attacking us.) Gumu then headed for the police post at Koilo. He thought that there were a lot of Japs wandering about, especially at Tasimboko, but that no new parties had landed.

With our aircraft attacking enemy shipping in earnest, we had a few quiet nights, and two or three of our smaller vessels were able to elude the Japanese Navy and bring up some much-needed supplies. The only trouble was it was so quiet that we stayed awake wondering why. Japanese rice was now a prominent feature in our diet; we held a sweepstakes on the number of currants each man got with his rice. The constant activity, together with the meager rations, burned up all my nervous energy, and I was often so tired that I could not sleep, even when I had the opportunity.

As a change from my normal afternoon report compiling, on 29 August I had a great "session" with two visitors—Dick Horton and Henry Josselyn, freshly arrived from Tulagi. Lucky devils, they were now sub-lieutenants in the RANVR. (At least they thought so: they were wearing naval shoulder boards on their Marine uniforms, though they weren't quite sure whether their commissions had come through.) Dick had a marmalade-colored beard, and Henry a scraggy sandy job. I rocked with laughter, but the joke was on me, for I had forgotten my own, which they found just as funny! They had had a great time scrapping on Tulagi with the Raiders, and so were burning to do something more active, but they weren't sure whether they would be allowed to carry on fighting with the Marines or be used as reliefs for some of the other coastwatchers. In addition, Walter H. Brooksbank, the civil assistant to the RAN's director of Naval Intelligence, arrived at Lunga with Macfarlan's relief, Lt. Lawrie Ogilvie, and there was much discussion and conferences with Colonel Buckley about the proper function of the coast watch.

Next day I took three of the lads down to Kukum, where they were to join the 1st Raider Battalion when that unit came over from Tulagi. (The Marines planned to have it execute a landing at Tassafaronga.) One of the destroyer transports, *Colhoun,* was lying close in to shore when the day's second air raid warning went. The Bettys sneaked down in the eye of the afternoon sun and landed a couple on her stern; she went down clean as a whistle in under three minutes, and we had the ghastly job of picking up the oil-covered survivors, many of whom were dangerously wounded by the explosion of her depth charges, which had not been on safety.

News arrived that the missionaries had been allowed to return to

Ruavatu, although it was feared that that was only to collect their belongings. I assumed that Ishimoto was at the bottom of it all, and I was very worried about them. Sergeant Andrew had got in touch with the party, proposing to spirit them away and hide them at Paripao, but the fathers refused to disobey the Japanese, who had now been reinforced by the troops from Marau. It was some consolation that Laena, the former bosun of the cutter *Lofung,* had played the local idiot and carried the Marau party's machine gun up to Bokoagau, so that he could keep tabs on them.

From information at our disposal on 1 September, it was clear that another Japanese attack was pending. The Marines were not the strong force of the seventh of August. We had had a lot of casualties, malaria was beginning to incapacitate units, and everyone had been working the twenty-four hours round. Since every Marine was needed for the front line, it was decided to try to get in some native labor if that was in any way possible. The laborers could relieve the Marines by unloading supplies, whenever supply ships managed to reach us through the Japanese naval ring, and do many quartermaster jobs. Unloading drums of gasoline was a wearisome job, but it was one that the Solomon Islanders were used to from peacetime days, and they could do it speedily and efficiently. I sent out orders for the collection of a gang.

All Modern Conveniences

I celebrated the first day of the new month by getting down to the Lunga River for a swim and a bath, which were much needed. The best technique, I soon found, was to sit in the river with my clothes on and, after having a good soak, to soap them all over. Then I took them off, anchored them with a big stone, and repeated the performance on myself. By the time I finished, my clothes were neatly rinsed and could be laid out to dry while I enjoyed a swim or just lying in the cool water.

One of the old Japanese shacks near the Lunga River contained a portable iceworks. It was now operating again as "TOJO ICE FACTORY / UNDER NEW MANAGEMENT /—J. Genung, Sgt., USMC, Mgr." Most of the ice went to the hospital, but occasionally we got a block by skillful arrangement through the souvenir net.

As we had decided to get in native labor and as the scouting organization had expanded so greatly, I had to get a new camp area for my men and organize a proper rationing system. Because of the strict rationing it was difficult to get enough rice for them, and, as we had no bread, they did not find the rest of the Marine rations very filling. The camp had to be accessible both to the front line, for getting the lads in, and to D-2, so I could keep an eye on them, and yet be as far away from the airstrip as possible—none of them liked air raids. It was a tall order.

The Resident Commissioner Calls

On 2 September we sent the Grumman Duck over to Malaita to get the resident commissioner. It wasn't working very well, and when he came the following day Mr. Marchant had a hazardous trip. He looked pretty skinny after his last few months in the bush, and his corduroy shorts were ripped from top to bottom, done in by the jet of water on landing. (His pith helmet, or "Bombay bowler," struck quite a note, however: we had all got used to tin hats or to the liners.) There followed long conferences with Colonel Buckley and the Australian naval people, straightening out the overlap of their setup with ours. It took hours to convince Mackenzie that, as I was still responsible for civil administration on Guadalcanal, the scouting net would have to remain my responsibility. In the end, however, it was agreed that it would be so, and that his function would be to gather information from the coastwatchers in the islands that were still occupied. It worked much the best this way, as our scouting system was by now part and parcel of the D-2 section, and all the scouts could now work in close cooperation with Marine units.

For scouting purposes we divided the island into five main sections, each containing a company of scouts. They were responsible not only for keeping us fully posted on the enemy situation in their area, but also for rescuing and bringing back any of our pilots who might have crashed and for bringing in as prisoners any stray Japs who could be overcome by force of arms or by guile. Any Marine patrols were to be passed through their territory and given every assistance. Gallant old Vouza, who had recovered completely, took over Tasimboko, the danger area; he greatly amused Colonel Buckley, who, in my absence, had asked him to bring in a prisoner. Vouza asked him when he wanted one; "Oh," said the colonel, "tomorrow will do." "What time?" Vouza asked. "Oh, about ten o'clock," Buckley said, and sure enough at 1000 the next morning Vouza arrived with a Jap neatly trussed to a bamboo pole. On being taxed with cruelty, Vouza said that the man couldn't walk fast enough, so they had decided to carry him!

Ammunition was badly wanted, and we were rather cross at the Navy for sailing off and leaving us alone. They had, of course, been pretty busy, but we knew nothing about it, and when we heard on the radio one night that they had been awarded some decorations the Marines had a good old grumble. We all felt pretty lonesome during those days of no retreat and no apparent help. It all came down to: Would we ever get off the island alive? If so, how? A morbid rumor started that the latest tune on the "Hit Parade" show was called "Say a Prayer for a Pal on Guadalcanal." Captain Moran cheered everyone up by electing himself "Hero, Self-Appointed," and after that he always added "H.S.A." to his signature.

The first night of the RC's visit was fairly quiet, but that was apparently only politeness to visitors. A day later he was given a good example of Guadalcanal's evening entertainment. We had just settled down for the night when we were suddenly covered with dust from a salvo from three destroyers or cruisers. Our rickety marquee rocked and heaved, and sustained further damage; the chief blow, however, was the loss of the destroyer transports *Little* and *Gregory,* which had returned a few hours before with two companies of Raiders from Savo. Some of our planes went up, but they saw nothing, as it poured with rain. We all got sopping wet.

The day raids were not so bad, because Read, Mason, and Kennedy were giving us enough warning for our fighters to get into the air and intercept them, but at night another nuisance had developed. It was an enemy scout plane, which, after gaining great height, shut off its engine and glided in over our area. The first that one would hear of his visit was his peculiar engine starting up again, followed immediately by the explosion of a solitary bomb. This quite often caused casualties, and always annoyed everyone. From the peculiar noise of his engine he was soon christened "Washing Machine Charlie," or, more technically, "Maytag Charlie," after the popular brand in the States.

After matters had been arranged to his satisfaction and he had experienced all manner of excitement and discomfort, the resident commissioner staggered back to Malaita in the Duck with a bag or two of supplies and a good idea of the luxurious life we were leading! I am glad to say he approved of what I was doing.

Up to now we had heard very little from the Japs beyond the Matanikau. Our patrol activities had been indecisive, and no line had been established. Then, on 6 September, a haggard Marine fighter pilot turned up at the western perimeter. His name was Richard Amerine.

Forced down in the water off Cape Esperance, Lieutenant Amerine had a hard time with the currents, which made him drift around in circles. Finally, he managed to creep ashore and hide behind a log. Two Japs were searching the bush for him; at dusk they gave up and, to his horror, sat down on his log for a rest. In his cramped position the pilot's choice of plan was rather limited—he grabbed a rock and, raising himself as noiselessly as possible, bashed one man over the head. Luckily he was the one with the pistol. Amerine was immediately set upon by the other, but, after a desperate struggle, finally strangled him. He had kicked off his shoes and trousers while swimming ashore; reluctantly, he took the pants from one of his victims.

The pistol had only three bullets in it. In due course the lieutenant found an enemy soldier whose boots seemed about his own size, and with new footwear and two shots left he continued on his way. Hundreds of Japs went by, carrying quarters of beef, while Amerine hid, starving. Looking for coconuts near the beach, he saw what he thought was some natives; they turned out to be Japanese, and he had to use his second bullet to get away. Before reaching our lines he was surprised by a Jap sentry, who raised his rifle to his shoulder, only to be drilled by that precious third shot.

Amerine came in suffering from sores, malnutrition, and shock. I saw him in the hospital; he was about to have his first good sleep in a week, but he insisted on telling us everything. Afterward, Colonel Buckley asked if he had anything to add. "Oh, yes," Amerine said. "What a pity, if I'd only had my net, just think how many beautiful butterflies I could have caught." It turned out he had studied entomology at the University of Kansas.

19

Attacked on All Sides

T HE 1ST RAIDER BATTALION, a specially trained unit (some of the officers and sergeants had completed Mountbatten's commando course at Inveraray, in Scotland), had borne, along with the 1st Parachute Battalion, the brunt of the fighting on Tulagi and on Gavutu and Tanambogo. They were sent over to Guadalcanal for a rest, but the word "rest" had passed out of our vocabulary.

The Tasimboko Raid

The Raiders' commanding officer, Col. Merritt A. Edson ("Red Mike," as he was known to his men), was a tough, shrewd leader who had developed his initiative against desperadoes in Nicaragua. He was a deadly shot, and wore a pair of pearl-handled revolvers. Another accomplished soldier was Edson's executive officer, Lt. Col. Samuel B. Griffith II, with whom Dick Horton and Henry Josselyn had become firm friends; we shared a shelter during a couple of air raids, and "batted the breeze" about the fighting in Tulagi and about Inveraray and Scotland.

From scouting reports by Andrew and others on 31 August, it appeared that most of the Japanese to our east were concentrated round Tasimboko. We had very little idea of their strength and dispositions, however, until two scouts, Selea and Vura, returned on 3 September from a three-day reconnaissance to that area. From their report I concluded that there were about three hundred enemy soldiers occupying strong defensive positions west of Tasimboko village. Colonels Twining and Thomas[1] drew up a plan to land the Raiders at Taivu Point and come in on the Japs from the rear.

At midday on 7 September, only hours before the force was due to depart, Vouza brought information that there were far more troops at Tasimboko than we had thought. I advised Buckley that there had been a sudden increase in the size of the garrison, and Edson might be facing two to three thousand well-armed Japanese. The D-2 staff, however, while conceding some increase in strength, had a low opinion of the enemy's combat readiness, and the operation proceeded as planned. That evening the Raiders embarked in two destroyer transports and two patrol craft for the attack on Tasimboko. With them, over from Tulagi, was Dick Horton, who knew the area well. Selea and Olorere went along as guides, but I doubted the usefulness of scouts for amphibious operations, apart from locating the landing area. Vouza, who loved a scrap, had talked his way into going. I insisted that he not go ashore.

Vouza returned on one of the APDs late the next day. He had guided them into Taivu but had stayed on board. The Raiders, enjoying both naval and air support, had surprised the rear guard of a large enemy force and destroyed a massive quantity of equipment, ammunition, and stores, which were stacked as if the Japanese had just arrived. Though most of their troops had already moved off into the bush, Edson estimated that no fewer than four thousand men had very recently been at Tasimboko, and he came away with a healthy respect for the value of my scouts' intelligence. As Marines could not be spared, I sent Deke and a scouting party to destroy the rest of the Japs' equipment.

Raiders' Ridge

Aerial photographs had revealed that division headquarters, with all the tracks leading to it, stuck out like a sore thumb. We had taken a lot of casualties there, from both bombing and shelling, and on 9 September General Vandegrift ordered a move of his command post to a razor-backed hill—actually one spur of a long grassy ridge—about a mile south of Henderson Field. The lower slopes of the hill had convenient clumps of large trees, under which the division's various staff sections could be hidden.

Looking back on it, this was a most inopportune time to move, as the Japanese obviously were preparing for something big. My scouts had reported that an enemy force of five thousand men was moving through the jungle, south to southwest from Tetere, in an arc that would leave it in a commanding position in the hills south of the airfield. These were the troops Edson had missed at Tasimboko. To the west, the Matanikau line was growing more active, and forces of unknown size had landed in Rhoades's area.

For three or four days it was absolute hell, digging in at the new command post by day and then returning to the old area for the night. We were all exhausted when we started. I did not like the new site very much: it was far less accessible for my scouts, and the forward (southern) slope did not seem well protected. We were so busy with operations that I took the risk and kept as many scouts as possible at D-2 to get our "Ops" dugout completed. The one member of the section who had any pretensions toward either carpentry or engineering was a Marine named Barr, a strong, silent woodsman. He and the scouts worked day and night with a hammer, a Japanese saw, and a few picks and crowbars. There wasn't a flat piece of ground anywhere, and a floor had to be leveled for our rickety old marquee; at least it was well hidden by trees. In a morning bombing raid on 11 September the Japs laid a stick right on the ridge, and nearly scuppered the road to the new CP. The nighttime shelling—it sounded like cruisers—started up again; this time, it seemed, they were trying to plaster the whole area, and the new command post in particular. I wondered why.

The relocation of division headquarters was accompanied by a move of Edson's men to the southern part of the ridge. Ostensibly this was to provide them a rest area, for they had not had a night off since the August landings and were completely exhausted. Both his battalions[2] were seriously under strength: the Raiders were down to about three hundred, the Parachutists even fewer, and many of those who were left had malaria or stomach trouble. In reality, however, the move was part of defensive preparations against a Japanese attack from the south against Henderson Field.

On 12 September, with the CP in a half-finished state, the Raiders were "resting" round about us. It was an uneasy rest, and the ever-alert Edson kept sending out patrols. That night his suspicions were justified. South of the command post the Raiders' forward positions were attacked by the Japanese; these were obviously not stragglers, but part of a well-organized force. There was a mêlée in the jungle on the right bank of the Lunga River, and one Raider company got almost inextricably mixed up with a Japanese force. (It took them till morning to unravel themselves and retire.) Then an enemy cruiser and three destroyers opened up, and the whole thing became pandemonium.

As if that weren't enough, at 0800 a jeep suddenly arrived from the 5th Marines down at Kukum with Reverend Stibbard and half a dozen native pupils, who had endured a seven-day bush walk after the enemy had taken over his mission station at Maravovo. He was in a dreadful state, as they had neither eaten nor slept for three or four days and two of his lads had been shot by the Japanese en route. Rowley, his offsider, with whom Stibbard had temporarily separated, arrived with five other boys two hours later; I could hardly recognize him, with his shrunken face and his eyes popping out of his head. All I could do was give them six feet of floor space and tell them to lie down and stay down.

After that, everything began to happen very quickly. It looked as if we were the mugs again. Edson, well up with the game and knowing we could not form a continuous defensive line, had his chaps digging strong points all afternoon; the remains of the Parachute Battalion were committed on his left, almost in the D-2 section. At 1600 a company of Pioneers, apparently the only screen to the southwest between us and the river, withdrew through the CP before a large enemy force, believed to be at least twenty-five hundred strong, that was advancing to the attack.

The ridge on which the command post was being erected extended southeast about fourteen hundred yards before dropping steeply into the jungle. From the battle that ensued, it was given various names, but I always remember it as Raiders' Ridge. It was impossibly steep for normal defense, and quite out of the question for maneuver. The headquarters camp commandant, Colonel Gannon,[3] handed out more weapons to us chair-borne types and ordered all my scouts into the command post defense line. This was indeed an honor, but it signified that the situation was extremely grave. Gloom was rampant, and we knew we were in for a dirty night.

D-2 was buzzing with messages, but everyone, when he had a chance, sneaked down to the Ops dugout for a little determined digging. The Raiders' line was less than two hundred yards from us, and we were getting the Japanese "overs." My post, which I shared with a paratroop captain, was just below the Ops dugout, where the land fell steeply; a half dozen scouts held the line in the jungle at the foot of the hill, covering a gap and trying to prevent infiltrators. Earlier that day, our artillery, which had been emplaced on the Matanikau front, had been hastily pulled up, and soon the registration shots were whistling directly over our heads. The shells only just cleared the treetops; one, coming in a bit too low, blasted off the top of a tree just above the scouts and about level with our dugout. They had a narrow escape. The sky was full of tracers, and mortar explosions lit up the trees.

Our line fell back until it was just forward of the command post. Edson, lying on his belly only ten yards behind the line of attack, directed the whole thing. We heard the Japs yelling as they charged the Raiders with bayonets. It was a hell of a night.

Dawn broke to find the forest, our beautiful cover, a mass of leafless skeletons, mere firewood. A sigh of relief went up that we had withstood all that the Japanese had thrown at us throughout the night, but we had not reckoned with the snipers who had sneaked into our lines, and all that morning we had to operate on our bellies as bullets went whistling above. A loud bang revealed a sniper caught in what was to be General Vandegrift's new closet.

Several attempts were made to get a scratch breakfast to the men, but every time a few of them collected to pick it up somebody got winged by a sniper secreted in a thick glade right inside our position. My lads searched all day, and eventually got him.

There were several suicide efforts. Near D-1 (Administration and Personnel), a Japanese officer dashed out in the clear morning light and cut a sleeping Marine to ribbons with his sword before a Marine officer dispatched him. Another enemy soldier drew the attention of Marine Gunner Sheffield Banta, who was calmly typing. As calmly, Banta pulled out his pistol, shot the Jap dead, and, so the story had it, went on with his work.

It was a bit too hot for some of the newsmen, who were anxiously inquiring when the next boat would leave. A garrulous correspondent, whose name I did not get, arrived off a plane, saying that he had come all the way from London to get a story. I told him he had got here just in time. A bullet whanged past, and he only just got his head down. As he rammed his feet in my face, I discovered that he was wearing purple pajamas under his khakis. We found out nothing further about him, however, as he disappeared in the direction of the airfield and was not seen again!

By 1530 the last sign of resistance was over. We had lost an awful lot of men. Raiders and paratroopers sat around with hunched shoulders, faces gray and drawn, far too tired to speak. They were whacked to a standstill, and could not have lasted much longer. A few lucky ones read their mail, which had come the previous day. The slope at the south end of the ridge was a ghastly mess: the Japanese had charged time and again, only to be repulsed, and there were dozens of them lying there in grotesque attitudes in death. There were Marines there too.

Our artillery had arrived in the nick of time, for the Japs had a considerable number of mountain guns, and they were just about to open fire when our first salvo landed on their batteries. We were very lucky. Their headquarters, which was hit early on, had been hurriedly evacuated, yielding up a rich haul of code books and other important information. It was evident that we had been attacked by almost a whole brigade. They had marched at least twenty miles to the ridge, manhandling their guns.

Later we found out that the force landed at Tasimboko had been a strongly reinforced brigade of about five thousand men, commanded by a General Kawaguchi.[4] While we were busy on the ridge, one of their battalions attacked the strongly entrenched 1st Marines on the Tenaru, and was badly mauled. A sortie against the 5th Marines on the western perimeter fared no better. The attempt to attack us on three sides at once had narrowly failed.

Only Just Coping

The next three or four days were almost as bad as the battle, especially for us at D-2. There was no time to recover and no respite, as we were hard at work analyzing all the information and moving the CP back to our old spot. This time we dug in properly, but we still worked at Raiders' Ridge and then trudged down the hill to sleep. Everyone was desperately hungry, as the cooks had been continuously on the move, and the occasional cup of coffee and some crackers were about all we could get. The naval shelling continued, but we were so tired that we turned over and went to sleep in spite of it. "Too tired to write," I scribbled in my diary on 15 September. It was a dangerous state in which to be.

We were in very poor condition. Expected reinforcements could not get in, and trouble sought us out at every turn. As if fighting for our own survival wasn't bad enough, signals poured in asking for assistance all round. Rhoades was in dire distress, but as the western end of Guadalcanal seemed to be filling up with Japs it was impossible to assist him. There was no news of the Ruavatu missionaries, and the mob at Gold Ridge was hungry again!

At last, on 18 September, the 7th Marines managed to sneak in, bringing with them a good whack of supplies. We were terribly excited, and licked our chops at the prospect of a square meal. After getting Stibbard safely away to Vila on the convoy (Rowley and the pupils would be sent to Bishop Baddeley on Malaita), I returned from the beach, only to find two more people to look after. One was Butcher Johnstone, last seen going south in the *Ruana;* the other was John Mather. Mather, a great big, cheerful chap who had been a planter in the islands, had been working with the Australian forces. They were to report to Colonel Buckley, but were not quite sure what they were supposed to do. Johnno was in good form: when we got back to the old command post to sleep, he started looking a bit shifty and, fumbling in his pocket, whispered that he was in a dilemma. He had half a bottle of whiskey with him, but did not know what to do with it, as it would not suffice to give all the D-2 officers a drink! After a whispered conference in the dark, he sidled up to the colonel and gave him a good slug; his duty done, we then sneaked off toward the latrines and had a good crack at what was left. It was my first drink of the real McCoy, and very good for morale!

For the next few days I didn't know whether I was on my head or my feet. There were countless different matters to deal with, and the operational situation got no better. The 7th Marines, who had taken over Raiders' Ridge, were having sleepless nights with snipers and parties of stragglers. We also seemed to have drifted into intermittent action with the Japanese in the Matanikau area; it appeared to be a deadlock, for they held the commanding heights across the river and none of the Marine units could get across without casualties. This situation involved me in the problem of how to get an attacking force round the enemy's landward flank. Unfortunately, most of the land to be traversed was trackless virgin bush, and very few scouts knew anything about it.

Then Eroni arrived. He had sneaked through the fracas in his tiny launch with Capt. Marion Carl, a Grumman pilot, as passenger. Carl, one of our leading aces, had come down in the water off Aola and been rescued by Eroni's men. It was arranged for Eroni to take Pfc. Harry M. Adams, a Marine radio operator who had been working with Mackenzie, to Marau. There the two of them were to run another coastwatching post, with a special lookout for enemy submarines, which had begun to turn Marau into a "torpedo corner." There was a slight holdup over Eroni's departure, and a certain amount of soreness, as Mackenzie not only had been annoying about giving the necessary assistance (I had been so busy that I did not have stores ready for Eroni to take with him) but also had failed to get permission for Adams to go, and that rubbed Colonel Buckley the wrong way. The two men finally departed on 21 September.

Snowy Rhoades was having an awful time. With the Japanese spread all over north Guadalcanal, he had packed up and flitted to Tangarare, the more southerly Roman Catholic mission station. On the way he had run into Bishop Aubin, whose headquarters at Visale had been occupied by the enemy. The Japs had elbowed the missionaries out of the way and forced them to seek refuge in the bush. In accordance with the bishop's neutrality policy, the Catholics had not hidden any stores, and the Japanese had smartly confiscated everything. As a result the bishop had nearly died from dysentery, and his whole party was in a very weak state.

Another little job I had to attend to was to lecture the 7th Marines the following evening. Colonel Buckley had asked me to go and chat with their colonel about night tactics and noises, as his men were spooked by opossums in the trees—they sounded like snipers—and their jittery shooting kept other units tense too. When I arrived, I was alarmed to find all the officers and some of the NCOs drawn up on a grassy bank under the trees. Though quite unprepared—for a few moments I was bereft of speech—I managed to say something apposite and ended by making them laugh. They kept asking questions for another hour. I hope it did them some good.

The air boys were having a great time round the north end of Guadalcanal, bombing and strafing landing craft and dumps of supplies. The

Japanese were definitely building up in that area, and we could not stop them. There was even an enemy party on the north end of Malaita; I helped John Mather to make up a plan for attacking it that would give Bengough a chance to participate.

We had at last stopped moving backward and forward, and had settled at the old command post. As there had been no air raids all day, John and I did the work lying on our stomachs in a slight depression on top of the coral ridge above D-2. This, much to his embarrassment, had been christened "Mather's Hole." On the second day after he arrived, the air raid warning went and John, in his breezy way, sauntered up to the top of the ridge and said, "I think I'll have a dekko at what goes on from here." "No, you bloody well don't," I replied, "you jolly well come down here." After some rude banter, Mather eventually climbed down and joined us below ground. During the raid, bombs fell all round, and after it was over we had the greatest pleasure in showing him the hole that had been made by a light antipersonnel bomb on exactly the spot he had chosen! He stood and looked at it for about ten minutes, his mouth open in shocked amazement.

On 23 September, Colonel Puller and his battalion[5] set off to try to outflank the Japanese at Matanikau. Puller, a fellow pipe smoker, naturally appealed to me. He was a tough old soldier, and if anyone could get round the Japs he was the man. Peli went with them, and later Selea went out with the Raiders. The scouts were getting pretty thin on the ground, as they were attached to operations on both our eastern and our western sides, and there was still all the normal coverage to do outside the perimeter.

Dick Mangrum, now a lieutenant colonel, called to see us that afternoon, as there was no alert and his planes did not have to scatter. He brought with him a senior officer, Col. Charles L. Fike, the executive officer of MAG-23 and Mangrum's SBD wing commander. The colonel appeared greatly interested in the Solomon Islanders. One of his many questions unintentionally raised a laugh. He asked me whether they had been able to write before the advent of the white man; I replied, quite unwittingly, that they could not have done so as they had no paper. Colonel Buckley and the D-2 watch nearly burst themselves laughing! "He's got you there, colonel," they said, and I am certain that our guest was never quite sure whether I had pulled his leg or not.

Mangrum told us the air boss, General Geiger,[6] was tearing out his hair over a new dive-bombing squadron. The squadron had attacked the enemy's nightly destroyer resupply runs off Cape Esperance, but had not much to show for it. When the destroyers returned on 24 September, the SBDs once more attacked, again with little results, and the old brigadier, shaking in his camp chair with rage, told the pilots to keep going out until they had sunk something! They went at it again and again, badly damaging two ships and forcing the others to turn back from their destination.

For a couple of days it was relatively quiet, and Art Claffey and I went over to Henderson Field to return Mangrum's visit. By the side of the runway the Japs had left a small hillock, on top of which they had erected a wooden shack with a traditional-style roof. This, duly christened "the Pagoda" by the marines, became "Air Ops." Beside it was the radar van, which, owing to its unfortunate habit of warning us of a raid ten minutes after it occurred, had given rise to the expression "Go on, someone, buy the radar boys a cream puff." They had a shaky bamboo mast that could just be seen from D-2. When enemy planes were in the area, they hauled up a Japanese flag, and it was "Condition Yellow." When you saw someone rush out, haul down the red and white, and, if he had time, haul up the black flag, it would be "Condition Red," which meant that planes were overhead. (Incidentally, if you weren't a damned fool you were underground by now anyhow, having seen them overhead yourself!) It was nice to see so many aircraft scattered round the strip. I was especially interested in the torpedo bombers: they were called Avengers, but, owing to their shape and the fact that they carried their torpedoes inside the plane, some wag had described them as pregnant dormice!

The "Tokyo Express"

For the next two weeks there was a lull in the land fighting east of the Matanikau, as organized enemy units had been either exterminated or thrown back in considerable disorder. Our job, therefore, was to repel boarders and stop the Japs from landing more fighting units on the island. This was not so easy, as they had temporarily abandoned the remains of Kawaguchi's force to the east and were busy consolidating to the west and north. We could keep the seas covered with our planes during the day, but the Japanese had many methods of sneaking troops in during the night.

They had landing craft bases hidden at different points from Bougainville down to Guadalcanal. On the lines of "grandmother's footsteps," their barges would pop out as soon as it was dark and make one stage farther south along the sound, whose waters became known as "the Slot." Kennedy and Kuper were kept busy trying to locate these boat stages. The Japs also used fast destroyers and even cruisers to sweep close in to shore and land their troops, who were cast over the side, together with sealed drums full of rice, and left to swim ashore. This sort of thing was difficult to detect. Our naval strength was not such that we could risk battles with this nightly service, known by us all as the "Tokyo Express," and consequently we were wide open to being shelled. The enemy warships would drop their human cargo near Cape Esperance, steam down at high speed, throw a couple of salvoes at us, and disappear again, out of range of our dawn patrol.

The Japs to the east were mostly wandering about in search of food, which worried the islanders. In order to preserve their sense of martial superiority, they would attack us at night; the uncertainty of their activities kept the Marines, in large numbers, on the alert twenty-four hours round the clock.

None of us got very much rest, but we were able to get some semblance of order restored at D-2. We actually got a new tent with a raised wooden floor made of Japanese bed boards, and were still busy digging a proper dugout for the duty crew. Each morning everyone would start working on it, but as the day wore on Marines and scouts would gradually be drawn off for other jobs, and Tabasui, who had now become an assistant quartermaster, would be left to work on his own. He adopted the job cheerfully, and soon became clerk of the works, foreman, and labor force, all rolled into one. All the Marines used to stop by and razz him, but without him we would never have got the job done.

Mackenzie and Horton had been laboring away at a similar task. They were very proud when they finished theirs first, and the two of them dragged me out of bed to go and christen their new toy with a hell-brew made of ethyl alcohol tempered with grapefruit juice. After a death-defying jeep ride down the muddy edge of the airfield in the pitch dark without lights, we arrived safely under ground, and the honors were done. What a drink! It was lucky that "Washing Machine Charlie" was having a rest that night. I eventually got back safely to D-2 without getting lost, much to the annoyance of everyone I stumbled over in the dark!

During this lull I managed to get my scouting organization brought up to date and put on a regular pay basis. As many of the men were in other parts of the island and obviously could not be brought in, Daniel Pule did most of the hard work, writing notes to all the section leaders to get the nominal rolls completed.

My education in American slang and customs was developing with the assistance of the enlisted men at D-2. I no longer asked whether breakfast was ready, I merely said, "When's chow?" I also found out that when it was ready the master cook would announce, "Chow is down," not "Duff is up," as in the British Army. The sergeant major of the Headquarters Company was a hatchet-faced Brooklyn native called Hank Moran. To start with, I couldn't understand a word he said. When I called to find out if my scouts were being adequately fed, Moran would tell me, "We's cookin' wid gas, on de front boiler." (This indicated that things were going well.) I threatened to start a "front boiner" club!

Then there were the particularly Marine expressions, linked in many cases with their great tradition. The greatest of these was "the word." Some of the earliest Marines had continued to shoot from the maintop of John Paul Jones's flagship long after everyone else had given up. Their excuse afterward was that no one had passed "the word." Hence you asked what "the word" was—on reinforcements arriving, for example, or when we were going to be relieved. If it was merely the latest rumor you were inquiring about, however, or the latest figures for Japs at Tasimboko, you said, "What's the scuttlebutt?" or "What's the dope?" It probably originated at "the head," the Marine term for latrine. Following the nautical vein, senior officers would wave you into their bell tent from the mud outside with "Happy to have you aboard, sir!"

Someone would make a naïve inquiry such as, "You Marines serve on board ship, don't you?" The reply would be, "*Hell*, yes!" Or, if someone asked them if they had anything to do with the Army, the reply would be, "Them dogfaces? *Hell*, no!" The way they said it exhibited their pride in their Corps; it had bags of expression! We also had the more local forms of American to deal with. There was the boy from "Okie Finokie" (Okefenokee), who told me, in his Elizabethan drawl, that his captain "done gone went" to HQ. Then there was "Wimpy" Wendling from Kentucky, who told us all about "shilling-on-the-stump moonshine."

During the frequent periods of waiting for attacks, we had plenty of time to "bat the breeze." In the circle one night was Lieutenant Colonel

Twining, who had taken over Operations (D-3) as Thomas had been promoted to colonel and become General Vandegrift's chief of staff. We had been discussing the well-worn topic of colonialism in America, and had just about got the Boston Tea Party put "on a paying basis," when Twining suddenly cut up rough. "What's the matter, Bill?" Colonel Buckley asked. "It was our goddam tea they threw in the harbor!" Twining replied, in injured tones. On another occasion it took us some little time to convince the Wisconsin native that they grew apples in California.

My little black dog with the funny prick ears, Suinao, had been grand company in the bush; as I could not leave him behind, he had joined the Marines, and had got more or less used to military life. He would trot at my heels when we were on foot, but when I was jeep-borne he preferred to balance aggressively on the flat bonnet. As for air raids and bombardments, he soon learned to sense danger; like everyone else, when we got Kennedy's morning message—for example, "22 Bettys, yours 1100," meaning that twenty-two bombers would be over us in, say, twenty minutes—he would seek out the nearest tree, do his business, and be ready to go down below as soon as Condition Red was sounded! The detonations of bombs or shells used to hurt his ears, and the poor creature would sit in my lap, whimpering gently, and let me hold my hands over them. On patrol, however, he was usually the first to sense danger, and if there were Japs within two hundred yards he would pause like a pointer, his hackles would rise, and he would emit an almost soundless growl. He was a fine companion, and most of the Marines were quite prepared to put up with him. It was not long before he was christened "Sui, the jeep hound."

Someone, in a flash of brilliance, suggested that eating fish would make up for the lack of fresh stuff in our diet. There was nothing wrong with the idea, but to catch a regular supply of fish for fifteen thousand men under front-line conditions was a major operation. I paid a visit to the beachmaster, Commander Dexter, of the Coast Guard.[7] He was quite keen, and we decided to do some experimental trolling from a landing craft. It was with a certain amount of misgiving that we went down toward Matanikau three days later. I felt that we were being watched by a thousand eyes, and if the engine stopped the Japs would be only too eager to dispatch us. Fortunately, we got back all right; unfortunately, we caught nothing, because the boat was too fast and noisy and there was oil on the water from the many ships that had been sunk in the neighborhood. We decided that hand grenades thrown into the water whenever shoals of fish appeared would fill the pot much quicker. For this purpose the grenades were designated "Nobel spinners"!

Extramural Operations

The lull enabled us to get all available scouts out checking the state of the Japs to the east. After a bit we had a pretty clear picture, but it seemed that the only static lot was the party at Gorabusu. This consisted of the fifty men who had settled at Taivu Point and who, just before the marines arrived, had sailed down to Marau, where they had interrogated the Catholic fathers and brothers. After their lugger was sunk, they had walked up the coast, accompanied by my scout Laena, who was still keeping an eye on them. The party was still in radio contact with the Japanese Navy, and it was not beyond the bounds of possibility that they were being contacted from time to time by submarine. It was decided that they should be put out of action, together with any other small parties in the area. The troops would come from Tulagi; I was to be responsible for scouting out the details, for getting our force into contact with the Japanese, and for supplying the necessary scouts and carriers.

On Sunday, 27 September, Colonel Buckley and I were sitting outside D-2, quietly discussing the Gorabusu "do" with Colonel Arthur,[8] whose Marines were slated for the job. Suddenly, the quiet of that peaceful afternoon was rudely shattered by Japanese planes, which scattered a mass of antipersonnel bombs throughout our area. We dove for our new dugout just in time, and when we emerged we found that bombs had gone off on either side of us, only twenty yards and twenty-four yards away. One had made holes through everything in our operations tent, including our beautiful, up-to-the-minute information maps and the colonel's cot, which had already suffered on several previous occasions. The other bomb had landed three yards from where the door of our tent had been; our gear, camp beds, bed boards, and tent had been blown back against the coral ridge and smashed to smithereens.

Of the eight officers using the tent, most lost everything. What we collected hardly filled half a kit bag. Of my gear, all I salvaged was a small haversack full, together with my three volumes of Shakespeare and my diary, which were badly splintered. Three red-hot pieces of jagged metal had entered the bottom of my kit bag and gone systematically through everything, ending up in a canvas mend-all at the other end. Everything had to be thrown away, but I kept a handkerchief that had been in the path of the shrapnel: when unfolded it displayed a charming lacework pattern! I thought I had saved my bedding roll, but the kapok mattress was full of hot splinters, and after twenty minutes it was on fire. What hurt me most was the loss of two good pipes and my RAAF wideawake hat. They were irreplaceable.

As we had no warning we were very lucky that no one in the section was killed, but the officers now had no tent, no floor, no nothing—just a big hole. The kunai grass, which had been eighteen inches high where it wasn't trampled, had been shaved off close to the ground as clean as a whistle for fifty yards on either side. As a final insult there remained but two articles on our telephone-wire wash line. These were a pair of knee-length woollen stockings, to wear with shorts, which I had acquired from a departing correspondent and which I had just washed. They had been sheared off about six inches above the ankle, and the feet were nowhere to be found. Jolly mean, I called it. We were all highly indignant. It was Sunday, too! There were more than fifty planes, which had come over in two waves; our only satisfaction was that the bombers were thoroughly shot up by the Grummans, and several didn't get back.

By some mischance of fate, Eroni and Pfc. Adams had not yet got to Marau to open up the antisubmarine radio watch. They had set out in Eroni's launch, but it was grossly overloaded, and they were forced to return. I then got a landing craft under our Coast Guard coxswain, Ray Evans, to escort them to Aola. Adams set up the wireless there—it was my old set, carried down from Paripao—but it would not work, so he had to bring it in for repairs. Bingiti brought him up in the small launch. Evans returned to Aola with Adams and the repaired set, together with five Raiders, under Sergeant Pettus,[9] whom we had borrowed from Colonel Edson. They had orders to make a preliminary reconnaissance of the Japs at Gorabusu and, as we could contact them through Adams, do any specific scouting jobs that we might find necessary. Thus, unknowingly, Adams and my old set became the nucleus of our second line of defense, based on the cadet's house behind the station.

On 1 October Admiral Nimitz,[10] Commander-in-Chief, Pacific

(CinCPac, as he was known telegraphically), who had flown in the night before in a Flying Fortress, held a "formation" at General Vandegrift's hut at six thirty in the morning. Everyone was very pleased to see him, and we got the idea that he was quite pleased with the Marines' performance. The admiral started by pinning a Navy Cross onto General Vandegrift's breast. The general went quite pink in the face, and appeared "fair dumbfounded"—it seemed he knew nothing about it. Colonel Edson got a Navy Cross for Raiders' Ridge; Colonels Cates and Pollock, for the Tenaru.

The air boys were well represented. Colonel Mangrum was awarded the Navy Cross, for the huge tonnage of shipping he and his men had sunk under such trying conditions. Major Smith, the leading fighter ace, Major Galer,[11] the CO of VMF-224, and Captain Carl, who would have equaled Smith's performance had he not had to spend a few days with Eroni at Aola, were similarly decorated. Everyone was in combat dress with helmets, except for the admiral, who wore the standard combination cap, and the fighter boys, who had on the dark blue baseball caps that they wore in the air.

Operation "Bunch o' Nuns"

As for Rhoades, his position was getting "wusser and wusser." He and Schroeder were both suffering from malarial fever, and with Bishop Aubin and his party also at Tangarare their food situation was pretty bad. Snowy had no freedom of movement—he was liable to be picked up at any time —so he could not give us much useful information. I managed to arrange for a Catalina to go round and rescue them, but the trip had to be canceled a couple of times owing to a shortage of planes for reconnaissance.

Following these delays, the bishop started agitating to have the fathers and sisters evacuated as well. This put me in a very awkward position, as he had previously refused to evacuate and had promised me that he would not call for help. Now, when we had practically no facilities for this sort of thing, I had to go and ask General Vandegrift to divert combat materiel to get him out.

The general, quite rightly, was infuriated that we had to consider a rescue mission in the middle of a war. "A goddam bunch o' nuns," he kept muttering. Rhoades's last signal, however, sounded a note of urgency: "Bishop requests also evacuation of native nuns, as if left behind will be raped." That tipped the scale in the prelate's favor, and another Catalina was approved.

Then we discovered that Mackenzie, unbeknownst to anybody and without authority, had arranged with Bengough[12] for the *Ramada* to go and pick up Rhoades, Schroeder, and Bishop Aubin and his party. This was even more confusing—now the general would think that Mackenzie and Bengough intended to land the missionaries at Lunga and leave the rest to him. He saw red, and Colonel Buckley and I had to take Mackenzie in to be hauled over the coals.

As the *Ramada* had already left Malaita, the Catalina was canceled. The schooner was unarmed; her sides and awnings were painted black and gray, respectively, and she was marked with two white crosses for identification. *Ramada*'s diesel engine gave her a speed of six knots. She was captained by Peter Sasambule, one of the senior native skippers, who could find his way blindfolded into almost every anchorage in the Solomons. He arrived on 3 October with three Japanese in custody, whom Bengough had picked up from a crashed airplane; two of Bengough's lads, Baethisara and Tome, remained on board as guards until I could transport them. Peter was not at all keen when he heard what his orders were, but he was slightly reassured when told that Dick Horton would accompany him.

The trip was rather risky. As they had to go past so much enemy-occupied territory, they headed out into the open channel early in the afternoon with the intention of making a horizon circle, and with one of our fighter planes keeping an eye on them. They had been gone only two hours when Kennedy signaled that six Japanese destroyers had been spotted about 140 miles away.[13] This meant that the enemy would be at the north end of Guadalcanal by 0400. The Dauntlesses and Avengers, though not equipped for night flying, kept going out until well after dark; they harried the Japs quite successfully, and early next morning Snowy signaled that the *Ramada* had arrived safe and unharmed.

With enemy destroyers in the vicinity, we kept our heads pretty low that night, but did not receive the expected shelling. (The troops they had landed no doubt would attack us at some later date.) When we were lucky enough to expect shelling, as opposed to being blown out of bed by it, I had the technique "wrapped up." Taking a waterproof cape to lie on, I would turn in on the parapet of our dugout, and when either we got the word or the first salvo exploded, or a star shell illuminated the scene, I would roll almost automatically over the brow. If awake, I would make my way into the dugout; if still comatose, I'd get swept in by the crowd.

While we were getting Horton and the *Ramada* away, a signal came in that Macfarlan, at long last, was coming to join us. The following morning a truck arrived with several scouts; they had a white man with them, but he was not the one we were expecting. Mac had had a touch of malaria, and the party had proceeded without him. They brought a U.S. Navy flyer, Bill Warden,[14] who had made a forced landing in the Slot near Ysabel on 7 August. Taken south by the current, he fetched up in the Russell Islands, luckily at a different bay from that occupied by the Japanese. A few days later he paddled across to the northwest coast of Guadalcanal, where friendly islanders brought him to Rhoades and he was taken in by Father de Klerk at Tangarare. The Japanese were starting to close in, and Warden, having recovered from his privations on Catholic chicken and pineapple, felt it his duty to report for service. Against all advice he walked to Gold Ridge, rigged up in Father de Klerk's rather clerical clothes; it was no wonder that when he arrived no one could recognize him! As the scouts had managed to avoid meeting any enemy troops, and as they had brought in some carriers, I got busy collecting rations to go back to the hungry hunters at Gold Ridge.

Later, the *Ramada* returned safely with Snowy Rhoades, well bearded; Lafe Schroeder; a rescued airman; Bishop Aubin, dressed in white and clasping his umbrella; six priests; six European nuns; and the native nuns. Our supply ships, having run the gauntlet of the Japanese Navy, were off-loading fuel and supplies and onloading hospital cases and prisoners as fast as they could. Landing craft went busily back and forth from the shore, and the screening destroyers steamed silently up and down the channel.

Into the midst of this activity came the tiny *Ramada,* loaded to the waterline with her heterogeneous cargo. As they dropped anchor, the fighter plane that had escorted them dipped low in salute to a good job, well done. We were standing by in a landing craft to direct unloading, and soon we had the fathers scrambling up the bosun's ladder onto the *Fomalhaut,* one of the cargo ships. Next were the sisters, who, in spite of the climate, were in typical nuns' robes; in any case, most were of such an age as made it impossible for them to go up the bosun's ladder. After a lot of shouting and waving of arms, the little mail boat was lowered and the nuns transferred to it. It was then smoothly hauled up the tall side of the ship by block and tackle, to the resounding cheers of all around. As the boat reached the deck, the anchor came up and the convoy slipped away into the gathering darkness.

The native nuns remained on the *Ramada* overnight; at D-2 we sarcastically speculated whether they were really safer with Sasambule and his crew than they would have been with the Japanese! While Rhoades and company were swept away by Mackenzie, I took Bishop Aubin to call on General Vandegrift.

The general had worked up a good head of steam. When the bishop arrived, however, his wrath evaporated: the poor man, who had undergone great privations, looked haggard and emaciated, and on his last legs. General Vandegrift could not help but be kind to him. He greeted the bishop with the greatest courtesy, poured a generous dram of Old Crow, and even managed (as I had daringly urged him) not to mention the "bunch o' nuns." The bishop stayed the night; bright and early in the morning we got him and the native sisters off to Malaita in the *Ramada,* en route picking up Rowley and his pupils, who had got as far as Tulagi. Thus was satisfactorily completed Operation "Bunch o' Nuns."

Since the beginning of October the weather had changed. We had several days of heavy rain, during which the whole area was turned into a sticky bog of black mud. It made life in our sleeping quarters intolerable, but whenever we could we got down to the Lunga River and washed it all away.

There was no rest for the wicked. I provided detailed instructions for Evans, who had to go and pick up the Raider recce party from Aola. Once the Japs attacked us from the west it would be a fight to the death, and we might not be able to spare anyone for operations like Gorabusu. Then the carriers for Gold Ridge had to be got away; poor old Mackenzie, who was just as overworked as we were, got very snappy because they had to leave before he had got his letters ready for Hay, who was to continue to operate Macfarlan's teleradio as an air warning post at Gold Ridge.

Back at D-2, Rhoades and Schroeder gave us their information on the occupied northwest. We made them put it on our map while two stenographers took down everything they said. Snowy had had a rough time, with malaria and stomach problems into the bargain; he was in poor shape, but he had certainly earned his keep. We did not vote him many marks for his beard, however, as, although it had grown well, it was part blond and part gray! Although he had lost a lot of weight, the addition of a khaki-topped naval cap gave Snowy a jaunty air, and he cut a great figure when I took him to call on the general, who congratulated him on his work.

Mac Arrives at Last

Not to be outdone, Macfarlan, accompanied by four scouts (Deke, Vura, Tabasui, and Sepo), finally came in from Gold Ridge at 1630 on 5 October. He was dressed in his "fin de siècle" whites, but the pièce de résistance was his terrific black beard: in Australian slang, it was a real "boomer." Mac got a wonderful reception, and it was definitely "old home week" at D-2 as he, Snowy, and I got down to swapping our experiences. The next day, while we were busy getting the two of them suitably clothed, the reconnaissance party returned from Aola with splendid coverage of Gorabusu and the two or three other small Japanese posts nearby. Legu Legu also reported in, having patrolled as far as Koli Point with a company of Cates's marines. As expected, they had met few enemy troops, since most of the Japs were well off the coast.

To complete the picture, John Mather, who had managed to get across to Malaita in the Grumman Duck after about six false starts, returned at last with a master plan for putting the Japs there out of action. He had done his best to explain to Bengough how things were with us, but it did not stop the latter from writing me a note casually asking me to send him over a thousand cigarettes! As the twenty-seven of us at D-2 had carefully shared out two hundred between us the day before, and we were lucky to get them, I wondered whether Bengough thought I was a magician!

The Japs' efforts to build up their forces on Guadalcanal for another attack had been unremitting; there was no doubt that something pretty solid was looming. One positive development in the situation was that our air force was becoming much stronger, and the daily raids of between fifteen and thirty enemy bombers were regularly losing a significant number of planes. We had no need to exaggerate the number of aircraft shot down, as Read, sitting close to their home airfield, used to let us know how many got back the same evening. Since 7 August, Japanese losses in the air had amounted to three or four hundred planes.

Although the Japanese planes continued to hammer away at Henderson Field, they were beginning to show an interest in mowing us down too. Every now and then a group of Zeros would zoom in at low level and let fly with explosive bullets, all over the shop. If they thought they were lowering our morale, they were wrong. If anything, they raised it. You couldn't do that sort of thing to Marines without inviting a reply. Everyone opened up with whatever they had, rifles and machine guns, and even we at D-2 would dash out and bang away with our pistols as the Zeros dived across no higher than the top of the coconut trees. "*Hell,* yes!"

It was a highly dangerous sport, but there is no doubt that it paid off, for quite often a Zero would crash through the palms, untouched by our bigger guns, and hit the ground with a satisfying thump. I used to enjoy it most when I was down at the naval base: I would sit with my back to a coconut tree and take them from left to right with a tommy gun as they strafed the plantation house at Kukum, which was Commander Dexter's headquarters. Dexter himself had a monster weapon, well dug in and protected by sandbags. It was a three-barreled Jap machine gun, a veritable Chicago piano, and until the ammunition ran out it did great service.

My education in American slang was added to by the arrival of Snowy Rhoades. He kept talking about the bush, going into the bush, hiding in the bush, etc., and Colonel Buckley said to him one day, "Hey, Snow, what is all this bush?" Snowy, in quite serious vein, described at length the country behind Lavoro. The colonel laughed and said, "Oh, you mean the boondocks." (The term "boondocks" was apparently used fairly generally in America for "unimproved ground"; thus, by extension, "boondockers" were boots specially made for pioneering, and to go "boondocking" was to make a bush trip.) Rhoades, completely stumped, pulled his pipe out of his mouth and sat eyeing the colonel suspiciously. In return, Snowy obtained the everlasting admiration of the Marines for the delightful intonation he gave to a much-used Australian word. He would tell a long tale of the iniquities of the Japs in his area, and at the end, raising his eyebrows slightly, he would softly mutter, "B-a-a-astards." Everyone at D-2 practiced it for days!

Macfarlan, Rhoades, and Schroeder were to be sent off on leave via Tulagi when opportunity offered, as none was in good shape and it looked as if life was going to be pretty tough. They had had their share. The pressure of work at D-2 was relentless, however, so, wearily waving them goodbye, we got down to it again.

20

Backs to the Wall

COLONEL THOMAS, the new chief of staff, was very keen to step up the information that we received through my scouts from outside the perimeter. I was humbly glad that he attached such importance to it, but, quite apart from the steady drain of casualties, most of the Marine units were being decimated by malaria and stomach trouble, and we could not afford to waste our efforts. At any event, I was hastily ordered to get on with the Gorabusu show as soon as possible; grabbing stores and ammunition, I was off to Aola in double-quick time on 7 October. Major Enright,[1] who would direct the attack, and I had arranged code words for signaling and rendezvous for the arrival of the troops at Aola. With Adams and the teleradio there, we could contact division headquarters.

The Attack on Gorabusu

Thomas told me that if plans had to be changed I could issue instructions and inform him afterward.[2] That suited me down to the ground. We were making the trip in an ordinary personnel landing craft (LCP) with a diesel engine; it was not the ideal vessel for a longish sea trip at night, but I was reassured by the presence of Ray Evans, who was becoming our own private coxswain. A petty officer in the Coast Guard, in which his Welsh father, a master mariner, had also served, Evans was a real seaman, and it took a lot to worry him.[3] There were seven others in the party: Cpl. Ralph E. "Wimpy" Wendling; Cpl. Vernon C. Stimpel; Pfc. Gerald F. Koepplinger; Pfc. Warner; Michael, the cook; and two scouts.

Saying goodbye to Commander Dexter at Kukum, we were off just after 1700, bumping along in the gathering darkness into a steady southeast wind and showers of rain. There was no cover in the boat, and we all were soon soaked to the skin. It was only our weapons we kept dry. Evans and I worked out a distance-time reckoning, but at 2130, when we headed in toward land, there was so much rain about that making a landfall was impossible. We went on at half speed until at 0030 a rift in the rain revealed a rock near Rere Point, which I recognized; knowing that there were no Japanese between Rere and Aola, we hugged the coast and got in safely an hour later. Andrew, Daniel Pule, and the rest of the Aola detachment were on the alert, and we soon had our stuff unloaded and carted up to the cadet's house.

At 0730 there was an alarm. Three Japs had appeared on the far bank of the Aola River; they had probably heard us the night before in spite of the storm, and were busy trying to discover if there was anything to be seen. Evans and Wendling rushed down to take the guns off the landing craft, which had unfortunately broached to on the beach, while the rest retired behind the station. Luckily, Adams and the teleradio were well hidden in the bush about a mile away. By 1130 the Japanese, having seen nothing outrageous, had been allowed to return to Gorabusu.

Up at the cadet's house I had Daniel and Andrew put all the latest information from Gorabusu onto sketch maps, which could be used by the attacking force. The district headman, Kilua, came in; he was sent off to mobilize all available able-bodied men to serve as scouts and carriers and to collect food supplies for us.

Evans was wrestling with the landing craft on the beach. This was one of the fairly early models, known as a Higgins boat; it had neither a bow ramp nor a proper stern cable. He had nearly got it off the sand when the governor broke down. That was that—there was no possibility of its returning to Lunga. If the Japs chose to walk down to Aola and found the boat there before we attacked them, the fat would be in the fire. This was all duly reported, but we got on with the job.

Apart from the Marines' weapons, we could muster only fourteen good rifles. There were also a few Japanese weapons, which might or might not fire but which could be used with bayonets. Putting out an elaborate night watch, most of whom were unarmed, we turned in on the concrete floor to sleep as if on feather beds, knowing that we would not be shelled or bombed. It was a marvelous treat, and I found that a tin hat made an excellent pillow. There were several false alarms, caused by land crabs' creeping over the recumbent figures; luckily no one got shot! The watch covered all tracks entering the government station, and, as far as gathered later, the Japs stayed home.

In the morning everyone was on the qui vive. At 0820 we sent a signal by Adams to say that all was prepared, while Wendling took a patrol along the back road to have a look at the Japanese. Wimpy, a Kentucky highlander, could shoot straight and walk the hind leg off a donkey but, as he put it, couldn't spell worth a damn. With him went Warner, Daniel, Gumu, and Bingiti; Daniel and Gumu were old hands at the game after Captain Brush's show, and Bingiti had gained his experience on Tulagi. We were all rather happy that we were not going to get bombed that morning, and after the patrol had gone the rest of us sat out in the sun and watched the considerable friendly air activity with a certain amount of academic interest.

After lunch, one of Michael's classic repasts made up from rations and local produce, we got a message that the operation would proceed according to plan. Wimpy returned safely from his patrol to say that all the Japs appeared to be in camp. By 2300 the watch was out and everyone mustered on the beach waiting for our Marines to arrive. Just before midnight we heard a vessel, which being so early might not have been friendly, but it was difficult to know how far sound carried. At 0050 on 10 October a landing craft successfully answered the challenge, however, and at 0130 Lieutenant Colonel Hill[4] came ashore. He had apparently taken over from Major Enright at the last minute. The colonel told us that the Marines, in eight landing craft, were being towed by two converted tuna fishing boats, which were now used primarily as supply vessels between Tulagi and Guadalcanal. ("Yippees," they were called, after their designation, YP.) They were supposed to land everyone before daylight. Unfortunately, the tow lines weren't long enough; in the swell, one of the LCPs had its bow wrenched out off Taivu Point, and fifteen Marines and three Navy crewmen were drowned. The first lot of Marines landed about 0830, and were dispersed all round Aola. The second YP and its remaining landing craft got in about 1230, leaving the enemy in no doubt as to what was going on. At least we thought so.

Instead of our fourteen rifles we now had nearly five hundred, but not all to attack Gorabusu—we needed some to hold Aola while we were doing it, and in case we drew the attention of larger parties farther up the coast. Our plans were soon worked out, and Colonel Hill departed at 1450 to attack the smaller parties farther west toward Ruavatu and Koilotumuria and to cut off any retreat from Gorabusu. With him went Daniel in charge of eight scouts, with thirty carriers to haul the teleradio and ammunition boxes. The Gorabusu force, a greatly reduced company of about ninety men from Company C, together with my little party and the other section of scouts, left at midnight.

I did not know it then, but Gerry Koepplinger was one of the best pistol shots in America. Colonel Buckley had sent him along to see that I got back unscathed. He didn't let the colonel down.

The Marines' company commander, Capt. Richard T. Stafford, was a tall, well-built young man, keen as mustard on his first independent action. We had six or seven miles to go, but had to do it all in the pitch dark. Unfortunately, after the rain of the last few days the track was pretty muddy, and, as there were deep rainwater ditches dug on either side, chaps soon were disappearing in the blackness. I quickly realized that moving a whole company in the dark was quite different from taking a patrol of half a dozen men. We therefore stopped, and I made each man put a piece of highly phosphorescent rotten wood in his belt at the back, so he could see the Marine in front of him. My lads scouted ahead silently, and although within the company the noise was terrific it was pretty quiet two hundred yards forward with the scouts.

The chaps I felt sorry for were the mortar plate men. They had to use two hands to carry their plates, which were very heavy, and they had a thin time of it slipping about in the mud. On the whole, however, we managed quite well, and there were no alarms. At 0530 on 11 October the machine gun platoon separated, to take the eastern position. Thirty minutes later our support platoon with the mortars broke off into the bed of the

Gorabusu River, which luckily was dry as there had been no rain in the bush. This was a made-to-order operation. The scouts were there before the detachments, waiting to direct them to their correct positions.

Meanwhile, Captain Stafford and I with the two rifle platoons went right round the flank to the west. We were closer in than I expected, but the cover was fairly thick and we were assisted by a sharp rain shower. It had been arranged for the machine gunners to give us the signal by opening fire shortly after 0630, but there was a considerable holdup as they did not think very much of their fields of fire. The scouts went backward and forward with messages, with the rain pouring down, while we lay in extended order on our sloping line of departure. I was getting pretty anxious at the delay, as I was worried that the Japs would send out a foraging party before we got organized. Owing to the slope our bodies acted as miniature dams, and every few minutes we had to raise ourselves off the mud and let the accumulated water run away. It was also difficult to keep the rain out of our weapons.

In spite of the downpour I could feel myself sweating. Apart from the butterflies in my stomach, the coldness of the rain was also giving me the gripes. I feverishly thought over every little detail we'd planned. The operation must not fail. It was already light, and even if the Japs didn't go foraging might they not, if the rain stopped, just walk out to see what the weather was like? Would those guns never open fire? Would our weapons work?

At last, at 0830, after what seemed a million years, the machine gunners opened up. We slithered into action and, when the Japanese returned our fire, took cover behind some felled coconut logs. Their fire was fairly thin, and after a bit we thought we had reduced resistance to the point where we could make a run in.

We should have waited longer. Captain Stafford put his head up above his coconut log for a look-see and took a bullet straight between the eyes. He was killed instantly. I was right next to him; this was not the time to falter, so I immediately went through, and the rest followed. After a short hand-to-hand struggle, in which I had a narrow shave with an enemy sword, the remaining Japanese fled into the arms of the machine gunners.

From the scouts with the machine gun platoon I heard that about fifteen Japanese had, as I had feared, left the area at dawn; the machine gunners had narrowly missed bumping into them. They had been left with a scout shadowing them in order not to rouse the main party; they were the cause of the delayed attack.

We killed twenty-seven in the bivouac area, some of them not even out of bed; but no one could identify Ishimoto. Some of the enemy were six feet tall, and all wore naval badges. There was a guard up a large nut tree, but luckily someone happened to look up before he opened fire, and he was brought down. Two sentries on the beach whom we missed were caught by the scouts later. My lads combed the area for any other odd Japs who might have been skulking in the brush. One platoon took up defensive positions to cover our withdrawal to the shore, where we were to be picked up. Meanwhile, the D-2 party and I sorted out much valuable Japanese equipment, which included a lot of radio stuff and marked charts obviously illustrating points on the route of the "Tokyo Express."

The Murder of the Missionaries

I had pretty definite evidence before we left Lunga that the Catholics from Ruavatu had been murdered, but no trace of them had as yet been found. We knew that the men we had just attacked had first taken them into custody. It was rumored that after the Tenaru battle the Japanese wanted to send one priest to urge the Americans to surrender, because they thought the whole invasion fleet had been sunk; the others would be kept as hostages. Later we found out that the missionaries declined to do this and so were ordered released. In late August, however, the Japs returned to Ruavatu and arrested them; taken to Tasimboko for questioning, the missionaries were accused of sending military intelligence messages to the Americans. They remained under guard in a small native hut at Tasimboko until about 3 September, when all were brutally murdered except poor old Sister Edmée, who had been left at Ruavatu suffering from elephantiasis and malarial fever, and escaped into the bush with the orphan girl in her care.[5]

Amongst the Japanese equipment we found the chalice and most of the altar cloths and vestments of the mission. The chalice had been used as an ashtray and one of the altar cloths as a blanket. The latter was wrapped round one of the Japanese, who was still in bed. It had given him no protection. My stomach revolted to see him. As at the Tenaru, the sight of the sprawling, inanimate bodies appalled me. Here I had taken an even more active part, but still I could not choke off my imagination. "Why, why?" "If . . ." "There but for the grace of God . . ." I quickly turned away and busied myself with equipment.

My lads, who had done splendidly, were exultant. Laena got back the machine gun that he had carried for the Japanese all the way from Marau. Solomon Islanders did not seem to suffer from morbid thoughts. In the small wars of their ancestors, success consisted of the total elimination of the enemy; that was not attempted unless the chances were really good, so there was nothing more to fear after the battle. They were all very short of clothing, and most of them had parked their lavalava with their haversack and valuables along the track, going into action naked except for their ammunition belt. As soon as the action was over they retrieved their belongings and soon were properly dressed—mostly in Japanese blackout cloth, which was the latest dash!

Having got the Marines and Captain Stafford's body safely embarked, I took the remaining landing craft, firmly requisitioned by Ray Evans, and went up the coast to meet Colonel Hill. He had found but one largish party, which he surprised completely, killing three but losing one of his own men, with one wounded. The rest of the enemy had plunged off the track into a bottomless swamp, from which the locals said there was no exit. He had wisely left them there to prove it. Large dumps of stores were discovered, as well as several three-inch antiaircraft guns complete with ammunition. They would have played havoc with our transport planes. What pleased Daniel's quartermasterly mind, however, was twenty one-hundred-pound bags of Japanese rice, which he arranged to send down to Aola to give the islanders a victory feast! Colonel Hill ordered evacuation of the area and a return to Aola. We had a fairly accurate tab on the stray Japanese, and scouts were left to eliminate them as opportunity offered.

An Unexpected Shower, and Other Surprises

Setting off back to Aola, we immediately found ourselves under the middle of a fierce air battle. Some twenty Bettys, chased away from Lunga, were being pounced on by Airacobra fighters overhead. They jettisoned their bombs in the sea right in front of us. Evans did wonders with our landing craft as we all did our best to shrink into the bottom of the boat. Luckily all we got was the spray. The air above became an absolute mêlée, and bullets and empty cartridge cases fell all round. Then planes started to crash into the sea about us. One of ours came down in a terminal dive at terrific speed. The pilot cleared his plane a bare hundred feet from the sea, hitting the water so hard that all his clothes came off. We picked him up but he died ten minutes afterward. Another pilot we rescued had gashed his eye very badly—in fact, it was hanging out—but when we got to Aola Eroni, good doctor that he was, stuck it back in and covered it with gauze and plaster. The flyer was a lucky chap, for he was back in action a month later! We also picked up another of our own pilots and one Japanese, both in poor condition.

I was quite relieved to get back to Aola: we were all washed out, but it seemed safer somehow! A message came from D-2 via Adams that Colonel Hill's men could stay on at Aola for a day or so if I thought it necessary. It also intimated that Lunga was under pretty solid attack from the west, and they wanted no nonsense from the east. The colonel agreed to wait until the next day and give his men a rest. They had earned it. All was quiet that night, but we kept a two-hour watch just in case.

In the morning Daniel took a patrol back to Gorabusu to see whether the remaining Japs had turned up. There was no sign of them, but more charts and some interesting notebooks, which we had overlooked, were brought back. Colonel Hill's transport turned up just after noon. It consisted of only one of the Yippee boats; the other one had broken down. After a lot of frenzied radio messages, division HQ accepted my suggestion that one company walk back along the coast to Tenaru and clear our eastern wing. The company was quite pleased; the colonel wasn't, but he left one LCP to get those of us from D-2—"Buckley's crystal ball outfit" —back home. I doubt if Ray Evans would have let him take it with him.

That evening, with a company of Marines to guard us, we had what might be described as almost a party at the cadet's house. There was nothing to drink, but we all gathered round the old wood stove in the kitchen while Michael produced a meal to end all meals. He hadn't had very much to work on, but one of the star numbers was pawpaw, hollowed out, stuffed with C-ration hash and beans, and baked in the oven. To go with this we had some pannas, small cigar-shaped yams that, when broiled on top of the stove, tasted like floury potatoes. A pigeon or two appeared from somewhere, and Michael produced a marvelous fruit pie all cooked in a couple of ordinary mess tins baked in the oven. There was a great argument as to whether it was "deep dish" or not.

The funny thing was that we could hardly wait until it was ready, and as the savory smells came from the kitchen we all gradually edged nearer and nearer in order to be first in line. Soon everyone was round the stove advising Michael. There was nothing peculiar about it, we were just normal human beings with a very abnormal hunger; as soon as chow was ready, we fell to and massacred the lot in very short order. As we had been absolved from guard duty that night, we sank blissfully onto the concrete, and most of us were soon noisily asleep. What a beautiful night!

At 0215 on 13 October the alarm went—the sound of diesel engines to seaward and to the northeast. Although it might have been one of our own submarines, we deduced it was a Japanese sub attempting to contact Gorabusu—which had, of course, gone off the air the day before. We got a signal off pretty smartly in case a plane was available at dawn, but we held our breath in case the sub either shelled Aola or landed a party. At dawn we breathed again—all quiet to seaward and nothing stirring.

Hiking, up to Date

In the morning, Lt. Thomas Leineweber and his ninety-two men departed on their patrol up to Tenaru, enemy permitting. I sent along one section of scouts and another of carriers. The former, besides accompanying them the whole way, were to contact the other scouts in each area, who would keep them in touch with enemy movements and show them the paths. In charge went a cheery rascal called Bunga, a retired sergeant of police. Either he was color-blind or he knew nothing of camouflage, for he paraded in a pair of vividly colored undershorts covered with two-inch black and white squares! They were delayed by the headman's carrier party, who were still celebrating our victory, but got away about 1030.

I spent most of the morning straightening out affairs with Andrew and Daniel, and was just beginning to feel pleased that everything was in order again, when a message came in from Adams that an enemy cruiser-destroyer force had been sighted. The pleasant feeling vanished; now, I thought, we would "cop it." I decided that we had better be off quickly enough to reach Lunga by daylight. Hastily bidding farewell to Adams and Eroni, who with the teleradio working properly could at last proceed to Marau, we scrambled on board our Higgins boat just before noon and made our way up the coast. Off Koli Point we found ourselves in the middle of another big air raid. Evans stopped the engine, and we again tried to look as small as possible. Two transports and two destroyers were lying off near Tenaru. At first we weren't sure whether they were ours or theirs—"Whose?" we whispered—but then they put up a great barrage and evaded serious damage, which left no doubt as to whose they were. Everyone heaved a sigh of relief, but we nearly jumped out of our skin when an empty belly tank jettisoned by a bomber hit the water behind us with a tremendous thwack. I had to laugh at the way we all reacted instantaneously.

Sitting with our fingers crossed, we were puzzled by what appeared to be a giant pall of smoke over Henderson Field. We found out later that it was a cloud of fine alluvial dust churned up by the aircraft warming up their engines before takeoff. On subsequent operations we were glad to see this pall, as it indicated that we still had some planes left!

As soon as the raid died down, we sneaked in, signaling our number in all directions to be on the safe side. In fact, we spent the next two hours on the beach, while another two waves of bombers came over. Ray and Wimpy were hurt that they had missed lunch! We learned from the D-2 observation post, where we sought refuge, that we were now being steadily shelled by six-inch howitzers firing from the Kokumbona area. This was a new game. Although they had not yet dropped anything into D-2, the heavy shells were exploding steadily on the rise just above the HQ mess, and on the road between D-2 and the airfield. Mackenzie's place at the other end of the airstrip was also catching it. It was no good getting excited or surprised, we just had to get on with it.

21

Nip and Tuck

W E GOT BACK to D-2 late on 13 October, just in time to report our doings and turn in, dog tired. In our absence Colonel Buckley and the others had gone flat out, and they were dead beat too; but he let me know that our naval forces had successfully attacked the enemy on the night of 11 October and had sunk several cruisers and destroyers.[1] The Japs were determined to wrest the place from us; for this reason, he said, scouting information was becoming even more vital, because we had to find out whether they had landed more troops. I also heard that a U.S. Army regiment had arrived;[2] I remarked that I hoped they were used to this sort of thing!

The Bombardment

Little did we know, as we collapsed on our blankets, that we were in for our worst night yet. Japanese planes kept coming over in ones and twos, and the Matanikau artillery continued its steady pounding; but there was better to come. The first intimation was a star shell, which went off right above us and lit up everything as bright as day for at least half a minute. Before it went out, the first salvo landed with a crash on our ridge. It was the heaviest stuff we had seen. The ground shook with the most awful convulsions, and there was dust and smoke everywhere. Our tent was in confusion, as a jagged piece of red-hot steel snapped off the tent pole above our heads; it went right through the remains of my digger hat, which had been hanging up there as a mascot. The top of the tent collapsed over us, together with a few tons of earth that had been blown out of the immense shell craters.

In spite of the confusion, everyone—including Suinao, who was first down and insisted on the best place in the dugout—got out safely, except a clot who was dead to the world (me). One shell fragment went through the top of my mosquito net. I had got to the dangerous stage, where I was aware of things but my brain was too tired to react. Luckily John Mather came back and dragged me out. I managed to crawl below, but promptly fell asleep again and kept falling over on the chap sitting next to me. Despite my stupor, I thought I heard every salvo land. Each time one did, the whole dugout shook and the earth between the coconut logs of the roof fell into everything. We were soon unbearably gritty, but there was no respite, and we spent the whole night down below.

The morning revealed a sorry spectacle. Within a hundred yards of our dugout were six tremendous craters, any one of which could have hidden a jeep, and there were more on top of the ridge. We found several tremendous shell base plates, solid pieces of heavy steel with a diameter of over twelve inches. The small stuff was eight-inch and five-inch. Several spent splinters, some up to twelve inches long, had landed jagged and red hot inside the scouts' dugout, and my poor lads were very scared. Luckily their only casualties were burns. I shall never forget the sound of those salvoes landing; Wimpy likened it to a hundred-ton door clanging. The field had fared even worse: there was hardly a plane left fit to fly. We were in a proper mess.

The "word" went round that we had been shelled by two *Kongo*-class battleships and some cruisers, which had lain off some sixteen miles away near Savo Island. Certainly the shells had exploded before the warning sound of firing was heard. Apart from four PT boats that had arrived on 12 October, we had no Navy in the area. We had just about got cleared up and had something to eat when heavy air raids started. As if we had not had our share from the night shelling, an antipersonnel bomb landed three yards from the end of our dugout and blew it in completely. Michael, my cook, and Lieutenant Ogilvie, Macfarlan's replacement, were both buried. It took us some time to dig them out. Ogilvie was the worst: he had had his back against the dugout side, and was suffering from hemorrhage and concussion. Poor Michael was lacerated all down one side from his ear to his foot by earth and stones, and his eardrum had been blown in. I took him down to the hospital; it was full of casualties, but a bed was found for him, and I was assured that he would make a good recovery. I hated having to leave him there. When I got back, the colonel was sounding off: all our beautiful maps had been ruined again, and so had his cot! None of us, least of all my unfortunate scouts, liked this sitting down and taking it one little bit.

In the midst of all this, David Trench, who had joined the Colonial Service with me as a cadet, arrived, now gazetted in the Defence Force. He and Dick Horton had been on a reconnaissance to the Russell Islands, but they had dropped the teleradio in the water and David was forced to come back. I was terribly pleased to see him, but I was very disappointed when I heard that he was temporarily attached to Mackenzie. I had hoped he would stay with me, as I had asked repeatedly for his assistance because the work had been piling up.

The Enemy Lands Reinforcements on Our Doorstep

That night we were again shelled by cruisers; it was little comfort that most of the stuff fell on the airfield. The Japanese were really turning on the heat. In the morning we learned the reason why. At Kukum I found Dexter, face white and drawn, hastily evacuating his base and moving it east to Lunga Lagoon. He said nothing—he just pointed over his shoulder beyond the Matanikau, and there, as calm as you like, were six large enemy transports unloading troops and supplies between Tassafaronga and Mamara plantations, only a few miles away. There was no nonsense about landing craft; the ships had their bows almost on the beach, and on each side soldiers were rushing down the gangways. Through the glasses I could see them mustering on the beach. There were thousands of them. Japanese destroyers were cruising up and down between Lunga and

Tulagi; one passed not more than five thousand yards off shore. There was nothing one could say or do.

The Zero fighters were keeping our heads down; for a while we had only one dive bomber available. By 1030, after a superb ground staff effort, a number of Wildcats and Airacobras got into the air, together with twelve SBDs. The fighters did their best to keep the Zeros on the move, while the dive bombers sneaked in and inflicted some damage on the transports. The beach was no place to be, as the Zeros kept strafing it, but I managed to stay safe enough at Dexter's "Chicago piano," which claimed one plane during the day. Later on more SBDs were repaired and a few Flying Fortresses arrived from Espíritu Santo. All the transports were set on fire eventually and three of them started to sink, but not before they had unloaded most of their walking cargo.

One magnificent effort that morning was made by Maj. Jack Cram, General Geiger's pilot, who had obtained permission to use the general's Catalina, the *Blue Goose,* to attack the transports.[3] They tied on a couple of torpedoes with hastily made wire slings, and he sailed into the fray. To his right were the Japanese destroyers; to the front, the antiaircraft gunners on the transports; to the left, the enemy artillerymen ashore. Into this blazing inferno Cram flew, dipping in a shallow dive to obtain top speed. We held our breath as, with charmed life, he held his course. Shouts of pure joy went up as one "fish" detonated against the nearest transport, then he stood the Catalina almost on her tail as he wrenched her out of the ring of fire. The Zeros chased him home, but he managed to land the plane safely. General Geiger complained about the large number of holes in the *Blue Goose,* but then, smiling, said, "Well done."

Late the next afternoon more F4Fs and SBDs flew in, but we were now almost out of fuel. The shelling had taken its toll. There being no chance of unloading a transport even if one could arrive safely, in a last desperate effort five huge flat barges had been loaded with drums of fuel and towed up from the New Hebrides; but none made it, as the convoy was attacked by enemy planes and one vessel sunk. On 16 October another barge, being towed by the converted destroyer *McFarland,* was lost in sight of Tenaru when some Vals planted a direct hit on the ship's stern. Wasting no time, they bombed the barge as well, setting the fuel alight. It was almost dusk, and there was our valuable fuel slowly burning away. Colonel Twining, with great presence of mind, ordered artillery to fire on the barge, which sank it and put out the fires. Then, in the encircling gloom, Dexter's Higgins boats rounded up as many of the drums as they could and brought them in. Luckily the tide was taking them eastward, and we were able to collect the remainder the next day.

My Own Worries

All normal life was completely disorganized. If you set out on a jeep journey, there was no knowing when you would return. On the fifteenth Koimate and Chaku brought in Freshwater from Gold Ridge. I had to go down to the perimeter to collect him. No sooner had I got there than a raid started, and we scuttled down into a nice deep shelter with some engineers. I hoped things would be quieter than at D-2, but I was disappointed —there was a tremendous explosion and the side of the shelter moved, closing the entrance. We just managed to wriggle out, to find a huge hole and the jeep knocked over on its side, but otherwise undamaged.

I sent Freshwater's carriers straight out again, as they were not used to bombing and I doubted whether we could feed them. The unfortunate Bilge was out of touch with the situation, and when he called the rations we had sent inadequate I snapped back at him. I felt very tired, nervy, and irritable, and rather cross that he had come in when we were so busy. It wasn't his fault, poor man! All the civilians up in the hills were moaning because I did not send them rations for their laborers. It was difficult to make them understand how precarious our own supplies were.

At dusk, having parked Freshwater, I was tapping away on the typewriter, trying to finish the detailed report on Gorabusu before dark, when Daniel and Bunga picked that moment to turn up with Leineweber's patrol, all ninety-three of them. I was pleased to hear that they had had a clean run from Aola; it meant that side was clear. At the same time, no arrangements had been made to feed or bed them, and their parent unit was in Tulagi. It took me until 2200 to find an area and get them settled. They were nobody's darlings, and everyone was intent on his own survival for another night. It made me feel responsible for their arrival, as if, like the baby in *Alice in Wonderland,* I did it to annoy!

The mystery of Ishimoto remained unsolved. If we had not actually killed him,[4] we had at least put him out of action by capturing his two teleradio sets and his arms and rations. One mistake the Japanese frequently made was talking to the islanders, and other people who they did not think mattered. Amongst our information on Ishimoto was a report that he had tried to get the locals to protect the Japs from the Americans. The Japanese, he said, could not now retake the island; he wanted to go back to Japan, but the Emperor had forbidden any of them to do so. In addition, he not only told one scout, acting as an innocent villager, that he received messages from the post at Vioru, but more or less admitted that submarines had called and brought them supplies. In a letter, Clarry Hart wrote that Ishimoto had said his real job was to protect civilians and prisoners of war against assault and pillaging by Japanese troops. (He was, as Hart noted, not overly successful, as there was plenty of pillaging, little of which could be put down to war necessity; nor did he protect the fathers and sisters from Ruavatu.) Ishimoto would have been a valuable prisoner, but we had had no luck in finding him alone when we had sufficient force to capture him alive.

Even getting the scouts fed was a problem, as they came in at all hours. My lads took a dim view of the operational schedule, but I kept them out and on the job as far as possible. On 16 October Koimate took ten other scouts up the Tenaru River, to split three ways and keep an intensive watch for flanking patrols.

As we got more deeply involved on our western boundaries, patrolling the rest of the perimeter became ever more important. I was given the go-ahead to enlist another hundred scouts. (Most of those enlisted had already done well as scouts, though in an unarmed, unpaid capacity.) And so we took over the patrolling of a large area up the Tenaru and Lunga Rivers and down to the coast on the eastern side. All this intense activity, daily air raids, and an increasing pile of reports awaiting writing—what a life!

"Reverse Lend-Lease"

I started on a real night's sleep, but was roused at 0430 on 17 October to make maps and indicate targets for a little "reverse Lend-Lease" shelling. Two brand-new destroyers had been detailed for the purpose, and I was delighted. Major Nees[5] of the 11th Marines came along to call the targets, including several six-inch howitzers beyond the Matanikau that had been throwing in such a lot of old iron. We had to wait an hour at the beach while the Grummans knocked down seven Vals and a Zero out of a mob that had come on the scene rather earlier than usual. The destroyers were unharmed, though one had her rail bent by a near miss. Major Nees and I went aboard the *Aaron Ward,* David Trench aboard the *Lardner.*

Leaving Nees to explain things to the captain, I clambered up to the director turret with the gunnery officer. As we steamed into position, I realized what a terrific treat it was to be on board such a clean ship. Our unironed "dungreens" and muddy boots looked positively scruffy compared to the immaculate Navy attire. My eyes goggled, as we passed through the wardroom, to see a snow-white tablecloth and real silver laid out on the table. Ashore we had forgotten such things. My cup was filled to overflowing when the gunnery officer telephoned down for a sandwich for me. Up came a real fried egg and some bacon between two beautifully toasted pieces of real bread. I could hardly believe my eyes!

Going close in to Kokumbona, we steamed along parallel to the coast as far as Mamara, where the Japanese had recently landed so many stores. Major Nees called out the target numbers from the bridge, while I directed the rangefinder onto them. Each time I did, all five five-inch guns immediately swung round onto the target, and the gunnery officer, removing his cigar, nonchalantly said, "A couple of salvoes, do you think?" "Yes, rather," I replied. And so we steamed up and down, with the *Lardner* coming on behind us.

After being on the wrong end of naval bombardments for so long, I thoroughly enjoyed the performance. Each ship fired a thousand rounds before breakfast, and we were not interrupted from the air. Shore batteries fired on us, but they were outranged. We started huge fires at Tassafaronga; up the coast there were flames, black smoke three hundred feet high, and tremendous ammo explosions. We picked the right spot, and did enormous damage.

After it was all over we sat down to a colossal breakfast in the wardroom, Nees and I really feeling quite ill at ease using civilized implements again. Meanwhile, Wimpy and Winter had been down in the waist of the ship taking movies of the spectacle. I expect Wimpy told some tall tales of the hardships on Guadalcanal, for as we clambered down into the Higgins boat for the ride back the sailors lined the rail and threw down cigarettes, candy bars, and magazines, all rarer than fine gold on shore.

Wimpy, a turkey drumstick protruding from each pocket, was wreathed in smiles.

Back at D-2, everyone was highly excited. Shore observation had given us "A+" for our shooting, and morale had shot up by leaps and bounds. They were just as pleased with our loot, which was carefully shared out. We took not the slightest notice of another air raid! (I refer to raids with monotonous regularity. I don't think we ever got used to them, but they were part of life on Guadalcanal. The Japanese air forces just kept on coming, and our fighters kept on knocking them down.) There was no doubt that something big was brewing, but it was not being brewed by us, and as I listened to the noise from the Matanikau front I had again the sense of impending tragedy. I felt very depressed in spite of the elation at the damage we had just caused to the Japanese.

I had managed to call at the hospital to see Michael nearly every day. He was picking up well, but he was getting rather fed up with being carted down into a dugout every time there was an air raid. Michael was very pleased when Wimpy and I told him about our shoot: "Altogether Japan 'e catch'm bigfella kill."

Pistol Pete

Although we had been successful in destroying enemy supplies, we hadn't had much luck with the Matanikau howitzers, collectively christened "Pistol Pete" or "Stovepipe Charley." Several of them had been knocked out, but the Japs seemed to have lugged the rest into widely scattered, well-concealed gullies, where we could not hit back. Fortunately their shelling was not coordinated, as they went after the same areas each night and everyone kept clear. The 6th Naval Construction Battalion had roped one area off and erected a warning notice, but the end of the airfield was still being sniped, and the fighter boys and their planes did not like it one bit. Another "landing area" was down near Mackenzie's end of Henderson Field. To drive there, you waited until a shell landed, then drove like mad before the next one came in. It wasn't the casualty rate that worried us, but the interminability of it all, and the effect on everyone's nerves.

The scouts on perimeter patrol were having considerable success in mopping up small isolated enemy parties and bringing in large quantities of deserted equipment. Here Chaku appeared to be in his element: with another armed scout and two or three retainers, he harried a mob of about thirty Japanese, picking off stragglers and separating one section from another by assimilated attacks until there were none left. He brought in six machine guns and several baskets of ammunition.

Trying to solve the howitzer problem, we had all gone over the aerial photographs with a fine-tooth comb, but most of the land where the gunners calculated they were hidden was virgin bush, and nothing could be seen. As we had been promised another destroyer shoot, I spent hours with Lester, one of the D-2 experts, working to plot all the possible sites. One night he and I were hermetically sealed in the blackout tent, preparing a target plan; suddenly, Lester, who was nearer the brailed-up tent door, disappeared, as a ghastly rattle developed overhead. Sweeping out the light with one hand, I fell straight through the tent door and made a dive for our dugout from ten yards away. I couldn't see Lester anywhere, but I could feel at the back of my neck that something very large was about to drop very close. The entry to the dugout had a bend; I literally flew down the passage and landed in a mass of shoulders and feet, having passed the unfortunate Lester, who had been crawling slowly into the dugout. At that moment everything heaved up with a tremendous bang: it was a thousand-pound bomb, which had landed seventy yards away. The bomb did not go off until it was twenty-five feet deep; it left a queer, bottle-shaped hole in the ground. Two minutes later the plane that had dropped it was hit in the tank and disappeared, blazing, into the sea. We *were* lucky!

The unceasing enemy air activity was followed by offensive action all along the Matanikau front. The whole area was in an uproar, and we had to hit back. On 22 October another shoot was scheduled, with the destroyer *Nicholas*. We went out at 0630 and fired a thousand rounds at four howitzer positions, but although the shooting appeared to be good something was still firing when we got back. We had just come ashore when the *Nicholas* was attacked by Zeros and Vals. She opened up with zest, the Grummans intercepted, and two of the dive bombers went into the sea.

Colonel Buckley told me that we were going to attack the Japanese on the Matanikau. To make it effective, every available Marine would have to be thrown into the line; no one could be spared to make roads to evacuate wounded, or to take up ammunition and rations. We discussed the feasibility of raising carriers to do the job—he wanted three hundred of them—and finding a camp site where they would be fairly free from bombing attacks. With tents being bombed to bits daily, they would have to dig foxholes and fix up some sort of shelter over the top with coconut fronds.

The other change we planned was to use the schooners, then tucked away in the mangroves at Marau, instead of landing craft, for reconnaissance parties and for evacuating the remaining civilians, who could not be fed. The Japanese diaries from Gorabusu showed that landing craft were very noisy and easy to pick up. To find out at what rate the Japs were reinforcing Guadalcanal by barge, Horton had made his trip to the Russell Islands (he returned safely that day) and Josselyn had been installed on Rendova, where it was hoped he would be able to tell us what traffic was passing down the Slot. These operations, both involving long passages, were done with landing craft; remarkably, they did not raise any suspicion on the part of the enemy.

The decision to concentrate all our efforts on the Matanikau front was obviously the right one, for between the air raids and the malaria our ground units were getting very thin. This gave my scouts the chance to volunteer for one or two more "guerrilla operations." After his success near the Tenaru, Chaku was sent off to destroy the enemy radio post at Vioru on the south coast, and the Aola section was given permission to dispatch the remnants of the Gorabusu party, which they had been shadowing at Gegende.

These small operations could deal with "refugees," but there would be trouble if the Japanese again landed a large force to our east. On 23 October Lieutenant Colonel Carlson,[6] who had led the Makin Island raid, arrived; we discussed in detail plans for his 2d Raider Battalion to make an extended offensive patrol from Aola westward, to oppose sudden landings and eliminate the considerable number of stragglers. This complex operation required complicated logistic arrangements, for the Raiders would have to bring along their rations and ammunition. I would meet them at Aola, and then Tabasui, with fifty scouts and a hundred carriers, would take them to the Tasimboko border; from there Vouza, with like numbers of men who knew that area, would bring them through to the perimeter. Carlson was a first-class leader, who had learned to live off the land. It was agreed that John Mather would be attached to him.

Things Brew Up on the Western Front

Wimpy, Koepplinger, and others at D-2 had been doing a lot of whispering with their friends in the 5th Marines. The latter had realized for some time that Tojo had merely been probing our defenses, and that he was about to throw his kitchen sink at some point along their line. Where it did come it was least expected, but nevertheless we were ready for it.

On the morning of 23 October, as the B-17s were taking off from the New Hebrides to bomb a big target to our north, machine-gun and mortar fire began to rattle all along the Matanikau. Just to help matters, it poured with rain, which bogged down all our transport. As the sun was going down, the Japanese tried to force the sandspit at the mouth of the river with medium and light tanks backed up by infantry. Gleaming wet from the rain, they were beautifully silhouetted against the setting sun. Hastily the Marines brought out 37-mm antitank weapons and half-track-mounted 75-mm guns. They soon got the range and knocked out nine tanks; the sandspit was so narrow that the rest had to retire.

The ground attack went on half that night, and the Japanese left behind several hundred dead. After a solid bombardment they tried the same thing two nights later, but again failed. We also had our casualties, and the Matanikau was bitterly held. This was but a prelude for an attack on our southern flank, between the Lunga and the Tenaru, where Lieutenant Colonel Puller's understrength battalion was battling like mad. We had just built a new fighter strip near the Tenaru, from which P-38 Lightnings, strange but speedy birds with twin fuselages, had recently begun operations. The Japanese went flat out to get it, and they very nearly did.

Things looked pretty bleak. There was talk at D-2 of our having to go into the line, but we had no time to dwell on possibilities. Intermittent enemy artillery fire continued all day and D-2 was bracketed several times, which made life pretty uncomfortable. I spent the time dashing out between salvoes, working on the camp area for the carriers who we hoped would volunteer. It was a good thing Trench was there to help. We really needed three or four officers to operate a native labor force, and another one or two to help with the scouting organization; but there was little chance of getting them.

At D-2 everyone was working, more or less, twenty-four hours a day. Apart from special jobs such as organizing the labor camp I had to take my turn at the telephone watch, collecting alarms and situation reports from all fronts and collating information from coastwatchers. At night, action continued and the horizon was continuously lit up. I didn't like the look of things at all.

By the time the sun set, the twenty-fifth of October had become known as "Dugout Sunday." Instead of sending only bombers, the enemy sent mixed raids over us all day long; they were mostly strafing Zeros. It was a relief to think that the Japanese might be getting short of bombers, but they were probably trying to tire our fighter pilots out. It was money for jam, however, and a field day for everyone. The Grummans chased the Zeros down to the P-39s, and if they missed them everyone on the ground opened up till the sky was red with tracers. Yells went up every time a Zero "bought it." One in particular I saw, blown to pieces in midair. The tail plane floated down, turning over and over like a falling leaf. And so it went on all day.

Things got blacker and blacker. Five enemy ships came close during the afternoon to pepper us; several flights of various aircraft responded, sinking a cruiser and damaging two destroyers. The rest escaped under cover of darkness; they had, I thought, probably landed troops somewhere. The rain made it very difficult for the returning dive bombers, who were being worked very hard. We didn't seem to have much navy left, while on land we had our backs to each other (except to the east, where we had very few troops left to outflank), and we were being attacked everywhere.

Information filtered in about the B-17s' target, which turned out to be Rabaul. It got a good pasting. Five to six hundred Japanese lay dead on our Matanikau line and to the south. That night our southern front was completely engaged; we managed to hold them off, but it was a very close go, and I did not see how we could hold out against a fresh lot of invaders. In the midst of this raging battle, Colonel Thomas called, asking me to make an urgent reconnaissance to Aola. He had briefed those who were going, and I had full authority to make whatever arrangements I liked, as long as I got off as quickly as possible.

22

Advance to the Rear

Wɪᴛʜ sᴏ ᴍᴜᴄʜ of the Imperial Japanese Navy about, I did not rel-
ish another trip in an open boat, but orders were orders. During
the night I got the team together, and after a lot of barefaced scrounging,
we got away just after 1600 on 26 October. I had Wendling, Koepplinger,
Banco, and Burnham from D-2; Beato and Allen from the scouts; and
Michael, whom I had more or less sneaked from the hospital, feeling a
trip to Aola would probably do him good. The technical experts consisted
of Captain Longley, from the 1st Marine Air Wing; Lieutenant Pratt, a
Navy engineer; and Lieutenant James and Chief Petty Officer Fortune,
the landing and anchorage experts from Commander Dexter's headquarters. Longley looked like a Victorian Englishman, with his pink cheeks
and large black mustache verging on a handlebar. Pratt, a tall, husky
"character from Utah," told us all about Salt Lake City. He was a breezy,
independent type—he may have been in the U.S. Navy, and on Guadalcanal, but he continued to wear his cone-heeled Texas riding boots. James
was a fresh-faced reserve officer, and "the Chief" had served in destroyers
in World War I.

Return to Aola

Our job was to survey locations for landing points and an airstrip. Although I had not been briefed on the overall mission, it appeared we were looking to establish a second line of defense in case we lost the battle for the Lunga perimeter. As I later learned, however, we were the point men in what one historian aptly termed "the singularly ill-considered effort" to create a second perimeter and airfield.[1] This plan, which was opposed by Generals Vandegrift and Geiger and by senior naval aviators in the South Pacific, was the child of the amphibious force commander, Admiral Turner,[2] who persisted in the belief that defense required dispersal of ground forces along the coast to deal with the Japanese. Turner's harebrained scheme would divert critically needed manpower and materiel from Lunga in the weeks ahead.

It was a clear, moonlit night, so when at 1945 we arrived at Aola I sent Beato and Michael swimming in to let Andrew and his lads know who we were. Recognition was quickly established, and in no time we had settled ourselves in the cadet's house and laid out an all-round defense. Andrew reported no enemy troops in the immediate vicinity; although it was already dark, I sent him off to alert all his scouts to scour the area for ten miles around and report it clear. Daniel Pule came in at 2000 with the news that there were about thirty Japanese at Paripao and more at Gegende, where some of those that Colonel Hill had driven into the swamp were still surviving. The local headmen were sent for, to bring in carriers and summon the bosuns of the vessels hidden at Marau.[3]

Early the next morning Lieutenant James left for Marau in the Higgins boat with his party and the bosuns, to pick up any schooners found to be serviceable. The rest of us spent the day doing reconnaissances, from Aola to Kombito plantation and from Kombito to Luvenibuli; every hour the scouts reported that all sides were clear. At 2230 a vessel was heard outside Aola Bay, but there was no light. An hour later another vessel passed and then, in response to our signal from the beach, came into the bay from the direction of Bara Island. Captain Longley exchanged flashlight signals with it for some time. We had been given Navy code, but could not interpret the one they were using; it was, however, fairly obvious that they were friendly.

After this exchange, the vessel buzzed off and brought in a second. We signaled them where to land the party, but it cheerfully replied, "We have no boat." Longley, weary by now of dotting and dashing, was about to signal, "For God's sake, go to bed, we haven't got one either." I stopped him just in time. There was not much swell, so I peeled off my clothes and swam out a thousand yards to the beastly thing. It was one of our newly arrived patrol torpedo boats; worse, it had overhanging sides.

At first it looked as though I would be shot out of hand, but before I got sucked under the propellers they handed me a boat hook and hauled me to the deck. Standing there, stark naked and dripping wet, I had to explain to the skipper, Lieutenant Taylor, what everything was about. He said they had been told there was a wharf where he could land the Marines. With bitter laughter, I replied, "There are the remains of one, at Aola plantation."

Fifty-nine Marines, led by Lt. Stephen Sekowski, transferred from the other vessel, a YP, to the deck of the PT boat. Clad only in a towel, I somehow got it maneuvered close enough to the end of the old wharf to let them jump from the bow onto the four-inch beams (I had previously removed the planking). We managed to get them off—even at low tide, I remembered, Palmer's wharf used to have two fathoms of water fifteen feet from the end—and they were shepherded back to the government station for bivouacking.

Fortified by some much-needed coffee, Sekowski and I got down to work straightaway, preparing maps and plans and arranging rendezvous, carriers, and guides. Andrew and Daniel, who now knew the form on this sort of operation, did most of the work like seasoned campaigners. (As Andrew would say with a smile, "Me savvy do 'im.") The idea was to have another shot at cleaning up enemy stragglers and then patrol back to Lunga along the coast. As the day wore on, all the headmen turned up with their carrier parties and were briefed as to their jobs. Different sections would carry ammunition boxes and rations, and act as stretcher bearers if need be. The latest reports placed the Japanese remnants at two parties of thirty or forty, but I could not believe there were so many, unless they had made their way down from Tasimboko. Still, it was better to be safe than sorry.

At dusk I was greatly relieved to see Lieutenant James return with the *Rob Roy* in tow, and the news that two other schooners would arrive shortly under their own steam. It had taken longer than expected to get the vessels dragged out of the mangroves and put in working order. They would proceed to Tulagi with their crews for refitting. All was serene at Marau, but our anxiety as to how our friends were faring at Lunga was not alleviated by the thuds and cracks that came all night from that direction.

The delay meant that we should have to spend another day, so James could complete his part of the reconnaissance at Aola, but they had already signaled this through Adams at Marau. He and Eroni were getting on famously. When I sent Harry Adams supplies I got profuse notes of thanks signed "Respectively yours."

It took us an hour or so in the morning to brief the carriers and scouts in detail and pair them with the right section of Marines, but they all set off in good time, with Sergeant Andrew and the cream of the Aola detachment in the van and the headmen themselves bringing up the rear with the ration parties. In the afternoon we sped down to Rere Point, which had been mentioned as a possible location for a landing place and secondary airfield; the swampy ground, however, made it impossible. The highlight of the trip was finding one of the Java sheep. It was promptly requisitioned, and that evening we had a colossal repast of roast mutton, our first fresh meat since May. All was peaceful again at night—what a contrast to Lunga—and I had a lovely sleep.

The next morning, 30 October, was beautiful and quiet, broken only by the passing of B-17s and of a cruiser and a destroyer that we "hoped" were ours. At midday Evans took us up the coast to meet Sekowski on the beach near Koilotumuria. He had got into position at dawn, but his show was a bit of a farce, since, when they were about to attack, one of his men said, "Hold your fire, there's a European." This gave the alarm, and the Japanese dispersed very smartly. Most of them were in their underwear.

The Marines killed one and wounded three, but the rest disappeared again into Colonel Hill's bottomless swamp. (Wimpy, who was there, reported that one of them had blond hair, was six feet tall and of solid build, and looked like a Dutchman. They had held their fire because they thought he might be a prisoner of war.) The Japs had no proper defenses, and no trace of food other than two small bags of rice. Four rifles, three swords, and two pairs of binoculars were all their equipment; they were probably in a pretty poor way. From their huts, Wimpy reckoned there had been ten to fourteen men. An antiaircraft gun, found by Colonel Hill's party but not put out of action, was destroyed; two cases of ammunition were brought back for identification, and another twenty-one cast into the sea. Wishing Lieutenant Sekowski the best of luck on his patrol, we returned to Aola that afternoon, taking four of his men who were down with malarial fever. Wimpy's report quite rightly advised that, as the range was seldom more than ten yards, machine guns had no place on such an operation.

The Battle for "Fighter One"

As we left for Lunga at daybreak on 31 October, I remember thinking that I could do with a clean undershirt and some new socks. The main thing on my mind, however, was what had happened at Lunga and whether we would find it occupied by the enemy. In the event, however, we got back safely. On the way we noticed at least forty oil drums on the beach at Volonavua. It might have been fuel or Japanese rice, but we did not waste time finding out.

In the five days we were away, more than twenty-five hundred Japanese were reported killed to the south and in the battle for "Fighter One," the new airfield. Fighter One was still ours, but early that morning a sailor —luckily armed—who was trying to iron out some shell holes with a bulldozer captured two enemy soldiers quietly sitting at the end of the runway. During interrogation they told Captain Moran that they had orders to go for the gap and rendezvous at the airfield, which they had done! On the bright side, we had at last crossed the river and taken Matanikau; there was no news concerning the Japanese invasion force, but Trench had been out with the cruiser *San Juan* and several destroyers, and they had shelled enemy positions without opposition.

With more than nineteen hundred Marines down with malaria during the month, they'd had to throw in an Army outfit, whose commanding officer, Lieutenant Colonel Timboe,[4] had been a newspaper editor in Devil's Lake, North Dakota, in peacetime. I heard later that he arrived at Lieutenant Colonel Puller's command post in the dark, to find Puller firing away with the rest. Asked where the gap was, Puller supposedly replied, "I've got about seventy men there and another seventy there, and all the rest's 'gap.' Now get cracking!" Puller, who was usually referred to as "Chesty," was a redoubtable warrior with a chin like a bulldozer blade, who puffed away at a little black pipe. Timboe told me afterward that though he came from Devil's Lake, that night he thought he'd found the devil's cookpot!

A New Unit Appears

I reported in at 0930, just in time to meet the first wave of my labor and carrier force. A hundred and eighty men had been shepherded in; they were all quite cheerful and prepared to work. I was more than busy all day getting them signed on and settled in their bivouacs. I was very tired, and disappointed that Trench had suddenly been grabbed for another coastwatcher job. It was a mercy that our fighters prevented the Japanese bombers from reaching us that day, or I would never have got the work done. Finally I returned to D-2 at dusk, only to have them telephone from the perimeter that another eighty volunteers had arrived. It was a nasty business going down in the dark, past trigger-happy sentries. All we could do was mark out foxholes for the men and start the digging right away; they needed no urging! At 2030 I got back to D-2 absolutely fagged out, having been challenged six times and nearly drowned in a huge bomb hole full of rainwater.

Although the intention was still to use the carriers to evacuate casualties and haul ammunition to the front line, a new problem had arisen. The small number of Marines who were held in reserve had been unloading ships, but they were now kept in the line so long that when they came out they were falling asleep standing. In any case the number of our reserves continued to shrink. It was essential to get the ships unloaded quickly, and that job was ideal for the Solomon Islanders. I spent most of the next day doing what I could to arrange rations for the carriers. The chief problem was the lack of rice, on which employed islanders normally fed. There were no suitable alternatives.

The other difficulties I foresaw were making the locals understand what required doing, and explaining to each and every Marine who would be dealing with them that they were independent bushmen who had simply no idea about American methods and efficiency. Another problem was that all Americans, however busy, loved souvenirs. The islanders brought things in, and they would probably want to take other things out. It was a case of "needs must when the Devil drives," however, and everyone would have to manage somehow; there was no time for training.

On my return from the new camp area, I heard that Sekowski had run into some Japs near Koli Point, and that a boat had been sent to Suagi to pick up two wounded, one a Marine and the other young Dovu, who had taken a bullet through his shoulder. There was also a huge pile of letters containing moans from Hay and the other civilians. I was so tired when I first read them through that I felt quite angry. Three days later, however, the resident commissioner sent a firmly worded signal to Gold Ridge: "Please advise Hay Campbell Andresen Freshwater U.S. Forces regret they are unable maintain them in supplies. If they wish to be evacuated arrangements will be made for this. They should get in touch with Clemens for this purpose."

Hay, of course, had been signed on as a coastwatcher, and he was entitled to rations. The main difficulty was sending the stuff out regularly, as usually the only people going out were scouts on reconnaissance. Ken was doing the decent thing and letting the others have their share, but he was also busy getting native laborers together to send down to us, and they also expected something to eat. He was quite right, but it was hard to explain that it took the best part of a day to tell the quartermaster people what it was all about, in order to justify the issue of rations. Then the rations had to be packed up in loads, and carriers got down to the perimeter; with Trench away and me dashing off to Aola, there was no one who could spare the time to do it all. As regards the others, their demands were quite reasonable when looked at objectively, but they could not realize—indeed, they couldn't be expected to—how hard won our rations were, and what a job it was even to get the stuff landed. We were only just hanging on at Lunga, and there wasn't very much we could have done for them even if we had had the time.

All the missionaries remaining on the island had been warned to collect at Marau for evacuation, but the miners hadn't yet made up their minds. To put it quite brutally, either they would have to come down to Lunga and work, or they would have to be evacuated somewhere where they would not be a ration liability.

The results of our reconnaissance had been quickly appraised, and at 1700 Colonel Thomas called me in again. "Good show," he said. "How soon can you go back to Aola and prepare to make arrangements for a landing?" I had been half expecting this, but to actually get the instructions nevertheless made me feel quite numb. I told him I would get away first thing in the morning, though I knew that it would be a miracle if during the night, when everyone was defending himself, I managed to collect the party, the rations, and the ammunition. There was no doubt about the set of the colonel's jaw, however, and I could not let him down. It meant another sleepless night.

23

Hammer and Tongs

B Y WORKING ALL NIGHT, we managed to get away for Aola at 0550 on
2 November. Most of the party was the same as before, with the addition of Sgts. Robert Howard and Francis Massaro from D-2 but minus
Longley and Pratt. Seeing a large convoy (ours) making up channel, I
heaved a sigh of relief and went to sleep on the bottom of the Higgins boat,
in spite of the vibrations.

Night Watch

The day's work consisted of constructing three huge beacons, twelve-foot-
high log pyramids six hundred feet apart along the beach. In addition,
four tracks were cut from the beach to the main government road to facil-
itate landing. Howard and Massaro—the latter had a handsome black
beard—sketched the area, making several copies. At dusk it set in to rain,
and everyone got very wet. Andrew had his scouts out, so the working
party returned to the cadet's house, where we sat round a roaring fire try-

ing to dry out our clothes. Michael, who had fully recovered, was in charge of the cooking; that was a good thing, as I had missed every meal at Lunga and was in need of a square feed. Russo, coxswain Evans's assistant, kept us amused with New York Italian stories.

By 0300, when we went down to light the beacons, the rain had died down a little; it soon began to pour again, however, and we stood there on the beach, wet and miserable. Then an alarm was raised when the Kombito villagers misinterpreted their orders and lit dozens of other fires, which turned the place into a veritable "Blackpool by night."

Although it was calm, there was a big swell on the beach, and distant sounds were heard to seaward; but there was no sign of any landing force. Dawn broke to find us still standing there, our teeth chattering, so Howard and his kerosene-tin coffee service were greatly appreciated by all. I had about given up hope of any landing when, about 0830, a Wildcat swooped down and dropped us a message: "Stand by—will inform you when to expect arrival."

We were rather angry at a night's work gone for nothing, and a soaking into the bargain. I began to wonder what had caused the big swell on the beach. Was it the enemy? At 1030 a Dauntless dropped the laconic note, "3 a.m., 4th November." I certainly hoped it would be—if not, we would run out of firewood, or "draw the crabs." We had to build the beacons all over again; it was harder now, as the timber was thoroughly wet. That done, we gorged on one of Michael's famous meals, then sat in a row along the verandah of the cadet's house with our feet up, too tired to move, as transport planes flew low over the water in tight groups, surrounded by fighters. Watching a three-ship convoy pass by, heading westward, Chief Fortune mused, "Oh, the irony of it all."

That night the beacons burned brightly again—luckily it did not rain —and at 0345 there was a welcome sound of engines to the southeast. Dawn revealed two APDs entering the bay and transports farther out, guarded by destroyers. The first mob off the four-stackers was two companies of Carlson's Raiders, who rushed ashore with fixed bayonets and spread out in defense. They had wisely been told to treat their landing as opposed, and the landing boats were emptied in rather under five minutes. As they dashed past, Howard, who was standing smoking his pipe, asked one Raider what he was looking for in the bush. "Nips, of course," the man said. Howard laughed and told him there weren't any for miles around. Another one of the new arrivals noticed the mass of pink scars on Michael's chocolate-colored skin. "What kinda disease is that?" he asked. Before I could explain, Michael's eyes lit up, and a grin spread across his face. "Bomb bomb disease," he replied.

Colonel Carlson and John Mather came ashore, and we got down to business. As we had planned, the Raiders would act as a security patrolling force between Aola and Lunga; it was arranged that the scouts in whose area Carlson was operating would attach themselves to him and supply him with up-to-date information on the enemy. He would leave at dawn the next morning; I agreed to muster as many carriers as possible, so the Raiders could take the maximum amount of ammunition. As an added precaution I sent a patrol of scouts to see whether the coast was clear toward Marau.

Later, landing of other troops began in earnest from the *Fomalhaut* and two large transports, protected by the destroyers outside. The men were ashore by 1500, but artillery, trucks, heavy equipment, and supplies continued to roll in till after dark. I met the three component commanders, Marine, Army, and Navy: Colonel Sturgis, whose 5th Defense Battalion was well armed with guns, antiaircraft and otherwise; Lieutenant Colonel Haines, commanding officer of the 1st Battalion, 147th Infantry; and Captain Carney, a flyer whose outfit was known as Acorn (Red) One.[1] Most of Carney's men were technical experts, and I was quite alarmed to find that only half of them were armed.

Eating Again

With the troops ashore and secondary supplies rolling off, our work was finished for the time being, so Wimpy, Koepplinger, and I sneaked on board the *Fomalhaut* and went straight to the canteen. We reveled in the delights on sale, none of which we had seen for a long time. It was lots of fun. We had long ago given up fancy notepaper in favor of Japanese message forms, and as for the aftershave, phew! We settled for some candy bars and a gallon can of ice cream. Taking them ashore, we sat Indian style round the can on the beach and attacked the ice cream with spoons, the only culinary weapons we carried. It did not last long. With everyone busy digging in, it was a quiet night, but in a tragic mishap an Army private was shot by mistake in the dark and killed.

The Raiders left at dawn on 5 November, with a scout section in advance and a long tail of carriers in the rear. It was the very epitome of Carlson's battalion motto, "Gung Ho," which meant approximately "work together, chaps." Their rations were almost entirely rice, bacon, and raisins. This suited my lads admirably.

The transports returned to discharge their remaining supplies and machinery. Then a convoy of transport planes, heading up channel low over the water, failed to give a recognition signal in time. The ships dispersed and opened up on them. They were quite right to do so; luckily no one was hit. Afterward the transports came in again and continued unloading until the piles were ten feet high all along the beach. I hoped and prayed that our fighters would keep Japanese aircraft away from such a magnificent target. The landing must have been carried out with a fair amount of secrecy, for no enemy planes or ships came to investigate.

I toured the security layout with Colonels Sturgis and Haines. Captain Carney decided to build his airfield on the far side of Aola plantation, and the Marine and Army command posts were located under the plantation's coconut palms.

Operation "Recalcitrant"

All my available scouts were out on patrol round the perimeter. Late in the afternoon, Lance Corporal Kimbo reported that his section had seen a couple of Japanese in hiding near Koilotumuria. I doubted whether by themselves they were very harmful, but if they saw what was going on at Aola they could well pass on the information. Wendling happened to be with me at the time; he read my mind, and his eyes lit up. "All right, Wimpy," I said, "take four scouts and bring me back some prisoners."

Wimpy departed on his little operation as soon as the sun was up the next morning. He was very proud of himself. I spent most of the day advising the triumvirate of commanding officers on many matters, trying tactfully to explain how we did things at Lunga. None of them really appreciated what was going on up there. I badly wanted to get them to move all the supplies off the beach as quickly as possible; in the end, however, that was achieved only by bringing in more Solomon Islanders to help us. I decided I had better return to Lunga and report that we had completed our mission, before I became completely involved with the Aola force.

At 1700 Wimpy returned with his patrol, brandishing a Japanese sword that was nearly as big as he was. The four enemy soldiers they had found had been killed. He regretted not bringing any prisoners; the only man he could have captured had been "kinda recalcitrant." I was secretly rather cross with him, but as he had obviously done well I did not have the heart to say so.

One of the rivers that Wimpy and the scouts had to cross was in flood, so they hacked down a few trees and built a raft, with which they made a precarious crossing. They located the Japanese in a small hut, into which they poured a vast volume of fire from about a hundred yards. Two men ran out, wounded; these were quickly dispatched. On closing in they found one of the other two apparently dead and the remaining one, who supported himself behind the doorpost, wounded. The wounded man was an officer, and he could understand English. Wimpy asked him several times to surrender; this the man refused to do. He then offered a bar of chocolate, but as he advanced with it the officer suddenly drew his sword and struck down at him. Luckily Wimpy had his finger on the trigger, and that was the end of his recalcitrant prisoner.

Close Acquaintance with a Torpedo

Colonel Sturgis was quite concerned at being what he called left alone, but I had my orders, and I could not be in both places at once. I had done my best to paint a picture of what went on at Lunga, and to show him how lucky he was so far to be undetected. All I could do was to leave Andrew as his liaison officer. He would keep the colonel posted as to what the scouts were finding out and see that the native laborers were handled properly.

The next morning, 7 November, was bright and sunny; we got away about 0700, wondering what we should find. We didn't have long to wait. Off Koli Point the boat lookout sounded a warning of white water to starboard. I pooh-poohed his suggestion that it was a reef: we were a mile or so off shore, and heaven knows I had traveled that way often enough. We were still wondering what it was when I spotted a small cargo ship ahead. Just as I put the glasses on her, a huge spout of water erupted; this was followed by a tremendous explosion, and she started to sink.[2] We quickly realized that the vessel had been torpedoed, and that our white water was in fact a torpedo's wake. Several destroyers were soon on the scene, dashing about madly and dropping depth charges, which nearly blew us out of the water. Dive bombers also joined in. Wimpy stood precariously on our stern, waving a huge American flag that Evans wisely always carried, in case we were suspected.

We beached our boat ten yards from where two or three people were bending over a long, silvery object. It was another torpedo, all hot and steaming.[3] Young Cobb, the bomb disposal officer, was examining it and cautiously trying to put it out of action. We all heaved a sigh of relief that we hadn't had to argue with a surfaced submarine.

At Lunga, as usual, there was a vast quantity of things to be done. I reported to Colonel Thomas that the landing at Aola had been safely made, but that I was not altogether satisfied with the camouflage and security. This opinion I put forward very tentatively, as it was really not my business and I didn't want to rub the Aola chaps the wrong way. I felt, however, that it was for their own good, and for the general good, that their presence there should not be suspected, for some time longer at any rate. Later I found out that my anxiety was fully justified.

I was glad to hear that the Catholic missionaries from Avu Avu had reached Marau safely, and that one of the fathers was prepared to go to Gold Ridge to fetch Sister Edmée. After the terrible time she had, hiding in the bush and, finally, learning what had happened to her co-workers, her nerves were almost gone—Hay wrote that she was reduced to a hopeless state every time a plane went over—but she had picked up wonderfully since she had arrived. Ken said he was endeavoring to use his last-war French with her, but most of it was not the sort of French that missionaries would understand. They must have reached some modus vivendi, however, as he reported that she was mending his clothes and sewing on buttons for him! It was, he wrote, one of the strangest experiences of his life, living on a mountaintop with a nun. Hay also very kindly sent us down one of his precious last bottles of Australian whiskey—not, may I say, without many prior broad hints and some urging! He added that he was practically dry, as Sister Edmée did not drink and it was an old family tradition of his never to drink alone—at least not much.

Amongst the pile of letters was an envelope containing six British captain's pips. I threaded them onto a piece of string and hung them up in our tent, as the Marine shirts had no shoulder tabs and there were no military tailors within range. (It also would prevent them from being scattered by a chance bomb!) Since August I had been wearing a set of Marine captain's bars, given to me by Colonel Buckley. They were easily recognized, and that saved a lot of explanation, especially at the front line.

A Narrow Squeak

As regards the military situation, it had been a near thing, but our prospects were momentarily looking a little better. The outcome of the struggle for Guadalcanal really depended on what the enemy had left to pit against us. On land, we were just about holding things. I was told that it was Japanese warships that had passed down the channel the first night we burned beacons at Aola, and the landing force had had to retire. The Matanikau, however, had at last been taken, and the front pushed well west of Point Cruz. (We had first crossed the river before the end of September, but the unit involved had been cut off, and eventually had to be evacuated by boat.) Since then the position had changed hands several times. The Japs had continued to land troops, but our navy had managed to run the gauntlet and land further Marine and Army reinforcements and some decent-sized artillery.

I had thought that the Japanese had landed all their reinforcements to the west; now I was amazed to hear that they had put troops and substantial materiel ashore at Koli Point in the early hours of 3 November, under cover of their combatant vessels. Carlson had arrived in the nick of time to stop them from heading toward Aola, as they had evaded another Marine battalion sent out to engage them. Two of our cruisers and a destroyer had provided offshore gunfire support. We had been amazingly lucky that our beacons had not "drawn the crabs" that first night, and lucky too to have kept well off shore on our return to Lunga. It was also very fortunate indeed that we had got the native laborers in while the coast was still clear. The biggest snag was that the Matanikau drive had to be slowed down until the situation in the east was stabilized.

Affairs at sea were still in the balance. I learned that our carriers had engaged a large enemy force off Santa Cruz on 26 October, and the Japanese had sustained severe losses in aircrews and planes. But we had had significant losses too, including the sinking of the *Hornet* and heavy damage to the *Enterprise*.

As before, Bettys and Zeros continued to rain their daily blows, and at night the Tokyo Express continued its operations. Now, however, a more cheerful spirit prevailed, though I noticed for the first time what a hollow-cheeked and herring-gutted mob we were becoming. I had seen this first at Aola, where all the newly landed soldiers looked so fresh-faced and well nourished, and everyone's aim was to see that they did not miss three good meals a day. The officers at Aola commented that the Lunga types never refused anything. Even Colonel Buckley had lost a lot of weight, but he never lost his cheerfulness.

We spent most of the night yarning at D-2 about our different experiences of the last few days; then I was up bright and early to see how the labor show was getting on. Daniel, though very disappointed at being taken off scouting, had got a semblance of order into the camp, and the islanders were doing very useful work unloading supplies at the beach.

I returned to headquarters at 0645 on 9 November to find that Admiral Halsey[4] was presenting decorations. General Vandegrift introduced me to him in the most eulogistic terms and told him what I had been doing. The admiral had a very firm handshake. "Well, Clemens," he said, "you carry on. We are only up here for one thing, to beat these goddam little yellow bastards. If you have any difficulties, just bring them to me, and I'll do my best to solve them." They then went to breakfast, which Halsey enjoyed so much that he sent for Butch Morgan and thanked him profusely for the excellent meal. Butch was unused to such praise; he shuffled his feet, wiped his walrus mustache with the back of his hand, and muttered, "Aw, shit, admiral . . ."

As soon as Admiral Halsey had departed, Colonel Thomas called and told me to return to Aola, taking Major Murray[5] from D-1 and Major Evans from D-2, in order to get that place put on a pay basis. We left at 0820; by 1300 we were inspecting the Aola defense area, and Murray was impressing on the commanding officers the seriousness of the situation. Andrew, who had now been promoted sergeant major, reported all clear from all patrols. We declined Colonel Sturgis's invitation to his mess, preferring to have a meal cooked by Michael at our usual headquarters.

Jim Murray had been terribly hard worked, and the comparative peace and quiet did him good. He too commented on the fresh pink faces, compared to the walking skeletons at Lunga. I could not but feel sad at the sight of the old government station completely militarized. We spent the next day helping to get everything straightened out, and left for Lunga at 0250 on 11 November.

The Bottom

When I got back to D-2 Colonel Buckley's cheerful grin was gone. He took me aside and told me that things were very black indeed. I was to keep the information to myself. The Japanese had a huge force gathering to blast us off the island, and the *Enterprise,* our only carrier still in action, was being repaired in Nouméa. We had reinforcements ready to bring in, but if their landing were opposed it would be touch and go what happened.

Luckily, the first elements of these got through, and that morning three transports began unloading off Lunga Point as fast as they could. They were given no rest, however, by either bombers or fighter planes. Five Vals, two Zeros, and four Bettys were destroyed in two raids by lunchtime, but not before the Bettys had dropped some bombs in our ration dump. We had to laugh when Colonel Buckley rang up the quartermaster colonel to ask what damage had been done. He replied in a sad voice that his two chief casualties were tomato sauce and tinned loganberries, which had left a horrible blood-red mush in the middle of his beautiful dump! After the second raid, Charles Widdy strolled in, having sneaked in uneventfully on a transport plane. He had returned to discuss the formation of a properly organized labor battalion.

Heaving a sigh of relief, and thankfully leaving a vast pile of signals, mostly about evacuating civilians, I took Widdy up to the labor camp to discuss problems and requirements. I was very glad to see him, as I could not continue to run everything much longer and the labor would be one less problem to handle. Several sections of laborers were now carrying rations up the hills behind Point Cruz to our advancing front line and bringing casualties back. There the real need was for officers, as the men did not like being under fire on their own. We tentatively agreed to try to get the underemployed Butcher Johnstone over from Tulagi, and if possible to bring in Clarry Hart as well.

Arrangements had been made to collect the Catholic evacuees at Marau. Missionaries from San Cristobal were included. One of the reconditioned schooners would bring them up to Aola, where it was hoped they could be put on board a ship. I sighed as I casually glanced at the other signals—there was far too much to deal with for me to handle them quickly. It could be better done, I decided, on the morrow, when I had had a few hours' sleep.

Off Again

It was almost midnight when Colonel Thomas summoned me to his tent. I was in a very sleepy and slightly protesting condition, just rested enough to sleep properly. I woke up when I learned that the Japanese invasion force was preceded by battleship task forces and they were headed directly for our area. He ordered me to leave forthwith for Aola, to warn Colonel Sturgis to hide and camouflage everything and to stand by for possible attack.

One good thing was that the *Ramada,* which I had managed to hang onto since the bishop's evacuation, was in good working condition. She had been refitted in Tulagi, and was ready for her first trip. I took Evans, Koepplinger, Michael, and a couple of scouts, in addition to the native bosun and crew of four. We got away, without running lights, at 0315 on 12 November. The wind and sea were calm, so as soon as we had set the course I turned in down below in the cabin, leaving Evans on watch. The next thing I knew I was awakened off Koli by a boot on my shoulder and Ray Evans's plaintive voice: "Captain, do you see what I see?"

I scrambled up on deck. There were ships all around us—we were sailing straight through a task force. We counted at least three cruisers and ten destroyers in the immediate vicinity; I hoped we had some more somewhere. I expected us to be blown out of the water any minute; they must have been warned that we were leaving, or we would not have survived to tell the tale. As we found out later, it was nearly our entire available strength, waiting to prevent the enemy from landing troops at Cape Esperance and Tassafaronga.

We got to Aola at 0820 without further incident, and I saw Colonel Sturgis immediately. Their peaceful calm was interrupted—everyone "turned to" and got cracking on camouflage and an emergency withdrawal plan. One thing that required a lot of attention was their beautiful roads. There was so much mud at Lunga that all our roads were black and didn't show up from the air. At Aola they had made beautiful, dazzling white roads out of coral rock, which stood out very clearly. Captain Carney was very proud of them, so he was not at all keen on covering them with earth, as I suggested. The air lookout tower of occupation days was repaired and a telephone installed, and native laborers helped Colonel Sturgis move his command post back behind the cadet's house. He wanted very much to move into it, but I was quite firm in saying no: it was an obvious bombing target, and we were still using it as scouting and reconnaissance parties' headquarters. In any case, the district officer had to have *somewhere* to go!

Hanging On Like Grim Death

About coffee time, a signal came in from CACTUS that the Japanese battleships had been sighted only 300 miles away. That would place them off the coast before midnight. Their guard destroyers were but 195 miles away. Six transports at Lunga[6] were feverishly unloading reinforcements, but they were being sniped at by enemy artillery. A second signal reported that more than twenty bombers attacking the ships had been shot down by ack-ack fire,[7] and our shore installations were also under bombing attack.

At Aola it was bright and sunny, with practically no swell. Apart from the steady drone of diesel-engined vehicles, all one could hear was the gentle splash of the surf and the rustling of coconut palms in the breeze. It was a peaceful scene—it was hard to imagine that there was a war on, let alone that our nemesis was so near at hand. But the news of the enemy battleships, which had spread like wildfire, had taken the silly grin off most faces, and preparations for defense went on apace.

Our job done, we settled down to the long ordeal of waiting to see what happened. I hung round the radio shack until 1700, but although

Colonel Sturgis had asked that we be kept informed we got no further news. There was no doubt it would be a dirty night at Lunga. After supper, Koepplinger, Evans, and I couldn't sleep, so we sat up talking of everything else, trying to avoid the subject. Gerry Koepplinger told me that some wit he had met that afternoon had told him it was common knowledge that Lever Brothers had already decided to charge the United States government five shillings for every coconut palm cut down to extend Henderson Field. This story was quite baseless: as far as I know neither Lever's nor any of the other corporate or individual owners in the Solomons received even one "brass razoo" as war compensation for their ruined coconut plantations, from either the Americans or the British. Nor did they get anything for their houses.

Nemesis at Lunga—The Naval Battle of Guadalcanal

Nine o'clock came, then ten o'clock. There was no news. The sky was clear, and all was quiet. The silence was overbearing. I finished all my tobacco and sucked on an empty pipe. Midnight, one o'clock passed. What had happened? Was the enemy heading for Aola? We knew from past experience that when it wasn't raining the flashes from naval gunfire lit up the sky, and could easily be seen from the cadet's house. Then, about 0130 on 13 November, the opening chords of a clangorous fugue fell upon our waiting ears. There were tremendous flashes, followed by thunderous explosions from the direction of Lunga Point. The Japanese had arrived.

The outgunned American force sallied to meet their challenge. As far as we poor souls knew at the time, our big stuff was but two heavy cruisers. David and Goliath. My God! If you have ever seen a naval action at night, you will know how I felt. I had seen warships exchanging red-hot shells at eight thousand yards, and even where we were we knew, from the din and the flashing sky, that this was the biggest battle of them all. The awful thing was that there was nothing any of us could have done to help, not even had we been at Lunga. We just had to hope and pray, knowing that our fate depended on the outcome.

The tremendous racket continued most of the night. Just after dawn a vessel came into the bay, accompanied by a mangled destroyer.[8] They were, thank goodness, ours. Instructions were given them to proceed south, and they headed out and away shortly afterward. I was relieved when Sergeant Major Andrew reported at 0800 that all was clear and as far as could be ascertained no one had landed within ten miles on either side of us during the night.

So far, the scouts round Aola had borne the brunt of the security patrolling, and they needed a rest. Although there were still dumps of supplies to be dispersed, I talked to Colonel Sturgis and eventually persuaded him to send out Marine and Army patrols with single scouts as guides. This gave the others the chance for a good feed and some sleep.

Everyone was, of course, too busy at Lunga to signal us a neatly documented account of what had happened. The resourcefulness of the average "gyrene," though, soon overcame this little difficulty, and unofficial reports began to filter through. The battle had been little short of amazing. Our cruisers and destroyers, under Admirals Callaghan and Scott,[9] had gone bald-headed for the enemy force and sunk seven or eight.[10] We had taken horrible losses—half a dozen ships sunk, including the light cruisers *Atlanta* and *Juneau;* both admirals dead; and five more vessels damaged, several badly so—but one of the Japanese battleships had been hit and torpedoed. SBDs, TBFs, and B-17s attacked her all morning, and by late afternoon she was thoroughly wrecked, off Savo Island. She had made a mess of the *Aaron Ward,* in which we had shelled the Japs ashore; the destroyer had to be towed to Tulagi. We had held them for the moment, but I remembered that it was Friday the thirteenth, and we probably had no naval replacements. The battleship was still afloat at dusk.

There was nothing we could do at Aola but sit and wait for the next round. We wondered how the chaps at D-2 were getting on, and wished very much we had been there. Everything was quiet again that night, and it was not until about 0200 on 14 November that the flashes and heavy gunfire came. In the morning, we heard that cruisers, destroyers, and probably the second battleship had bombarded the airfield and destroyed a large number of planes.

Later on, we got the joyful news that the *Enterprise* was back at sea. She was just in time, for Japanese naval forces appeared to be everywhere, and our aircraft were attacking warships and transports from the Bougainville Straits to the Russell Islands. Every available plane was on the job. Finally, at 1900, we got an official message that the leading section, at least, of the enemy transport force had been put out of action and we were safe for the moment. Seven large transports had been sunk or damaged north of the Russells, and the sea was littered with survivors.

"Ramada *with telephone wire*"

Late at night I got an urgent message from the communications officer, Colonel Snedeker,[11] appealing to me to bring up as much combat telephone wire as I could. I managed to get fifty reels together and loaded on the *Ramada.* Rumor spread wide and fast at Aola, but it was obvious that the Lunga bombardment had shot our telephone system to pieces. We decided, probably wisely, not to proceed until dawn. It was just as well that we waited, for the gunfire that night was the heaviest so far. There was no doubt that the Japanese were quite determined to wipe us out, regardless of cost. It was a question of who could hang on the longest.

Signaling, from far off, "*Ramada* with telephone wire," we got to Lunga at 0945 on 15 November. We were challenged but allowed to come in. I thanked my lucky stars that there were no ships about. We came ashore in time to see the four remaining enemy transports, beached at Tassafaronga and Mamara, being hammered by our planes and shelled by a destroyer.[12] We heard that we had lost more ships in last night's action, in which two of our battleships had taken part. One of them had been badly damaged. It was believed that at least fifteen thousand Japanese troops had been lost at sea during the battles. Another enemy battleship and several more cruisers were reported sunk.[13] Yet, in spite of the bashing they had received, the Japs were still landing men and supplies. Up at division headquarters there was pandemonium, as most of the main telephone lines had been cut and many units were completely out of touch. I heard many grim stories of the last two nights' battles.

This was not the war of August and September. It was a stark struggle for survival, and no one knew where it would all end. Hundreds of Navy survivors wandered about dejectedly, looking for somewhere to park. There was no spare clothing left at Lunga; I saw one sailor clad in rubber boots, an undershirt, and a poncho, strapped on with a piece of telephone wire, for trousers. Others had only their undershorts. The sick bay was full to overflowing.

In spite of this desperate situation, the sun was shining, and everyone looked relieved and cheerful, as if the worst were now over. It was evident that we had dealt the Japanese a solid blow and stopped them from landing troops to retake Guadalcanal. What was even better was that we had established superiority with an inferiority both in numbers and in size. Our naval squadron had achieved success in spite of being outclassed. Our flying boys were also on top of the situation, and nearly every wave of enemy planes was pounced on and many sent scuttling into the sea. The Japanese transports at Tassafaronga were now blazing wrecks. That afternoon, the dive bombers administered the coup de grâce to a huge ammunition dump near Mamara. It blew sky high, and the thud of the explosion could be felt on the beach at Lunga Lagoon.

As for the land situation, more Army troops had arrived and supplies were being unloaded in vast quantities. We had all the gear we needed, and unless the Imperial Japanese Navy could mount another full-scale attack we hoped we could settle down to cleaning up the enemy troops between Cape Esperance and the Matanikau. The chow had improved greatly, too: I had actually seen some fresh butter. It would be a great treat. A vast amount of work was waiting for me concerning scouts and laborers; there was also the welcome news that my lads had wiped out the Japanese at Vioru on the south coast and demolished their radio sets.

Native Labor

By 18 November Johnstone had arrived from Tulagi, and with Widdy was doing his best to get the native laborers properly organized. We had, of course, to arrange for the labor force to be properly put on the ration strength; the next thing was to find Widdy and Johnno some transport. It was agreed that Hart should come to assist them, and messages accordingly were sent out to get him up. The number of laborers, which was more than three hundred, was increasing; as they had worked, some of them, for more than a fortnight, the question of what they were to be paid had to be resolved.

It was found, almost by accident, that the Marines had brought a large amount of money in Australian shillings and florins (two-shilling pieces). That it had managed to survive damage for so long was, to me, amazing. I would have to start paying the scouts. Up to this time, all the old hands had received six months' pay in advance; but the larger part of the force had volunteered, and had joined at various times, and no arrangements had yet been made about signing them on or paying them. I had also made several promotions as the force had expanded, and there was the question of what pay they were to receive. All this entailed many signals back and forth to the resident commissioner's headquarters on Malaita. As he had been away consulting the high commissioner in Fiji, it all took time.

During the last two days our fighter strength had been greatly reinforced. It was almost a pleasure to drive down to the labor camp, knowing that the morning raid was being intercepted over the Russell Islands and there was no need to cease everything and take cover. The weather had been quite unusual the last two or three days—bright and sunny, with no rain—and the dried mud was everywhere. It got into eyelashes, round necks, and even between the teeth, so it was a sheer delight to go down to the Lunga River and soak there until it had all drifted away.

As I had been so busy and not in a position to reply to his signals, Hay had sensibly got Campbell and Sister Edmée, together with a dozen islanders from San Cristobal, started on their arduous journey down to Aola for evacuation. I sent frantic signals to Bengough asking him to arrange that Campbell's launch be sent to Aola from San Cristobal as soon as possible in order to take Campbell and his party back there.

Ken complained that, since Vouza's patrol was entirely committed with Carlson and, as a result of Carlson's attacks, the number of Japs scattered about to the east was increasing, it was very difficult to get rations up to him. He suggested that if we shipped them through Aola he could send there for them. At the last minute another forty-five men from San Cristobal, who had been working for Andresen and Campbell, were attached to Campbell's party. This meant that they could not all be taken south in one trip. I wanted if possible to avoid asking the Aola force for rations for them, so I frantically signaled Bengough again to see whether he could send another ship as well.

The problem of dispatching our small boats on these tasks was, in a way, made more complicated by the fact that, as a result of the intense air activity of the last fortnight, we had rescued fighter and dive bomber pilots and crews scattered all over the place. Picked up and succored by the people on Guadalcanal, San Cristobal, and Malaita, they were gradually finding their way back to the various headquarters, where they were anxiously awaiting transport back to Lunga and further action. Many had also been picked up by Kennedy on New Georgia and Kuper on Ysabel, but they were returned through Tulagi. At the same time, it was convenient to have a couple of native pilots traveling with the best boat crews, for with something happening at Lunga every day the crews were a little afraid of crossing open waters alone and undefended.

Bringing back pilots to fight another day was one of the great advantages we had over the Japanese. I cannot quote actual figures, but I believe that between August and the end of November more than two hundred of our pilots were returned to duty, through coastwatching posts and the helping hands of Solomon Islanders. Japanese pilots were not so lucky. Very few even had parachutes. Those who survived a crash were often dealt with by the islanders in their own way, and that could not be avoided. Those who were captured were brought back to Lunga as prisoners. They all said that if they had succeeded in returning to Rabaul they would have been segregated from those who had not been to Guadalcanal, in order that the news of their awful defeats not leak out. The number of pilots, either ours or theirs, recovered by the Japanese was extraordinarily small; this no doubt was a factor in our gradual increase in superiority over their air force, since the quality of its pilots and crews rapidly declined.

Postmortem

At D-2 they were very busy sifting out all the reports of the naval battle. It was believed that the Japanese had lost twenty-six ships (in fact, it was seventeen), with twelve more badly damaged. Apart from the two battleships and other combatants, it was almost certain that all eleven of their transports, containing full combat rations and supplies for the fifteen thousand or so on board, were destroyed. We had lost nine ships sunk and nine more damaged, one of them the battleship *South Dakota*.

There was no doubt that the Japanese had for the time being utterly failed in their effort to recapture Guadalcanal, and unless they could immediately produce that effort again it was unlikely that they would have much chance of victory. Our morale had gone up tremendously—everyone felt that, barring accidents, we could hold the island and eventually drive off the enemy.

On 19 November there was a small alarm of an enemy transport off Malaita. Aerial reconnaissance revealed that it was a floating hulk, a relic of the destroyed Japanese transport fleet. It provided an excellent practice target for the flying boys.

Fresh Faces

The aloneness we had felt in the dark days of September and October was wearing off as fresh Marine and Army units continued to pour in; the Marines had a great time ribbing the "doggies" and selling souvenirs for more useful "gismals," such as cigarettes, clothing, and food.[14] The Army units were part of the Americal Division, which original plans had landing on Guadalcanal ten days after the Marines. Here they were, nearly three months later. "A miracle," we called it!

The attack on the Japanese beyond the Matanikau was proceeding with redoubled vigor. Most of our 1st Marine Division men, who looked like lean and aged veterans, had been withdrawn from the exhausting front and replaced with 2d Division Marines and Army units, under Army Brig. Gen. Edmund B. Sebree. More and more native labor was being required here as time advanced.

It was just as well that the Marines were withdrawn, as malaria was taking a tremendous toll. Almost two thousand men were out of action with it in October, and in November the number rose to more than three thousand. Though I never took atabrine as regularly as I should have, a steady prewar routine of quinine had perhaps inoculated me against malaria, for I managed to evade it.

Lieutenant Colonel Carlson was still busily involved with the sizable remnant of the Japanese force from Koli Point. All information pointed to the fact that originally about fifteen hundred men had landed.[15] They had suffered heavy casualties from the bombardment by our three warships. Carlson had attacked and broken them up, and they were now in full flight toward the Matanikau via the headwaters of the Tenaru and Lunga Rivers. He lost no opportunity in harassing them.

John Mather, doing valiant service for the Raiders, was yelling for more and more carriers. It was very difficult to help him, as we had collected most of the able-bodied people from the immediate vicinity for the labor force. The best I could do was send John some extra scouts to help with recruiting on the spot.

We began to get a stream of VIPs from down south. They came up in transport planes, which evacuated the wounded. (Heretofore they had been full on the way up with bombs and drums of gasoline to keep our combat aircraft going.) There were senior officers of Admiral Halsey's command and of units that were about to be sent up to reinforce us, together with officers of the Commonwealth forces. I was introduced to most of them, and had to explain how we ran the island outside the Marine perimeter! Amongst these VIPs was Col. J. I. Brooke, GSO 1 (i.e., chief operations officer) of the 3d New Zealand Division. He stayed with General Vandegrift, and when he first arrived he declared his intention of watching his first Pacific air raid from the top of the general's dugout. I thought immediately of John Mather's first effort! The colonel was quite used to air raids in the Middle East, but it did not take him very long to discover that ours tended to be rather different, and he soon developed that rabbitlike tendency with which we on Guadalcanal were so familiar.

Senior officers of the Royal New Zealand Air Force also put in an appearance, including Victor Goddard, chief of New Zealand Air Staff. I confess that when I met him for the first time, in khaki and with his cap off, I completely failed to comprehend the significance of his blue and black air commodore's rings! The RNZAF was bursting to go into action, and Squadron Leader Fisher with No. 3 Squadron of Hudsons arrived on 20 November. Everyone was very pleased to see them, as it meant that the dive bombers could be relieved of all the long-range ship patrols and could concentrate on strikes only. These lads had been worked very hard, and had to compete with malaria, jaundice, and "the bends" into the bargain.

D-2 had expanded so greatly that it was hardly recognizable. Amongst others we now had two officers and several enlisted men interpreting aerial photographs. This was a fairly new science, and occasionally they made mistakes. One of these, committed by their headquarters, was to issue to the Aola landing force maps of Aola Bay indicating a sixty-foot wharf to the westward side of the bay! This puzzled me for a long time, until I realized that the beach had started to shelve and that what they had picked up from the air was the still-intact wing member of Ekins's Catalina, which had slipped down until it lay just above the surface of the water. I pulled their legs about it, especially as the wing member was, as far as I could remember, more than sixty feet long!

There were certain other additions besides, and to accommodate us all there was now a vast operations room, which had been dug out of the ridge behind our old Ops tent. Fred Kidde was off on attachment to a newly formed eastward offensive force under the command of General Rupertus,[16] and Art Claffey was very pleased with himself at having returned all the way from the New Hebrides sitting on a thousand-pound bomb inside a DC-3 transport. Wimpy and Massaro quite typically had "acquired" cots from the Army; I didn't mind, because they got one for me, too![17]

Captain Moran was in his element. The captured material and documents had piled up tremendously, and he had sorted out some interesting "dope." Some of the Japanese diaries were interesting and amusing, but others were rather grim. The Japs considered themselves invincible, and they went into long explanations making every excuse for their defeat except their own inefficiency.

One captured document purported to be the draft arrangements for our surrender to Lieutenant General Hyakutake.[18] Amongst other matters, it stated that General Vandegrift would be escorted to Kokumbona, where, in a touching ceremony, he would be asked to hand over his sword. "It would have been kind of embarrassing," he said, "as I forgot to bring my sword with me!" Diaries revealed that some of the howitzer crews had died of starvation, while the quartermasters on the beach, who were completely out of touch, lived in hideouts under piles of rotting rice bags.

Another document, of a totally different character, had been written by a medical dresser. It recounted what he termed an interesting lecture, given by a doctor at their headquarters. He revealed that two Marine scouts, who had gone missing some time before on the Matanikau front, had been tied to trees and used as demonstration specimens. With no disgust or horror whatever, the dresser described in detail how the medical officer had carried out vivisection, lecturing the while on the anatomy of the human body. There were no words of emotion for the Marines, nor any reference to their reaction or their horrible fate. All he could say was how interesting a scientific demonstration it had been.

Although still very lean and hungry, we had begun to get three meals a day. As a result, the morning tea club died a natural death. I kept our apparatus for a long time after. The kettle was an elegant Japanese aluminum one, with the lid secured by a chain and a naval badge, consisting of an anchor with a cherry blossom superimposed, on the side. Our drinking vessels, also Japanese, were blue enamel pannikins with the rising sun trademark on the bottom. We used to bring back limes from our extramural operations and, provided we could get ice from the Tojo Ice Factory, make a health-brew of lime squash in our tea kettle. It was eventually stored away for some time, and invaded by ants. Not content with building their mud home inside, they attacked the aluminum, which became full of strange blisters and holes, and my historic relic of life on "the Rock" had to be thrown away.

Rumors always traveled very fast on Guadalcanal. The latest one, toward the end of November, was that eggs would be arriving. To Marine "chow hounds" it was the most important news for months.

Catching up with all the signals and reports, and the letters and demands from my remaining parishioners, was an uphill job. I found I could not stick to it for more than two or three hours at a time. We had all got so used to dodging into a dugout whenever there was an air raid that I felt quite strange working on without them, and instead of concentrating I'd find myself staring up into the sky. We still got the air warnings, but our fighters usually managed to attack their planes while they were still far away.

In catching up with my paperwork I had great assistance from a lad who has not so far been mentioned. His name was Peachey, Private Peachey, and he was formerly a university lecturer in French and German. So, what did they do with him? They sent him to the Pacific! Fred Peachey had lived in England and in Europe for some time, and had been educated at Marlborough College and Paris University. He was our "boffin," the backroom boy, who wrote many polished reports. He also had a rich and wide range of language, culled from both sides of the Atlantic. If you rang up D-2 you would usually get from the other end, "TEXAS TWO, Private Peachey speaking, sir," in the most faultless English, with a slight trace of the Oxford accent. Peachey, who was growing bald, was already married, and he became quite incensed when he got the news that his wife had been given a commission in the newly formed lady Marines! This organization had not yet obtained a euphonious acronym such as SPARS or WAVES, but amongst the Marines a title, quite vulgar, was soon found for it, on which officialdom frowned. It was, excuse my French, BAMs, or Broad-Assed Marines. This gave rise to some unmerciful ribbing, as Peachey himself was not all that narrow across the rump! He got a well-deserved commission in the field, however, in a later campaign.

My old, and only, pair of boots had finally come to pieces and worn right through the sole, but I hadn't had time to notice it. Early on 21 November I went down to see Colonel Coffman,[19] the quartermaster, to get a new pair, and to thank him for all the trouble he had gone to in getting rations for our extramural operations at all hours of the day and night.

The colonel presented me with a long cigar. It was a custom to which I had not altogether got accustomed. At first it had struck me as odd that the Marines were prepared to smoke them at all times of the day, though admittedly the cigars that we used to smoke before the war were much stronger than these. I was used to smoking them after meals, and that usually meant after dinner, but here it seemed quite in order to smoke them after breakfast. (Colonel Waterman,[20] who commanded the 1st Service Battalion, even smoked them *before* breakfast, although as often as not he just kept one in his mouth, chewing and rolling it from one side to the other.) I didn't smoke cigarettes, and I was, as usual, short of pipe tobacco, so who was I to complain? And so I lit up. Colonel Coffman's ration dumps were in the middle of a leafy grove, and it was rather pleasant to lean back in a camp chair and contemplate the blue sky, quite free of enemy planes, through the checkered green canopy. We talked about "before the war" and about plantations, and what was produced in the islands. I told him all about coconuts, and copra, and bêche-de-mer. As I rose to say goodbye, he asked me whether anyone had ever thought of growing rubber in the vicinity. I told him he was at that moment sitting in the middle of a rubber grove!

The following afternoon I was down at the naval base settling some difficulties over the schooners. The fuel oil was too heavy for our high-speed diesel engines. I was caught there about 1900 by a most irregular air raid, but Dexter's successor, Lt. Cdr. George W. Holtzman, had the situation well in hand. We retired to his well-equipped dugout, while the night sky was made horrible with flashes and flares. Always the perfect host, Holtzman produced some cartridge-case goblets, into which he poured what he called his antipersonnel cocktail. It was a liqueur made of Coca-Cola syrup and pure alcohol. We sipped it elegantly, to the fanfare of ack-ack guns and falling bombs.

Diggers on the Scrounge

Widdy had gone across to Malaita to discuss with the resident commissioner the establishment of properly organized and officered labor battalions. Until they were in place, we had to get most of their rations and equipment by gentleman's agreement. Down at the labor camp, Johnstone and Hart were doing great work; Johnno found it a little difficult, however, not because the Marines were uncooperative but because they were so busy getting the laborers to their jobs that they had little time to draw equipment.

Colonel Buckley was highly amused by what he called the boys' "motorized operations." Johnstone, who had always claimed to be one of the first Diggers ashore at Gallipoli, would drive around darting his eagle eye over everything. If he saw a case by the roadside, he would stop and examine it, and if he thought it was useful he would pop it in the jeep and drive off, with never a backward glance! Hart, who apparently had not had much recent experience at the wheel, would drive along in a grand manner—meaning that quite often he was well off the road—and come back with a strand or two of barbed wire or telephone wire dragging behind him. Clarry soon developed his own scrounging technique. Stopping conveniently near an unloading truck to disentangle a snagged piece of wire, he would engage the unsuspecting soldiers in conversation. Before long, he would have checked their load, and with a careless air he would say, "I don't suppose you've got any so-and-so?" Then off he'd go with his couple of cases!

Old Clarry was the best intentioned of men. When I wrote him from Aola at the end of October, he replied, in all seriousness, that he had four or five cases of books at Kau Kau, mostly novels, and would be glad to pass them on to one of the camps, where they would probably be welcomed! Perhaps some boat in the vicinity could come and pick them up, or perhaps he could deliver them somewhere. What did I suggest? It was jolly kind of him, but had he been at Lunga he would have realized that there would be no time to read books until we got on board the boat for home. Another of his earlier letters, commenting on the way the Japanese had ill treated his property, mentioned the loss of part of his stamp collection. "Some of the bastards," he wrote, "also appear to be stamp collectors as they pinched a lot of foreign stamps from a drawer here valued at about £20; I drew Ishimoto's attention to the loss but he did not do anything, and I could not point out the man who took them." I remembered that we had found a bundle of stamps wrapped up in a silk handkerchief at Gorabusu, but had not had time to do anything about it. Rooting around in Captain Moran's "museum," I found the bundle and sent the stamps over to Clarry Hart. He was immensely pleased.

Many of the scout detachments were working with different Marine and Army units, and those outside the perimeter reported through Adams or Hay. The heavy work of interrogating each scout when he came in, therefore, had slacked off considerably. But something new was always developing. As an example, after the trouble we had had with the Japanese howitzers, a new system had been worked out for spotting them. A scout would set out in the afternoon with a piece of apparatus known as a smoke pot. When the switch was set, it would produce a column of dense gray smoke for more than twenty minutes. The scout, having made a previous reconnaissance and discovered a gun position, would plant the smoke pot at a fixed distance due south of the position. In the morning, at a prearranged time, he would start the smoke off and run like mad. The SBDs would then come over and drop their bombs at approximately the same distance due north of the smoke column.

It did not always work out so simply, and Chaku, returning from the successful raid at Vioru, had a much more exciting story to tell. He came across an artillery piece in the middle of what he called "the big Japanese road." This was the track cut out of the jungle by General Maruyama[21] in his outflanking operation during the October battle. The gun had a caliber of approximately 105 mm. Chaku was about to shoot the crew of four when SBDs and our howitzers began to pound the surrounding area and the Japs retired below ground. Following their telephone line to a shack containing ammunition and stores, he shot the three soldiers he found there, cut the telephone wire, and carried away a long piece of it, together with a Japanese machine gun.

Two days later, Chaku just managed to avoid being killed when the party of fifty that he was shadowing deployed into the bush, forcing him to jettison the machine gun and run away. By this time he was near the Tenaru River, so he went and reported in at Gold Ridge. Hay had some smoke pots dropped, but when Chaku returned to the site he found that the gun had unfortunately been moved. Before he could begin to search for it, a hungry straggler fell out, from a column of about eighty; the scout shot him, then followed them. When the party stopped near the airfield, it was near the prearranged time; as they were the only target offering, he switched on his smoke pot, but though the Dauntlesses came over they did not drop any bombs.

Determined to eliminate them somehow, Chaku went to the village of Garokiki, where he collected about two dozen men and laid an ambush for the Japanese. Unfortunately the enemy saw them and fled, but they managed to shoot six of the party; the Japs had no arms, and only rotten rice for food. Another small party, this one armed, returned down the road and engaged Chaku's mob, who had not time to disperse; after a short action, however, Chaku was again the winner. He then boldly advanced up the road, but got surprised by another eight armed Japanese, who rushed his amateur soldiers and put them to flight. Chaku cursed them roundly and sent them home. Two enemy soldiers stopped to look at a body that he had thrown in the bush; the scout put them down with a single bullet. Then a completely fresh mob came up the road, and Chaku had to make himself scarce. He was shot at, but vanished silently into the jungle. Sometimes the smoke pot service was more effective, but it certainly was a dangerous business.

After Johnstone and Hart took over the labor force, Daniel returned to Aola to lead the patrol that was shadowing the few surviving Japanese from the Koilotumuria-Gorabusu crowd. When this six-man party wandered into Paripao in search of food, Daniel devised some quite novel tactics to deal with them. As the Japs sat round the steps of a native house, he sent a scout in to sell them a chicken, while he and the rest took up positions covering the doorway at the back of the house. The chicken seller insisted on and got five Australian shillings for the skinny bird, then retired and collected his rifle. Busy with their chicken, the enemy soldiers suspected nothing till a shot rang out and one of their number fell to the ground. The rest fled through the house, to be caught by Daniel and his lads. Result—six Japanese, five shillings, *and* their chicken!

24

All's Well That Ends Well

W ITH THE JAPANESE NAVY subdued, equipment and gear rolled in every day, and many new units made their appearance. When I could get away from D-2, I dashed madly from one headquarters to another explaining the local setup and answering questions about bush warfare. Continuous air raids and night shelling were things of the past, and we almost became enthusiastic at the thought of having everything needed to defeat the enemy. There was always "Washing Machine Charlie," but we could still laugh at him, although occasionally some unfortunate was killed. We began to think, rather cautiously and without speaking about it, that the day had almost come when we could leave things to someone else.

Thanksgiving Day

Thursday, 27 November, was Thanksgiving Day, my knowledge of which was restricted to what I had learned from my history books. The pundits at D-2 were arguing whether the day appointed by President Roosevelt was the correct historical date or not. I was very busy that day, and had not thought very much about its significance, so when I arrived late at the mess I found everyone "with their feet well in the trough."

I was confronted by a huge—repeat, huge—plate of turkey, cranberry sauce, real live spuds, and pumpkin pie, and everyone was doing what Macfarlan would have called "giving it a nudge." I licked the platter clean, and did likewise to an almost larger second helping. Afterward there was apple pie, with real apples and, of course, real pastry! I sat back, bloated but bewildered, not quite sure whether it was true. If it was, I could give thanks for the first real, normal meal in months and months; if not, it was a most satisfying dream! I heard that they had made a special point of getting the ingredients up in time. This was, of course, achieved only by air; but it was certainly worth it, to judge from the happy Marine faces around me. Back at D-2 there was no other topic of conversation. Howard, incorrigible as usual, said, "Gee, captain, why don't you all celebrate Thanksgiving Day in England?" There was an amused silence as I racked my brains for a reply. The joke was on him, for all I could find to say was "We didn't have to leave!" Everyone roared.

By the end of the month, I had more or less caught up with arrears of reports and other paperwork, thanks to the great assistance of David Trench. We also had paid off, on 23 November, the first lot of Solomon Islanders who had labored so valiantly down at the beach. They had been asked to work for only one month. Owing to the lack of proper records, the payout took far longer than expected, and it was pitch dark before we finished. Some of the men said they had not expected pay for their share in beating the Japanese, but I deemed it best to pay them all and save arguments afterward.

David and I had an anxious moment or two. We were assisted by Capt. Freddy ("Big Bad") Wolf, one of the D-2 officers, who was no more an accountant than Trench or I. The three of us counted a hundred pounds in silver shillings several times and all got different answers. When we finally gave up, there was a general agreement that we were ten pounds short. In the morning, after we had been through all the lists, we found that we had paid off more men than we thought, and all was found correct!

VIPs

On the twenty-ninth I got word from the resident commissioner that the high commissioner for the Western Pacific was coming from Fiji to pay us a visit on 2 December. I had to make all the arrangements. I spent a whole day trying to get an amphibian plane, which could land in the harbor at Auki, to go and collect Mr. Marchant, who was to be with us for the visit. Major Sampas,[1] the responsible officer at 1st Marine Air Wing and a great friend of coastwatchers, with the best will in the world, did his utmost; but the three available planes all had holes in them, and it took a lot of hard labor to get one good one into the air.

I suddenly realized I had to smarten myself up. That meant I'd have to get some shoulder tabs somewhere, if I wanted to wear my beautiful new pips, and shave off my beard. The beard was the easier job: there were several willing helpers around with map scissors, and it was soon off, to the accompaniment of a lot of jovial leg pulling. I must say I felt quite strange without it! The shoulder tabs weren't so easy, but we managed somehow, and the mob at D-2 decided that I would pass muster, but only just.

On the day appointed, the Duck behaved itself and the resident commissioner arrived safely about breakfast time. He was quite disappointed to find me almost properly dressed, except for headgear, and the beard gone. About 1200 the high commissioner, Sir Philip Mitchell, duly landed on Henderson Field with his staff in an RNZAF Catalina. He also wanted to know where the beard had gone. Back at division headquarters, Sir Philip impressed General Vandegrift greatly by presenting him with a huge flask of whiskey. On the general's protesting that he could not accept all of Sir Philip's stock, the latter replied, quite nonchalantly, "Oh, it's quite all right. I've got another one just the same size."

There followed much feverish discussion of plans for what was now called "The Solomon Islands War Effort," in big capitals. In the late afternoon, I took Sir Philip round to the native camp, where he inspected the few scouts who were not out on duty. They remained stolidly at attention, at order arms. As I had expected, he commented on it; I was ready with the reply that, though they could all shoot straight, there had been no time to teach them rifle drill. Then too, instead of bayonets they were all wearing bush knives in rawhide scabbards with the hair still on, and consequently could not fix bayonets either!

Appearing satisfied with my reply, Sir Philip then told me he had heard from General Vandegrift that my lads had killed a very satisfactory number of Japanese. "Look here, young Clemens," he said, "you realize you've been killing Japs without a license?" For a moment I didn't understand. "Well, General Vandegrift says you have four hundred armed men and are doing a damned fine job." "Yes, sir," I replied, "but it's up to you." He told me to cheer up, that he had decided to regularize the situation by gazetting my scouting organization as a special battalion of the Defence Force, and would soon be sending me three British cadets who had done their military training and some Fijians and New Zealanders who had been trained as commandos. Then the high commissioner asked me an awkward question: how had I been paying the scouts and laborers up to date? I told him that, early on in the piece, I had seized all the evacuees' money and paid everyone in advance as far as I could. "Since then, sir," I said, "I have 'arranged' to get them paid up to the end of November, and if arrangements can be made to pay them henceforth, no difficulties will arise on that account." (The general knew quite well that I had asked him for some Australian silver to pay cargo unloaders and had signed for ten thousand pounds "for intelligence received." But I wasn't putting *that* on the books!) Sir Philip looked straight at me, and I saw a ghost of a twinkle in his eye. "All right, you young devil," he said. And that was that. We moved on to the native labor setup, and I explained how they were getting the rations and ammunition ashore and up to the front, and how they brought casualties back from the front line. I introduced Hart and Johnstone, and Sir Philip talked to some of the islanders.

Guadalcanal No More

Later on in the day, I was called to General Vandegrift's hut. Sir Philip told me that the general was very pleased with what we had accomplished and, as the Marines would be moving out shortly, had suggested that I be given some leave. He had accepted the general's suggestion, and approved the leave; would I get ready to depart Guadalcanal with him in the morning? "Yes, sir," I replied weakly, hardly appreciating what it meant.

I walked back to D-2 almost in a dream. I could hardly control my feelings. Was I really leaving the island? I could hardly comprehend that the long ordeal was really over, or was it? We had got used to being left alone with our troubles. Going on leave? It would be only as far as Australia. I had no plans, but I could foresee a long program of eating ahead. That was about all our battered brains could think of!

I spent the whole night talking with the mob at D-2. Their ideas of how I should spend my leave were pretty lurid, and they all wanted to come too! Joking apart, we had all got used to each other, faced danger, made plans, and been on "shows" together; I felt as though I were leaving Colonel Buckley and the Marines to do it, although I knew that their days on the island were numbered too. There wasn't very much packing to do, and I joyfully handed over the sheaves of signals and letters that were our records. David Trench carried on the good work.

To Andrew and Daniel, who had come up for the occasion, I bid a sad farewell, giving them messages for Vouza, and Eroni, and all my gallant section leaders, true veterans of Guadalcanal. Without their wonderful assistance, I certainly would not have survived to tell the tale. I was rather sad at missing young Dovu, who as I have mentioned had been brought back from Suagi on 1 November with a bullet through his shoulder. He had been amazingly lucky. It had passed just under his collarbone, struck nothing vital, and passed out through his shoulder blade, leaving a neat hole the size of a silver dollar. I had managed to see him only once in hospital, for the blighter, as soon as the surface of his wounds had healed, had "gone over the hill" and reported for duty with Vouza and the Raiders! He was still doing a great job. Michael, my personal retainer and cook to the Aola expedition, was quite overcome by the occasion, but he had Suinao for company, and he intended to await my return at Aola.

As for the civilians, most of the Roman Catholic missionaries had gone south or over to Malaita. Sister Edmée had safely reached Aola, in convoy with Campbell, whose cutter had come from San Cristobal to collect him; there Father de Theye from Avu Avu had met her and taken her to Malaita. Father de Klerk was still helping the scouts at Tangarare. Brother James Thrift was looking after the mission property at Marau; Eroni and Adams were still checking on submarines nearby. At Avu Avu, old Father Boudard, having managed to avoid every opportunity for evacuation, carried on his life's work, quite independent of wars and civilization.

The schooner service was running smoothly. Six or more were now running stores and personnel to coastwatchers and small boats, and bringing back pilots from Malaita, San Cristobal, and Ysabel. They also traveled up and down from Aola to Lunga, thereby releasing Navy boat crews and craft for other jobs.

Sir Philip's Catalina took off at 0900 on 3 December. As we moved off down the runway, I sat in the gun blister aft and had my last view of Wimpy, Koepplinger, Howard and Massaro, Michael, and, of course, our revered colonel. I felt very sad leaving "Buckley's crystal ball outfit," as when I returned it would be gone, never to be the same again. Our battered plot, the CACTUS area, looked very strange from the air. Queer new growths were appearing amongst the old familiar shell holes.

There was an air of finality about that departure, for though there would be many more scraps the worst was over on Guadalcanal. As it faded over the horizon, that city of sleepless nights, I could almost feel the strings that tied me to it break. It had been my "home" for ten short months, but what had passed in that time was still almost beyond comprehension, and like a dream.

As we passed high over San Cristobal, I wondered how Michael Forster was getting on. He had been so near, and yet so far from it all. Although he had probably not seen any Japanese, apart from their planes and ships by the score, he must have had an anxious time, and probably had felt as much alone as I had. Later I found out that he had taken his delight in keeping up the forms of government, and when relieved he had neat piles of monthly returns, all of them up to date, ready to forward to the secretary when normal government was restored. Michael's only consolation during the occupation, apart from the occasional companionship of rescued pilots, must have been the choice tinned foods washed onto his shore from sunken ships. At the bottom of San Cristobal we passed Santa Ana, where "the Baron" was still holding out. He, too, had picked up several pilots, and had them returned to base. He was the father of Geoffrey Kuper, the coastwatcher.

I still felt quite bewildered. Was it all a crazy dream? We were flying fairly high, and the vibration of the plane's engines had a peculiar effect on my ears. I felt completely detached from anything that had happened. Time ceased to exist. The steady drone was like a music staff over which my senses played a tune. My mind flitted over the happenings of the last few months; as I thought of the shelling, or the bombing, or even the talk at D-2, I could hear it all again. It was quite eerie. I tried to think of Sydney and what it would be like when I got there, but my brain would not function in that direction. It basked in the past, or merely free-wheeled. The reaction had set in. I was not alone anymore. I was not on watch. It was peace indeed. I gave up the unequal struggle and drifted into a beautiful sleep.

And so to Vila in the New Hebrides, where I met the Australian naval personnel who had picked up my signals when I was in the bush. In the bay lay a host of Liberty Ships, built in four days and loaded in six, waiting as many weeks until wharves could be built for their unloading. We stayed overnight, and I celebrated my safe arrival with the first bottle of British beer since the March before. Then on to Nouméa, capital of New Caledonia, where I said goodbye to Sir Philip and his party. And finally to Sydney, where a good time was had by all!

Epilogue

Thus far, with rough and all-unable pen,
Our bending author hath pursu'd the story;
In little room confining mighty men,
Mangling by starts the full course of their glory.
—*Shakespeare, King Henry V, epilogue*

THE BATTERED REMAINS of the 1st Marine Division were relieved by the Army about a week after I departed. Not more than two-thirds were left of their original number, and some were so weak that they had to be helped up the cargo nets. On relinquishing his command, General Vandegrift issued a divisional circular, which was also passed to all coast-watchers. It read as follows:

In relinquishing command in the Cactus area, I hope that in some small measure I can convey to you my feeling of pride in your magnificent accomplishments and my thanks for the unbounded loyalty, limitless self-sacrifice, and high courage which have made these accomplishments possible.

To the soldiers and Marines who have faced the enemy in the fierceness of night combat; to the Cactus pilots, Army, Navy, and Marine, whose unbelievable achievements have made the name "Guadalcanal" a synonym for death and disaster in the language of the enemy; to those who have labored and sweated within the lines at all manner of prodigious and vital tasks; to the men of the torpedo boat command slashing at the enemy in night sortie; to our small band of devoted Allies who have contributed so vastly in proportion to their numbers; to the surface forces of the Navy associated with us in signal triumphs of their own, I say that at all times you have faced without flinching the worst that the enemy could do to us, and have thrown back the best he could send against us.

It may well be that this modest operation, begun four months ago today, has, through your efforts, been successful in thwarting the larger aims of our enemy in the Pacific. The fight for the Solomons is not yet over, but "tide what may," I know that you, as brave men and men of good will, will hold your heads high and prevail in the future as you have in the past.

/s/ A. A. Vandegrift
Major General, U.S. Marine Corps.

I was not there to see Carlson's Raiders march in. Yes, they marched in. I wish I had been there to salute them. When I returned from leave, however, waiting at D-2 was a page from Carlson's little notebook, with a handwritten letter for me:

Dear Clemens:
We are at Tini—en route to Binu and have contacted Vuza (great fellow).

I am sending Tabasui back as he is not familiar with the Binu area. Tabasui has done top work for us. Please tell him how much I appreciate it.

We are pushing on and hope to nip them in the rear.

Yours
Carlson

Although I say it myself, I was sure Vouza would do well. In fact, he was a damned good company commander. He was awarded a Legion of Merit for that patrol.

Late in December, it was time for Ken Hay to be sent south because we could not go on providing rations for civilians. Hay, who it will be recalled was exceedingly overweight, had to walk down and be met at the perimeter. Several attempts to get him down were made, but they were interrupted, mostly by operations, and it was not till January 1943 that he eventually made it. Ken was so out of condition that he sat down and would not budge till he felt better. Getting impatient at the delay, the colonel in charge of the Intelligence section of the Army's newly activated XIV Corps sent a young lieutenant to see what the holdup was.

The lieutenant, seeing this very fat man with an enormous paunch, tried to get him going. Ken replied, "I can't, I am knocked up!" To an Australian it meant he was so tired he could not walk, but to Americans it meant something else. The lieutenant rang his colonel: "Mr. Hay, sir, says he is knocked up, and believe me, sir, he looks as if he was!"

It was not until February 1943 that the Japanese were beaten, and Guadalcanal again became free. The war in the Pacific settled down to a steady but grim routine; Guadalcanal saw some part of every force sent out by the South Pacific command to attack the Japanese—including the last, which went to Okinawa—and it saw many of the wounded returning. But the late summer and autumn of 1942 will always be remembered as its apogee, especially by the islanders, and by those of us who had some attachment there.

Throwing the Marines into Guadalcanal was but a stopgap measure, done with the only troops available, to prevent the Japanese from going any farther and cutting off Great Britain's southern Dominions. The 1st Marines were, I believe, on the U.S. East Coast when called upon, the 5th were on the West Coast, and the 7th away in Samoa. They met as a division for the first time off Fiji, and a few days later they were landed, some thousands of miles from any assistance and with no base, on an unknown and hostile shore.

As you have read, we did not have much to share, but we shared it, white and black alike. The Solomon Islanders were not required to slug it out in the firing line, although, in extremis, many of them did so; but they did not only the scouting work but also all manner of other important jobs, including, in later days, the control of malaria, which had put so many men out of action. Outside the perimeter, they sheltered and returned to circulation a remarkable number of pilots, who lived to fight another day.

The Marines were of America's best. They never said very much, but they did an awful lot. Together we lived and worked with but one aim—to get the job done as quickly as possible.

When a group of men from different places and callings share an experience—especially one like this, where the shadow of death was ever flitting by—they frequently coin some joke or phrase, or commemorate it in some way peculiar to themselves. In a public house I know, there hangs an illuminated scroll, signed by all the men in one of the Japanese prison camps who had been to the same school. It was smuggled out, and now hangs in its place of honor. I believe that the "Rats of Tobruk" coined themselves a brass commemorative medal.

We were no exception. Early on in the piece, when we were without food, barbed wire, and, as we wrongly surmised, any visible means of naval support, there was a great deal of griping. We all felt abandoned; what more natural, then, than to blame the top brass of the Navy? We called those blokes every name under the sun. It was agreed that their guiding principle was "F——k you, George, I'm all right!" We, of course, were George.

Colonel Twining got Capt. Donald L. Dickson, R-1 of the 5th Marines and a talented combat artist, to design a medal of our own. They and their co-conspirators, including me, discussed what the inscription should be. The division's on-scene historian, Lt. Herbert C. Merillat, suggested "Let George do it," an expression that had become quite common among the Marines. It was decided that the motto should be in Latin, and I was asked to translate it. (In Twining's recollection I was the only one there who knew the language, though I'm sure that Herbie Merillat, who had been a Rhodes Scholar at Oxford, did too.) My loose rendering, "Faciat Georgius," was approved. From there it was but an easy step to the Guadalcanal George Medal, which was "awarded" to a fortunate few, of whom I was lucky to be one. It was issued with a formal citation signed by Colonel Buckley, the Grand Master of the Order.

The medal, minted in Australia out of old iron that was come by in a way known only to real Marines, has on one side the motto "FACIAT GEORGIUS," over which a hand, emerging from the sleeve of a naval dress uniform, is dropping an exceedingly hot potato into the outstretched hands of a tired Marine, with our operational nom de plume, a cactus, in the background. The reverse graphically illustrates one of the expressions most used during the campaign. "The shit just hit the fan" was the rude operational code for all manner of disasters, and the preliminary to a demand for help. On the medal, a fan whirs merrily to the one side, while a cow, tail uplifted, is busy beside it. (Speaking heraldically, she may be described as "rump rampant"!) Below is the inscription, "IN FOND REMEM-BRANCE OF / THE HAPPY DAYS SPENT / FROM AUG. 7TH 1942 / TO JAN. 5TH 1943 / U.S.M.C." The ribbon was made from old and faded jungle-green herringbone twill, or "dungreen," as it was called.

During the campaign, I learned a lot about America and Americans and, I hope, cleared up a few misconceptions about Great Britain. My primary reason writing for this book was to give a measure of recognition to the part played by the Solomon Islanders in the Pacific war, and especially to those who stood by me so loyally on Guadalcanal. At the same time, however, it belongs just as much to the Marines, the "First to Fight," who were there, on "the Rock," and whose redoubtable spirit helped make the island of Guadalcanal free again for men to walk about in peace. Good luck to them all, *wherever* they may be.

A Few Words on Reflection

I will always remember a bon mot of Colonel Twining's, first heard during one of our daily sessions taking shelter from Japanese bombs. He said, "We were confronted with oversized problems, the unthinkable, the unforgivable, and the unavoidable."

A district officer's normal job was to look after fifteen thousand Solomon Islanders, some missionaries, and some planters and traders. They were all scared out of their wits when thirty thousand Japanese arrived; then came nineteen thousand American Marines, and the last named were the only lot who had food. The task was so oversized as to be unthinkable. The Japanese were unforgivable, the subsidiary problems quite unavoidable. I could have added, "The nigh impossible, dealt with day after day."

At the end of a paper prepared for the Australian Naval Historical Society on the Battle of Savo Island, I wrote, "It was the inaugural engagement of a bloody and desperate campaign which I shared with General Vandegrift and his marines, and the 9th August, 1942 only the first of terrible days to come." The commanders on either side might well have raised their hands to heaven, crying out, like the Psalmist, "For all the day long have I been plagued, and chastened every morning." I was there, and I can vouch that that was the way it was. Some of us were fortunate in surviving. Well over twenty-five thousand Japanese did not.

MAPS

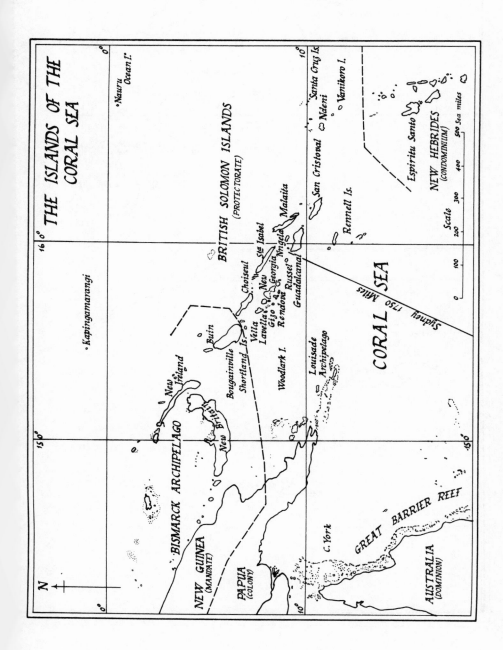

THE ISLANDS OF THE CORAL SEA

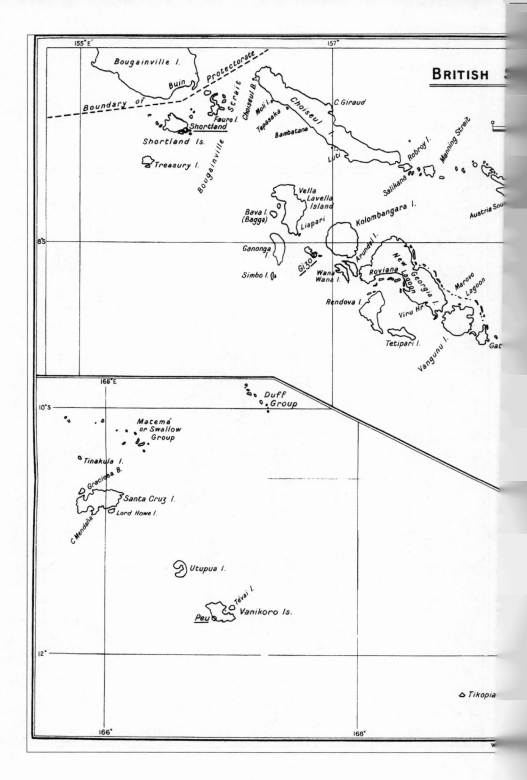

155°E
Bougainville I.

Boundary   of   Buin   Protectorate

Shortland Is.

Shortland

Fauro I.

Treasury I.

Bougainville   Strait

157°

Choiseul B.

Moli I.

Tepasaka

Bambatana

Choiseul

Luti

C. Giraud

Robroy I.

Salikana

Manning Strait

BRITISH

8°S

Bava I.
(Bagga)

Ganonga

Simbo I.

Vella
Lavella
Island

Liapari

Gizo

Wana
Wana I.

Kolombangara I.

Arundel I.

Roviana

New Georgia I.

Rendova I.

Viru Hr.

Tetipari I.

Vangunu I.

Maroyo
Lagoon

Austria Sou

Gat

166°E

10°S

Tinakula I.

Graciosa B.

C. Mendaña

Santa Cruz I.

Lord Howe I.

Matemá
or Swallow
Group

Duff
Group

Utupua I.

Peu

Tévai I.

Vanikoro Is.

12°

Tikopia

166°

168°

w

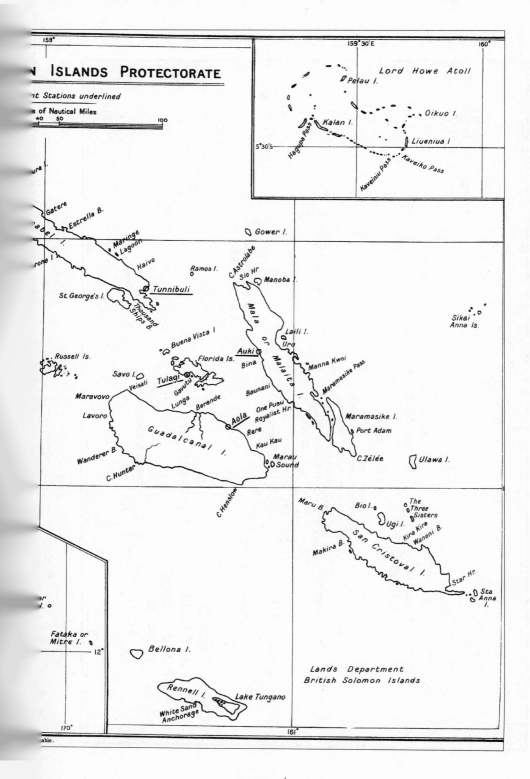

N ISLANDS PROTECTORATE

nt Stations underlined

e of Nautical Miles

40 50   100

Lord Howe Atoll

Pelau I.

Kalan I.

Oikuo I.

Hagupa Pass

5°30'S

Liueniua I.

Kaveiniu Pass   Kaveiko Pass

Gatere
Estrella B.

Gower I.

Maringe
Lagoon

Haivo

Ramos I.

C. Astrolabe
Sio Hr.

Manoba I.

St. George's I.

Tunnibuli

Thousand
Ships B.

Mala
or
Malaita

Laili I.
Uru

Sikai
Anna Is.

Buena Vista I

Russell Is.

Florida Is.

Auki
Bina

Manna Kwoi

Maramasike Pass

Savo I.

Tulagi
Veisali   Gavutu

Maravovo

Lunga

Berande

Baunani

Lavoro

Guadalcanal I.

Aola
Rere

One Pusu
Royalist Hr.

Maramasike I.

Port Adam

Wanderer B.

Kau Kau

C. Hunter

Marau
Sound

C. Zélée

Ulawa I.

C. Henslow

Maru B.

Bio I.

Ugi I.

The
Three
Sisters

Kira Kira

Wanoni B.

Makira B.

San Cristoval I.

Star Hr.

Sta.
Anna
I.

r
d. o

Fataka or
Mitre I.

12°

Bellona I.

Lands Department
British Solomon Islands

170°

Rennell I.
Lake Tungano
White Sand
Anchorage

161°

able.

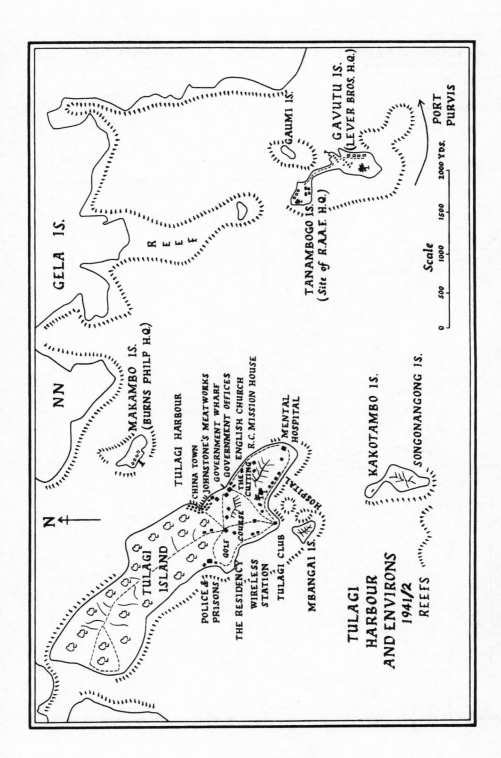

GELA IS.

NN

N

MAKAMBO IS.
(BURNS PHILP H.Q.)

TULAGI HARBOUR

CHINA TOWN

JOHNSTONE'S MEATWORKS

GOVERNMENT WHARF

GOVERNMENT OFFICES

THE ENGLISH CHURCH

R.C. MISSION HOUSE

THE CUTTING

MENTAL HOSPITAL

TULAGI ISLAND

POLICE & PRISONS

THE RESIDENCY

WIRELESS STATION

TULAGI CLUB

GOLF COURSE

HOSPITAL

MBANGAI IS.

KAKOTAMBO IS.

SONGONANGONG IS.

REEFS

GAUMI IS.

GAVUTU IS.
(LEVER BROS. H.Q.)

TANAMBOGO IS.
(Site of R.A.A.F. H.Q.)

PORT PURVIS

Scale

0   500   1000   1500   2000 YDS.

TULAGI
HARBOUR
AND ENVIRONS
1941/2

REEFS

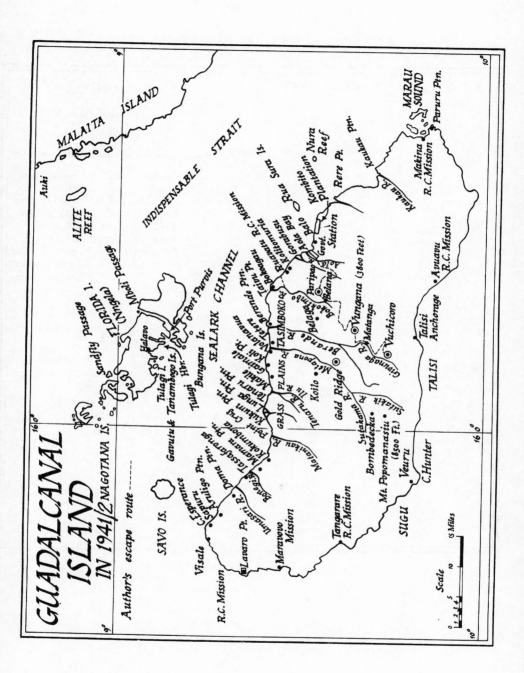

GUADALCANAL ISLAND IN 1941/2

Author's escape route ------

SAVO IS.

MALAITA ISLAND

Auki

ALITE REEF

Sandfly Passage

FLORIDA I. (Nggela)

NAGOTANA IS.

Mboli Passage

Port Purvis

Halavo

Tulagi I.

Gavutu & Tanambogo Is.

Tulagi

Havi

Bungana Is.

INDISPENSABLE STRAIT

SEALARK CHANNEL

Visale

C.Esperance

Sopriligo Ptn.

Doma Ptn.

Tasaerunga Ptn.

R.C. Mission

Lavaro Ptn.

Lunasa R.

Maravovo Mission

Tangarare R.C. Mission

Kohinbgia

Mananara Ptn.

Point Cruz

Kukum Ptn.

Tenaru Ptn.

Koli Pt.

Volonawa

Matbibi

Mataniko R.

GRASS PLAINS

Tenaru R.

Gamiala R.

Berande Ptn.

Taivu Pt.

Taisangagulo Ptn.

Tasimbolo R.C. Mission

Buchtomuria

Kolitonbusu

Gorabusu

Aola Bay

Balo

Rua Sura Is.

Kombitto Plantation

Nura Reef

Rere Pt.

Kaukau Ptn.

Tasimboko

Belaga R.

Paripao

Berande R.

Koilo

Gold Ridge

Sutakona R.

Sulaziz R.

Bombedecka

Mt. Popomanasiu (8500 Ft.)

Veuru

C. Hunter

SUGU

TALISI

Govt. Station

Viungana (3800 Feet)

Matanga

Vuchicoro

Cinunaga R.

Talisi Anchorage

Avuavu R.C. Mission

MARAU SOUND

Makina R.C. Mission

Paruru Ptn.

Kautau R.

Scale

0 1 2 3 4 5   10   15 Miles

160°

9°

160°

16°

10°

10°

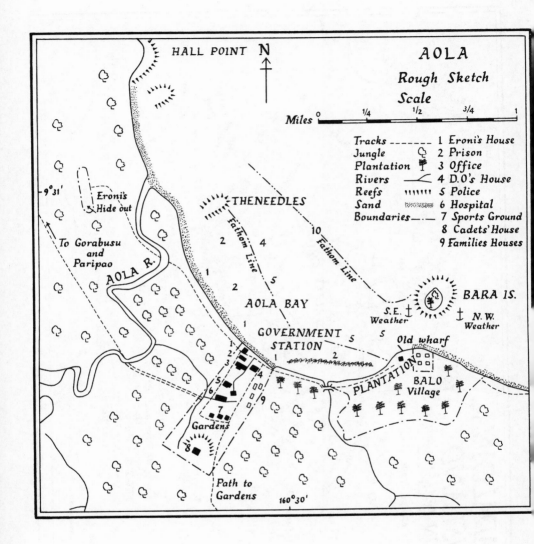

HALL POINT **N**

AOLA

Rough Sketch

Scale

Miles 0   1/4   1/2   3/4   1

Tracks	- - - - -	1 Eroni's House
Jungle		2 Prison
Plantation		3 Office
Rivers		4 D.O's House
Reefs	՛՛՛՛՛՛՛	5 Police
Sand		6 Hospital
Boundaries	—·—·	7 Sports Ground
		8 Cadets' House
		9 Families Houses

THE NEEDLES

9°31'

Eroni's
Hide out

To Gorabusu
and
Paripao

AOLA R.

Fathom Line

10

Fathom Line

2   4

1

2   5

AOLA BAY

BARA IS.

S.E.
Weather

N.W.
Weather

1

GOVERNMENT
STATION

5

Old wharf

5   5

1
2
3
5
6
4
7
9
8

Gardens

PLANTATION

BALO
Village

Path to
Gardens

160°30'

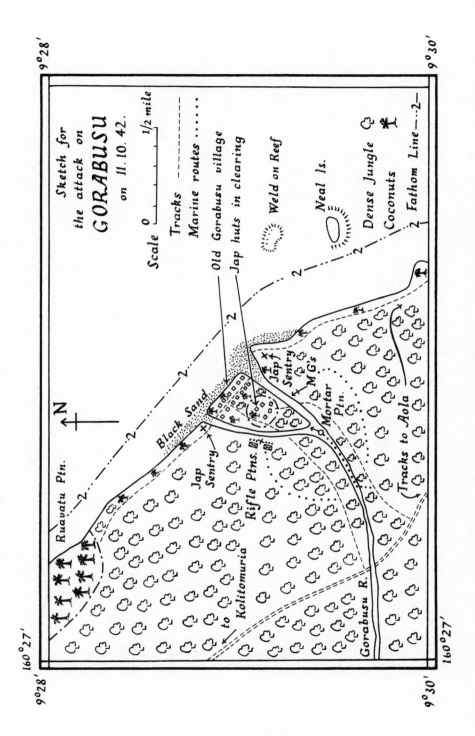

Sketch for
the attack on
GORABUSU
on 11. 10. 42.

Scale 0 _____ 1/2 mile

Tracks – – – – –
Marine routes ·······
Old Gorabusu village
Jap huts in clearing

Weld on Reef

Neal Is.

Dense Jungle
Coconuts
Fathom Line –··–2–··–

N

Ruavatu Ptn.

160°27′

9°28′

Black Sand

Jap
Sentry

to Kolitomuria

Rifle Ptns.

Jap
Sentry

M.G's

Mortar
Ptn.

(Tracks to Aola)

Gorabusu R.

9°30′

160°27′

NOTES

Chapter 1. "And there we were . . ."

1. Both firms were instrumental in the commercial development of the Solomon Islands. Lever's main business was producing copra, the dried coconut meat used in soap and cosmetics manufacturing; its properties were managed by Lever's Pacific Plantations Pty. Ltd. Burns Philp received an annual subsidy from the Australian government for providing shipping services, including carriage of mails, between Sydney and the Solomons.

2. Robert S. Taylor had been a shipboard wireless operator during World War I. In 1943 Bob returned to the Solomons, did a tour of duty, and went on leave. On his way back, the Liberator in which he was flying was lost in a rainstorm. There were no survivors.

3. The police force, which was under the Police and Prisons Department, was an armed constabulary that served as both a police and a defense force. It comprised the officer commanding armed constabulary and the superintendent of prisons, which had been combined; a sub-inspector of constabulary and gaoler, also a European; two sergeants major; and 112 other ranks. There was a central prison at Tulagi and a small local jail in each district; the establishment consisted of a clerk, fifteen warders, and a wardress at Tulagi, and one warder at each district prison.

4. The Shortlands and Vanikoro district vessels were not involved in the events of this narrative.

5. J. A. Johnstone, a plantation employee in the early 1920s, later became the butcher at Tulagi. He was usually called Johnno, or Butcher Johnstone.

Chapter 2. In Harm's Way

1. Only two managed to get away in this manner. One, Paul Kneen, went miles into the Queensland bush, where he was not known, and joined the AIF under a false name; he was killed in New Guinea.

2. On 25 January the *Kombito* had arrived at Berande. Ken Hay was told she was taking all those residents who wished to evacuate and would transfer them to the motor vessel *Kurimarau* in the Russell Islands for the trip to Australia. On

27 January 1942, *Kurimarau,* with seventy-three people onboard, had sailed from the Russells for Sydney.

3. A. N. A. Waddell and W. H. Miller, the district officers in the Shortlands and Gizo, respectively.

4. F. E. Johnson, treasurer and collector of customs, and W. V. Jardine Blake, accountant.

5. The staff of the RAAF's Tulagi Advanced Operational Base averaged twenty-four men; it included wireless operators, boat crew, a medical orderly, and an armorer, under an officer in charge from flying officer to flight lieutenant in rank. The detachment of the 1st Independent Company, AIF, numbered about twenty; it was headed by a lieutenant.

Chapter 3. Clearing the Decks

1. In all, more than two thousand workers in the central and western Solomons, about three-quarters of them on Guadalcanal, were returned to their home islands.

2. J. Cramer-Roberts, manager of gold-mining interests on Guadalcanal.

3. Father Wall had dragged part of them to shelter, but some crates had been lying on the wharf since evacuation day. Of course, they had been quite untouched by the bombing.

Chapter 4. Visitors, Welcome and Otherwise

1. I never did find out his real name. Elsewhere in my diary he is referred to as Yip Tim. That must be the name I wrote on the vouchers he used to claim his charter fee from the BSIP treasurer in Sydney. It may or may not have been his correct name.

2. Father Claude A. Palmer was then visiting Visale. He was stationed at a mission in north Malaita.

Chapter 5. A Watcher in the West

1. The regular habitués of Tanambogo were our bêtes noires, the Kawanisi four-engined flying boats, known as "43s." They were very large and heavy, and, knowing that there was no opposition, they never bothered to fly very fast.

Chapter 6. A European Murdered

1. My diary entries show that I believed this ship to be the *Mako.* Horton, however, clearly places *Mako*'s arrival sometime in late March 1942. (See D. C. Horton, *Fire Over the Islands: The Coast Watchers of the Solomons* [Sydney: A. H.

and A. W. Reed, 1970], 29-30.) He notes that they had almost no prior warning, that *Mako* docked after the morning raid, and that her master insisted on leaving that night. Horton also mentions that she was en route from Australia with drums of fuel for the Catalinas; though her primary mission was one of supply, Hamer and Russell had arranged to embark some unfit AIF troops, "and also a group of civilians who had escaped from Bougainville . . . in a small and unreliable motorboat. . . . The group . . . included Rolf Cambridge. . . . *Mako* left towards midnight . . . and steamed at full speed for Sydney. . . . [They] arrived in Sydney on 7 April."

Horton's "small and unreliable motorboat" probably refers to *Fico,* one of two cutters in which the seven refugees had come down from Bougainville. In an unpublished philatelic essay, Rev. A. H. Voyce, a Methodist missionary in the western Solomons, records an envelope from Rev. J. R. Metcalfe to his wife in Melbourne:

> [It] was handed by Mr. Metcalfe [who had stayed behind after the Japanese invasion] to Mr. Rolf Cambridge from Soraken, Bougainville, travelling out to Australia in a small vessel, the "FICO." After the war, Mr. Cambridge told me that this letter with other mail was taken to Sydney by him, and that upon reaching Sydney he "hailed" a post office van and handed over the mail without getting a receipt for it, though he later learned that the mail reached its destination. This [envelope] is marked PAQUEBOT SYDNEY 7 AP 42.

This appears to corroborate Horton's story in that Metcalfe's letter was posted on the same day as the evacuees arrived in Sydney. (Presumably they departed the Solomons in the *Mako.*) If *Mako* arrived in Sydney on 7 April, however, that fact must be squared with the entries in my diary: "Am informed 'Mako' duly arrived Tulagi 7th" (8 April 1942); "'Mako' goes by. 5 Jap planes over Tulagi" (9 April 1942). The only logical explanation is that another vessel arrived in Tulagi on 7 April, and it was that ship I saw, from a distance, sailing away two days later.

2. Kelemedi Nabuno Suno was employed by Solomons Gold Exploration Company, Ltd., whose headquarters were on Guadalcanal.

3. Charles Morris Woodford, *A Naturalist among the Head-Hunters* (London: George Philip and Son, 1890), 43, quoting Captain Simpson, RN (quotation marks in original).

4. Ibid.

5. "Yes, Sir, everything is quiet, but there is a lot of work. The bush villagers are not peaceful. Many headmen have come in and brought a lot of men to be tried in court; they have stolen, gotten in fights, or done some other bad thing. The Catholic missionaries [i.e., the fathers and sisters at Ruavatu] have not obeyed your order to go bush. They all say the bishop's order is, we are neutral, stay on the coast. Our local headmen say that everyone does not listen to their advice, and they have a lot of hard work keeping their people quiet. At the station, everything is no longer in good shape: I have moved your household to the top of the hill, and they all have planted a lot of food. Those at the lookout post do not sleep."

Chapter 7. In Which We Prepare for the Worst, and the Enemy Arrives

1. F. T. Stackpool, formerly dispenser at the government hospital on Tulagi.

2. The *Balus*, a squat wooden cargo vessel of about eighty tons, belonged to W. R. Carpenter and Company and was used to transport copra.

3. Postmortems have revealed that they had three fleets. The central fleet, the amphibious task force, was concentrated in the Shortland Islands, while the other two patrolled the waters surrounding the Solomons, one on either side of the island chain.

4. On this and subsequent events, see also Robert K. Piper, "The Royal Australian Air Force at Guadalcanal," *Australian Defence Force Journal* 87 (March/April 1991): 27-34.

Chapter 8. The Battle of the Coral Sea

1. The Tulagi strike group, from the carrier USS *Yorktown*, comprised twenty-eight dive bombers and twelve torpedo planes. The latter were second to attack, and no doubt it was the reflection from their aerial torpedoes that we saw.

2. *Yorktown* had launched four Wildcat fighter planes in response to a report that enemy aircraft from Tulagi were harassing the torpedo bombers, then on their second strike.

3. Lt. Leonard M. Davis, BSIPDF, the protectorate postmaster at Tulagi, had transferred to Auki with the resident commissioner in February.

Chapter 9. Some Unexpected Guests

1. These were two of the four Grumman Wildcats dispatched to Tulagi by the *Yorktown*.

2. Lt. (jg) Roy M. Plott and Lt. (jg) E. Scott McCuskey, respectively. In fact, Lieutenant Plott was ill that day, and his plane was flown by Ens. John P. Adams.

3. The actual results were one destroyer and three minesweepers sunk, plus a minelayer and another destroyer damaged.

4. These were undoubtedly the three minesweepers, which had just left Tulagi Harbor and were bound for the Shortlands.

Chapter 10. "The district officer has gone."

1. My diary for 16 May is silent concerning the arrival at Aola of this vessel, which may have been a native launch. Instead, the final entry for that day reports the return of the *Gynia*, with Malaita men who had been cooks for the AIF; it

would have been my responsibility to repatriate them. In an annotated transcription of the diary I wrote that *Gynia* arrived at midnight, and that she carried as well the small arms, ammunition, and teleradio. She must have come up from Marau Sound: I commented that "*Gynia* should have left Marau in the dark and arrived at dawn—makes guards nervy when boats arrive at night." It is, therefore, quite possible that the crew sailed the launch from Nggela to Marau and then transferred the cargo to the *Gynia*.

Chapter 12. "When creeping murmur . . . !"

1. This was exported by Dunlops of Virginia, who sold it under the brand name Emu; it was basically excellent tobacco, but for the South Seas trade had been so dolled up with molasses that I could not smoke it. Now that it could be bought no longer, however, its value appreciated week by week. It was the best coinage I had for buying food.

Chapter 13. "Devil b'long Chimi sing out!"

1. Dick Horton had had some brilliant ideas about using local leather, but had never been able to put them into practice.
2. On two nights out of five at that particular time, for example, there were 125 and 132 points of rain, respectively.

Chapter 15. "Oh! Lord, how long?"

1. Recent research has confirmed that the man's name was Ishimoto. A thirty-year-old linguist who was fluent in four languages, Terushige Ishimoto was a civilian interpreter for the Imperial Japanese Navy, with the pay of a lieutenant commander. He was assigned to the 81st Guard Unit, which reached Guadalcanal on 1 July 1942. Information courtesy of Stanley C. Jersey.

Chapter 16. Watch and Pray

1. From here one could see the river flowing in four directions, as it described a long loop that was bent back on itself, creating a secondary loop inside. It took me about twenty minutes to work out the course and draw a sketch map of it, it was so confusing.
2. A closer approximation of the pronunciation would be Tsaku.
3. When he had reported in, some days previously, Londoviko had fainted

clean away. An enemy party had gone to have a look at Marau, and this lad, after walking for three solid days, had just managed to intercept Eroni and prevent him from walking straight into the hands of the Japanese; then he had come back, another five days, to let me know the form. To me it looked as if he had a fairly acute case of appendicitis; fortunately, he did not, and he made a remarkable recovery.

4. Early on, we had dispersed Eroni's drugs and medical supplies to three different places, one near me. When he wasn't scouting, Eroni visited these "clinics" from time to time; in his absence, a dresser at each place carried on as best he could.

5. With the increased intensity of our bombing, I was pretty well tied to the teleradio. As Matanga was built on the river shingle and there were only two or three trees suitable for holding the aerial, I had had to set up the apparatus in the village church. The twenty-sixth of July was a Sunday, and I had forgotten the morning service. While I was receiving traffic from Bengough, everyone filed in, and soon parts of the message were blotted out by the sound of "Ave Maria"!

6. He claimed that the beach at Halavo was being used as a landing ground for seven Zeros. They were probably floatplanes.

7. These were B-17s of the U.S. Army Air Force's 11th Bombardment Group (H), which had landed on Espíritu Santo, New Hebrides, only one day before. The group's commander, Col. LaVerne G. Saunders, led the initial formation of nine Flying Fortresses against Guadalcanal.

Chapter 17. The Marines Have Landed

1. I found out subsequently that it was a transport, the *George F. Elliott*. She had been struck by an enemy plane and eventually had to be sunk.

2. Four of these turned back before reaching the target.

3. This must have been the *Australia:* HMAS *Canberra* had been scuttled at 0800, a victim of the Battle of Savo Island.

4. Chaku's behavior had been excellent, but I could not let him go. As I had no alternative, I made him work.

5. I had tried to touch Macfarlan for a pair of shoes; he had sent me over, more as a joke than anything else, a pair of sharp-pointed, thin-soled black shoes, suited more to business circles than to bush walking. They were really a size too small, so I kept them for my grand arrival at Lunga.

6. This incident is of no great importance, except that in the division history I am described as having consumed a whole bottle of brandy. (See George McMillan, *The Old Breed: A History of the First Marine Division in World War II* [Washington, D.C.: Infantry Journal Press, 1949], 47.) I wish it had been!

7. Why on earth I ever expected to find such amenities I cannot imagine. I can ascribe my peculiar feelings only to my having been alone for so long. The

Marines, of course, had landed in combat gear, and were lucky even to have enough to eat, let alone any trappings of civilization.

8. I found that what we called "boots" the Marines called "shoes."

9. Lt. Col. Frank B. Goettge.

Chapter 18. Out of the Frying Pan and into the Fire

1. The sources differ considerably as to the strength of the enemy patrol and the number of Japanese killed. (See Richard B. Frank, *Guadalcanal* [New York: Random House, 1990], 678-79.) The figures given here are those in my diary.

2. The 1st Battalion, 1st Marines.

3. Twelve SBDs of VMSB-232 (Maj. Richard C. Mangrum) and nineteen F4Fs of VMF-223 (Capt. John L. Smith).

4. Lt. Col. Edwin A. Pollock, commanding officer of the 2d Battalion, 1st Marines.

5. See Don Richter, *Where the Sun Stood Still: The Untold Story of Sir Jacob Vouza and the Guadalcanal Campaign* (Calabasas, Calif.: Toucan Publishing, 1992), 170-85.

6. Col. LeRoy P. Hunt, who commanded the 5th Marines.

7. Viv Hodgess was now custodian of his regiment's beer supply!

8. It was Butch who introduced me to hotcakes and syrup for breakfast—we had little else—and spared us a kettle of boiling water for the 6:00 A.M. morning tea club. We had the stuff neat, unless a lime appeared fortuitously, brought in by one of my men.

9. Actually, the American pilots concerned found it hard to believe that the missionaries had been allowed to remain and would have been most surprised had they seen the brethren.

10. The pilots may have seen the Japanese barges, but as no real target offered, they probably kept their bombs in reserve.

Chapter 19. Attacked on All Sides

1. Lt. Col. Merrill B. Twining and Lt. Col. Gerald C. Thomas were assistant operations officer and operations officer, respectively, of the 1st Marine Division.

2. The parachutists were now attached to the Raiders for operational purposes.

3. Lt. Col. James J. Gannon.

4. Maj. Gen. Kiyotaki Kawaguchi, commander of the 35th Infantry Brigade, Imperial Japanese Army.

5. Lt. Col. Lewis B. Puller was commanding officer of the 1st Battalion, 7th Marines.

6. Brig. Gen. Roy S. Geiger, commander of the 1st Marine Air Wing.

7. Lt. Cdr. Dwight H. Dexter, USCG. Dexter ran and maintained all the landing craft. He had a busy enough time keeping his battered command together —it usually suffered from night bombardment—but he always had a welcome sandwich available.

8. Col. John M. Arthur was commanding officer of the 2d Marines.

9. Platoon Sgt. Francis C. Pettus.

10. Adm. Chester W. Nimitz.

11. Maj. Robert E. Galer.

12. Bengough was acting resident commissioner at the time.

13. Actually, six destroyers and a seaplane carrier. Part of a ten-ship "Tokyo Express," they were headed for Tassafaronga.

14. Machinist William H. Warden.

Chapter 20. Backs to the Wall

1. Maj. William K. Enright.

2. Colonel Thomas told me that a senior officer would be in charge of the troops but that I was in charge of the operation. As a humble captain, I naturally had qualms about telling a superior what he had to do and seeing that he got it right. "If you have any trouble," Thomas said, "just say you're my representative, and if he doesn't like it, tell him to call me on the radio!"

3. After he departed Guadalcanal on a well-earned leave, Raymond J. Evans was given a commission and awarded the Navy Cross for gallantry during the rescue of Lieutenant Colonel Puller's battalion west of Point Cruz on 27 September 1942. It was during this action that Evans's close friend, Coast Guard Signalman First Class Douglas A. Munro, was killed as their Higgins boats shielded Puller's Marines from withering Japanese fire; Munro was the only Coast Guardsman during World War II to be awarded the Medal of Honor. Ray Evans received both his commission and the award the same week as he was married.

4. Lt. Col. Robert E. Hill, commanding officer of the 1st Battalion, 2d Marines.

5. See Don Richter, *Where the Sun Stood Still: The Untold Story of Sir Jacob Vouza and the Guadalcanal Campaign* (Calabasas, Calif.: Toucan Publishing, 1992), 251-59.

Chapter 21. Nip and Tuck

1. This was the Battle of Cape Esperance. Actual results were one cruiser and one destroyer sunk, plus one cruiser and one destroyer damaged.

2. The 164th Infantry, under Col. Bryant E. Moore, USA, landed on the morning of 13 October.

3. All the torpedo planes at Henderson Field had been wrecked or damaged by the shelling.

4. It now appears we had. See Richard B. Frank, *Guadalcanal* (New York: Random House, 1990), 291, 702.

5. Maj. Charles M. Nees.

6. Lt. Col. Evans F. Carlson.

Chapter 22. Advance to the Rear

1. Richard B. Frank, *Guadalcanal* (New York: Random House, 1990), 420. See also 724.

2. Rear Adm. Richmond Kelly Turner.

3. The bosuns were in local villages, with one of them on guard in turns. I had to see them to tell them the plan. Lieutenant James knew no pidgin, and they had to collect their crews, so it was best that I spoke to them.

4. Lt. Col. Arthur C. Timboe commanded the 2d Battalion, 164th Infantry.

Chapter 23. Hammer and Tongs

1. Acorn was the Navy code name for a unit designed to construct, maintain, and operate an advance land- or seaplane base and its associated airfield. "(Red)" denoted importance and priority in transport.

2. The *Majaba,* an eighteen-hundred-ton converted auxiliary vessel, was torpedoed by a Japanese midget submarine. Fortunately, she was not sunk, and the tug *Bobolink* was able to tow her to Tulagi. See Richard B. Frank, *Guadalcanal* (New York: Random House, 1990), 501, 742; Samuel Eliot Morison, *History of United States Naval Operations in World War II,* vol. 5, *The Struggle for Guadalcanal* (Boston: Little, Brown, 1948), 226-27.

3. This may have been the one fired at the destroyer *Landsdowne,* which was anchored nearby unloading ammunition for the Marines. *Landsdowne* took part in the depth charge attack on the submarine. See Frank, *Guadalcanal,* 742.

4. Vice Adm. William F. Halsey, the new commander, South Pacific, had flown in the previous day.

5. Maj. James C. Murray Jr.

6. Admiral Turner had brought in seven vessels, in two groups, but the transport *Zeilin* had been damaged by the Vals the previous day, and was returning under escort to Espíritu Santo.

7. Actual results were eleven of sixteen torpedo-carrying Bettys and one escorting Zero. They attacked about 1400.

8. The destroyer was probably the *Sterett.* See Frank, *Guadalcanal,* 442; Morison, *Struggle for Guadalcanal,* 244-45, 251.

9. Rear Adm. Daniel G. Callaghan and Rear Adm. Norman Scott.

10. The figures, as so often happened, were greatly overstated. Actual Japanese losses were one battleship (*Hiei,* which sank during the night) and two destroyers.

11. Lt. Col. Edward W. Snedeker.

12. This was the *Meade.* See Frank, *Guadalcanal,* 488; Morison, *Struggle for Guadalcanal,* 283-84.

13. The Japanese lost three vessels: a battleship (*Kirishima*), a heavy cruiser, and a destroyer. We lost three destroyers. Other ships of both sides were damaged.

14. "Gismal" or "gizmo" was a peculiarly Marine word that had no doubt been picked up overseas, although no one quite knew where. When I had gone to Palestine after the war and learned Arabic, I wondered whether it might not have been a corruption of the dog-Arabic *shuismu,* meaning, roughly, "what's 'is name."

15. In fact, the number of troops landed was far fewer, about three hundred, but provisions for two thousand men also came ashore, and this may have influenced our estimate. Actually, there were in excess of three thousand Japanese at Koli. See Frank, *Guadalcanal,* 415, 420-24.

16. Brig. Gen. William H. Rupertus, the assistant commander of the 1st Marine Division.

17. When Lieutenant Colonel Buckley's Japanese stretcher finally gave up the ghost, by the purest coincidence the 164th Infantry was coming ashore. Somehow the regiment's personal gear landed before the men, and next day Colonel Moore came and complained bitterly that two hundred cots had disappeared. Buckley sympathized, and said he knew nothing about it, but the entrance to his tent was laced up tight!

18. Lt. Gen. Harukichi Hyakutake commanded the Japanese 17th Army.

19. Lt. Col. Raymond P. Coffman.

20. Lt. Col. Hawley C. Waterman.

21. Lt. Gen. Masao Maruyama, the commander of the Sendai Division.

Chapter 24. All's Well That Ends Well

1. Maj. Michael Sampas performed the first closeup aerial photographic reconnaissance of Guadalcanal, rescued 39 pilots and 61 crewmen, and evacuated 237 others. See Robert Sherrod, *History of Marine Corps Aviation in World War II,* 2d ed. (San Rafael, Calif.: Presidio Press, 1980), 112, 140 n. 34.

GLOSSARY

AIF	Australian Imperial Forces. That part of the Australian Army serving overseas.
Airacobra	Bell P-39 or P-400 (export version) single-engined fighter plane
APD	Destroyer transport or high-speed transport. The APDs were converted flush-deck destroyers ("four-stackers") from the World War I era. They carried small landing craft.
ARP	Air raid precautions
Asdic	British sonar (from the initials of the Anti-Submarine Detection Committee)
AV	Auxiliary vessel
Avenger	Grumman TBF single-engined torpedo bomber
BEM	British Empire Medal (officially, Medal of the Order of the British Empire)
Betty	Allied code name for Mitsubishi G4M Navy type 1 twin-engined medium attack bomber
BSIP	British Solomon Islands Protectorate. Name changed to Solomon Islands, 1975; gained independence, 1978.
BSIPDF	British Solomon Islands Protectorate Defence Force
CACTUS	Allied code name for Guadalcanal
Catalina	Consolidated PBY twin-engined flying boat
CBE	Commander of the Order of the British Empire
CMG	Commander of the Order of St. Michael and St. George
CO	Commanding officer
CP	Command post
Dauntless	Douglas SBD single-engined dive bomber or scouting plane (literally, "scout bomber, Douglas")
DCM	Distinguished Conduct Medal (Br.)
DH	District headman
DO	District officer, officer in charge of the district

DSC (U.S.)	Distinguished Service Cross (U.S. Army)
DSC (RN)	Distinguished Service Cross (Royal Navy)
DSIO	Deputy supervising intelligence officer
DSO	Distinguished Service Order (Br.)
Duck	Grumman J2F single-engined biwing amphibious utility plane
Flying Fortress	Boeing B-17 four-engined heavy bomber
Hudson	Lockheed twin-engined medium bomber
Kawanisi	Kawanisi H6K Navy type 97 four-engined flying boat; Allied code name "Mavis"
LCP	Landing craft, personnel
Lightning	Lockheed P-38 twin-engined fighter plane
LOM	Legion of Merit (U.S.)
MBE	Member of the Order of the British Empire
MC	Military Cross (Br.)
MID	Mentioned in Despatches (Br.)
MM	Military Medal (Br.)
NCO	Noncommissioned officer
NLO	Naval liaison officer
NMP	Native medical practitioner. The government employee who served as the doctor in each district. The NMPs were graduates of the Central Medical School in Suva, Fiji.
OBE	Officer of the Order of the British Empire
PC	Police constable
P.O.	Petty officer
RAAF	Royal Australian Air Force
RAN	Royal Australian Navy
RANVR	Royal Australian Naval Volunteer Reserve
RC	Resident commissioner
RCM	Roman Catholic Mission
RNZAF	Royal New Zealand Air Force
SDA	Seventh-Day Adventist Mission
SSEM	South Sea Evangelical Mission
Val	Allied code name for Aichi D3A Navy type 99 single-engined dive bomber

VMF	Marine fighter squadron
VMSB	Marine scout-bombing squadron
Wildcat	Grumman F4F single-engined fighter plane
WRANS	Women's Royal Australian Naval Service
WT	Wireless telegraph or wireless telephone. Prewar name of the coastwatchers' means of communication with the outside world, by Morse code or voice, via the teleradio.
YJX2	Twenty-four-hour watch on "X" frequency kept in Vila, New Hebrides (modern Vanuatu), by the RAN, which passed on coastwatchers' messages to the Fox Schedule for broadcast to all Allied ships
YP	District patrol vessel (literally, "yard craft, patrol")
Zero	Mitsubishi A6M Reisen (Zero fighter) single-engined fighter plane; Allied code name "Zeke"

INDEX

Note: (SI) after individuals' names indicates Solomon Islander

335

143–44, 178, 194, 231; mission station
at, 47; Japanese occupation of, 231
Vololo, 173, 175
Volonavua, 12, 115, 197–98, 206, 209, 272
Vouza, Jacob Charles, 12–13, 18–20, 23–24,
111–12, 115, 138, 139, 150, 152, 178,
192, 195, 197, 206, 211–12, 214,
221–22, 225, 265, 305; capture of,
209–10; awarded Legion of Merit, 30;
knighted, 26
Vuchicoro, 177–80, 182
Vungana, 154, 158, 165–66, 168–69, 177,
179–85, 188–89; move to, 153–56; conditions at, 155–57; inaccesiblity of, 176;
return to, 178; provision problems at,
164, 181; departure from, 196
Vura (SI), 44, 206, 214, 225, 243

Waddell, A. N. A., 41, 57, 196
Wai-ai, 50, 65, 163
Warden, William H., 241
"Washing Machine Charlie," 222, 234, 301
Waterman, Hawley C., 297

Webster, Jack, 78–79
Wendling, Ralph E. "Wimpy," 235, 247–48,
255, 257, 262–63, 266, 268, 271–72,
278–81, 295, 306
Whaling, William J., 22
"Whaling Group," 22
Wheatley, Hugh, 42
Whitehead, Jim, 203
Wickham, H., 41
Widdy, Charles V., 16, 18, 20, 22, 58,
195–96, 198–99, 284, 290, 295
Williams, Robert H., 16
Wilmot, Billy, 89, 91–92, 94–96, 98, 111, 198
Wilson, C. E. J., 41
Winter, Mike, 202, 262
Wolf, Freddy (Big Bad), 302
Woodford, Charles, 93–94

Yandina, 72
Yorktown, 8, 116, 120
Ysabel, 33, 65, 66, 89, 102, 139, 163, 167, 241,
292, 306
Yuama (Japanese), 151

Martin Clemens was born in Aberdeen, Scotland, and educated at Bedford School and Christ's College, Cambridge. In 1938 he went to the Solomon Islands in the Colonial Administrative Service, and after learning his trade on Malaita became District Officer, San Christoval. In 1942 he went to Guadalcanal, where he soon took over the district and coast watching. When the U.S. Marines arrived Clemens was ordered to join them as British Liaison Officer, and he integrated his force of Solomon Islanders with the Marine units as intelligence gatherers, scouts, guides, and carriers.

After the war Clemens was posted to Palestine, then to Cyprus. In 1960 he retired to Melbourne with his Australian wife and their four children. He helps run the family's sheep and cattle properties in Queensland and is active in philanthropic and civic organizations.

The Naval Institute Press is the book-publishing arm of the U.S. Naval Institute, a private, nonprofit, membership society for sea service professionals and others who share an interest in naval and maritime affairs. Established in 1873 at the U.S. Naval Academy in Annapolis, Maryland, where its offices remain today, the Naval Institute has members worldwide.

Members of the Naval Institute support the education programs of the society and receive the influential monthly magazine *Proceedings* and discounts on fine nautical prints and on ship and aircraft photos. They also have access to the transcripts of the Institute's Oral History Program and get discounted admission to any of the Institute-sponsored seminars offered around the country.

The Naval Institute also publishes *Naval History* magazine. This colorful bimonthly is filled with entertaining and thought-provoking articles, first-person reminiscences, and dramatic art and photography. Members receive a discount on *Naval History* subscriptions.

The Naval Institute's book-publishing program, begun in 1898 with basic guides to naval practices, has broadened its scope in recent years to include books of more general interest. Now the Naval Institute Press publishes about 100 titles each year, ranging from how-to books on boating and navigation to battle histories, biographies, ship and aircraft guides, and novels. Institute members receive discounts of 20 to 50 percent on the Press's nearly 600 books in print.

Full-time students are eligible for special half-price membership rates. Life memberships are also available.

For a free catalog describing Naval Institute Press books currently available, and for further information about subscribing to *Naval History* magazine or about joining the U.S. Naval Institute, please write to:

Membership Department
U.S. Naval Institute
118 Maryland Avenue
Annapolis, MD 21402-5035
Telephone: (800) 233-8764
Fax: (410) 269-7940
Web address: www.usni.org